# LETTERS FROM AND TO
## JOSEPH JOACHIM

*Joseph Joachim, 1867*
*From the painting by G.F. Watts, R.A.*

# LETTERS

FROM AND TO

# JOSEPH JOACHIM

SELECTED AND TRANSLATED

BY

## NORA BICKLEY

WITH A PREFACE BY

## J. A. FULLER-MAITLAND

NEW YORK
VIENNA HOUSE
1972

This 1972 VIENNA HOUSE edition is reprinted
by arrangement with The Macmillan Press Ltd.
International Standard Book Number: 0-8443-0043-8
Library of Congress Catalogue Number: 70-183496
Manufactured in the United States of America

# PREFACE

FOR the world at large, the name of Joseph Joachim stands for the illustrious violinist (probably the greatest of all time), who set up the highest possible standard of artistic playing, who never for a moment swerved from his high ideals, and whose influence on the music of his time was great beyond all possibility of assessment. In England more especially, from the time when, advertised as "The Hungarian Boy," he was made a counter-attraction to the opera of *The Bohemian Girl*, to the date of that famous celebration of the sixtieth anniversary of his first London appearance held in the Queen's Hall in 1904, he was the champion of all that was best in pure music, and it is probable that the enormous increase in musical taste which came over the whole country during the time of his artistic career is due, directly and indirectly, more to him than to any other individual; for the "Popular Concerts" with which he was more intimately connected than any one else, as their primary attraction and as a guiding influence on their director, were among the most important agents in the improvement of public taste in London.

To a smaller number of people, Joachim ranks as one of the composers who, in other circumstances, might have attained a world-wide acceptance; his works, though few in number and perhaps a little austere in expression, hold a permanent place in the affections of those to whom they appeal, and there are not wanting signs that if his life had been devoted to composition rather than to the noble work of interpreting the best music in the best way, he would have been numbered among the great creative masters.

Until the publication of the letters from which this volume is a selection, it was only a still smaller number who realised to the full the beauty of Joachim's character, his power (so wonderful in a public performer) of self-abnegation, or the depth of his sympathy with those he loved ; his clear and simple vision of what it was right for him to do, corresponded with the way in which he would give out a musical phrase. So, and no otherwise, it seemed good to him to read a musical strain, and his interpretation created the idea that thus, and thus alone, it must have been conceived by the composer. There was a simplicity and directness about it that seemed childishly self-evident, and as if it might just as well have occurred to anybody else to do it that way. The intensity of his perception in artistic matters left no room for the affectations and traces of self-consciousness that spoil a goodly number of otherwise fine artists; and in the momentous decisions of his life the same directness and simplicity are to be seen. If only other people had been as simple as himself many of the trials he had to undergo would never have existed.

It is only a year since the great collection of letters to and from Joachim was completed by his son, Johannes Joachim, and his biographer, Andreas Moser; the three large volumes contain considerably over 1000 letters, and these, it is understood, do not include by any means every letter that could have been published. Nor does this collection include the correspondence with Brahms, which was published a few years ago as the fifth and sixth volumes of Brahms's *Briefwechsel*.

In that collection there are over 500 letters, about 25 of which have been taken into the present volume. In this it is clear that the translator's object has been to let the letters themselves present a more or less continuous narrative of the great man's life, keeping a just proportion among its different parts. It has sometimes been felt that in the German collection, as in the German biography, too little has been admitted that bears on Joachim's relations with England and the English public. It is obvious from his letters that many of his intimate friends came very near resenting his annual visits ·to London, and it is doubtful if any of his English friends quite realised what it cost him to give them the music and the personal intercourse which for many of them gave new life to every spring. In this selection the greatest omissions seem to have been made in the German correspondence, so that the balance is to some extent adjusted.

There is surely nothing in the history of music more beautiful than the relations of Joachim first with Schumann, then, after that master's tragic end, with Frau Clara Schumann and Brahms. To grasp fully the character and depth of this intimacy, the reader is strongly recommended to study the biography of Brahms by Kalbeck, and that of Clara Schumann by Litzmann ; the latter is well translated, and those who only read English must live in hopes of a translation of Kalbeck's big book making its appearance some day. Yet with both of these dear friends there arose, at different times, small differences which meant a virtual estrangement for a time. Only those who appreciate the tenderer side of Joachim's character can thoroughly sympathise with his sufferings in each case, or with his joy when the clouds were removed; the letters which concern the deeper tragedy of his married life are quite wisely not given, but the touching announcement of the wife's death sent by Joachim to a nephew shows that, had time been granted, the two great artists might have been reunited at the close of their lives.

In reading the account of the famous split between the partisans of the classics and the school of Liszt, the dispute which may be considered as the other great trial of Joachim's life, it is necessary to remember the difficulties of the situation to one who felt it to be his first duty to guard the older music from attack. Joachim was convinced, sooner than any one else, that Schumann and Brahms were in the royal line of the great composers. This does not seem a very strange position in the present day, but the "moderns" of that time, with Liszt at their head, were never tired of sneering at Schumann, and though they professed to uphold the classics, yet it was clear to every one that they were working for their own glorification rather than in the cause of legitimate music. It was their assertion that opinion in Germany was unanimously on their side which roused Joachim, Brahms, and one or two more, to make the famous protest which appeared in 1860. Right or wrong, the attack began from the "modern" side, and the deliberate falsehood had to be contradicted by some one. By an unlucky mistake the protest was sent to the press before the numerous musicians who had expressed their willingness to sign it had an opportunity of doing so. While the verdict of the public concerning Wagner has reversed that of Joachim himself (Brahms, be it remembered, was an ardent admirer of Wagner's music, although personal relations between them were of course out of the question), yet Joachim's antagonism to the principles that underlay the more ambitious of Liszt's compositions has not been without practical endorsement by later musicians, for the vogue of Liszt's symphonic poems seems to have passed away, and no very definite ideal seems to have been accepted by the present representatives of modernity in music. The letter to Liszt in which the severance was definitely made, will be found on pp. 146-148 of this volume, and it may surely stand as a model of what such a letter should be. Quite explicit, without any desire to shirk the difficult explanation, yet expressed with perfect courtesy and that feeling for others which was perhaps the dominant note in Joachim's nature, it is a worthy landmark in musical history.

This note of sympathy for others rings out in every letter of the selection now published, and it is hardly fanciful to say that it is what gave to the artist's ensemble playing its inimitable quality. For him, and through him, for the members of his quartet-party, the music was everything, personal display absolutely nothing. The same characteristic made the career of the ordinary virtuoso, fêted by society, especially obnoxious to him. It is supposed that the immediate cause of his determination never to accept private engagements for a fee was due to some little *faux pas* perpetrated by a London hostess early in his career ; but all who knew will realise that the disagreeable side of such a career would, for him, far outweigh the monetary advantage to be gained thereby.   Yet it was in private that his playing most profoundly impressed the privileged persons who made up the audiences at the many artistic reunions that took place in the course of every visit to London.   In such surroundings he produced an impression that could best be described by combining the German and the English meanings of the word *genial*, that is, he displayed both genius and geniality in the highest imaginable degree.   One side of him, that which appealed to the public at large, is for ever silent, as that of all musical interpreters must be after they are dead ; but a faithful picture of the other side remains in the letters of which the following are a sample.   They have been translated so skilfully that it is difficult to believe them to be a translation, and it is to be hoped that Mrs. Bickley will one day turn her attention to the work of translating the whole of the correspondence with Brahms.

J. A. FULLER-MAITLAND.

# LEADING DATES IN JOACHIM'S CAREER

| | |
|---|---|
| Birth at Kitsee, Pressburg, Hungary . . . | June 28, 1831. |
| First appearance in public . . . . . | March 17, 1839. |
| First appearance at the Leipzig Gewandhaus . . | August 19, 1843. |
| First appearance, London (Drury Lane Theatre) . | March 28, 1844. |
| Marriage to Amalie Weis . . . . . | May 10, 1863. |
| Appointment as director of the Berlin Hochschule . | 1869. |
| The Joachim Quartet founded, with Schiever, De Ahna, and W. Müller . . . . . | 1869. |
| Celebration of the fiftieth anniversary of first appearance, Berlin . . . . . . . | 1889. |
| Celebration of the sixtieth anniversary of the same, Berlin . . . . . . . . | 1899. |
| "Diamond Jubilee" celebrations, for sixtieth anniversary of first appearance in England . . | May 16, 1904. |
| Death, Berlin . . . . . . . | August 15, 1907. |

# ILLUSTRATIONS

JOSEPH JOACHIM, 1895.

From a photograph by Frederick Hollyer.

# LETTERS FROM AND TO
# JOSEPH JOACHIM

*To Joseph Böhm in Vienna*

LEIPZIG, *October* 15, 1844.

Dear Professor—It is certainly not owing to forgetfulness that I have not written to you for so long, for whenever I think of my visit to London[1] and of its success I remember you, my honoured master, with the deepest gratitude, for it is you above all whom I have to thank for it.

I am glad, for your sake, that you will really see your dear Ernst this winter. Now that I have the honour of knowing him myself I can easily understand your affection for him ; he is really the most charming person imaginable and certainly the greatest virtuoso. I hope to see him soon, as he is coming here in a few days. I have heard Prume,[2] too ; I did not much care for him. His tone seems to me pretty but not great, his bowing not particularly good, his interpretation not very intelligent, and his composition not at all original. But his right [left ?] hand is very good, and indeed, on the whole, he is a remarkable violinist. He is going to Vienna next season, too. The Gewandhaus concerts have started here again already. I wrote to you last year to tell you how excellent they were.

[1] For an account of Joachim's first visit to London in the spring, see Moser, vol. i. p. 60.

[2] François Prume, student at the Conservatoires of Paris and Lüttich. At that time he excited universal enthusiasm, although dissenting voices were not lacking.

I am practising a Quatuor brillant in B minor (Opus 61) by Spohr at present, which I like very much. I play Paganini a good deal also, as well as old Bach, whose Adagio and Fugue for the violin alone I played in public in London.

My Concerto for the violin will soon be finished. I am composing songs under Hauptmann, the effects of which ought not to fail in houses where there are lots of rats and mice.

Remember me, dear Professor, to your wife, and do not quite forget your most affectionate pupil,

JOSEPH JOACHIM.

## To Ferdinand David

[LONDON, *April* 12, 1847.]

Honoured Master—You gave me permission to write to you from here, and nothing could give me greater pleasure. First of all I must thank you for your letters of introduction, which have been very useful to me, as Herr David in Cologne, as well as Madame Dulken[1] here, received me most kindly. I have played in public here several times already, and on the 27th I am playing at the 5th Philharmonic concert, which has given rise to many difficulties. I have no choice but to give the Beethoven Concerto (as Ernst played the *Gesangsscene* at the second concert). I find the Philharmonic concerts are not worthy of their reputation, for after hearing the Beethoven Symphonies in Leipzig, their performance here is not very edifying. Even the tempos in my opinion (which is probably mistaken) are quite wrong. Ernst did not play the *Gesangsscene* correctly ; he modernised

---

[1] Louise Dulken, Ferdinand David's sister, a first-rate pianist. Died 1850.

the cadenza (although he used the same harmonies), put in some very difficult passages, left out the beautiful modulation in the passage in the Allegro (in F) entirely, made modern conclusions to every one of the solos in the Allegro, and played the staccato passage in thirds so that he had to take it rather slower. I consider Ernst to be a *very great* violinist, and he seems to me to be incomparably greater than Sivori as virtuoso, artist and man. The latter plays the most astonishingly difficult things, but he is often out of tune, and is altogether a great charlatan. There is a superfluity of foreign violinists here. Ernst, Sivori, Pott [1] (who is to play in the next and 4th Philharmon.), Gulomy [2] (of whom one hears nothing at all), and Rossy,[3] sixteen years old, who brings good recommendations from Rossini and is said to play badly, so people tell me who ought to know.

At the 3rd Philharmonic concert Madame Dulken played a Quintette of Spohr's with flute, clarionet, bassoon and horn, which was really magnificent. But it was a pity that the heat made the wind instruments go up so that they were at least an eighth of a tone too high. . . . Ole Bull is said to be making a lot of money in America. Parish Alvars told me that Ole Bull was giving concerts over there in a riding school at a shilling entrance fee. Parish Alvars also told me that he, I mean Alvars, was coming to Leipzig next winter to produce a symphony which he had nearly finished. He is really a splendid fellow, and I am looking forward to seeing him in Leipzig. Now

---

[1] August Pott, a pupil of Spohr's. In 1836 he founded the Mozart Memorial Fund with the proceeds of a concert at Salzburg.

[2] Jerome Louis Gulomy, *Hofkapellmeister* at Bückeburg from 1853. Died there 1887.

[3] Carlo Rossi, pianist. As a violinist he was a pupil of Menzel's in Vienna. Has lived at Venice since 1851.

allow me to ask you some questions, as I hope you will send me a few lines.

Is it true, as I have heard here, that you are coming over here next year? What news of our dear Gade? Is Herr Hiller still in Leipzig? Was Herr Schumann's journey successful?[1] Doctor Mendelssohn is expected here for certain.

Won - ne o se - lig o    himmlisches Glück

etc.[2]

I am just going to Herr Klingemann's[3] to see whether he has arrived yet. Farewell, and do not forget your ever grateful          J. JOACHIM.

*To his brother Heinrich in Vienna*

LEIPZIG, *November* 19, 1847.

I still owe you my thanks for your kind and consoling letter,[4] and send them now from the bottom of my heart. It is fortunate for me that God has granted me such dear kind people, whose sympathy does me so much good, and whose love for me I am learning to realise and value more and more.

So far as music is concerned, everything here is dreary and desolate since the great spirit who tended

[1] To Berlin for the performance of the *Peri*. See Litzmann, *Clara Schumann*, vol. i. p. 423 (trans. G. E. Hadow).

[2] Incorrectly written from memory from Schumann's *Paradise and Peri*, in which the passage (No. 26) is in G major and the text runs: "Wie selig, o Wonne, wie selig bin ich!" (How blissful, O joy, how blissful am I!).

[3] Karl Klingemann. Died September 25, 1862. Mendelssohn's friend, and Secretary to the Hanoverian Legation in London. A charming account of his life, written by his son, is to be found in his correspondence with Mendelssohn. Essen, 1909.

[4] On the occasion of Mendelssohn's death, November 4.

it has gone from us.  His works, which I am now studying zealously, are my best consolation, and it gives me the deepest delight to spend my time amongst them, owing them, as I do already, so many happy hours.  Then, if I go to the piano and play a specially beautiful passage in which his noble spirit seems perfectly rendered, I am sunk in a blissful melancholy which words fail me to describe.

I think I shall stay here over the winter, at any rate, and compose some things for next spring (in London). . . . The postman has just brought me a letter from dear mother in which she asks me to come to Pesth, father having written to the same effect the day before yesterday.  In spite of my great desire to do so, and although I had quite made up my mind to go there, I was obliged to admit, after maturer considera-tion, that it would be injurious to my artistic develop-ment, and in spite of my unwillingness I had finally to decide not to leave here just yet, as I do not know a soul there, musical intercourse with whom would not do me more harm than good.  I am glad now that I had the courage to write at once yesterday to dear Rechnitz[1] that I could not manage it, for otherwise, I think, after mother's loving letter to-day, my longing to see my people, from whom I have been separated for so long, would have conquered me.  Are you going to Pesth soon?  If only I could be so near my people! . . . Your                          JOSEPH JOACHIM.

*To his brother Heinrich in London*

LEIPZIG, *March* 27, 1848.

. . . I shall only remain in Leipzig another month at the most.  But *in no case* will I go to Paris, sorry as I

---

[1] Joachim's brother-in-law, a doctor.  He died at an early age.

am not to carry out your wishes.   I do not know any one in Paris, and should be quite alone.   Secondly, I do not know of a single musician with whom I wish to be associated, although there are plenty I should prefer to keep at a distance.

Moreover, there are no concerts there in the summer, living is dearer there than in Germany, troubles might break out again at any moment, and above all, I long more than ever for the warm, close intercourse with my nearest and dearest whom I have not seen for so long.   My God, how good it will be to see my dear parents and brothers and sisters again !   I expect to be in Pesth by the beginning of May to spend the summer there and to occupy myself chiefly with writing for the violin, to finish the Concerto I have begun, etc.   Then perhaps I can arrange to go *via* Holland and Paris to England at the beginning of next year, *to astonish the nativ's, if possible.*[1]   Write and tell me what you (and Bernhard [2]) think about this. But God knows what will have happened to Europe and to us by that time.   Perhaps we shall be hearing cannons and not violins then.   In these times we cannot reckon with certainty on the next day.   You will have heard, of course, of the terrible events in Berlin, and of the good news about our country.   I congratulate you on the free constitution obtained by the Austrians, and I hope we shall long be able to rejoice in this freedom.   May Germany march boldly forward on the open road and soon become a united state which can claim the position it is entitled to hold !  . . .

---

[1] Written in English in the original.

[2] Joachim's uncle, Bernhard Figdor, who lived in England and afterwards in Paris.

JOSEPH JOACHIM, 1848.

From a drawing by Friedrich Preller, senior.

*To his brother Heinrich*

PESTH, *July* 2, 1848.

. . . As to your questions, I will answer them at once. First of all, it is all right about my appointment,[1] for I have had letters from Fanny[2] and Doctor Klengel about it, in which I am told that everything will go on as before. I have a salary of four hundred thalers, three months' leave and a good deal of freedom besides, and another good thing is that all my superiors are personal friends. For this I have to give lessons daily at the Conservatoire (I do not yet know for how long, but in any case for not more than two hours), play with the orchestra at the opera (generally two or three times a week), and also at all the twenty concerts, and play solos twice, and in the church for a quarter of an hour every Sunday. It will suit me very well to be tied down to regular work, so that the work I do for myself will be a recreation ; and, as far as pecuniary matters are concerned, I shall be glad, especially just now, if I do not have to live on my few remaining gulden, if there are any left. . . . Be so good as to let me know what my balance is. But at your convenience. Father would like to know, and I cannot tell him ; he declares I must have some money. But I do not know where it could come from, for what I earned last year by playing in London was not such a great sum, and I have been drawing from it up to the present. You will laugh at my business letter ! ! ? But that is enough of such matters. As to publishing my compositions, my dear brother, I must stick to my refusal. It is a matter of principle with me not to

[1] As teacher at the Leipzig Conservatoire. He entered upon this on August 1.
[2] Fanny Wittgenstein, *née* Figdor. See Moser, vol. i. p. 11.

publish anything until I am, to a certain extent, satisfied with it myself. One should present nothing to the world of which one might say, I could have done it better. If everybody were of this opinion the world would be spared a lot of rubbish. Believe me, one is always the best judge of one's own work ; I know that from my own experience. What a few well-meaning cousins, aunts, and friends think about it cannot possibly influence my opinion, because I know how much allowance one has to make for the involuntary indulgence which invariably biasses the judgment of relations. All the same, I hope to be able to carry out your wishes quite soon, for I take more and more delight in composition, and it would speak badly for my powers if, with such a good will, I could not succeed in putting something together which I could lay before a publisher. . . . The Landtag will be opened here on the 1st. Kossuth wanted to resign a few days ago, but it has not come to that. The Slavs and Croats still look threatening. Who knows how things will end here? To all appearances the rebels are being appeased from high quarters and the Innsbrück Chamber is playing a false game. . . .

### To Bernhard Cossmann

LEIPZIG, *May* 11, 1850.

My dear Cossmann—Your honoured father, whom I had the pleasure of seeing here, was to tell you in his letter of my safe arrival, and I preferred to keep back my letter to you until my visit to Liszt at Weimar, so as to tell you all about that at the same time ; and I hope you will treat me with your usual indulgence and, in consideration of my being such a notoriously bad correspondent, not take this delay amiss. For I really ought to have thanked you long ago for your kind and sympathetic friendship, of which I had such splendid proofs in Paris, if such things can be repaid at all by a mere formality! I am to tell you from Liszt, with whom I spent several unforgettable days, that he regards your appointment as settled, although it has not yet been officially discussed in Weimar. In musical matters Liszt is so almighty there that he can always get what he wants, and you can be assured that he wishes sincerely to see you appointed there. He has an extraordinary affection and esteem for you, but this will be nothing new for you, to whom beautiful Paris is now paying homage, although another would be proud of it.

Herr von Ziegesar [1] (a very pleasant man) told me, too, that he hoped to see you in Weimar in September. I liked the place very much; it is a friendly little town, and I am sure the people are easy to get on with, and above all you will have Liszt there. Since I have come to know him better, my former antipathy to him has been transformed into an equally strong liking for him. Am I perhaps less of a Philistine since my visit to Paris? Has he really modified his method and style so much? Or is it something of both? At any rate, I like him so much that I am already looking forward to going to Weimar again soon. Everything is as usual here. Now that I have considered matters here with unprejudiced eyes, I am of your opinion, my dear friend, with regard to many things, and if it were not for my relations, the Klengels and David I do not think I would stay here much longer. In any case I will make good use of the summer for fiddling and composition, so as to be well prepared for January and Paris. You cannot doubt

[1] Manager of the Court Theatre.

that it would give your friend great pleasure to find you there. Remember me most cordially to your friends and mine there, but especially to your dear brother and his Jeannette, of whose kindness and hospitality I have grateful memories. Do not forget, too, to tell our dear Morena and his family that I often think of them, and will not forget my promise to send news of myself; tell him to think of me sometimes. Will you remember me also especially to Mad. Wartel and the Café Europa Club and to whomever else you think fit. Write and tell me when and to what address in Baden I am to send the *Wilhelm Tell* Fantasia.[1]

Farewell, dear friend, and continue to think kindly of your                                           JOACHIM.

Have a good time in Touraine, but *compose* too, and do not forget your mission for the violoncello.

J. J.

### To his brother Heinrich

LEIPZIG, *the last day of September* 1850.

. . . In a fortnight's time I migrate to Weimar. Through the influence of my friend and patron, Liszt, the Archduchess has made a post for me there as music director, which is for the present no better financially than the Leipzig one, but where I shall, firstly, have a much more honourable position, and secondly, extraordinarily little to do (perhaps to play once a week at the opera under Liszt's conductorship), and thirdly, the prospect of a *five months'* leave yearly (next year from the end of March to the end of August), etc. But the chief thing which attracts me to Weimar is the life and co-operation with Liszt, for

---

[1] For violoncello, by Cossmann.

every time I see him I like him better and I feel sure
that he is a true friend to me, who would not advise
me to take the post if he did not think it were for my
good. He lays great stress on the charming and
practical way in which the Court at Weimar interests
itself in artists, and he thinks it would be of great
use to me on my tours, particularly in Russia, as the
Archduchess is a sister of the Emperor Nicholas.
Be that as it may, in any case I shall be able to work
more and with greater freedom in Weimar than here,
and that is essential if I am to pay you a visit in the
spring. . . .

## To Franz Liszt

[LONDON] *May 22, 1852.*

Most honoured Doctor—You must think me the
most ungrateful fellow in the world, who does not
know how to value your permission to write to you!
And you would have good cause to think of me in this
way if the busy life in London, rehearsals, concerts,
or any such things had kept me from sending you
news of myself. But nothing of this kind prevented
me from writing; what did prevent me was a certain
shyness about telling you, of all people, who had such
high hopes for me, that, up to the present, I have
hardly accomplished anything. If it were not that
it is torture to me to think you might have doubts
of me, I should hardly be able to bring myself to
break my silence now. In spite of all my efforts
and the greatest waste of time I have, indeed, accomplished nothing here. I have had no opportunity
either of testing myself with the orchestra before a
large audience, or of fulfilling wishes of a higher kind,
such as, for instance, getting to know and understand

Berlioz more intimately.   Add to this that mediocre
talent is frequently honoured here beyond all reason,
and that the wretched musical conditions are hardly
ever relieved by a performance of any considerable
merit, and you will forgive me for not writing, because
I was afraid my words might remind you too much of
the composer of the " sick poodle walking round the
Park at Weimar," [1] and I know you cannot bear him.

By your greeting you have sent a ray of light into
my London fog, for which I thank you from my heart.
It came to me in a letter to Madame Pleyel.   I have
only seen this artist at one rehearsal and one concert,
because I happened to be taking part in both.   She
gave me great pleasure when she made up to me for
her indifferent performance of Mendelssohn's Trio
in D minor by her much more successful rendering
of some of your compositions.

The clear, bold, assured way in which she overcomes the most difficult passages in the *Patineurs*
is astonishing.   If only, in addition to her brilliant
tone, she had more tenderness and power of modulat-
ing the expression, she would remind me vividly of
the composer.   She made an extraordinary impression
on the audience at the second Ella Matinée with her
arrangement of the Schubert songs and the Prophète
Fantasia.   I also played at the concert, for the first
time here, and played the Schubert Quartette, which
was not yet known over here.   It made no impression ; people thought that, as a novice in instrumental
compositions, they could dismiss Schubert with a
lofty doubt as to his capabilities in that direction.
It is extraordinary how seldom people here allow
themselves to form an unbiassed judgment ; they are
so ruined by the commercial cries of the speculators

[1] Joachim himself.   Cf. Moser, vol. i. p. 105.

(in whose hands music rests entirely) that they regard the names of musicians in exactly the same manner as they do those of business firms whose bills they would dishonour or accept according to whether they have heard their names often or seldom. Beethoven has been established here for a long time, and so Opus 1 and the 9th Symphony are received with equal enthusiasm! How helpless I feel myself to be here, with the desire but without adequate means to fight against such perverse conditions. I should like best of all to clear out of here at once and go to Altenburg, to you! You have doubtless done a lot for the progress of music in the meantime, and I am missing many things in being so far away! Raff was so good as to give me news of my friends in Weimar, which pleased me very much. I intend to write and thank him from Dublin. I start for that town in an hour and shall remain there for the next week, as I am engaged for two concerts. After my return I am to play here in the old Philharmonic hall, and if I can give you good news of myself, then I will write to you. You will learn much more about the musical doings from the papers and from Berlioz than I can tell you now in my haste.

I have had plenty to do the last few days, as I have announced that I am giving a concert on June 25, and I have had to see to all the necessary business connected with it before leaving for Dublin. Do not be vexed with me for these hasty lines. I could not start in peace without having written to you! I will only take the liberty of asking you, honoured Doctor, to pay my respectful duty to those in your immediate neighbourhood.—Ever yours,

JOSEPH JOACHIM.

### *To Herman Grimm* [1]

WEIMAR, *December* 10, 1852.

Dear Grimm—After reading your *Armin* [2] with your friend [3] nothing could have delighted me more than to receive your letter authorising me to avail myself fully and unreservedly of your friendship. The powerful intellectual life breathed by all the characters in your *Armin*, the rhythmical swing of the language and the exalted spirit of it—all this has greatly excited me and has brought the author vividly before my mind just as I saw him here that first time [4] "*in Mitte göttlicher Bekannten.*" [5]   I have carried that vision with me ever since, and had I been obliged to banish it from my heart I should have done so with the deepest sorrow.   Your letter tells me I may keep it; there is nothing in it to make me fear that such a time of painful tension, ending (as here when we are playing quartettes and a melodious string breaks) in the destruction of all inner harmonies, can ever occur again.

I thank you for it!

I am looking forward now with great pleasure to my visit to Berlin, where I am to appear in public for the first time on the 13th of this month. [6]   I start to-morrow, and so I shall be calling on you a few hours after this letter reaches you, to tell you all about the

[1] Son of Wilhelm Grimm, the pioneer, with his brother Jacob, of the scientific study of German folk-lore.   Herman was the author of various books on literature and art, and later (1873) was appointed Professor of the History of Art at Berlin University.   Died 1901.

[2] *Armin. A Drama in Five Acts.*  Leipzig, 1851.

[3] Gisela von Arnim, afterwards Grimm's wife.

[4] For an account of Grimm's first meeting with Joachim at Bettina von Arnim's in the "Elephant" coffee-house at Weimar, see Grimm's *Fünfzehn Essays* and Bülow's letters to his mother at that time.

[5] "In the midst of godlike friends."

[6] At a concert given by the Stern Choral Society.  See Moser, vol. i. p. 128.

joys and sorrows that have fallen to our lot in Weimar since you left us.—To our happy meeting!

JOSEPH JOACHIM.

*From Herman Grimm*[1]

BERLIN, *February* 4, 1853.

Dear Joachim—It is late at night. A little while ago I was at Bettine's; other people were there. A piano was being played downstairs, and a violin sounded with it. I could not make out what was being played, but I felt a loathing for the chatter going on around me. I thought of your room at Weimar with the vine outside the window, and I longed to be there to see the soft spring sunshine through the leaves and to hear the tones of your violin. It gave me pleasure only to think of it. I should like to write so many things now which will surely never be so clear to me again. But I pass my days amidst such a confusion and noise of people that even when I am at last alone the sounds continue to ring in my ears until I have to go back to them again. I cannot understand how I have managed to bear it up to now, and why it has not driven me distracted.

Why do you not write to me? I will not remind you of the promise made on the steps of the inn, because that kind of promise is always forgotten. But I think we know one another too little to be silent for so long and too much to break off all intercourse again. This is not meant in any sense as a warning, but perhaps (I can imagine the possibility) you would have written to me, only you did not know how to begin your letter.

---

[1] It was Grimm's habit to write his letters in Latin writing and to use no capitals at the commencement of his sentences.—TR.

Frau von Arnim and Giesela have been here since last Sunday, but up to now I have not quite succeeded in breaking through the net in which I had allowed myself to become entangled during their absence: the demands of numerous people on my evenings. I hope a more peaceful time will come soon. They are both well. Armgard does not come for another week. Giesel tells me that when you were here you would have liked to discuss many things with me but that you had promised Bettina not to do so. I confess I can understand how you came to promise this, but not how you managed to keep your promise. Farewell. —Yours,                                    HERMAN GR.

Lincksstrasse 7.

### To Franz Liszt

HANOVER, *March* 21, 1853.

Dear and honoured Master—Instead of worrying you with a long-winded explanation of the reason why you have not heard from me for such a long, long time, I prefer to send you my Overture to *Hamlet* in the first joy of having a complete copy of it in my hands. I do this in the hope that the work may make clear to you what I trust you have never doubted, that I have had you, my dear Master, constantly in my mind. Your farewell words, which you called out to me when in the midst of friends on that last evening at Weimar, still ring in my ears; they re-echo in my heart like music which will never die. I have had ample leisure here to listen to this *voix interne*; I have been very lonely. The contrast between that atmosphere, which your untiring efforts are always flooding with new sounds, and this place, which seems dead to all music under the management of a phleg-

matic northerner from the time of the Restoration,[1]
is too harsh! Whichever way I turn there is no one
who has the same ambitions as myself; not one,
instead of the phalanx of friends at Weimar all
thinking alike. The gulf that yawned between my
most eager desires and any hope of their fulfilment
filled me with despair. I turned to *Hamlet*. The
motif to an Overture I had "intended"[2] to write at
Weimar came back to me. But writing it down did
not help me; I tinkered at it again and again, and at
last after your letter (because joy gave me strength) I
worked it all out again. But who knows how childish
my *Hamlet* will seem to you, great Master! Let it
be so! I dare to address you again in these notes
because I know you will not fail to recognise the
earnest endeavour in my work. Yes, I am sure you
will look through the score, considerate Master as
you always are, and will advise me, just as though I
sat beside you, dumb as usual, but eagerly drinking in
your words of musical wisdom. But if you cannot
spare any of your valuable time to write to me, let me
know by a few lines that I have not become estranged
from you! Otherwise I shall come myself before May.
From my whole heart, your          JOSEPH JOACHIM.


### To Woldemar Bargiel

[HANOVER, *April* 7, 1853.]

Dear, good Bargiel—Your wish to see something
of my work falls in splendidly with mine to tell you
the results of my private work in Hanover. So I am
sending you an Overture which has long been my
confidant here, and which has survived many meta-

---

[1] Marschner.
[2] That is to say, he had already begun to work at the Overture at that time.

C

morphoses in myself before it attained to its present form. You will not mind my sending you the rough draft; it would delay matters very much to have another copy made. Your musical feeling will easily help you to make out any doubtful notes. A clean copy of the work is in Liszt's hands, who has not yet written to me with regard to it, although he is the only one who knows it besides myself. There is no one in Hanover in whose musical understanding I have sufficient confidence to show him anything which means so much to me. So do not accuse me of vanity if I beg you to write to me soon about the Overture; if I were vain I would hardly send you such a very unattractive copy. A rough draft like this is really a kind of artistic confession to him to whom it is sent; it reveals our train of thought unadorned, and lays bare our weaknesses to the recipient. I hope you will agree with this and consent to undertake the duties of a confessor. I shall await the absolution which I may receive from you, my dear, conscientious Padre, with the greatest suspense!—I need hardly justify myself to you for my choice of a hero for my musical experiment. Hamlet is generally regarded as unmusical material; people maintain that Hamlet is too introspective. But this introspection is merely a refuge from the constant tumult of his mind. The feelings which drive him to it, the strong and constant need for action, the sombre grief because this great longing for the realisation of his inner life must wither impotently when opposed to external circumstances, these feelings must have tormented every human heart; they are universal, therefore they must be musical. Music is the purest expression of feeling, only that which is superficial, unnatural or self-conscious is foreign to it.

Beethoven is the eternal example of this. He, more than any other, has a deep understanding of the human soul. He is the Shakespeare of music (and not Händel [1]). His themes are his only friends throughout his whole spiritual life; they accompany him everywhere as his intimates, and so they inevitably bear the stamp of his rich and sensitive nature. Hence the variety and vitality of the forms which entrance us in his modulations, which ring in our ears like sounds heard long ago. But where have I got to, from my *Hamlet* Overture to Beethoven! O Humour! This gives you a fine opportunity.

To more congenial matters.
"The Arnims are people of fine intelligence." Your are right, dear Bargiel. But they are also charming people, with so much good-will, so much tact, that it often surprises one to see the extent to which they can identify themselves with the nature of others; they respect every kind of independence, and that makes their own individuality all the more delightful; they never encroach on the spiritual rights of others. That is not often the case with "intellectual" people, and for that reason intercourse with them is generally a trial to musicians. But why say all this to you when no doubt you have realised it for yourself long ago! I would rather ask you, who often go *unter den Zelten*,[2] sometimes to send news of the people of "fine intelligence" to one who has no such pleasant shelter for his leisure moments, namely to me, as I really take a childish delight in the thought that I am often remembered kindly there.

[1] Gervinus, in his introduction to Shakespeare, 1849, had at that time only sketched out the parallel between Shakespeare and Händel; his book, *Händel und Shakespeare*, only appeared in 1868.
[2] The name of the street in Berlin in which the von Arnims lived.

The day after to-morrow I have to go to Hamburg to play at the Philharmonic concert.   A variety of trifling matters has prevented me from settling to any serious work here lately ; and besides that I have been restless because Liszt has not written to me about my work.

When I come back from Hamburg (where I shall be from the 8th to the 10th) there is a Court concert, probably my last " official " duty here.   I am going to Göttingen at the end of April ; from there I shall make a short trip to Weimar in May, and perhaps a fort-night later a journey to Pesth to see my parents again—the first time for ever so long !   Perhaps we shall meet sometime during the summer.   If you write to me again tell me about your plans and your compositions and about the Arnims, etc., etc.   It would give great pleasure to your ever devoted

JOSEPH JOACHIM.

### From Franz Liszt [1]

[WEIMAR, *middle of April* 1853.]

Very dear Friend—" To be or not to be ; that is the question " as regards art, which is the beginning and, as it were, the birth-cry of our immortality, just as it is with regard to dogmatic belief and our hopes of a future life.   You resolve this great question with an emphatic affirmative, by a serious and beautiful work, greatly conceived and broadly developed, which categorically proves its right to exist.

After a careful reading of your score of the Overture to *Hamlet* I do not hesitate to offer you my sincere compliments, as much on the distinction and integral worth of the ideas as on their noble and vigorous presentation.   Various circumstances, which I need not explain to you in detail, having decided me

[1] Written in French in the original.—TR.

to take no more part in the activities of our theatre since the last performances of Wagner's works (as I have already informed the few people whom it could concern), I have, unfortunately, not yet had an opportunity of having your Overture performed; but, unless any quite improbable events should cause me to leave here, I count on not letting next month go by without giving myself the pleasure of hearing in its entirety this remarkable work, which, among other merits, has that of bearing a strong resemblance to you as I know you and love you. When I have had it rehearsed you will perhaps allow me to make detailed observations on it; meanwhile, I must thank you very cordially for the dedication, which will please our orchestra very much, and for which I am grateful to you.[1]

You do not answer me with regard to your coming here in May for the concert which must take place then on the marriage of Princess Amélie. Mr. de Ziegesar will write to you shortly on the matter, and I hope that, if you are not prevented from doing so by a journey to London, you will give me the pleasure of seeing you again in Weimar.

As to news which would interest you, no doubt you know already that Mlle. Max d'Arnim (Armgarte's sister) is marrying Comte Oriola, Colonel of a regiment at Bonn, where she will live.

Cornelius has just spent a fortnight at Altenburg, —always the same, excellent and charming. His last Masses for four voices with organ accompaniment are very good and worthy of high esteem.

*Benvenuto Cellini*[2] will be performed in May, in Italian, at Covent Garden Theatre in London.

---

[1] The score of the *Hamlet* Overture bears the dedication : " Dedicated to the members of the Weimar Orchestra "; it was not printed until after Joachim's death in 1908.

[2] Berlioz' opera, which he had composed that year.

Hans surpasses even you in epistolary laziness, for he has not written me a single line from Vienna. From the news I have of him through Löwy, my cousin, and Haslinger, I know that he has given two concerts, and I have no doubt of the good results to his reputation and of the valuable lessons he will draw from this trip. Some rather bitter newspaper articles about him need not make him uneasy, and I hope he will succeed in maintaining a worthy and dignified bearing as becomes one hailing from Weimar. I have particularly advised him to do nothing to influence the press and to pay court to no one. There is nothing to be gained by making the way smooth for MM. Drey., Willm., Litt., Schul., Leop. Meyer, only to be attacked by the first cad that comes along. "To be or not to be; that is the question," and false pretences help not at all.

But I hope he will earn the right to exist, and not simply to appear and disappear again with the advertisements and notices of his concerts. You know that I am attached to Hans as if he were my son, and up to the present my affection has not brought ill-luck to any one.

Raff leaves Weimar on the first of June next. His *Alfred* will be performed again on April 16. He also has a good chance of being appointed second director of the orchestra at Munich in the place of V. Lachner, who goes to Hamburg in the autumn. I am trying to get him this post, which I think ought to suit him, and I have written to Dingelstedt and to Comte Pocci, *Musikgraf* at Munich, to recommend him as he deserves.

Klindworth is making remarkable progress, and I think you will be pleased with him when he goes back to Hanover.

Have you read the great work of which Wagner has just had a hundred copies printed for his friends —*The Nibelungen Ring*—a dramatic work for three days and a preliminary evening?

If you like I can send you a copy.[1]

For light reading I recommend you the *Soirées de l'orchestre* by Berlioz, and a charming article on *Indra*[2] by Kossak.

Until we meet again soon, very dear friend, most sincerely and affectionately yours,  F. LISZT.

## *From Robert Schumann*

DÜSSELDORF, *June* 8, 1853.

Many thanks for your dear letter and for the music enclosed with it, especially for your Overture, which interested me deeply from the very first bars. I was greatly surprised. As you had not told me the name of the tragedy I had imagined a lively Overture for the concert hall, and found something so very different. As I read it, it seemed as though the scene gradually grew before my eyes and Ophelia and Hamlet actually stood forth. There are very impressive passages in it, and the whole is presented in the clear and noble form which befits such a great subject. I should like to say so much to you about it; but words only express one's feelings imperfectly. Music should, in the first place, appeal to the sympathies, and when I say that your work has appealed to mine you may believe me. As to what should interest the musician apart from the poet in us, for this you have amply provided. The artistic interweaving of the subject, the way in which you repeat in a new manner what

[1] This rare edition was in Joachim's possession at the time of his death.
[2] Opera by Flotow, which was being performed everywhere at that time.

you have said before and especially the handling of the orchestra and the way in which you use it for rare effects of light and shade—all this [seems to me worthy of high praise.   And there are daring passages suitable to the theme, here and there, as for instance the sharp interval in the third bar (the E♭[1]), which sounded somewhat harsh to me at the first reading. But in the course of the piece this very interval seems particularly characteristic and not to be replaced by any other.   Other passages which especially please me are the first introduction of the principal subject in F major (is the hautboy emphasised enough here?), then the introduction of the same subject in D major (in the horns), before that the resolution

Indeed, the whole of the longer moderato in the middle must be delightful — and then the last few pages with the deep tones of the horns, and the final chords—and then the whole of it.

So accept my congratulations on the completion of the work.   Do not alter anything until you have heard it several times.   I should like very much to have the Overture performed at one of our first concerts.   Perhaps you would help us to do this by sending us the score and the parts, if you have them?

I found my name written in your hand on the score of the Beethoven Concerto.   I conclude that you wished to make me a present of it, and I accept it with pleasure, the more so as it reminds me of the magician and necromancer whose skilful hand led us through the heights and depths of that marvellous

[1] Jansen, in *Letters of Robert Schumann*, 2nd ed., p. 374, reads D♭ – E♭ (*des-es*).

structure which the majority explore in vain. And when I read the Concerto I shall often think of that memorable day.

Good-bye, dear and honoured friend. Keep me in your thoughts. R. SCHUMANN.

I entered upon my 43rd year to-day.

[*In Frau Schumann's hand*] Please accept a heartfelt greeting from me too, dear Herr Joachim. We are still living in the memory of those glorious hours you granted us.

See that those hours of the past are renewed in the early future. CLARA SCH.

### *To Arnold Wehner* [1] *at Cassel*

[HANOVER] *September* 10, 1853.

Dear Friend—The first half of the Overture [2] in question is sketched out on the paper for the orchestra, and now I will just give myself a little pleasure by writing to you and your dear wife before I pay the necessary calls which I have put off until to-day. You good, kind people, who were so indulgent to my unbearable ways and moods at Göttingen, you must not be left another moment in doubt as to the devotion and gratitude of your "foster-child" (I hear that they honour me with this epithet at Göttingen). The time—it is already a fortnight since we parted—has flown because of my many and varied experiences: in Düsseldorf these consisted of *Märchen* and other visions which have left something more than a passing impression on me. Schumann's character, which I have been able to study closely for the first time,

---

[1] At that time Director of the Music Academy at Göttingen.
[2] To *Henry IV*.

seems to me splendid. His slightest words bear witness to his absolutely uncompromising honesty, combined with a charming sympathy, and at the same time he has such a naïve innocence that, in knowing him more intimately, one cannot but feel at ease with him. It is as if Florestan's foster-brother stood before us in the flesh. His mind is always so full of music that I can bear him no grudge for being unwilling to let outside matters clash with these sounds, although it was owing to this that I, for instance, misunderstood him sometimes at first. There is no conceit in him, but his thoughts are noble. You know the touching manner in which Clara interprets his ideas. It gave me extraordinary delight to play Robert's compositions with her, and I often wished that you could have been there to enjoy it too ; perhaps this will be possible another time. But I must not fail to draw your attention to the new Sonata (D minor) which will shortly be published by Breitkopf and Härtel, and which we played from the proofs. To me it is one of the finest creations of modern times, in the wonderful unity of its feeling and the significance of its themes. It is full of a noble passion—almost harsh and bitter in its expression—and the last movement might almost remind one of a seascape, with its glorious waves of sound. You must play it ; best of all with me some time ! I am not sure yet whether this will be at Cassel—I am still waiting to hear from Liszt. But I am expecting a letter from Weimar at any moment, and of course you will hear as soon as I hear anything definite myself. I have seen no newspapers here as yet, and so I have learnt nothing about Karlsruhe from them. Berlioz is expected here next month for some concerts ; this is the only news which interests me or which will interest you.  Brahms' silence is worse even than mine.  Our friend, Student Brinkmann,[1] comes to see me every day, and has become quite the lawyer without forfeiting any of his enthusiasm for music.  A great compliment!

Your dear likeness in daguerreotype hangs in my room and reminds me of happy times!  Later on Shakesp. and Beethov. are to come on one wall, Raph. and Moz. (together with the former's "Violinist") on the other; and opposite, Gluck and Sophocles.

Altogether, my rooms will be "homely"[2] this winter, and I think you must come and see them for yourself some time.  Won't you, dear Arnold?  Our concerts only start in January, but I hope there will be plenty of rehearsals before then.

Now you have a hasty sketch of my doings since I left you, you dear friends.  I will soon write and tell you things more in detail.  But I hope you will be satisfied with this word from me for to-day.

Say all that is affectionate for me to your honoured parents and your household, but especially to your dear wife.—From your          JOSEPH JOACHIM.

Remember me to the great master of the violin[3]; and *write* to me if you would give me real pleasure.

## To Bernhard Cossmann

KARLSRUHE, HÔTEL ERBPRINZ, *September* 26, 1853.

Dear Friend—The pleasant task has been laid upon me by Liszt of writing to you in his name, as he is setting the wind and percussion instruments

---

[1] From Göttingen.  Brinkmann was a friend of Joachim's for many years, and, after an eventful life, died a lonely death abroad in his eightieth year.

[2] Joachim uses the word *wöhnlich*, an expression peculiar to Hanover.

[3] Spohr, Frau Wehner's uncle.

going most energetically with his baton. But before I speak for him I must send you hearty greetings and wishes in my own name. Do come as soon as possible to help swell the number of comrades in art and life who are gradually coming together in this pleasant Karlsruhe. Even if you have a warmer climate in the south of France, I am sure you will find warmer hearts here, in spite of the undeniable charm of your hostess, to whom I should like to be remembered if she has any recollection of me.

Liszt asks me to enclose the programme as arranged at present with the request that you should arrive here *at the latest* next Sunday; but you know that the sooner you come the greater gain it will be for your friends, and I hope you will take this into consideration. In reply to your retrospective question, Liszt says that the theatre at Weimar began on the 17th of last month. The Karlsruhe Theatre, in which the concerts are to take place, is a most attractive building, in which I heard Cherubini's *Wasserträger* yesterday. The Opera left me cold in spite of many musical and even dramatic beauties; it even bored me at times. I was amazed to find how much I must have altered since a few years ago when so many things in it delighted me. Now I seem to miss more especially that natural, joyous something which, in Mozart's most antiquated forms, charms us with its eternal youth. Doubtless Cherubini also experienced emotions and he has expressed them in his music, but like one who has been incommoded rather than inspired by them. But why should I write all this to you to whom I have so much to say which nearly concerns us both! Let all this be compressed for to-day into the heartfelt cry: Come soon, dear friend!—Your truly devoted                                JOSEPH JOACHIM.

[H. W.] Ernst is coming; Monday October 3 is the first concert. Bülow started yesterday for Switzerland, owing, unfortunately, to the news of his father's death! I tell you this so that you may have the unpleasant news before you come to Karlsruhe. You will find Bülow here; he is coming back on Saturday.

*From Johannes Brahms*

[DÜSSELDORF] *October* 17, 1853.

Dear Joseph—Dr. Schumann is putting my things through with Breitkopf and Härtel with such earnestness and determination that I feel quite bewildered. He thinks I ought to send the first works to them in six days' time.

He suggests the following programme for the sake of variety:

Op. 1. Phantasie in D minor for piano, violin, and 'cello (Largo and Allegro).
Op. 2. Songs.
Op. 3. Scherzo in E♭ minor.
Op. 4. Sonata in C major.
Op. 5. Sonata in A minor for piano and violin.
Op. 6. Part-songs.

Write and tell me what you really think of this. I cannot make up my mind. Do you think the Trio (you will remember it, I expect) is worth publishing? Op. 4 is the only one I am really satisfied with. But then Schumann thinks one ought to begin with the weaker things. He is right in that—either start with them or *leave them out altogether* and strive not to fall again in the future.

Could I begin with the C Sonata?

Dr. Schumann thinks the F♯ minor and the Quartette in B♭ could come after any of the works.

When the Trio has been copied I should like to send it to you; of course, I have corrected some of its weak points.

Do console me soon with a few lines.—Your

JOHANNES.

In great haste!

### To Johannes Brahms

[HANOVER] TUESDAY [about October 20, 1853].

My dear Johannes—You ask me to tell you in what order you should let your music cry out to the world the fact of which you have long been joyfully conscious : *I am!* I am unspeakably touched by this. In the course of the summer (as you know) I had so accustomed myself to regard all I love most as lost to me that I had quite made up my mind to give you up to the Schumanns as a matter of course, because I realised that the grand, cloud-topped mountain must necessarily hide the hill, however friendly a shelter the latter may offer. I forgot that you live on a height which affords you a view of goodness of a less magnificent character ; and so, my very dear Johannes, it is more fitting that I should ask your pardon than express my thanks.

To come to your question, it really seems to me immaterial (from the higher standpoint, and therefore from yours) with which of your works you first cry to the world : *I am!* A heavenly vision remains a heavenly vision, even if it begins by merely showing the world—its big toe. He who is filled, as you are, with the holy spirit of music can produce nothing which does not bear his sign. But if you wish fully to bare your musical brow to the world of music when you first address it (and my standpoint is still too "idealistic" for me to desire anything else) make the two Sonatas (in C and F♯) Op. 1 ; then you can go on as follows :

Op. 2. Songs.
Op. 3. Scherzo.
Op. 4. Phantasie in D minor.
Op. 5. Violin Sonatas.
Op. 6. Part-songs.
Op. 7. Quartette.
Etc., in infinitum ! ! !

But I would *willingly* defer to the great master whom we both revere. I am strongly of the opinion that Härtel ought to bring out three works simultaneously; however, I do not know whether that would be practicable.

I am hourly expecting a letter from Schumann. Remember me to him and his second self, and also to [Albert] Dietrich. And do you remain my friend, as I shall always be your faithful and devoted

JOSEPH JOACHIM.

In haste.

*To Arnold Wehner at Göttingen*

[HANOVER, *October* 25, 1853.]

Will you be able to read this scribble written late at night with a steel pen?

There are moods which lead us along strange unaccustomed paths, with such mysterious power that we cannot find the way back to that road on which we prefer to travel—and it is some time before the compass of our emotions points out the surest way to avoid destruction in this wilderness—the way to our friends.

This may perhaps excuse what would otherwise be

inexcusable, even in such a notoriously bad letter writer as myself: my not having sent news of myself again. The coming of your wife and yourself to Karlsruhe gave me indescribable pleasure. I think you must have had some pleasant impressions of that time as you still speak of it at Göttingen, although you have just come from Cassel. If you had only come further with us to the Three Kings which stands so beautifully on the banks of the Rhine at Basel and where we fared so well! You, too, would have rejoiced in Richard (a true Lion Heart!). When one is hurled, as we were at Karlsruhe, on to a lot of bare, colourless sandbanks (Schindelmeister, Guhne and Co.), which stretch out into the ocean of music, one longs for a good, hard, jagged rock which raises its corners decently to heaven, and on which, if the waters become overpowering, one can at least save oneself from death by drowning. Wagner is one of those rare people who act as they do because the truth within them (or at any rate what they take to be the truth) will not permit them to do otherwise. You know that without having seen him; but you do not know that his every movement and every tone of his voice are like heralds proclaiming the completeness and nobility of his soul. When you hear him read his *Siegfried* you realise for the first time that, what his writings express in the crudest manner is, when freed from the disturbing tendency to move in a labyrinth, nothing less than a purely artistic enthusiasm, which ignores custom and recognises emotion only. As you and I guessed long ago, it is much more painful to him also to be discussed in a certain quarter than to be ignored, and I do not think I am misunderstanding him when I compress his intentions into the words: it would be the most distressing indication of his having been misunderstood

if people took to expounding works of art instead of
creating them.  He has written a good deal merely
in self-defence which people have taken as foundations on which to build!  But compression is not my
strong point!

I agree most heartily with what you say about
journalism.  I myself have been so stupefied by it
that I am now treating myself with the healing waters
of Schiller's aesthetics.  Am I not a good doctor? . . .

*From Franz Liszt*[1]

WEIMAR, *November 2,* 1853.

My very dear Friend—Now that I have been back
in Weimar for the last ten days I should like to have
a chat with you, as I know you will not grudge me so
much of your time.  My stay in Paris was cut short
by a week owing to the very urgent letters I received
from here which obliged me to return at once.
Wagner stayed on there three or four days after me
(for he had promised to meet his wife there), no thanks
to the papers which announced that he had been
forbidden to spend more than forty-eight hours in
Paris!  This, however, is not the first any more than
it will be the last or the worst of the lies which will be
circulated among the public with regard to Wagner.

As to news from Paris, I have none, except of
the energetic rehearsing of Meyerbeer's new opera,
*L'Étoile du Nord* (at the Opéra Comique), for which
he tells me he has only made use of four or five pieces
from the *Feldlager in Schlesien*, all the rest of the three
acts being quite new.  Also, the complete success of
the instrument which I have often mentioned to you,
and to which they insist on giving the name of *Piano-*

---

[1] Written in French in the original.—TR.

D

*Liszt.* It has three keyboards — plus a keyboard of two staves with pedal attached — and, without too much volume of sound or difficulty, it produces a harmonious and well - proportioned combination of piano and organ. It pleased Berlioz, who heard it, and in a month's time the instrument will be at Weimar, whence I shall not stir for the whole winter.

Now I have to work at and develop the new effects which this instrument can and ought to produce, which will be at least a year's work.

We also heard in Paris, Wagner and I, two of the last of Beethoven's quartettes (E♭ and C♯ minor) played by MM. Maurin,[1] Chevillard, etc. These gentlemen acquired a special reputation last winter by their performance of B.'s last quartettes, which seems to me well deserved.[2]  Sax[3] produced for our benefit the next day his large family of Saxophones, Sax horns, Sax Tubas, etc., etc.  Several of these (especially the Saxophone Tenor and the Saxophone Alto) will be exceedingly useful, even in our ordinary orchestras, and the *ensemble* has a really magnificent effect.

Hans is now in Dresden and will probably spend the winter in Paris. Remény has your room at Altenburg, and made a very successful début in the Weimar orchestra as leader of the first violins the day before yesterday at the performance of the *Flying Dutchman,* which I conducted. The hall was very full, the performance more satisfactory than the preceding ones, and the public at a sensibly higher pitch of

[1] Jean Pierre Maurin, born 1822.  See Wasielewski, *Die Violine und ihre Meister,* 1910, 5th ed. p. 571.

[2] With regard to the impression made on Wagner by the performance of the C minor quartette, especially, see *My Life,* p. 608.

[3] Charles Joseph Sax, from Belgium, born 1791 ; cf. Grove's *Dictionary of Music.*  Wagner (*My Life,* p. 761) speaks somewhat contemptuously of "the terrible man."

sympathy than ever before.   In ten days' time I shall
return to my desk to conduct *Wilhelm Tell,* and then
*Tannhäuser* and Dorn's *Nibelungen,* previous to the
performance of *Lohengrin* with Tichatschek and
Johanna Wagner.   This will take place I suppose,
when their Serene Highnesses the Grand Duke and
Grand Duchess revisit the theatre in a few months'
time, when the period of mourning is over.[1]   Until then
the Grand ducal lodge will remain empty, unlighted,
which gives it a very mournful appearance.

Klindworth will spend a fortnight in Hanover in
February before going to London, where he hopes
there will be a fair chance of success for him.   I
commend him to you once more most particularly, as
an excellent musician, a perfect pianist, and as one
belonging by rights and in truth to the category of
*real* artists, which unfortunately is so small.   If you
have an opportunity of obliging him I am sure you
will have no cause to regret it.

I have commissioned Pohl to publish his articles on
the Music Festival at Carlsruhe[2] in pamphlet form,
and I will send you a copy as soon as it appears.
The Musikfest has caused several good people to
expectorate who would have done much better if they
had remained silent.   Happily, this does not disturb
us in the least.   We have a lot to get through, and we
must continue to go forward.

Have you had your Overture performed at
Düsseldorf?   I have not had time to read the
newspapers for the last few days (overwhelmed as
I am by matters which are more than unpleasant)
and know nothing about it.   Write me a few words
when you have time.   And give me news of Berlioz'

---

[1] On account of the death of his father.

[2] Hoplit, *Das Karlsruher Musikfest,* Leipzig, 1853.

concerts at Hanover, and remember me most sincerely to him.  I still hope that he will be able to arrange for his concerts in Dresden, and in that case I count on seeing him here.  As our Court is in mourning it will not be possible for me to suggest that he should conduct one of his works here, as I should have very much liked to have done.  If you have the opportunity will you explain the circumstances to him.

Remény, of whom I am very fond, wishes me to assure you of his sincere friendship, to which I add the assurance of my very real, very cordial, and un-changeable affection.                            F. Liszt.

So as not to forget the friendly *Du* we used in Heidelberg, I must just add a postscript.  Just before I left Paris Wagner said to me, " I thank you most particularly for having brought Joachim to me at Basel "—you may rest assured that Wagner has the most friendly feelings for you.

I played Schumann's 2nd Piano and Violin Sonata with Remény with the greatest interest, and I agree most cordially with your praises of it.  What is Schumann doing now?  Did you see Brams [*sic*] at Düsseldorf? [1]

### From A. Dietrich

DÜSSELDORF, *November* 6, 1853.

My dear Friend—With this you will receive the manuscript copy of our three-in-one Sonata [2] and also the likeness of that wonderful pair of artists for Brahms and a copy of the *Musikzeitung*;  I am delighted with Schumann's short but pregnant article. This warm and enthusiastic outburst will do much to

---

[1] The Postscript is written in German.—TR.

[2] The sonata written as a greeting to Joachim by Schumann, Brahms, and Dietrich in collaboration.  See *Moser*, vol. i. p. 179.

open men's eyes, ears, and hearts to our Johannes; and I have no fear—as have many who do not know him—that, intoxicated by his sudden successes, he will make no more progress and imagine himself to be a finished master of his art already. That would be the sign of a weak nature—but Brahms is strong and determined, and the public and enthusiastic recognition accorded him by his master will strengthen him still more; he will have to remain worthy of it.

I miss Brahms very much and, for my own sake, I wish he could have stayed here, but I do not grudge him to you in the least! I would follow him at once and join you, if it were not impossible for me to leave the Schumanns, particularly now when a crisis is pending.[1] I am absolutely relying on your timely help in this matter, and in my opinion we ought to hold to our decision. Schumann, and his wife also, have no suspicions, and I fear that even if they are told in the most considerate manner possible it will be a crushing blow for both of them. I still hope that things may right themselves, or that the matter may be put off until a later date; the people in Düsseldorf are a vacillating lot, and if the next concert goes well and the *Glück von Edenhall* is successful with the public perhaps it will all simmer down. But if the contrary should happen I fear that there will be a sudden and violent crisis. I am very anxious and disturbed about it.

Before long I will send Brahms the music he left with the copyist and various other things. 1000 greetings to him. Farewell, and think of me! I hope to remain worthy of your friendship. Your faithful                              ALBERT DIETRICH.

---

[1] The disputes with the concert agents at Düsseldorf; see Litzmann, vol. ii. p. 46.

*From Robert Schumann*

[DÜSSELDORF, *November* 21, 1853.]

Dear Comrade-in-Arms—Since I sent a few 20-pound shells into the enemy's camp a few days ago, peace has been more or less preserved. I heard only yesterday that another comrade - in - arms had been secretly approached by the enemy, who wished him to blow me up by means of an underground mine, upon which the expression of the said comrade's face implied that he would far rather blow them up. Is that not amusing? But if you know anything of the conspiracy I should like very much to hear about it.

Something else, something tragi-comic, has happened to my wife and myself. We have a friend in whom we take a great interest. Now this friend said, rather gravely, to my wife that a few days ago a decision had been made which would affect his whole life. My wife came to me, somewhat upset, and pointed out that that must mean a rejected suit. I agreed with her, with some curses. But shortly afterwards there came different news and—just imagine—the contrary statement, that he had been accepted—whereupon the scales fell from our eyes and we saw what we had seen long ago—and our good wishes were redoubled. Dear Joachim, I will compose a Wedding Symphony with a violin solo and a Märchen for an Intermezzo ; I will write on it : "This Symphony belongs to Joachim." I will weave many things into it, including the many times you wished to leave Bonn, and that other time at Düsseldorf, which will make good musical crescendos, and the times when you were far away from us in spirit, so that we sought you as we might seek Franklin ; in short, it shall be my 5th, but in C major, not in C minor, and without a long Adagio.

GISELA VON ARNIM, 1846.

From a drawing by Herman Grimm.

Now give me your hand; if you promise me the wedding, I promise you the music for it. You scoundrel! To take us by surprise like this!

I should like to write much more. But I have fallen into a merry mood and cannot get out of it. So good-bye, dear bridegroom!          R. Sch.


*To Gisela von Arnim*

[Hanover, *November* 27, 1853.]

. . . Your long letter came as a wonderful gift to me. No one understands how to give of himself as you do; it was just as if I heard you talking beside me—I cannot tell you all that has happened since we parted, in the same way. The mechanism of letter writing is like a drag on all my words, and then I so seldom value external events sufficiently to remember them; I often have to ask myself—what did I do yesterday, before I realise that I came in contact with other people. It is different with you; everything you see has a relation to your inner life (and that is as it should be); thus what is a mere incident to me is significant to you. You get that from your mother. All external life is to you a reflection of the soul— there is sweetness everywhere, and, in the face of such beauty, I feel my weakness and dullness very deeply. But a musician like myself hardly ever sees the significance of anything except that which takes place in the depths of his soul—because this alone gives life to his music—and so he is often clumsy and unskilful when he tries to lay bare his thoughts, and he needs some one who can see past that right into his heart. . . .

I have been interrupted after all!! It was an old gentleman with whom I made an appointment for to-day—he came from Osnabrück on purpose to show me a rare Italian instrument.  Ah, people have no idea what little interest that sort of thing has for me ; they all imagine that when one has reached a certain point in any profession one can stay there and make oneself as comfortable as possible; they know nothing of the persistent worm of dissatisfaction with ourselves which is ever gnawing its way from heart to head.    I know no rest—my development was too unequal for that.    How enviable is a nature like Brahms' on whom work has the most soothing effect.    He is sleeping peacefully now, after his day's work, on my sofa in the next room, where he has already camped out for 2 nights—I am glad to think he is getting so much at home with me that he hardly ever leaves my rooms— when I have worked I am quite out of tune with everyday life.    Brahms has been here since Friday, when, on coming back from a late walk, I found the young green and gold tiger lying in wait for me, greener than ever by reason of his laurels and newly gilt by publishers who are printing all his things.    He was in splendid spirits and talked far into the night of old friends in the town of booksellers.[1]    You have really seen deep into his nature—he is egotistic and always on the look out for something to his advantage—but at any rate he is sincere in the expression of his feelings, with none of the false sentimentality with which others of his kind like to deceive themselves — and then anything he does seize is only used to help him in his efforts to become a great artist—that is saying much when one compares him with others. And I love him for it—you do not know what disgusting vanity I come across among my colleagues. So as not to end with this dissonance I will add that

[1] Leipzig.

I have prepared your 3 compositions for the printer—
they shall go to the publisher with the Concerto and
the *Hamlet* Overture. . . .

### To Robert Schumann

HANOVER, *November* 29, 1853.

This thick letter which the post will bring to you
in a foreign land, will no doubt alarm you; but it is a
musical letter which is easier to lay aside than a letter
in words. It must not take you from your Dutch
comforts for long! I have looked forward to sending
you the three pieces so that you, you generous man,
who have bestowed the richest gifts upon me, should
receive at least a small portion of the good fruit which
I have obtained from your wealth, so that you may
have proof of my good will, which, unfortunately, is
the only thing I can lay before you. At the same
time the 2nd piece, which should really be inscribed
Malinconia, contains the answer to the question of the
engagement; the final notes accentuated with blue
ink F, A, E, which alternate in the course of the piece
with three other notes have not only an artistic but a
human significance for me : their meaning is "*frei aber
einsam.*" [1] *I am not engaged.* People may feel themselves to be affinities, may believe that they are made
for one another,—and yet a hostile power may come
between them all their lives as though predestined.
That is what I have experienced. How? The
answer is better suited to a long evening talk than to
an account in a hasty letter. I am saying all this
only to you, for your sympathy gives me the greatest
pleasure. If you wish to hear more when we meet
again (which just Heaven grant may be soon!) I can

[1] Free but alone.

tell you all about it, but then you must promise to lie quietly on the sofa with your eyes closed if you are tired—and to listen only partly to me in the midst of your dreams. . . .

### To Gisela von Arnim, at Weimar

[HANOVER.]
*During Sunday night the 3rd and 4th [December, 1853].*

My mind must have been in a very morbid state, I can tell that by my frequent relapses; a crushing depression often steals over me.   Recently the whole of the summer with its solitary grief came back to me; I felt so forlorn, so desolate, indifferent among the indifferent who passed me by on their way to their Mammon, their pleasure.   You know nothing of all this, things seem much too bright to you, you have supernatural consolations, you can weep, sorrow is to you a transfiguration.   This is not given to me, I only feel how bitter everything is; I believe that what dissolves on the souls of others in melancholy healing dew, turns with me into hard cruel ice, the jagged edges of which merely wound.   I have often reproached myself for this and tried to overcome it, but its foundations must lie too deep; the fact that I so easily fall into these evil moods must be a part of my nature and comes perhaps from my Eastern origin. . . . You will see from all this that I am not made to be comfortable, I am prepared to fight with myself and with others, if need be, during my whole life.   Combat is life!   I wrote that to your Herman yesterday, and that I would be his comrade-in-arms and, as such, call him *Thou*.   That will please you. . . .

I began an Overture to *Demetrius*[1] yesterday and

[1] By Herman Grimm, Leipzig: Hirzel, 1853.   Performed for the first time, February 24, 1854.

I will try to finish it quickly. If one were only not
perpetually being disturbed by a thousand matters.
The letters I owe, more especially, burn in my conscience with an inextinguishable flame; hardly do I
fancy that I have sprinkled sufficient water on the fire
on the one side than, hui! up goes a tongue of flame
again on the opposite side; and yet the post brings
me letters abusing my dilatoriness every day! Added
to this I am continually swayed between my inclinations as virtuoso, conductor, and composer, so that what
with making plans and the difficulty I have in coming
to a decision I often get no real work done, just like
a housewife who never has the house straight because
of her mania for cleaning. But a spoilt child *unter
den Zelten* [1] will know nothing of such conscientious,
overworked labourers—unless it were from the *Frucht
und Dornenstücken.* [2] You lucky people who only need
to follow your inclinations, although you only do so
in the highest sense, your goodness is so infinite!

How glad I shall be if I am able to come to Berlin
for a few days at Christmas; I think this is sure to
be possible. Your mother has invited me to stay with
you if I should ever go to Berlin; I am delighted to
think she has such a kind feeling for me—but, all the
same, I should certainly not do so this time. You
must meet a number of people who would have
nothing in common with me, and they would be
curious, and then I should not be able to avoid intercourse with people who, if they did not try you,
at any rate would not interest you. And besides, to
be honest, I am afraid of gossip—it annoys me when
common people handle delicate fabrics with their
clumsy fingers. I am sure I must sometimes appear

---

[1] See note on p. 19.

[2] Joachim possessed the works of Jean Paul (the favourite author of Mendelssohn
and Schumann) as far back as in his Leipzig days.

philistine to you and your mother—but I am not really—the only reason why I am often careful to observe the conventions is that, as a rule, I value people too little to care for their indulgence on account of my art.   How often I have heard the silly remark: "A little carelessness is always excusable in an artist!" That annoys me; people should not be allowed the right to pardon anything.   And in my anxiety for you I have grown rather afraid of appearing so intimate with you in public: imagine, I had letters of congratulation from Bonn, from Wasielewski, and the Schumanns!  I was quite upset about it, until I saw the comic side of the affair!  I sent Schumann the *Abendläuten* and told him he was to abide by the notes F, A, E, which occur in it—you know what they mean.

You are right, when the 3 Gisela compositions appear I had better dedicate them openly.   I had the letter from Härtels (the publishers) to-day containing the answer to my suggestion that the Concerto, Overture, and the Paraphrases of your name should be printed; it began with such courteous thanks that I made sure it was a refusal—but no! in addition to the acceptance they requested me to say what fee I would require.   How Schade would rejoice over such exemplary publishers!

I am looking forward so much to the *Demetrius* Overture!  Your analysis of the play is excellent, and will be of great service to me in composing.  You have no idea of the blissfulness of the moment when the stormy passions and the waves of music meet in the heart, and the brain sees the crystallised columns of sound shooting upwards; they go on accumulating and arrange themselves side by side like organ pipes, getting bigger and bigger—and at last they become *one* sounding organ. But at present everything is still bubbling and fermenting mightily. I keep on hearing

It would be magnificent if only I had nothing in the world to do but to compose, and I hope that time is yet to come. But, all the same, I shall never be like my honoured friend and master, Schumann. He sits at his desk the first thing in the morning and draws (with much skill and wealth of design certainly) fantastic figures on the music paper, and the more the notes on the 5 lines twine themselves into labyrinths and the more he conceals the twists and turns, the more eagerly this fantastic builder rubs his hands with malicious glee and thinks : you will just have to pull the white thread, common sense, out of those brains of yours, that will help you to find your way about my work. Like every other poet, every true musical poet must discover the relation between the music in his own soul and the life around him, his music should re-echo with the eternal essence of the things he sees—ah, I know well enough how it ought to be, but my music is still on quite contrary lines— it is not free enough to loose the fetters which still bind it to the morbid in me. Be my theme. Help me to shake them off—you can do it ! . . . Your father's *Markgraf von Brandenburg*[1] gave me real enjoyment the other day : there is a true poet ; his works should be given to every musician one cares for ; or, if he happens to have his instrument in his hand or his pen, they should be laid on his desk : in Arnim's works there is an overflowing abundance of

---

[1] *Markgraf Carl Philipp von Brandenburg.* *Tragedy.* Vol. xx. in the collected works of Ludwig Achim v. Arnim.

feeling. I can still remember how delighted I was when I read in Jean Paul's *Titan* how Albano, longing to be one with the beauties of Nature surrounding him, tears the bandage from a wound in his arm, out of which the warm blood gushes. I have always longed to meet with passionate emotion like this—your father's poetry has it; in him it all wells up in generous abundance, like warm gushing heart's blood. That does me so much good. I love him unspeakably. The other day I read his play through at a sitting. What the d——! I will write polite letters to others, not to you! . . .

. . . You think your trip to Weimar was satisfactory—your mother, it appears, is particularly pleased with the Archduke's zeal.[1] Your portrait of the latter fits in with what I had already imagined him to be, but I should have thought he had *esprit* rather than real intellect; all the better for Hoffmann, Schade, and his own subjects if you think he has something more. But for God's sake do not imagine that I wish to stand up for the Princess[2] in opposition to you; I have nothing in common with her, least of all with *her* enthusiasm for my soul's favourite, Schiller. The only thing about Schiller which would appeal to the Princess's nature, as exhibited on its most bearable side in her chatter about the immortal Liszt, would be the superficial grandeur of his aspirations. The magnitude of his ideas satisfies her lust of power just as the pathos of Schiller's language suits her Polish sense of family pride and royal dignity (somewhat like an ermine mantle for her tongue, which might, possibly, be made to represent the purple)—of the intrinsic

[1] Karl Alexander, who had succeeded on July 8. Bettina tried to interest him in a monument to Goethe as well as to obtain his patronage for Hoffmann von Fallersleben and Oskar Schade.

[2] Liszt's friend, Caroline Witgenstein.

worth of the great man Schiller, in whom the love of
justice had grown to be the guiding destiny of life—
of the majesty of the mind which, in spite of all
obstacles, still believed in the growing seed of truth—
of Schiller's reverence for the individual arising from
his love for the universal—of the Schiller whom *I*
mean, the finicking Princess has no notion.   I think
differently of Liszt, as you know.   His appearance
certainly put life into the band of lazy dilettante music
directors who were enjoying their sinecures ; that had
to be done, and it required an impetuous nature such
as Liszt's to do it.   Wherever he has acted in an
unauthorised and despotic manner there will not fail
to be a reaction.   I have a weakness for the spoilt
man, although I cannot deny that there is no very
sharp distinction in his nature between pride and
vanity.   There is much in him also which is quite
incomprehensible to me—but I feel it my duty to
defend him against the charge of thoughtlessness
towards many of his colleagues—I can admit it to
you.   I have not yet replied to his letter !  I could
not get the right tone, and that is your fault, you
estrange me from my friends, you wicked enchantress !

I have scribbled such a lot to you; if you have really
read as far as this, I will add a few words of apology
in as good a hand as possible, so that you may read
them, at any rate, without straining your dear eyes ;
but I fear it will be in vain.   So I will just send my
best wishes for your recovery from your cold : to
continue your vivid metaphors on the subject, I might
say that as far as your nose is concerned it has been
as a fruitful overflowing of the Nile from which the
sun of your intelligence will draw rich nourishment for
your wits—but I will not go on, for fear the letters
should give one another colds.   I was to write as much

"nonsense" as I liked; you see, your wish is a command to me. . . . One thing more; shall I send you Brahms' book of legends before Christmas? You need only send one word—yes or no; you need not write a letter for which, I am sure, you will have no time now. But think of me a little sometimes, you can always find time for that!—Adieu! Ever your

J. J.

### From Hector Berlioz [1]

LEIPZIG, December 9, 1853.

My dear Joachim—I have had a letter from Elberfeld, in which it is suggested that I should go there and have some things performed at a concert. The writer of the letter, M. Abraham Kipper, adds that you will doubtless have given me particulars as to his position and his *establishment*.

I know nothing of these matters, however. What is there at Elberfeld? Is it a society for concerts like the one at Bremen? What is the orchestra like down there? Is it twenty-horse power or only ten? Are there any choirs? What ought the fees to be?

I know nothing and you know everything, and you keep your knowledge to yourself like a sphinx.

I shall be here until next Tuesday. My concert takes place to-morrow. All is well. In spite of their cold manner, the *Leipzikois* have swallowed the thing. *All* the papers have treated me splendidly. The opposition is furious, but we laugh at them. Liszt returns from Weimar to-morrow.

I have arranged for one or two concerts at Dresden for next spring, and I have an offer from Oldenbourg for the same time. Would it not be better to make the Elberfeld affair fit in with the two others?

[1] Written in French.—TR.

Be so good as to give me some details by return of post.

Brams [*sic*] has had a great success here. He made a deep impression on me the other day at Brindel's[1] with his scherzo and his adagio. I am grateful to you for having let me make the acquaintance of this diffident, audacious young man who has taken it into his head to make a new music. He will suffer greatly. . . .

As for my admiration for you, it has increased since I left you. And when I think of your musical *worth*, which is so complete, so brilliant, and so pure, I sometimes find myself exclaiming (all alone, and *à propos* of nothing), "Ah, it's stupendous, it's prodigious!"

Adieu. Remember me to our friends of the Hanover orchestra, of whom I have such pleasant memories. Give special messages to Müller.—Yours most sincerely,

HECTOR BERLIOZ.

*P.S.*—David is very kind, very friendly, and very prudent. He knows the people of Leipzig, and I could not do better than follow his advice. He is a true artist—and has intellect—which is never a disadvantage.

M. Otto Nieper in his last letter mentioned an article in the *Gazette de Cologne* in which you are supposed to have had a hand. . . . I am very curious to read it, but I *confidently* thank you.

*To Gisela von Arnim*

HANOVER [*about December* 11], 1853.

. . . Everything I do is done, unconsciously, for you, you dear, good Mamma. I will even call you

[1] Franz Brendel.

E

that if it gives you pleasure, as you say you would like best of all to represent my mother! I will agree to anything that pleases you.

But one favour you must grant me; of all my weaknesses spare the *one*, that I do not like to be reminded in my own person of the fickleness of human affections. Do not go on drawing such alluring pictures of how lovely it can and will be when I have forgotten that you were once my ideal which was to be with me through life. I still hold the fatalistic doctrine that one meets one's affinity once in a lifetime only. I know you have had far greater opportunities of studying the lives of other people than I have—you have even led a fuller and more varied life than I—but I also have already realised the fickleness of human nature, the yielding of the *Ego* to habit. Yes, I have been able to experience it and study it in myself, but as something which caused me pain. If you look forward, with a foresight in which you are *quite justified*, to the happy day in the future when there will be a charming Frau Concertmeister, do not, at any rate, expect me to take comfort from it. I would far rather have the most cutting remarks on my fickleness poured on my head, and I would enjoy the douche. Do not remove the cataract before the time; you may think it is ripe — but I can only entreat my spiritual doctor to subject me to no violent remedies.

Many thanks for your little friend's charming note —she seems really worthy to be called your friend. There is a delightful girlish vivacity in the way in which she talks about herself, *Demetrius*, music, dilettanteism, ending up with her cloak, and only covering two pages! To a dull person like myself this is extraordinarily charming. She has discerned *one side* of Bülow from his playing quite accurately ; a boldness which is not always justifiable and therefore sometimes renders his manner burlesque or objectionable (without euphemism : a kind of insolence).

I can do nothing to soften this side of his nature ; my skill is not equal to his, and he would very soon feel his superiority, and so I should be of no use to him.   So I keep his excellent qualities before me ; the constant activity of his mind, his enthusiasm, and his power of self-sacrifice.   He is just as likely, I imagine, to sacrifice his life to an ideal as to an actress's smile, and this is a precious inheritance from his father.   That is the French blood in him ; at Weimar I often called him Liszt's Camille Desmoulins[1] in joke.

I have not yet written to your mother.   I think it will offend her if I accept the Grimms' invitation instead of hers, and for that reason it will be just as well, perhaps, if I do not go there at Christmas. But in any case I shall come to the performance of *Demetrius*.   The inevitable development of the characters and the simple force of the language are very marked in the play and should be recognised by every one, even without the help of your excellent commentary.

. . . All your letters arrived safely.   I will tell you nothing about concerts and other events ; they would probably not interest you, at any rate, as far as I am concerned, I set no store now on applause at concerts. The lack of taste and judgment which came under my notice at the Court concert quite recently (it was last night !) was horrible.   And these people pour a watery chatter about art over one as though it were

---

[1] The young people were very familiar with the history of the French Revolution.   At that time Bülow had given Joachim the translation of Robespierre's writings and speeches which was published in 1852.

refreshing rain, and their silly smiling patronage the sun shining through it. Under such conditions my musical blossoms cannot fructify. But your letters, glorious lady, are like so many overtures full of the most lovely sounds! . . .

### To Gisela von Arnim

COLOGNE, *December* 20, 1853.

It is still early morning, day has hardly broken in the sacred town, which seems to vibrate like a violin. . . . I am staying for the first time for many a long day with relations; they have a marvellously *good* child, with whom I have made friends; that is a little pleasure strewn in my way like sugar plums on a stale cake. I loathe all the cheap time-worn compliments people pay me; I have no wish for such easy laurels. For me the whole of life consists in remembrance of the past. Nevertheless, I have forced myself to come to the decision not to go to Berlin for Christmas. If I do not finish the *Demetrius* in the week between Christmas and the New Year, I shall not be able to do so for some time; and I think you, too, would prefer to see me there when I have leisure. Then I shall stay four or five days in Berlin, and I shall have time to arrange the text of the Opera with you and Herman. I have been so worried latterly at Hanover by a crowd of small duties that I could not write to your mother about the rooms. Fancy, they wanted to force me into the Austrian army. To let myself be shot for the Habsburgs would chime in nicely with my sympathies! Added to that I had a letter from home which really grieved me, because it showed that my people are so far from understanding the only thing to which I attach any importance—the most *independent* development possible of my natural intellectual capabilities.   Only think, my mother wishes to marry me to a favourite niece.   In all seriousness is it not extremely funny that my personal freedom should be at the disposal of the State and the family?   I am writing you a lot of " things " just as they come.

*Wednesday.*

I was interrupted yesterday.   Since then I played in public last night.   They clapped furiously after the Beethoven Concerto.   I saw many mouths open during my Concerto, but not to praise—to yawn.

All the same I shall not be able to leave off composing—it is the one means by which I can let light on to my innermost feelings, and all others fail to satisfy me just now.   If I were only between my own narrow four walls now writing *Demetrius*!   But I shall be here until the day after to-morrow.   To-morrow I am giving a concert for a poor theatre manager who has no other means of supporting himself and his family.   May it be well attended! . . .

*From Hector Berlioz* [1]

PARIS, *December* 20, 1853.

My dear Joachim—It will be a real treat to me to return by Hanover and to take part in your concert on April 1.

I am sending Captain Nieper two songs (*La Captive* [2]) and something of mine (*Nuits d'été* [3]), and am asking him to be so good as to translate them. Mme. Nottes could sing these two Lieder (with

---

[1] Written in French in the original.—TR.
[2] Op. 12.   Reverie for mezzo-soprano with orchestra.
[3] Op. 7.   Six melodies for mezzo-soprano with orchestra.

orchestra) admirably, and to these could be added the *Symphonie Fantastique* or *Harold,* whichever you prefer.

I have another song already translated into German, which Schneider[1] has sung with the most unexpected good fortune at Leipzig. It is *Le Pâtre Breton* ; and M. Bernard[2] would give it with delightful effect.

I would add that should Mme. Nottes find the *Captive* too low for her (in D) I have the orchestra parts transposed (in E♭). And in that case it could be played in E♭.

I may tell you in confidence that I adore this work, but that it is very difficult to render satisfactorily because of the varying shades of rhythm and of mood (at the same time exalted and voluptuous) in which the singer must steep herself if she is to understand it.

If you can procure me some sort of indemnity for the journey on the occasion of the concert on April 1, it will be very useful to me, and I shall be greatly obliged to you. But I warn you that I shall come even without that if the Oldenburg concert remains fixed for April 8 ; as I have every reason to believe it will.

Adieu. As soon as you have any news for me write to me in Paris, 19 rue de Boursault.

Yesterday, at the concert of St. Cecilia, conducted by Seghers,[3] they performed my little oratorio, *La Fuite en Égypte,* in full for the first time, with the

---

[1] Karl Schneider (1822–82), known as the admirable interpreter of the Evangelist in Bach's Passion Music. From 1872 teacher of singing at Cologne Conservatoire.

[2] C. Bernard, baritone at the Hanover theatre since 1852.

[3] F. J. B. Seghers (1801–81), first-rate violinist and conductor. One of the founders of the Paris Conservatoire concerts.

overture and chorus. It was a great success and the audience encored the tenor solo.

Goodbye, with many expressions of my sincere affection, H. BERLIOZ.

*To Gisela von Arnim*

[HANOVER, *January* 11, 1854.]

. . . You do not know what it means to sacrifice your precious inner life to all kinds of external trifles. For the last week I have had a crowd of little annoyances like that to put up with, and now I am off again and am travelling to Leipzig to-morrow, where, after having refused for three years, I have been obliged to consent to play in public so as not to give the management and my musical friends there the idea that something has offended me. But, good heavens, why am I writing thus to you, you good spirit, whose image I like best of all to call up before me freed from all that troubles me, a pure spirit, one in thought and expression, as in the picture from Fiesole which you gave me. That, and the others, were my consolation, when I had to divide my attention on all sides, instead of living as I longed to do. I have not yet learnt to collect my thoughts again quickly, when external impressions have distracted me ; when I have times of depression they are generally due to this ; and then my inclinations, miles away from the possibility of having free play, make my weakness more clear to me than ever. But perhaps I shall have strength in the future to conquer what seems to be my arch-enemy. . . .

. . . What would you like to be called in the dedication of the three pieces (on your name)? The copies are now before me and are to go to the publisher in Leipzig. I suppose simply, Fräulein Gisela von Arnim, without *Hochwohlgeboren* and without *respectfully*! Is that not so? And perhaps you can think of a less prosaic title than " Three Pieces." At first I thought of writing " Reality and Dreams,"[1] but, apart from the fact that it sounds to me too pretentious, it might be capable of various interpretations, and I prefer the stupidest title to one which might cause people to imagine things. I shall be in Händel's town until Friday ; on the evening of the 13th I am going to a Court concert at Weimar. . . .

. . . Bülow has been staying with me for the last week. You are greatly mistaken if you think he influences me. More about that later on.

### *To Woldemar Bargiel*

[HANOVER] *January* 30, 1854.

My dear Woldemar—Your sister[2] who, with Schumann, unhappily left me behind in unmusical Hanover, tells me she has spoken to you of my reluctance to have my music played in public. I can, indeed, only confirm this, with reference to your kind proposal to have my compositions performed in Berlin. The manner in which they have been received up to now in other places, in Düsseldorf, Weimar, Leipzig, and Cologne, gives me no reason to expect that my compositions would be sympathetically received in Berlin, and as the aim of music is not exactly to experiment on the ears of the audience I will not be importunate with my music, but (as three works are appearing shortly with Härtel) I shall either wait until another musician is sufficiently interested in them to produce them of his own accord, or see if I

---

[1] *Wirkliches und Geträumtes.*
[2] Bargiel was half-brother to Clara Schumann. See Litzmann, vol. i. p. 2.

cannot present something newer and better. I am aware that everything I have composed within the last few years is too serious, I might almost say defiant in character, to please others, but I could not help laughing when the papers attacked my music for being formless, probably because they felt quite sure that I should consider it my duty to express in my music the Drama of the Future! I sin rather on the side of writing too rigidly ; every bar should be related to the whole ; that is my aim, but perhaps it is often too painfully evident. I fear that is the case again in my latest work, the *Demetrius* Overture. It is not all written out yet : during the last three weeks I have not been able to work at it, partly because the concerts obliged me to hear and play much too much other music, and because I was moving from place to place. For me, at any rate, the greatest concentration is necessary for composing, and I intend to live the life of a real hermit ; for the next few months I shall go nowhere (except to Berlin to attend a performance of Grimm's *Demetrius*). Perhaps you will get two Overtures as the result of this seclusion. I am longing to know what new things you have composed since the three beautiful piano pieces ? Could you not send me something? I hope you are convinced of my musical as also of my friendly sympathy under all circumstances, even though I am not a very zealous correspondent. So be kind and share your good things ; Brahms can play it to me if it's for the piano ; he is looking forward to meeting you after all that Schumann has told him about you, and he sends kind regards meanwhile.—Farewell! Your sincerely devoted                    JOSEPH JOACHIM.

You have no doubt heard from your sister about

Schumann's visit here.  Those were glorious musical days, which I would have liked you to have enjoyed with us.

### From Robert Schumann

DÜSSELDORF, *February* 6, 1854.

Dear Joachim—We have been gone a week, and we have not yet sent a word to you and your comrade![1] But I have often written to you with sympathetic ink, and there is a secret writing between these lines which will come to light later on.

And I have dreamed of you, dear Joachim.  We were together for three days—you had heron's feathers in your hands from which flowed champagne — how prosaic!  But how true!—

We have often thought of the days we spent with you; may there soon be more like them!  The kindly royal family, the excellent orchestra, and the two young gods in the midst of it all—we shall never forget it.

Meanwhile I have been at work again on my *Garden.*[2]  It is getting more and more stately, and I have put up sign-posts here and there so that people should not get lost, *i.e.* explanatory notes.  I am now among the ancients, with Homer and the Greeks.  I have discovered particularly splendid passages in Plato.

Music is silent at present—externally at any rate. How is it with you?  The Leipzigers showed more understanding for your Phantasia [3] than these prosaic humdrum Rhinelanders.  Yes.  I think so too—the virtuoso caterpillar will disappear by degrees, and a magnificent butterfly of a composer appear.  Only not too much mourning, let us have the goldfinch too sometimes ?

[1] Brahms.                [2] An anthology of passages dealing with music.
[3] Concerto in G minor, op. 3.

When are you going to Leipzig? Write and tell me! Is the *Demetrius* Overture finished?

I am enjoying the cigars very much. They seem to be a Brahms brand, and as usual very strong but good! Now I can see him smiling.

I will stop now. It is getting dark. Write to me soon in words and in music!

R. Sch.

My wife sends messages. Kind regards also to Herr Grimm.[1] He does not appear to live up to his name.

## To Herman Grimm

[HANOVER, *February* 28, 1854.]

Dear Grimm—From the moment I left Berlin my mind has been almost exclusively occupied with you. Your green book[2] was the only thing that mattered to me. I was forced to return to it again and again, to learn to know you better and better, and to rejoice in the calm and perfect harmony of your nature. How completely and entirely detached you are from those phenomena of which you are master, but which hamper me on every side when I do not ignore them. Let me repeat here, most emphatically, that to know you so much more intimately is a delight to me. I would tell you that I "revered" you if I were able to do so; but I can only love perfection; it draws the good in me to itself like a magnet. Everything in me that is akin to this higher power clings to it with eager desire to become like it and to draw strength from it, and, apart from all other considerations, I am your friend

---

[1] Julius Otto Grimm.

[2] A green notebook, containing Grimm's thoughts on God, the world, humanity and other subjects, more or less systematically arranged.

in this way, just as the light of your nature penetrates to me in spite of all obstacles. I am not too proud to tell you this, do not you be too proud to accept it. I believe firmly that I shall have only *one* aim before me during the whole course of my life.

I should have liked to enclose a copy of my *Demetrius* Overture for a certain box in your room, but Schumann has not yet returned it. If you think I was weak to send my work to the one man in whose pure artistic purpose I have absolute confidence, at any rate I have been sufficiently punished by the anxiety I have felt ever since. On Saturday I hope, at last, to hear the Overture played by our orchestra at a rehearsal. If I like it then I will send you the whole thing, and you can do what you please with it. I often thought of you on Sunday evening,[1] and I should have liked to have gone with Rudolf[2] and your sister to see the play. The critic in the *National Zeitung* finds fault with two things that seemed to me admirable : first, that you have sacrificed the historical interest of your characters to the human interest, and then, that *Demetrius* returns for the second time to prison. What annoys me in criticism is not what is said but the injustice of being judged by some one who does not even take the trouble to consider the subject on which he is passing judgment from the artist's standpoint.

[The conclusion is missing.]

### From *Albert Dietrich*

DÜSSELDORF, *February* 28 [1854].

Dear Friend—I have terribly sad news for you and Johannes ; you must let me off the minuter details

---

[1] Second performance of *Demetrius*.      [2] H. Grimm's younger brother.

for the present; I am not calm enough yet to be able to write them. In a recent letter to Brahms I hinted that Schumann's nerves were in a bad state. This has become worse from day to day; he heard music continuously, sometimes it was of the most beautiful description, but often agonisingly hideous. Later on phantom voices were added to this, which, as he thought, cried terrible and beautiful things in his ear. Last Saturday week he was seized with violent despair for the first time. From that time Schumann's mind was obviously affected; the phantoms did not leave him a moment's peace. I went to see him three times a day. As a rule he was apparently calm, but sometimes he hinted at something frightful which the spirits were urging him to do—and he has attempted it—on Monday—yesterday—towards mid-day he managed to slip out of the house—Hasenclever, I and several others looked for him in vain until nearly half past one. About that time he was brought back by four boatmen; they had rescued him from the Rhine; he had thrown himself in from the middle of the bridge. Now, as before, he is apparently quite sensible, and yet his mind is so much affected that they do not think he will recover for some time, although the doctors have not given up hope. As you can imagine, his wife is overwhelmed by grief and despair, but they have managed to keep the worst from her; she seems to have a suspicion of it, however—but she is not to be told—she has not been allowed to go to him since, and is staying with Fräulein Leser in an agony of longing; neither I nor anybody else except the doctors and attendants may go near him—he will probably be taken to a good nursing home soon.

You can imagine what I have suffered; I was quite ill, and I am still often attacked by a kind of feverish ague. I hope I shall be able to send you better news before long. I will write to you again soon.

Schumann was not able to look at your Overture; I studied it thoroughly until Monday; I deeply admire your fine work. I should like to write a great deal about it—but it is impossible to-day.—Your devoted

ALBERT DIETRICH.

### To Woldemar Bargiel

DÜSSELDORF, M[arch] 6, 1854.

Dear Bargiel—Things seem to be turning out better than I had dared to hope. Schumann was no longer in Düsseldorf when I arrived; they had taken him to a pleasantly situated place near Bonn,[1] where, it is to be hoped, he will grow gradually calmer, as everything which might remind him of his unfortunate attack is carefully kept from him. Your sister, who has not yet been told the worst, is calmer than I imagined, owing to the presence of your mother and the care of loving friends. Music gives her consolation and confidence in the future. Before his final collapse, Schumann had some intervals of peace during which he wrote some Variations on a theme brought to him during the first stages of his illness by "angels as a greeting from Mendelssohn and Schubert." As though Schumann had had some sort of presentiment he had put all his domestic affairs in order, down to the minutest details ; latterly, he had even written the most precise instructions on all his manuscripts. In one of his earlier notebooks, which he filled with all kinds of remarks, there is the sentence : " *The artist should beware of losing touch with society, otherwise he*

---

[1] Dr. Richarz's private asylum at Endenich, which Schumann never quitted.

*will be wrecked, as I am.*" It made me shudder, and indeed I have no feeling but that of the deepest grief when I think of the ideal which has changed from beauty to horror in such a heart-breaking manner. But I will not describe your own feelings to you. I am expecting Dr. Hasenclever (Schumann's friend) to return to-day, and I hope to hear something reassuring from him. I go back to Hanover by the night train. —Sincerely yours, J. JOACHIM.

### To Julius Otto Grimm at Düsseldorf

[HANOVER, *middle of March*, 1854.]

Dear Grimm—I was delighted to find you had thought so soon of those who remained behind. There is not much to say about either of them, still less about Hanover—much, very much of the glorious sky of the last few days and the still more beautiful sun which burns in one with dreams of courage and the future (I nearly wrote "music"!); I went for a long walk to-day. You lucky ones are doing that energetically no doubt, and singing Swedish songs and looking at pictures. Well, my chief reason for writing is that in a month's time, please God, there will be a glimmer of hope for Schumann—only a glimmer because I do not believe much in magnetism. But listen: they tell me in Berlin [1] that there is a Count Sagadie in Paris (the name is not very clearly written, it may be Saparin) who by means of his magnetic power has kept people alive who have been given up by the doctors. He is said to have first discovered his power through his own child, whom he snatched from death: and as he is very pious and

[1] Probably one of the Arnims' circle of friends. The new practice of table turning, magnetism, and Count Franz Szápary's cures by suggestion, were occupying society at that time.

wished at one time to go into a monastery, he is devoting his life to the task of curing people for nothing.    The friend who told me about it mentioned several people *by name*, whom he knows personally, who have been helped by the magnetic cure, but he told me principally of a professor who had suffered from melancholia for eight years (as the doctors said, in consequence of a stroke and *softening of the brain, which they declared was incurable*), and he is now completely cured after being treated by Count Sagarin.    That is the account from Berlin —now what do you think, dear friend?    The matter seems to me at any rate important enough to be mentioned to Dr. Hasenclever.    Consult Dietrich about it, to whom I send sincere greetings, and, if possible, let me know what Hasenclever says— however resigned one may be to providence, personal anxiety is not to be silenced—one hopes and despairs in a continuous ebb and flow.    One of you three[1] might write every week; it would do you no harm and be of great use to me.    How is that splendid Frau Schumann—does she still play?    I wish I could take Becker's place.    Give her my respectful and sincere regards—and messages to the children and Frau Bargiel.

I see Wagemann[2] every day, he is a good, honest soul.    Bülow has been here—Berlioz is coming at the end of the month.    At the last subscription concert in Leipzig I conducted *Hamlet*; the *Demetrius* Overture will be rehearsed to-morrow, etc., etc.

I think of you and yours often, very often.

Always your devoted                              J. JOACHIM.

[1] Grimm, Dietrich, Brahms.                    [2] A cousin of J. O. Grimm's.

*From Julius Otto Grimm*

DÜSSELDORF, *March* 9 [*probably April* 1854].

. . . Indeed there has not been any very joyful news to give on the subject we have at heart—first of all, as soon as I got your letter I went to Dr. Hasenclever, but your suggestions about magnetism had no success whatever with him. The news from Endenich has been and is depressing—always the same—Schumann is calmer than at first, except for several less violent attacks he has had from time to time ; Frau Schumann is just as overcome as in the early days—often when she mentions him or plays something of his she breaks into sobs. It is a relief that she is no longer burdened to the same extent with verbal and written expressions of sympathy. We, that is Kreisler [1] and I, have spent some wonderful hours with her. She showed us many Manuscripts, among others that most beautiful one of all, the *Faust*—she at the piano playing the piano part —we following the score with eyes, ears, and hearts. All three of us have longed often and heartily for you and still do so, and we beg you to come soon. Your proposal to stay in Hanover is disapproved of most strongly by us—*Do come soon !* . . .

My dear cousin has kept me posted in you and your musical doings (Berlioz, Wehner, etc.)—and it is charming of you not to desert the people of Hanover who are so longing to be ennobled. . . .

The third chapter of this letter must be occupied with Kreisler. He commissions me to ask you, in case you have not been able to decipher his two letters, to send them back to him, so that he can write them again or have them neatly copied and

[1] Brahms. See Florence May, *Life of Johannes Brahms*, i. 93 : " ' Kreisler, jun.,' a pseudonym adopted by Brahms out of love for the Kapellmeister Johannes Kreisler, hero of one of Hoffmann's tales."

F

send them to you again; for the contents are of importance to him—especially those of the second letter—about his sister and her journey here. I imagine the hieroglyphics are not as bad as all that, as my cousin said in his letter, but Brahms is getting anxious, because he has had no answer from you up to now. . . .

During the last few weeks we two have been on the Rhine, *i.e.* Cologne, Bonn, Mehlem, Drachenfels, etc., etc., have drunk Rhine wine, and enjoyed ourselves generally. I only wish you would come and we could have another Scherzo like that, only a bigger one, in Trio. Kreisler is the most marvellous person. Hardly had he delighted us with his Trio than he had finished three movements of a Sonata for two pianos, which seems to be even more sublime. À propos! He begs you to send him his arrangement of your *Hamlet* Overture as soon as possible, he wants to revise and where necessary alter it, and above all to play it with Frau Schumann. Good Lord, I am scribbling so badly you will hardly—but Krösel[1] is pestering me so, he wants to go to Grafenberg, so that we can lie in the moonlight in the woods. He is as mad as he can be—as the artistic genius of Düsseldorf he has adorned his room with beautiful frescoes in the style of Callot, *i.e.* with heads of Madonnas and brats—so as to have something worthy of his contemplation whilst he is at work. . . .

*From Hector Berlioz*

HÔTEL DE L'ANGE D'OR,
DRESDEN, *April* 26, 1854.

My dear Joachim—Thank you for having given me news of yourself, I am really grieved that you

[1] Kreisler.

should have been bothered by my affairs. I will not refer to them again when they have sent me word,— but I do not want to think of it any more. I have written to M. de Platen,[1] who has not replied. I did not mention the question of money. I insisted on knowing when I was to go back to Hanover next winter to fulfil the engagement I had made with the King to let him hear *Roméo et Juliette*. As you can imagine, that is not a trifle to me, because of the time which will have to be spent at the theatre rehearsing the voices, because of the artists who will have to be procured from Brunswick and even from Hamburg (in accordance with the King's gracious wishes), and finally, because of my own affairs which I must arrange accordingly. I have to go to Bavaria this summer, and perhaps I shall go to Hamburg later, and I must fit in these various journeys. But, my dear Joachim, do not bother about this; now that M. de Platen has had my letter he will do what he thinks best. M. Nieper was to have come here to hear *Faust*, and he was to have sent the German words for *La Captive*; I have seen neither him nor his verses. *Faust* was performed magnificently, wonderfully, incomparably. What a pity that you could not be there to hear it! We are giving it again *this evening*. M. de Luttichau[2] at once asked me to give it again, before he left the hall last Saturday. The *Höllenfahrt* and the *Pandemonium* made a most extraordinary impression on the public. The bitter-sweet Dresden papers admit that it is *something*. I hope the performance will be better than ever this evening. Next Saturday we are giving *Roméo et Juliette, La Fuite en Égypte*, and the two Overtures to *Benvenuto Cellini*. The

---

[1] Count Platen.   [2] Manager of the Dresden Court Theatre.

orchestra, chorus, and soloists shów an ardour, a devotion, a patience, an intelligence, an enthusiasm, which would delight you.   And what musicians!! . . .

Adieu, I press your hand, or your hands (those two clever hands) with all the strength of my friendship and admiration.—Your ever devoted

H. BERLIOZ.

*To Gisela von Arnim*

[HANOVER, *end of April* 1854.]

. . . In short, I am not in the least alarmed by your description of Berlin in the summer, the heat will do me no harm, so long as your warmth does not suffer under it, I am used to dust, and I ask for nothing but a small, cheap, shady room, which is so ugly and so out of the way that no one will want to come and see me, and also—for some green outside the window.   Ought that not to be possible with the help of Herman and Bargiel?   Through force of habit something green has become a necessity to me— before every house I have had for the last eight years luck has granted me a few trees on which my musical thoughts could climb at times.   I have not derived positive happiness or content from this—I ought really to have accustomed myself long ago not to look for truth and beauty outside, but to *seek* them "in" me ; I have never found them—but there was such contradiction, such confusion between my inclinations and that which I considered my duty— that I *had* to feel unhappy.   So give up all idea of my being disappointed in my expectations—I could only be that through my own fault. . . .

*To Gisela von Arnim*

[HANOVER], *May* 1 [1854].

My dear Friend—I have just finished making myself a copy of your poem; I am returning you the original! Will there be anything left of it, since I have drawn so much delight from it in copying it?

I feel so strong since the spring; mentally, I have not felt like this for ever so long—I think I must have been really morbid—my thoughts were a burden to me; they seemed to me like a gloomy thicket, penetrated by no daylight, through which I laboriously cut my way for no particular reason, simply from a sense of duty and a fear of cowardice—Oh, we shall have lots to talk about. Divine power of thought; into what a spirit of torment we transform you, if the dark forest through which you lead us is not illumined by the blue sky and sun of action! Oh, I feel so calm now, so glad to be alive! I long for nothing but hard work and—intercourse with those I love. . . .

*From Richard Wagner*

ZÜRICH, *May* 30, 1854.

Dear Joachim—Your last answer did not satisfy me at all. One does not reply like that when one is reminded of a promise; you must still remember that when you were in Basel you promised to pay me a visit in Switzerland this summer? The Musical Festival[1] is, of course, only a side issue between us; for this year I am contemplating a tour through the Bernese Oberland to le Valais, and from there (after the music-making) to the Lake of Geneva as the only

[1] For an account of this unfortunate *Musikfest* and of the tour see Wagner, *My Life*, p. 612.

trip I shall allow myself, and I hoped that whoever cared to pay me a visit—would go with me. Hence the talk of the Musical Festival, in which, so far as I am concerned, I only mean to take part to the extent of the A major Symphony, as I thought it well to withhold all promises of a composition of my own. But—if you were with me then it could not hurt you to take up your fiddle when I am wielding the baton. But, you seem to have given my hasty invitation rather serious consideration. It would be very nice if your consideration became a little more frivolous, and you wrote " I am coming."

Think it over well, and if you find my request reasonable, bring one of your Overtures with you, of which Liszt wrote me much in a few words the other day.

Could you not inveigle poor Hans into coming too, in that case ?

If Liszt is still with you tell him he will shortly receive a long letter from me. The announcement of the completion of *Rheingold* has already gone off to him. Farewell, and—give me pleasure !—Your

R. W.

### To Gisela von Arnim

[HANOVER, *about June* 1, 1854.]

. . . I am going to Berlin on Saturday. Liszt left me last night. One illusion after the other is vanishing as I go through life ; that pains me, not because I become more and more solitary, but because it makes one sad to regard with pity the things one used to look up to with awe and reverence and hardly dare to criticise. With his gifts of heart and mind Liszt might spread happiness around him—and in spite of this he requires the most complicated machinery to hide from himself that he is, indeed, unhappy owing to his confusion of mind. There is a tendency to restlessness in his every action that has something unholy about it, in spite of all his moral aims. If only I could heal him!

### From Clara Schumann

DÜSSELDORF, *June* 9, 1854.

My dear Friend—Your letter and enclosure gave me very real pleasure. You must have known this when you wrote, for you will have felt with me the sadness of yesterday [1] which I had to spend without him, the man I love above all else. Accept my warmest thanks for the great sympathy and self-sacrificing friendship you have shown me all through this time of sorrow, may your feeling for me and my Robert remain the same in the future, it is a precious possession to us, for we both love and honour you deeply—you know that!

I was very glad to see your pieces in print at last, only I should have liked the composer himself to have accompanied them. It was a surprise to us all to hear that you were in Berlin, and a pleasant one only in so much as my brother will derive great enjoyment in every way from your visit. Brahms was rather hurt; although he had had his suspicions, he had hoped and we had all hoped to have you here for some time, but I think I am right in understanding from your letter that you are coming all the same, and then, of course, you will bring Woldemar with you.

Brahms is writing this with me. I am learning to understand his rare and beautiful character better every day. There is something so fresh and so soothing about him, he is often so childlike and then

[1] Schumann's birthday.

again so full of the finest feelings.  His is a youthful
and open nature combined with a manly earnestness
of purpose.  And as a musician he is still more
wonderful.  He gives me as much pleasure as he
possibly can, as you can imagine, and he does this
with a perseverance which is really touching; it often
oppresses me to think of how much he is giving me
and of how very, very poorly I can repay it!

My brother tells me in a letter of a Fantasia for
the violin which he has finished, and during the composition of which he thought of you!  I think he is
very anxious for fear you may not like it.  I should
be very grieved if that were so, but you would have
to tell him honestly ; that will be of use to him even
if it hurts him at first.

You have heard the latest news of my dear Robert
from Woldemar, and so I need not tell you over again.
The reports vary greatly, but on the whole they point
to a gradual improvement.  I am swayed continually
by hopes and fears, and at the bottom of my heart I
suffer more than I can possibly describe.  But I will
not lament to you!  You know him, and you know
how much he was and still is to me!

Please give Frau and Fräulein von Arnim my
sincerest regards—perhaps I shall see you all sooner
than we imagine at present!  Accept, dear friend, the
gratitude and respect of your    CLARA SCHUMANN.

### To Johannes Brahms

(*Received at Düsseldorf, June* 28.)[1]

[BERLIN], *June* 27 [1854].

Dear Johannes—How can I thank you for your
letter, and your music!  You see, dear friend, I had

---

[1] Written by Brahms at the top of the first page of the letter.

so accustomed myself to hearing from you from time
to time, that I sometimes felt quite miserable at the
thought that something had come between us and
alienated you from me—possibly my visits to Berlin!
And now your letter, full of the old, warm feeling, has
dispelled all my doubts, and my joy in it could only be
exceeded by one thing, by my delight in your genius,
which is shedding ever brighter and intenser rays.
Dearest Johannes, how every note of your Variations
gladdened me ; how I sunned myself in the wealth of
feeling and intellect contained in them! You dear,
modest fellow, you ask me for criticism, and I can
only tell you how much I have learnt.   I place the
Variations side by side with the deepest and most
beautiful works, not even excepting my favourite.   I
have not mentioned his name for fear of startling you ;
but he lived at the beginning of this century.   Each
Variation is a little temple to the glory of the spirit
concealed in the subject.   And however varied their
architecture may be, this spirit breathes the same love
through them all. . . .

## From Johannes Brahms

DÜSSELDORF, *July* 27, 1854.

Dear   Friend — I   am   very   grateful   to   Frau
Schumann for allowing me to give you the latest,
joyful news from Endenich.

Yesterday evening Fräulein Hartmann [1] came back
from Bonn.   On the ship, where we all, including
Frau Schumann, awaited her, she handed the latter
a bunch of flowers from her husband.

This time, at Fräulein Reumont's [2] suggestion, he

---

[1] Mathilde Hartmann, a singer and a friend of the Schumanns.
[2] Nurse at Endenich.

carefully selected some lovely roses and carnations (the last time he did not know for whom he was picking the flowers). Fräulein Reumont again asked him where they were to be sent and to whom. " Oh, you know quite well ! " was his reply. So he had not forgotten the ones he had sent before.

You know, a short time ago, he asked who had sent the flowers which were in his room. They told him Fräulein Reumont had put them there, and they will always tell him so unless he asks point blank whether his wife had sent them.

Fräulein Hartmann saw him walking in the garden. (She is altogether much to be envied !) He was led by the doctor, with whom he was conversing, to Fräulein Reumont's window; Fräulein Hartmann stood behind the curtain. Fräulein Reumont talked to him, and told him to pick some flowers. He looked very well, better than Fräulein Hartmann had ever seen him. He walked firmly and rather quickly ; he examined the flower-beds with his lorgnette, and he spoke amiably.

On leaving he waved his handkerchief, as he always used to do when he was in good spirits. Fräulein Hartmann would have liked very much to have had a chat with him, just as I should have done.

Tell all this to W. Bargiel, his mother, etc. Frau Schumann will not write about it, as I am doing so. Frau Schumann left you sooner than you expected, but after all it was quite natural ; after that fine letter from Endenich I expected her every day. We spent some time with her that evening. The next morning, when I went to see her, she danced round the room with joy. I have never seen her in such good spirits and so calm.

She told me about your new viola pieces ; can you

not send them to me? It would give us all, and me
especially, such pleasure. You never mention your
own work! Your *Heinrich* Overture is finished, but
I knew that long ago; what else are you writing?
Please give me a full account some time. How goes
the glorification of the people from whom I spring?
*Of course* I should keep your letter to myself. As for
my score,[1] I expect you had realised, and I begged
Frau Schumann to tell you, that I owe anything good
there may be in it to Grimm, who helped me with
sound advice. What is faulty or bad, which it will
not be hard to discover, was either overlooked by
Grimm or left because of my obstinacy.

I must just add that I want to let the low D predominate at the beginning, and that is why the F–B♭
in the clarinettes and bassoons is so weak. It has
always pleased me that it is all so short and concen-
trated, but I do not know whether that is quite the
right thing for the orchestra? Sometimes at the
Finale I feel as though it had come to an end, and
sometimes as though the Coda ought to be only just
commencing! Will you encourage me to go on with
the other movements? I feel so imbecile.—Yours

JOHANNES.

Remember me to Bargiel, Grimm, and the von
Arnims!!

*To Gisela von Arnim*

HANOVER, *September* 5 [1854].

. . . I have been out a great deal in the lovely woods
round Hanover; then . . . when I got home again I
often seated myself at the writing table, and took up
my pen, but that never wholly silenced the beating of

---

[1] The remodelling of the D minor Sonata for two pianos into a Symphony.
Later it became the Piano Concerto, op. 15.

my heart . . . at those times I could bear nothing but
music. . . .

. . . I should have continued my quiet life here,
even though mentally I knew no quiet (awaiting the
return of my chief, Graf Platen), but suddenly I was
startled by a *command from the King of Hanover* to
join him at the watering place, Norderney, at once.
So I must go there in a few hours. It is a critical
matter for me from more than one point of view. I
will write from there and explain; I only just have
time now to put my things together and to write and
put off my parents. It is hard to serve! . . .

One thing more I am sending which will force you
to think of me—the *Prometheus* of Aeschylus—which
I shall lend you. I have been re-reading it during the
last few days—and I have been dreaming the time
away with Goethe's *Poems*, too, your favourites. . . .

### *From Johannes Brahms*

DÜSSELDORF, *September* 12, 1854.

My very dear Friend—I have again delayed so long
in writing that I am afraid you will not get this letter
until you come back from Vienna.

Forgive me, and see how little you have missed.

I have nothing more to say to you than that I
received your letter with the overtures and thank you
most heartily for them. (As a matter of fact I never
have anything more to write to you.) As usual you
have regarded the movement of my Symphony through
a rose-coloured glass, I must alter and improve it all
through. There is a good deal wrong even in the
composition, and as to the instrumentation, I do not
understand as much about it as appears in the movement, the best part of it I owe to Grimm.

You gave us *great* pleasure by sending us the overtures. I prefer the one to *Heinrich* and Grimm —the *Demetrius*. I cannot understand how you can take any interest in my things, in little Variations and Sonatas like mine! I always see you before me so vividly when I play your things, deeply moved and exalted, as though you had just created them.

You do not say that I am to send them back soon, so I shall keep them until we meet, or until you write for them.

I have nothing new to tell you of dear Robert, his condition remains much the same, he continues to take walks to Godesberg, etc. I suppose you heard in Berlin that I had seen him? If you did not, let me tell you about it soon by word of mouth. Grimm saw him too. Frau Schumann spent four weeks in Ostend and came back very well. She plays with all her old power, but with more intensity, *more than ever* like you. Yesterday she played me my F minor Sonata, just as I had imagined it, but with more nobility, more tranquil enthusiasm and with such a pure, clear rendering and such a magnificent tone in the stronger passages : these are all little advantages she has over me.

To-morrow, the 13th, is her birthday; I have fulfilled a long-standing wish of hers and arranged Schumann's Quintette as a piano duet. Whilst she was at Ostend I took the manuscript out of the cupboard, so she knows nothing about it. I have been immersing myself in it deeper and deeper, as in a pair of dark blue eyes (that is how I seem to picture it). That is why I have not written this letter before.

My Variations have had two new additions, in one of which *Clara speaks !*

Härtels have offered to print it.   My dear, so long as Frau Schumann is here, I will not, indeed I *cannot* leave, but Grimm and I will be at Hanover by the beginning of October.   I shall probably go straight to Hamburg, I want to see my parents, and as I should have to go there in any case during the winter I would rather do so at once.   (I should probably see Frau Schumann there too.)

But, please God, we shall be together from the New Year onwards, *for certain.*

I long so much to see you and to live with you; I do not think the perpetual excitement here is good for me, I shall have to recover from it.

We must start playing regularly at Hanover.   I hope I shall play better now, and I have a larger repertoire in my head.

Money matters are not very grand with me, I cannot think of returning you the fifty talers yet.

I have bought Shakespeare, Aeschylus, *Faust*, a volume of Plutarch, etc., here!   That's what I do when I have a few talers.

. . . I wanted to learn to play the flute so as to accompany Frau Schumann, but Kuhlau's Sonatas bore her.   Are you going to pass through Düsseldorf on your way to Vienna?   We all hope *so much* that you will.

Grimm is going to be at Hanover during the winter, too; I am, of course, since you want me, and can put up with me.

My letter has become longer than I thought, however rubbishy and unnecessary it may be.

If you possibly can, do come through Düsseldorf. Write and say you are coming!

Love from Frau Schumann, Grimm, and most of all—from your                                          JOHANNES.

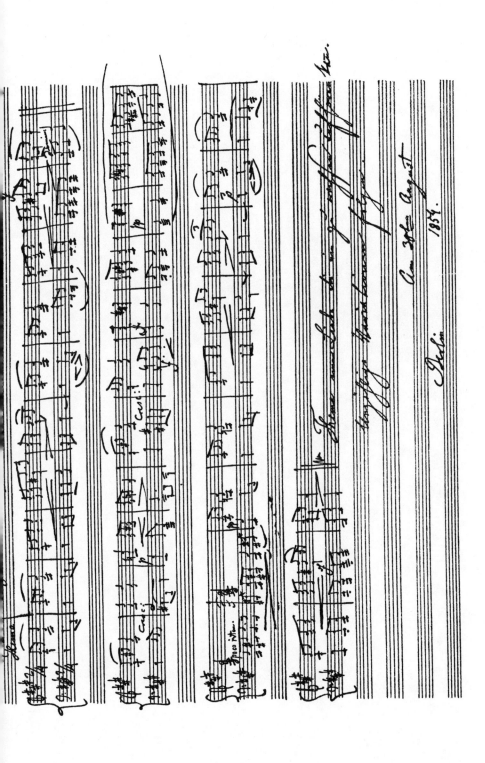

*To Gisela von Arnim*

HANOVER, *September* 14 [1854].

. . . Although I only spent two and a half days in Norderney, I went through a great deal there—yes, a great deal, although it all happened in my own mind. I think I have come through the excitement years calmer and more clearheaded than before. Let me tell you . . . I owe it to you . . . that my confusion of mind became clear, that I did not allow anything trivial to master that which should alone be of value to us—that quality of our spiritual nature which may not be blinded or shaken by any external influence. In the calm and secure possession of this the reverses and calamities which occur in every life, can only disturb our mental balance when they succeed in conquering that inner power.   I have not yet acquired that uniformity of judgment and sentiment which we should all possess—that divine calm of yours which soothes my inmost feelings.   Ah, and I was in so much need of external peace, too, just now.   You have no idea what I am sacrificing to my parents in starting on this new journey to-morrow and plunging into new surroundings—when there is so much in me that demands expression—and when my thoughts race round like mice on the table because the cat, peace of mind, who ought to be keeping order, is always on the road or in the train.   Well, I hope at last to order my external life somewhat more comfortably for the coming winter ; my own mind is so restless and active that I require peaceful surroundings.   " *Still und bewegt* " ;[1] when one understands Hölderlin's phrase one learns to love it.

But I meant to tell you about Norderney—it will

[1] "Calm and active."

be best if I copy out what I wrote to you a few hours
after my arrival in Norderney, but which I did not
send, as it seemed to me too childish . . . now that I
have conquered it I will tell you, so that you alone
may be *au fait* with my state of mind at the time,
for we must always be honest with one another.

Well then, Norderney, 7th. (A few hours after my
arrival that evening, after having travelled day and
night.) "At a moment when I have made an
important decision for my immediate future, I feel
that you alone have the right to ask me to justify
myself—you alone can say whether I have acted
rightly or wrongly. Listen and decide: You know
that I was commanded to come to this island by the
King of Hanover—in spite of my reluctance to put
off again the visit to my people I have obeyed the
command—it seemed to me that I ought to make
some sort of sacrifice for my salary, so that the means
of subsistence should not be given to me for nothing.

"When I wrote from Hanover I told you that the
matter was particularly unpleasant to me for one
reason ; this is, that in the letter from the Hanoverian
manager commanding me to come here, it was also
stated that Frau Lind[1] was giving a concert at which
I was to assist. I concluded from this that the King
would have told Frau Lind (whom he regards as a
miracle) of his intention to send for me, and that it
might be difficult for me to oppose his wish that I
should assist at her concert. But imagine my horror
when, at a little Hanoverian town on the way, I was
addressed by an obnoxious Philistine, who also got
into the coach, and who wanted to know whether I was

---

[1] It is hardly necessary to say that Joachim's early, unfavourable opinion of
Jenny Lind, to which he gives expression in this and other letters, afterwards gave
place to a juster estimate of her talent and personality.

Konzertmeister Joachim who was to play at the concert at Norderney, to which he was going. I must have looked so nonplussed that he put his hand in his coat pocket, and, taking the paper off a parcel of cakes, handed it to me, and there I saw the notice, piping hot from the printers, of 'a concert to be given by Frau Goldschmidt-Lind for the poor of Norderney, at which she will be assisted by Messrs. Mathys and Joachim from Hanover,' on September 8. I must confess that I was vain enough to feel deeply hurt and mortified. What! I said to myself, the King, my duty to whom I have always fulfilled so conscientiously that his wishes were as commands to me (not merely because of etiquette, as is the case with some of his other subjects), for whom, in my zealous obedience I have just regretfully given up a visit to my people, does not even esteem me so highly that he would consider it an indignity to let me make a long journey of one and a half days simply to join with a third-rate musician in filling up the gaps in a famous Prima Donna's concert! He does not even consider that it might hurt my feelings to be *commanded* to assist at a charity concert given by another. He does not even give me the opportunity of saying yes or no. I felt insulted; the musician in me was outraged at the *service* demanded. And so I came to Norderney in a great state of excitement, quite determined to tell the King I would not play. Nobody was there to apologise for having made use of my name without my consent. Frau Lind met the coach (but by chance, because in the course of conversation she told me she had called for a letter from her husband). She at once asked me to arrange with her the programme for next evening's concert, and she added that she had had no part in my summons here

G

(referring to a former refusal of mine in Berlin), that as soon as she had agreed to give a concert for the poor, the King had determined to make me come. I replied that I should have preferred it if she, as an artist, had anticipated my consent in such a cause rather than that I should be forced by a command to perform a 'good work,' and concluded by telling her that I would fulfil my temporal master's commands *à contre cœur*, and that under the circumstances I would resign. *And what I said to her I will stick to.* As is always the case with me, I was not furious with other people for long, but in my anxiety to be just I soon said, *I* am a fool myself; *I* had a wrong idea of my position, *I* was stupid not to guess at once why I was sent for, etc. I shall be consistent to the last— play as well as I can, not let the King suffer because it is *his* to command, *mine* to obey, so long as I eat his bread, but I shall exercise my right to *give up a position* in which such unpleasant occurrences are possible— and about which *I* so foolishly deluded myself. This is the decision I wanted to tell you about. Now tell me whether you think my decision a wise one—you, the one and only judge recognised by me."

So much for what I wrote to you from Norderney.

I am glad the stupid tale is finished. Laugh at it, at me—that I could be so puerile—yes, laugh still more; since then I have gone through various other tragic experiences (I will not speak of feelings!) —laugh more and more, because the end of it is that I am still in the service of the King of Hanover after all—not without the wish, certainly, to attain as soon as possible (but with no demonstrations!) to a quiet independence, even if it means sacrificing something.

I hate serving even the gentlest master. The
King, the Queen—all, were gentle, kind, and attentive.
Whilst I was still writing all that unnecessary pathos
to you on the evening of the 7th, the King had
commanded me to go to him on the following day—
I will not repeat all the sympathetic, courteous
things he said in the course of the interview, but
I will tell you this much, I could not have brought
out one of the politely obstinate declarations of
independence which I had prepared on my way
there without feeling myself to be the most un-
mannerly lout.    And yet, after I had said jokingly to
Frau Lind at the rehearsal (piano and pianist were
ear-splitting, an old retired German had officiated
as piano-tuner!) that the long journey had excited
me, and put me into a very bad temper the evening
before, and that I had seen everything in the worst
light, I was suddenly so horrified at my own in-
consistency towards a lady, that when I got home
I wrote her a letter telling her that I intended
to carry out what I had said the previous evening
—that I would cease to be Konzertmeister at
Hanover.    In short, I did one foolish thing after
the other in my wounded vanity, and although the
sea and the unaccustomed sight and sound of the
waves gave me moments of exaltation, although
the cry of the sea-gulls often sounded to me like a
mocking chorus, laughing at all those who did not
soar above the trivial, passionate herd as they did,
and fearlessly rejoice in the eternal spirit of the
elements—yet I was, on the whole, a miserable
wretch, full of confused and foolish thoughts —
" vacillating." . . .

Perhaps all this has bored you; to make up for
it a little I will copy an Aria from Gluck's *Armide*

for you . . . all that you feel about that is so beautiful and true. . . .

I heard Frau Lind sing the Aria at my request —and some lovely songs by Schumann—the rest was a horrible truckling to the public taste—and her peculiar talent lies in *coquetterie*, more than deep musical feeling and understanding — but she has great skill in *expression*. Added to this she has a thoughtless, superficial piety—she often invokes God when talking of the most ungodly things, such as money and fame. But she is very clever, she can be extremely charming, and she is much more clearheaded than I am. She knows *exactly* what she wants. "He who merely understands must always give way to him who wills" applies here in a different sense from that intended by Alfieri. . . . I will write to Herman from here to-morrow, so that he may know where I have got to again. . . . I am looking forward to the Danube, and to the girls with long plaits who live on the banks of the Danube. . . .

### From Johannes Brahms

DÜSSELDORF, *September* 17, 1854.

Dear Joseph—I am delighted to be able to write you this letter and send this enclosure.

Listen :

On September 12 (the Schumanns' wedding-day) a letter came from the doctor at Bonn, in which he said Herr Schumann had expressed to him the fear that his wife must be dead, as he had had no letter from her. In this letter of the 12th the doctor asked Frau Schumann to write a few lines to her husband. She wrote two letters;

in one she mentioned the dates (12th and 13th), in the other she did not. But Herr Schumann told the doctor quite of his own accord of the great importance he attached to those two dates. So they gave him the first letter.

At mid-day on the 15th a letter came from the doctor with enclosures. I handed it to Frau Schumann in fear and trembling!

Were her letters being returned or was it a reply? She opened the letter, and could hardly stammer, "from my husband"; she could not read it for some time. And then, what unspeakable joy; she looked like the Finale to *Fidelio*, the F major movement in $\frac{3}{4}$ time. I can describe it in no other way. One could not weep over it, but it fills one with a deep and joyful awe.

I was the first to read the letter after her. Now I am sending you, his dearest friend, the first news and a copy of the letter, and Clara sends you a greeting by this means.

What would I not give to have you here now; at the time and afterwards I wished for no one else.

I cannot read the last sentence of his letter ("so many questions") often enough; it is the best proof of what I believe to be the case, that he is only ill now through fear and imagination. He is afraid of asking irrational questions, and begs her, in that case, to draw a veil over them!

The doctor tells her he read her letter frequently during the day, and wept with emotion. As the doctor gave her permission to answer his questions, and send him what he asked for, she did so the same day. There is one more thing I cannot understand.

The doctor says in his last letter that Schumann

had expressed surprise at finding no mention of her successful confinement in her letter, and then the doctor adds that he had told Herr Schumann about it some time previously!! But they always said Herr Schumann never referred to his wife in any way!

Well, no matter; her second letter will explain everything to him. It will certainly not be long before we see him.

Of course Frau Schumann sent him his manuscripts. How beautifully he writes of the subject in E♭,[1] no mention of Schubert now! He had attacks of cramp at Godesberg.

Write and let me know how long you are staying in Pesth and Vienna, as the most vital news may come any day, and I shall write and tell you everything immediately. I will copy his letter for you.

Rejoice with me, beloved, there can be no more doubts now?—Your          JOHANNES.


### From Clara Schumann

DÜSSELDORF, *September* 21, 1854.

My dear Friend—I cannot keep to myself that which, I know, will give you the greatest delight! It is a *greeting* to you, dear Joachim, from my dearest Robert. He writes that I am to give it to you if I am writing to you. You will have had Brahms' letter before this, in which I copied the first letter from my dear husband. With how much greater pleasure would I send you the second one, received yesterday! He writes of the Fantasia for the Violin which you played so magnificently, and he asks whether your *Hamlet* Overture has appeared yet, whether the others are

---

[1] Of which Schumann had said it had been brought to him by Schubert's spirit.

finished, what you and Brahms have composed besides
—oh, and so much more.  And so a joy has come to
me for which I hardly dared to hope a fortnight ago,
and yet, believe me, it is terribly hard to bear it!  I
should like to pour my heart out to him, to be able to
tell him how he alone occupies all my thoughts and
feelings, and yet I have to be careful in my letters, I
must control the mighty beating of my heart and
suppress so much!  He says nothing about my going
to him at present.  I imagine the doctors are still
against it, and he readily agrees to everything they
tell him.  And so, in spite of all the promising
symptoms, he will make very slow progress, and I am
quite resigned to that!  I only pray God He may give
me the strength to endure the terrible agitations which
I have again experienced, and which lie before me in
the future.  My old friend, my piano, must help me in
this!  Oh, dear Joachim, I thought I knew what a
splendid thing it is to be an artist, but I only realise it
for the first time now that I can turn all my suffering
and joy into divine music, so that I often feel quite
happy!

But who should know that better than a magnificent artist like yourself!  How much better you must
know it than I, since you can *create*!

As to my other plans and doings, I can only tell
you that I am playing with great diligence (I would
do so a great deal more if I were allowed), and that
I am going to Leipzig on October 16, after that, on
November 11, to Hamburg, then to Berlin, etc.  I
need not tell you what I feel about so many journeys!
But I am driven to it partly by necessity, and partly by
the earnest desire that he, my beloved husband, should
find his house well cared for when he comes back to
us!  This will give me strength to carry out my plans!

I should so much like to know when I am to have the pleasure of seeing you again ?   Could you not pay us a visit for a few days ?   Please write and say that you can !   If you cannot, we shall meet on October 15 at Hanover, where I shall stay for a day, because I must see you, and talk to you, and press your hand with a *joyful* heart—on his behalf, too !

Now I must tell you something which I have been longing to say to you.   I agree in *everything* you have said about Brahms's Variations ; they are magnificent, and I can hardly wait for the time when my Robert will see and hear them ; I have studied them carefully and with ever-increasing enthusiasm.

You will not be annoyed with me, dear friend, because I felt as though you were sitting beside me with your kind and happy eyes, as you have so often done, and I had so much to tell you !   But I like so much to open my whole heart to you and Brahms— for you love and understand that wonderful man to the depths of his soul, to the vibrations of his inner- most feelings !

One thing more I must tell you, which has given me great pleasure.   I wrote to Robert about the little one and told him I had chosen three names, and that he was to choose from those the one he liked best, to which he replied, " If you want to know my favourite name you will easily guess it—the name of him who will ever be remembered ! " [1]

You will guess it too : it was the same one I had chosen.

Good-bye, and if you send me a few lines soon, you will give great pleasure to—Your

CLARA SCHUMANN.

[1] Mendelssohn.  As Joachim was not yet baptized at that time, he could not be godfather to Felix Schumann as well as Brahms, as Frau Schumann had wished.

### *To Woldemar Bargiel*

HANOVER, *October* 9, 1854.

Dear Friend—You have not heard from me for a long time—my excuse must be the restless life I have led since we parted, and which I have spent chiefly in railway stations. I have been back in my old nest now for about two days; it is lonely, cold, and autumnal in Hanover, in more senses than one. Where is my old, hot garret in the *Blumengarten*? Where are the *Zelten*, *Linkstrasse*, Grimm, the Arnims, we two, and Beethoven, Bach, and Gluck in the evening! All these good spirits live in my memory as though warm with life; and they will have to see to it that reality does not freeze me in my winter quarters. I am realising for the first time how horribly lonely it is in Hanover. How we would rejoice together over the news from Düsseldorf! Your sister, with her noble confidence, was far ahead of us all in wisdom. Whilst I was away, and before I left Pesth, I had the good news from Brahms and your sister herself—and your welcome letter, too, was so full of happiness. Oh, I enter into it all with my whole heart, and thank God — may He guard Schumann's entrance into active life again with a gentle hand. How much richer your life and mine will be when the dear master is with us again! Brahms seems, by his letters, to be beside himself for joy! I hope he will come here soon; I think he will accompany your sister, who intends to spend a day here on her way to Leipzig. You can imagine how thankful I am to have this to look forward to; delightful guests like these are a most beneficial stimulant. You ought to make up your mind at once, and start the autumn trip we discussed so often with Grimm with a visit to Hanover at that time—then you can go with them to Leipzig or else to the Rhine.   Apart from the pleasure you would give to your sister, Brahms, and myself, and which you would therefore bring with you, I cannot promise you anything in Hanover—but be generous and come!

I had hoped to hear my Overture here on my return from Pesth, but the copyist has not finished; besides that the musicians are all tormented by rehearsals at the theatre and so disinclined for music that it will be some time before the written notes are turned into music.   It is the beginning of the winter season.   Patience.

I am reading Gluck's biography,[1] and enjoying *Iphigenia in Tauris* in Lührss'[2] copy, which is still among my music.   By and by I will ask him for the scores of Gluck's other operas; not an accent in them occurs by chance, and yet there is *nothing* mechanical about them; deep feeling is expressed by the simplest means, as though the heroes were sighing or rejoicing in his own heart.   There is much to be learnt about instrumentation from his scores—Sincerely yours,

JOACHIM.

### To Gisela von Arnim

[HANOVER], *October* 20 [1854].

. . . Brahms has gone again, and I have not yet looked up the Detmolds, but I will do so soon, because when they met me they gave me a cordial invitation. Indeed, I intend to mix with people sometimes—one gets out of the way of it, and then, when it is a question

---

[1] By Anton Schmid, Leipzig, 1854.

[2] Karl Lührss, a prominent composer in Berlin at that time.

of going into society, one allows all sorts of things to
disturb and influence one that are really not worth it.
As for Brahms, who put up here on the black sofa for
a few days, I did not really feel at ease with him,
although I once more realised all his good, his unusual
qualities. I believe Herman has spoilt me — and
whereas I used to live, purposely, in a kind of twilight,
so far as my friendships were concerned, so as not
to be disillusioned in that which I cared for—now
my reason insists on seeing what my affection feared
to discover. Brahms is egoism incarnate, *without
himself being aware of it.* He bubbles over in his
cheery way with exuberant thoughtlessness — but
sometimes with a lack of consideration (not a lack of
reserve, for that would please me!) which offends
because it betrays a want of culture. He has never
once troubled to consider what others, according to
their natures and the course of their development,
will hold in esteem ; the things that do not arouse *his*
enthusiasm, or that do not fit in with *his* experience,
or even with *his* mood, are callously thrust aside, or, if
he is in the humour, attacked with a malicious sarcasm.
This immediately raises a barrier between him and his
companion, who has been rejoicing in the society of
the happy, brilliant young man whose whole personality
is stamped with intellectual power. I often had to
summon my sense of justice to prevent the warmth
of my feeling from cooling down. He knows the
weaknesses of the people about him, and he makes
use of them, and then does not hesitate to show (to
their faces, I admit) that he is crowing over them.
His immediate surroundings are quite apart from his
musical life, and from his attachment to a higher and
more fantastic world. And the way in which he wards
off all the morbid emotions and imaginary troubles of

others is really delightful. He is absolutely sound in that, just as his complete indifference to the means of existence is beautiful, indeed magnificent. He will not make the smallest sacrifice of his intellectual inclinations—he will not play in public because of his contempt for the public, and because it irks him— although he plays divinely. I have never heard piano playing (except perhaps Liszt's) which gave me so much satisfaction—so light and clear, so cold and in-different to passion. His compositions, too, are an easy treatment of the most difficult forms—so pregnant, rejecting all earthly sorrows with such indifference. I have never come across a talent like his before. He is miles ahead of me.

Frau Schumann has been here; I was glad to have such good news of him. Bargiel will have told you about it. He has asked after me in his letters, too; it was quite uncanny to read my name. He writes as a child would, with questions and narrative all mixed up together, like some one who is just awake and must first of all separate real things from the figures of his dreams. I have promised Frau Schumann to appear with her at her concert in Berlin, which is to be the middle of next month; I think this will help on her splendid purpose, and for that reason you will be glad of it too. . . .

*To Robert Schumann*

HANOVER, *November* 17, 1854.

Dear and honoured Master—A day on which a letter came from you would always be a happy one for me; but how much more so this time, when you are good enough to write to me after such a long time! And what a delightful letter it is, in which you tell me

that you often think of me and of the time you spent
with me. What a pleasure it was to me to read this
in your handwriting, which I know so well. Shall I
tell you how often I have thought of you, how often I
have played your music with your dear Clara, with
Johannes, with my colleagues in the Sunday quartettes?
You can imagine all that; you must know what you
and your music is to your friends. If I could only
play your D minor Concerto to you; I know it better
now than that time in Hanover when, to my great
annoyance, I did it such injustice at the rehearsal,
because my arm was so tired with conducting. The
$\frac{3}{4}$ time sounds much more stately now. Do you
remember how pleased you were, and how you laughed
when we said the last movement sounded as though
Kociusko were leading a Polonaise with Sobiesky: it
was so stately? Those were glorious days!

It is very gratifying to me that you still remember
my *Hamlet* Overture; your sympathy amply com-
pensates me for all the other people who do not like
it. I should like so much to send you the overtures to
*Demetrius* and Shakespeare's *Henry IV.*, but I fear it
would be more of a labour than a refreshment to you
to read the score from my manuscript copy, which has
many corrections in my bad writing, and you must
still take great care of yourself, so that your friends
may see you very soon. I will have a *beautiful* copy
made, and if you will then honour me by looking
through my works I shall be delighted. Your opinion
is always my highest reward when I have thought out
anything with devotion and care. The overture to
*Henry IV.* is not so gloomy now, but I am afraid it is
rather long and noisy. The chivalrous Percy and the
hot-headed prince who afterwards soars to the heights
of a splendid kingliness, seduced me to many a burst

of trumpets.   I have not heard it yet.   Your wife is coming before long to Hanover for a Court Concert, and then I shall have it played in her honour.   The other day she played Brahms' Variations on your F♯ minor theme most beautifully to me.   The depth of the composition and the wonderful harmonic beauties take hold of me more every time, and I am glad that your praise of it is in agreement with my judgment.   I heard your E♭ major Quintette again the other day ; it sounded so romantic and fresh—ah, if only you had heard it too !

Your music is often played here, their Majesties enjoy hearing your compositions so much, and they always ask me whether I have had news or letters from you.   They are certainly among those who think most often of your visit to Hanover—I will ask the Minister of the Interior whether a greeting from a musician is contrary to etiquette, as you have commissioned me to give messages to those who remember you.   But I should have a lot to do if I gave them to every one !

And now I must say good-bye to you for to-day ; I have already taken up a lot of your time.   If I may send you a line now and then it will be a great pleasure, dear and honoured Master, to—your ever devoted                        JOSEPH JOACHIM.

### From Robert Schumann [1]

ENDENICH, *November* 25, 1854.

Dear Friend—How glad I was to recognise your hand—and the hand which enclosed the letter.   Oh, if only I could go to you with Clara as we did last

---

[1] This letter, which is now published for the first time, contains many corrections and is illegible in places.

JOSEPH JOACHIM AND CLARA SCHUMANN.

From a drawing by Adolf von Menzel.

(*By permission of Herren F. Bruckmann, A.G., Munich.*)

January. I like to think of that evening when we went to their Majesties, Fräulein Clauss too,—and I was very pleased to hear they were so gracious as to ask after me, and to like my compositions. So many things pass before me, the merry supper with Brahms and Grimm and the musical mornings with you. Yes, I received from you Bettina's correspondence with Göthe; I am copying a good deal from it for my poet's garden of music. I suppose Clara has the extracts. She often supplies me with recently published compositions of mine, such as the Fantasia for the Violin which I heard you play so magnificently, and, to my delight, my collected writings, of which the first volume is corrected, and which remind me of happy, bygone days. Oh, if I could only hear my D minor Concerto played by you; my Clara wrote so enthusiastically about it. It is too good of you to wish to send me a copy of your Overture to *Henry IV*.

Will you be so good as to send Brahms the enclosed letter, and also one to my wife?

Write soon, as you 'promised to do; if only I had your [*sic*] old powers again. I am not so fresh and light-hearted now as I was at Düsseldorf; I still suffer from insomnia as I did latterly there.

Always remember your faithful and admiring

R. Schumann.

### To Herman Grimm

[Hanover, *beginning of January* 1855.]

Dear Herman—The other day I was summoned by the King to an audience; it lasted half an hour, with no other result than that the King asked me to remain in my post. I answered emphatically at last, "I *cannot*, your Majesty," and he went on urging me, saying finally (after having represented to me almost like a friend the difficulty I should have in keeping myself without a definite post) that I must think it over, and that my departure would be an irreparable loss to him and " his queen." So as not to respond harshly to such gracious words I had to say, " I have never ventured to imagine such a thing." The King seemed to take this as a compliance with his wish that I should remain in his service, for on dismissing me he said, " Next year (the audience was on December 30, 1854) we must often meet, and we must hear you play as before," etc., etc. Since then, however, the King seems to have heard that I want to leave Hanover ; by his command I was told that I was to put my wishes, in whatever form I preferred, in writing, and he would consider them, and if I remained in his service he would have no objection to giving me leave for a considerable period. In accordance with this I have decided to send in the following. Tell me what you think of it :

" I humbly request your Majesty to grant me leave of absence for two years with cessation of the contract at the end of the time specified in it, so that I may be free to continue my musical studies, and particularly composition (I do not like that, but it is the truth ; perhaps you will think of something better).

" As the undersigned intends to live in North Germany, he will gladly be at the disposal of His Majesty during the three months of the concert season, as often as His Majesty may have need of his musical services.

" At the end of the above-mentioned two years the undersigned, pending a new contract, will again be prepared to place his powers at the disposal of His Majesty for the concerts at Hanover. Whilst venturing to make these proposals to your Majesty," etc., etc.

What do you think of it? Please let me know. The other day[1] I heard my Overture to Shakespeare's *Henry IV*. for the first time. It sounded better than I expected. Br[ahms] and Frau Sch[umann] had planned the surprise for me—many thanks for *Rotrudis*: [J. O.] Grimm is delighted with it. I like it more than ever. The Wehners have been here a fortnight— weaklings! If only the Arnims would pass through here. *Write soon* to your J. J.

## To Woldemar Bargiel

HANOVER, *Thursday*, 18. 1. 55.

Dear Friend—An affectionate greeting from me first of all! I expect you are rather cross with me because of an all too lengthy pause in the score of our correspondence—but you know my talent for writing is not very productive and sometimes takes refuge in a pause, just as bad composers do. But I am going to bother you now with a request, namely, to send me the viola pieces which I have promised to send to an English publisher, together with the Variations.[2]

There is no hurry for the Overture, but there is for the pieces mentioned, as I should like to have them soon. The other day I heard my Overture to *Henry IV*. played here—I was surprised to find that most of the passages sounded as I had imagined them. If only you could hear it! Well, perhaps later on! I expect you have heard from your sister that she and Brahms planned the surprise for me at a rehearsal. We often thought of you, especially when the glorious news about Schumann came, which must have filled

[1] On January 3 at an orchestra rehearsal.
[2] Op. 9 Hebrew Melodies and op. 10 Variations for the viola, both of which were published by Breitkopf and Härtel.

H

your heart with joy, as it did mine. I did not write to you when I was at Endenich, because your sister begged me to give her the pleasure of telling you herself. More recently Brahms found Schumann much further advanced on the road to complete recovery. Things are going fairly well with me—in the prospect of being free to carry on my musical studies from April '55 to December '57; the King has graciously given me leave for so long. You can imagine how any one would look forward to it who, since his fourteenth year, had been fettered to theatre managements which obliged him to appear in association with any and every humbug. But please *do not mention what I have told you yet. Tannhäuser* is to be performed here for the first time on Sunday, I am very curious to know what impression it will make on me after two years (it is as long ago as that since I heard it in Weimar). My taste has changed very much since then. I should very much like to know what you are doing and writing; perhaps you will give me a surprise by enclosing with the music I have asked for something in music and words from your own hand. . . .

*From Herman Grimm*

BERLIN, *January* 24, 1855.

My dear Joachim—I have just left Schwarz, and as I walked silently through the falling snow, the flakes lay so pure and clear on my fur-covered hand, and when I came to the lamps I could see their beautiful, glittering shapes. What is more beautiful than such a delicately fashioned star, what is more artistic, and their number is infinite, so that if all the people in the world looked up to admire them millions would still fall unseen by any eyes. I think beauty has no further obligation than to come into being. Then it has attained its end and has no cause for complaint if it is unnoticed and the world treads it carelessly underfoot. I do not think beauty exists to be recognised and made use of, it is a moment sufficient to itself which meets with destruction as soon as it seeks to pass from that moment into time. For this reason all art is not beautiful in itself but it has the power of eternally recreating that moment for others; it conquers death, for it is forever awaking that which was dead and making it live for the moment.

Such were my thoughts. Perhaps I feel them more clearly than I can express them.

I have no news of Bettine. I think it is neither a good nor a bad sign, and I am not anxious, but I foresee the blank there will be for me when I can never see her again. How many will feel it in their hearts, as mankind once felt the cry, "great Pan is dead," how everything earthly will fall from her like dust, which no one remembers once it is blown away.

I can imagine how disturbing your affairs must be. Thank God when you have done with them and the cold-hearted wretches. What more does their praise amount to than that they sit by the hearth in which they have painted a fire to make those at a distance believe that it is really burning, and that they are warming themselves at it. The poor devils' teeth are chattering. . . . Your                                          HERMAN.

*From Herman Grimm*

SUNDAY, *January* 29, 1855.

My dear Joachim—The absolute lack of news from Bonn had put me in a great state of excitement, but since yesterday I have been in a state of mind about something else, not such a serious matter certainly, but which, I am ashamed to say, has upset me much more. My friend Hofrath Teichmann writes to tell me that, although the report on my play [1] was most favourable, Hülsen intends to return it to me in the course of a few days, because it does not lend itself to production. Matters being as they were, I had to come to a decision.   I knew quite well what was at the back of it.   Hülsen demands that his clients should pay him court somewhat, and I had preferred to negotiate with him by letter, without ever having called on him or made any other attempt to win his favour.   I begged Teichmann to delay the written refusal from the management, and, without saying a word of my intentions at home, I wrote to Humboldt [2] urging him, as my father's friend, to use his influence with the King, who made my first step possible, so that my second might not be in vain.   The letter went off last night, and I am now in a state of great suspense.

In itself the play is not worth the trouble.   But the notion of having spent so much time and loving care for nothing revolts me.   I could hardly sleep at all, and to-day I can only hold my thoughts in check with the greatest effort.   Then there are my mother's argus eyes, which see at once when anything is wrong with me, and question me covertly or openly.   I can tell you this pretence on the one hand and this anxiety on the other are almost driving me mad; and the feeling that I am not even going through all this mental strain for something which I can call good with my whole heart, makes matters much worse, instead of calming me.   Would you believe your sensible

[1] Probably *Rotrudis*.
[2] Alexander von Humboldt had access to the King almost every day.

friend to be capable of having seriously debated more than once whether this wretched world is not worth less than a charge of powder or a drop of some soothing liquid? Damn it all. Everything looks so black, I feel so discouraged and so physically weak that it would not take much to persuade me to trample all nine muses underfoot, and to spend the rest of my life adding up thalers and groschen in a bank, simply for the sake of having something to which I am indifferent to occupy my mind, and people about me who take no interest in me and yet give me food. This state of despondency, into which one can sink so completely from the highest thoughts, is a wretched accompaniment to human courage. I must have some one to whom I can confess my miserable weakness, I sometimes fancy I might get rid of it in that way.

And with all this there is not a soul here in whom I could confide, not one whom I should not immediately have to console much more than myself if I mentioned it; I am thrown back on myself. I cannot even write and tell Giesel, for I do not know what she is suffering, and I must not add a grain of sand to her burden. If you were here I should at any rate be able to make a little fun of this pod without peas.[1] But I cannot even do this. One is really no better than a dog who has a bit cut off his ears every day until they are gone, and on top of that is laughed at, and fears that now his ears are gone his tail will be attacked. The devil take the damned rabble that has the power to shake and harass one like this. Dear fellow, write me a few words and comfort me. I should like best of all to sell my play to a stationer's as waste-paper, and cut myself off from the theatre for the rest of my life, unless I sometimes went and stood in a corner of

[1] A play on the name *Hülse*, which also means "pod."

one and . . . a fine consolation. But it would be better than wanting to cry, anyhow.

I am not used to being so beside myself. Humboldt may have left my letter lying unopened in a corner. Or the letter may be lost in the post. How often that happens, and here I am sitting and waiting. I hate every one, and sit and grouse all by myself. The devil take such moods. I could sit and sneeze without stopping just for the sake of doing something which would send me quite mad instead of only partly so. Write me a few words and comfort me. Abuse my play so that I may at any rate have the consolation of knowing I have not been treated unjustly. I do not even know whether I wrote in the right way to H. I am so awkward and cold and stiff when I have to speak for myself. Oh, the *canailles*! they demand that one should be as they are before they will pass what one brings them. And on top of it all to feel that not a soul cares, that if I were to announce in the papers that I was going to put an end to myself, instead of trying to dissuade me, people would ask quite innocently when and where, and whether they could perhaps look on without risk. This is just imagination, and I am laughing at myself, it is contemptible laughter I assure you.

That is how things are with me. I wish I knew of a corner of the earth where I could get away from it all. But it is the same everywhere, and there is not a spot in the whole atlas where I would rather be than here, or where I should not dislike to be just as much, and yet I should not care if the devil took Berlin and me with it. What I write may sound fairly brave, but I am like a piece of sugar in a glass of water, you would only have to stir it round quite gently and I should fall to pieces.—Your HERMAN.

*To Johannes Brahms*

[DANZIG, *March* 3, 1855.]

My dear Johannes—I have something to tell you to-day which gives me more and more pleasure the longer I think about it.  I have succeeded in persuading our friend to give up her plan of going to England.  You will be surprised at my having taken upon myself to discuss the matter with Frau Schumann, so as to influence her actions, because I had always told you I thought it wrong to try and advise any one so conscientious in deed and omission as Frau Clara, whose every action arises out of the purest love and devotion to her Robert!  But then Frau Schumann only thinks of what she calls *duty*, and as she seems to me to have much too large (not to say false) an idea of this for human nature, I felt obliged, as her sincere friend, to oppose her blind zeal for self-sacrifice with my cold common sense.  For the present, as her family is secured from want, thank God, Frau Schumann's duty seems to me to lie in keeping her intellect vigorous for their sake, and in preserving her artistic faculties in all their purity for her Robert, not in destroying that beauty of soul, which so rejoiced him, by restless anxiety for gain.  And I insist that this is what *must* happen to any one who tries to make a financial success of concerts, particularly in England.  Frau Schumann, as an artist, must not devote herself entirely to the coarse demands of pleasure-seeking people (that is, the public *en gros*), who are probably a whole century behind Beethoven's conviction that music is the purest form of emotional expression, which inspires Frau Schumann as it does us.  Frau Schumann's sensitive nature has suffered enough by the way in which she has given herself up to the worries of concert giving, whilst anxiety for her family was destroying her peace of mind (at the expense of her health). If, after all this, she went to London, the perpetual torment of mental worries combined with physical strain would finish her—or else the fine energy, the noble intellectual vigour, and the tender inspiration which have so often delighted us in her playing would have to give way to an inartistic apathy which endures everything because there is no help for it—and I do not know which would be worse ! God preserve her from either. All this would fall with double weight on Frau Schumann in London—because, up to now she has deliberately endeavoured to drown this voice, which whispers to her sometimes, under the pretext of "duty." But her anticipation of such a state of things (she would not actually admit it to herself) often made her very *unhappy*, although she never sacrificed her courage to her femininity sufficiently to admit it. So it was my duty as a friend to dissuade her from the journey, and to overcome my dislike to interfering in other people's affairs (even those of my dearest friends) ! Was I not right, dear Kreisler junior ? And I hope you will lend a friendly hand too, and write to Frau Clara in Berlin that she must be sure not to go back to the old idea ! Frau Schumann has borne so much bitter trouble with such extraordinary courage, that she will be quite justified in devoting the summer to herself and her family in Düsseldorf, the more so as she will be able (since she must always do more than anybody else) to give lessons. Indeed, as regards pecuniary advantage, it would be much safer to give a few soirées again in Berlin next winter as we did last, at which (if we are up to the mark) there will be no lack of audience, than to undertake the journey to England. In England so much depends on chance—and nothing is certain except the vulgarity prevalent in artistic circles over there, which has a deteriorating effect on fine natures like our dear friend's. What would Schumann say if he found that his Clara had killed herself intellectually for the sake of money. It might drive him to despair later on. She could only go there some time under her Robert's protection, so that a fine nature might keep up her love for her art, which might be all too soon destroyed in London. Music is not an industry at which one makes a living as quickly as possible, but that is how it is regarded over there! It needs spiritual peace and insight in order to realise the beautiful without distraction, and not restless, vainglorious anxiety. There should be no brooding (*experientia docet*)! And so Frau Schumann must spend the summer at Düsseldorf so as to be near Endenich. That is the meaning, in a few words, of the whole of my discourse, to which I hope you agree. Write soon and tell me what you think, and strengthen Frau Clara in her decision. My leave lasts until the 9th, from then onwards letters will reach me in Hanover, before that in Berlin.

We had a splendid musical evening yesterday. Frau Schumann played magnificently (as I have not heard her play for a long time), and taught me to find new beauty in things long familiar to me. We had the last movements of the F minor Sonata. Besides this we played the sublime one's[1] G major Sonata full of the promise of spring. A pretty woman sang songs by Schumann and Johannes Brahms to the satisfaction of a friend of

---

[1] The friends used to refer to Beethoven as "*der Hohe*," that is, the great or sublime one.

the composers; the latter played Joh. Seb. Bach's Chaconne.

But Frau Schumann will have told you all this much better in the yellow letter. Good-bye, and remember your                    JOSEPHUS JOACHIMUS.

*To Clara Schumann*

HANOVER, *March* 18, 1855.

Dear Friend—My hopes of seeing you here for the next concert have come to naught — you do not know how hardened I have become during the years I have spent here to giving up my dearest wishes, or else you would know what it means when I say that I am quite overwhelmed by this fresh lack of consideration — not one of my suggestions are adopted—and besides that I have once more to suffer the indignity of having a charlatan set up as my rival before the public, without ever having given cause for such a humiliation by my behaviour.

So I must content myself with seeing you for a few moments at the station, for after your two last letters I dare not ask you to break your journey here for half a day!

I cannot take it amiss that you should want to be home as soon as possible after the latest reports. Your Robert's last letters are healthier and more delightful than any of the earlier ones; they rejoiced my heart. They even bear traces of his former charming sense of humour; so much so that I cannot as yet accept the doctor's words as those of an oracle; Dr. Richarz said himself he would rather promise too little than too much; but you can tell from the whole report how the charm of a noble, loveable personality has never left him, my dear friend,

even in his darkest hours—and it will remain with
him always to the admiration of us all, even if he does
not in the future shower the treasures of his mind
so plentifully upon us as heretofore. I think if I see
you passing by me here I shall soon follow you to
Johannes and to much good music!—Ever your
devoted                                    JOSEPH JOACHIM.

### To Clara Schumann

HANOVER, *Wednesday*, 4 P.M.
I am not sure of date. [*April* 4, 1855.]

Dear Friend—Many thanks for the splendid letters
—I mean yours and the beloved master's! How
vividly everything stands before his mind's eye! And
what pleasure it gives me to think that Johannes and
I often occupy his thoughts! Everything he says is
splendid, and the occupation he intends to take up is
most comforting. I have begun to practise hard so
that we can play the Paganini Studies,[1] which I am
dying to hear, in the summer. I hope to play them
at Endenich with Johannes some time.

God grant that this mental activity may soon fit
our dear friend and honoured master for intercourse
with the outer world; we must talk that over when I
see you again, which I am longing to do! I suppose
we shall see one another on your way to Weimar[2] (for
you must certainly hear *Genoveva*). I am not in
favour of a concert just now; Spohr and other music
have taken the edge off the public appetite, so that
we could not count for certain on a brilliant success,
and in Hanover one must either give brilliant concerts
or none at all!

[1] With piano accompaniment by Schumann.
[2] Although cordially invited by Liszt, Frau Schumann finally decided not to
go to Weimar.

But there is every prospect that the King and Queen will want to hear some music, and that we shall play in the Castle where we played last time. At all events I can assure you that both Their Majesties have the warmest feeling for you in spite of all Platens. The wife of the Lord High Steward, on whom I called to-day, told me repeatedly how often the Queen speaks of you, and she thinks it is only due to the remissness of Count Pl. in not notifying your arrival that the King has not commanded you to be invited to play. I am sure Wehner has not said anything against you at his conferences, he would not dare to do that! He leaves a great deal of good undone, but he would do nothing wrong if he really recognised it as such. I trust him so far. Liszt has not told me anything about *Genoveva*, and he is quite right; what a bad conscience I have with regard to the *Weimaraner!* And yet I hope I shall be able to hear the Opera; we must discuss that too.

I would gladly have given the Dutchman a favourable reply about the lessons; but an American and a Dane[1] already intend to go with me to Düsseldorf for lessons. I fear I might be undertaking too much if Myn-Her von Leiden were added to my woes.[2] If you take a special interest in the "honest" father of a family I will give him lessons; otherwise he had better remain at home. You have so often relieved me of the torment of making a decision; do it again this time. I have already sent a refusal to the Düsseldorf Musical Festival Committee. Write and say *when* you are coming through here, and forgive a hasty letter, honoured friend.—Your truly devoted

JOSEPH J.

Heartiest greetings to Johannes and Ludwig.

[1] Woldemar Tofte.   [2] A play on the name *Leiden*, which also means " suffering."

## *To Herman Grimm*

[HANOVER] *Sunday* [*April* 22, 1855].

Dear Herman—I shall only write you a few words
—for it is half-past seven, and the letter must catch the
post.   I thank you from the bottom of my heart for
your friendly letter—you are so good to me, and I feel
it so deeply, more than I can say.   It is one of my
dearest reflections, and one to which I often return,
that I am so bound in thought and sympathy to a man
of such pure endeavours, that this bond must grow
stronger in the course of years and in proportion to
my progress.   I am working hard and am only just
beginning to awake from a state of apathy regarding
my puerility, into which, as I now realise, I had long
been sunk.   One step in this connection is—do not be
alarmed—that in the course of the next fortnight I
shall become a Christian.   The secret is out, but *I
entreat you not to mention it to a soul*; it will take
place here very quietly and rather romantically.   How
I should like to have an opportunity of telling you.   I
wish you could come here soon, as you did last year
(together with Knabriel).   Cannot you see your way
to it?   If you knew for certain the date when the
Arnims would be passing through here, could you
not arrange to be here at the same time?

Last Monday to Wednesday I was at Bonn[1]; a
week ago to-day at this time I made up my mind to it
and went off.

[Conclusion of letter is missing.]

[1] At the Arnims'.

## To Herman Grimm

[HANOVER] *April* 26 [1855].

Dear Herman—I shall probably be here for another full week ; my baptism will only take place then. It is to be done quite secretly, which has been made possible by the fact that the King and Queen have taken over the duties of godparents. Wehner will have the church keys for the duties of sexton—the King, as he often does, will take a walk alone with his wife at mid-day, and will go into the church in which I shall be waiting with the clergyman. The King's simple *goodness* has delighted me ; not long ago (when I had audience with him with reference to musical matters) my remarks on Bach led him to ask me how it was I appreciated his spirit so well, seeing that I was born in a Catholic country, and when I told him of my Israelitish origin and other circumstances of my life, he wished to know what had prevented me, with my " Christian " nature, from accepting the Christian religion. He did away with my chief reason, my dislike of all outward demonstration in purely spiritual matters, by asking if he might be my godfather. I feel as if I had shaken off all bitterness for the first time and were armed against all the sordidness of Judaism, against which I became more inimical the more I had to conquer the disadvantages under which I suffered, at first unconsciously, and afterwards consciously, owing to my Jewish upbringing. The basis of Christ's religion seems to me to be a willing surrender to things spiritual and a joyful martyrdom for them—and in the face of this everything else appears unessential to me just now— I am so romantic that I wish Gisel and you could have been my godparents in some village church.

The day after to-morrow (Saturday evening) I am playing in public here three of Beethoven's Quartettes chosen from different periods of his work. It is for a charitable object (the family of the late Konzertmeister Hartmann of Cologne, whom I learnt to respect as a thorough musician at the Düsseldorf Musical Festival, where he and I played at the same desk). Last Saturday my *Demetrius* Overture was performed at Cassel—neither you nor I have heard it up to the present! Spohr writes that the audience was unsympathetic; he himself, although he acknowledges and praises the " Phantasie " on which the music is based, feels that there is a good deal which is " ear-racking" in the work, and quotes passages (which I cannot imagine sounding less natural to other ears than to mine) to which he cannot accustom himself "in his old age, as he was brought up on the harmonious music of Haydn, Mozart and Beethoven ('the earlier period ')." His letter is full of an old man's kindliness, and really touched me. Old Spohr's nature is honest and firm as a rock; he never let himself go in his whole life, and yet he has ready understanding for every earnest endeavour, so that I am pleased by his sympathy without being discouraged by his fault-finding.

Thank you for the head of Dante. I often look at it, but I have not been to the Arnswaldts' since I got your letter, so I have not shown it. Farewell. My kindest regards to your people and to Bargiel.—Your
JOSEPH J.

*To Clara Schumann*

[DÜSSELDORF, *June* 21, 1855.]

Dear Friend—Your kind letter gave me great pleasure ; Brahms had already told me that you were

so contented at Detmold, but I like best of all to
hear from yourself that you are thinking of me and
would like me to be with you, and I thank you for it
from my heart.   I have doubly to reproach myself
now for having seemed to you so ill-humoured last
time—if my serious mood was really so unbearable, I
apologise a thousand times ; but I am sure I could
never have given cause for the suspicion that my dear
companions were to blame—least of all you, dear,
honoured friend, who seem to have made sympathy
and self-sacrifice for those whom you care for the main
object of life !   If I am ever melancholy again I would
rather you scolded me for being capable of mistaking
such lively companionship for Hanoverian solitude—for
these unsociable habits only come from thence.   But
to turn to something gayer

*und    freu - den - vol - le - res* [1]

Johannes and I are playing a great deal ; for instance
we have played all Haydn's lively Sonatas.   You must
hear the one with the jolly Hungarian Rondo in G :
it is the most characteristic music I have heard for a
long time—one can really see the Hungarian Hussars
twirling their moustaches, and the Hungarian girls'
long nut-brown plaits getting entangled in the spurs
as they dance ; the violin often stumbles so heavily
after the rhythm !   We played Bach's E major
Sonata the other day too—but we nearly always play
in my room ; it makes us too melancholy to hear the
violin and the Erard without the living soprano voice.
Come soon again !   Whether I can really come and
fetch you remains doubtful only because Herman
Grimm may pass through here at the end of the month,
and I have invited him to pay me a short visit.

As soon as I hear definitely from him you shall

[1] " And more joyful."

know, but you can imagine that in this case the fee
is not my motive![1] The children are as merry as
ever, and Johannes' education is taking wonderful
effect—he has just told me triumphantly that the boys
are learning to turn somersaults!
To our meeting in the near future.          J. J.

### To Gisela von Arnim

[HANOVER, *circa December* 9, 1855.]

. . . My relations with Herman are really based on
the fellow-feeling of two artists, who both feel they
must defend the right against the world undeterred
by false pretences, and also on the bond of kindred
powers and common rights—no trivial matters, by
God. I realised the full meaning of this only the
other day when I had the pain of seeing (I went to
Liszt's concert[2]) a man whom I had often called friend,
in whom I had gladly pardoned colossal follies out of
respect for his powers, cringing contemptibly to the
public and acting with revolting hypocrisy towards
himself. Shame on those who are bent on succeeding
and cannot refrain from heightening the effect and
making themselves cheap with groans and shrieks of
woe to heaven because they know they are misusing
their powers. . . .

### To Clara Schumann

[HANOVER, *circa December* 10, 1855.]

. . . I have much to tell you, dear, sympathetic
friend, about Liszt and other matters. I have not been
so bitterly disillusioned for a long time as I was by

---

[1] Joachim was to assist at a Court concert at Detmold.
[2] On December 6 Liszt had conducted some of his Symphonic Poems and
choral works at a concert given by Stern's Orchestral Society.

I

Liszt's compositions ; I had to admit that a more vulgar misuse of sacred forms, a more repulsive coquetting with the noblest feelings for the sake of effect, had never been attempted. At the conductor's desk Liszt makes a parade of the moods of despair and the stirrings of contrition with which the really pious man turns in solitude to God, and mingles with them the most sickly sentimentality, and such a martyr-like air, that one can hear the lies in every note and see them in every movement. Meyerbeer, Wagner, the morbid side of Chopin's muse, not his proud patriotism but his sugary tenderness, Berlioz, all this is combined in one *sample*, without the disorder due to richness of material. I shall never be able to meet Liszt again, because I should want to tell him that instead of taking him for a mighty erring spirit striving to return to God, I have suddenly realised that he is a cunning contriver of effects, who has miscalculated.

You were right, dear Frau Schumann, whenever we argued about his nature. You must make up to me here for not having heard the B♭ major Sonata. Will you do that ?

Another letter will come from me in a few days with similar countless ? ? ? ? ?—The changeable and unchanging                                   J. J.

### To Gisela von Arnim

[HANOVER, *circa February* 4, 1856.]

. . . I have begun my composition for your Pantomime ; I will try and do it as well as I possibly can. But do not rely on being able to make use of it. You know what little sympathy my work has met with up to now—and yet my overtures came from the very depths of my being ; they welled up, un-

checked, from my own inner life—I created them
out of the most passionate of my hopes and desires.
They ought, therefore, to have reached the hearers'
hearts—and yet they did not; nearly every one
who heard them was repelled by them.  So what
will compositions of mine be like which have not got
those fiery elemental aspirations?  They will seem
empty and dead, and equally unworthy of your
enthusiasm for Ristori, and of that temperamental
actress herself, if the play is produced; and that I wish
with my whole soul for the sake of your dear innocent
joy in the matter.  Oh, if only I were sufficiently
simple and untroubled to praise myself whole-heartedly,
as you can, you dear soul.  But unfortunately I cannot do anything of the kind; there is nothing much
in me, believe it, Gisel; you overrate me, I am afraid.
I feel that what people used to love in me, a good,
kind, sympathetic heart, is freezing up more and more;
sometimes I even feel as though, when I am practising
Beethoven's music, I were playing it like a pedant
who insists on his room being tidy; and as God has
not provided me with rich mental gifts and a keen
understanding, I do not see what there is to recommend me and my work as a musician.

So do not expect anything good from my composition, and if you know of some one who you think
could provide passable music for your play, let him
write it, and do not be afraid that I shall be offended.
Others have at any rate the advantage over me of
possessing a certain amount of skill. . . .

## To Clara Schumann

[HANOVER, *February* 6, 1856.]

Dear Friend—You have been so good and kind to me again, and I—Hanoverian—have not yet replied to two letters! That is detestable and—unpardonable? If I were not putting this question to you, kind, indulgent friend, the answer would be "Yes," but I will at any rate try to give you an idea of the unpleasant time I have had since we parted, so as to make you more disposed to forgive me. Only think, my chief's continued double-dealing and other intrigues once more made my position here so unbearable that I was obliged to send in my resignation twice! I gave my reasons for wishing to resign, etc., etc., both in writing and at an audience with the King. In short, the whole transaction was most complicated and wasted much time.

Finally the King was gracious enough to declare that I should never receive my dismissal from him, but should be protected by him against unauthorised interference with my musical rights. Everything has been so arranged that at last my position is what I wished it to be, and is not dependent on the whim of an ill-disposed chief. It turned out that Count Platen had repeatedly given me false impressions of the King's wishes: for instance, that he did not want any of Mozart's music, and was unfavourably disposed towards a certain pianist [1] with whom I much prefer to play Mozart. As to the last item, the King belied it by his own behaviour towards this lady, which (as you know) has always been most charming and deferential. . . .

[1] Frau Schumann herself.

*From H. Kolbe* [1]

HANOVER, *February* 8, 1856.

Most honoured Konzertmeister—I take up my pen to express not only my sincere sympathy, but also the most emphatic disapproval of the way in which some of my colleagues have behaved to-day. Be assured that there are many in the orchestra who think the same as I do, and it is my earnest wish that all my colleagues may learn to appreciate what a distinguished artist you are, and with what great devotion you strive to attain the best possible results—an artist from whom all can learn.

I hope you will not be so indignant at what happened to-day that you will think you must leave us. The time will surely soon come when you will receive from all the musicians the full appreciation which is unfortunately accorded you now, in the degree which you merit, by only a portion of the orchestra.

It is hardly necessary for me to conclude by assuring you that I esteem and honour you most highly both as artist and man.—Yours most respectfully, H. KOLBE.

## To Ferdinand David

HANOVER, *February* 13, 1856.

Dear Herr David—Brahms, who has given me your messages from Leipzig, and who is staying a few more days with me, has also told me of the steps which you and Schumann's friends have taken in order to make his future more secure. I need hardly

---

[1] With regard to the reason for this letter, see the letter to Gisela von Arnim of February 29, p. 120. On the back in Joachim's hand is written: "I received this letter after the disagreeable rehearsal; it soothed me somewhat, for he is one of the most able members of the orchestra."

tell you how interested I was; it is splendid that a *practical* step has been taken to this end at last![1] Unfortunately, I soon realised that what *we* discussed that last evening at Leipzig, and what I in particular advocated, was not feasible; at least, I came to the conclusion that a *musical* combination which would represent Schumann's true ideals was not possible, as so much heterogeneous material would have to be drawn upon for the purpose; also, there is not that agreement among the public which would be necessary in order to attain the desired end. But if my idea cannot be carried out in its full artistic sense, it had better not be attempted at all, and we had better turn to the simplest and surest way of gaining the chief object we have in view.

Allow me therefore, I beg, as a former Leipziger, to associate myself with Schumann's friends and admirers, by devoting 50 Rthlr. out of my salary to the same object. Unhappily, it is not a great deal, but I am not able to do more—and I should like least of all to remain *quite* out of it. If you will let me know soon how much is still to come, and from whom, I shall be very grateful. I am most anxious that every one should do all they can to carry out the suggestion successfully as quickly as possible; for, in my opinion, Frau Schumann herself ought to be told the result before the end of this month. Even though what you and the others are doing is only intended to benefit Schumann himself, it will naturally not be without effect on the position of his family, and I think an early communication with Frau Schumann would influence her touring plans. Not long ago she thought of undertaking a journey to England from a sense of duty, although I

---

[1] Schumann's expenses at the asylum were to have been met by a yearly subscription from his friends. See Litzmann.

know how extremely fatigued she was after the concerts at Vienna and other places, and how much they affected her health.   She certainly ought to have absolute rest, at any rate for the summer, and if her friends told her that Schumann was provided for by his brother artists and admirers she would be free to consider a move to *Berlin* instead of the journey to London, so as to take, as soon as possible, the necessary steps in Berlin to insure for herself a permanent means of existence, which Frau Schumann ought not to find difficult, with her great talent and energetic character.

Write to me soon and tell me whether you agree with what I have said—and if you do, what I can do to help the matter forward.

I am very much taken up with music just now— there are rehearsals for the 9th Symphony every day this week, as I have been requested to coach the Singing Academy in it and conduct it on Saturday.

Besides that, Rubinstein and Brahms are here ; the latter plays the piano more magnificently than ever, and there is no end to the music.   He wishes me to send you his kindest regards, and I would add that I wish to be remembered to your family.—As always, sincerely yours,          JOSEPH JOACHIM.

### From Johannes Brahms

[DÜSSELDORF, *February* 26, 1856.]

My dear Friend—Thank you for your letter and the two enclosures.

I missed the passport at Minden and the other here.

I am to remind you that to-morrow afternoon (2 o'clock ?) the [Schumann] children are passing through Hanover. We are loading them up with bread and butter and oranges here; you are to see to the coffee. And then I want to remind you of what we have so often discussed, and beg you to let us carry it out, namely, to send one another exercises in counterpoint. Each should send the other's work back every fortnight (in a week's time therefore) with remarks and his own work, this to continue for a good long time, until we have both become really clever.

Why should not two sensible, earnest people like ourselves be able to teach one another far better than any Pf. [Professor?] could?

But do not merely reply in words.

Send me your first study in a fortnight. Shall I send you Marpurg?[1] I have it.

I am looking forward hopefully to the first batch. Let us take it seriously! It would be very pleasant and useful. I think it is a delightful idea.—Always yours,
                                                    JOHANNES.

### To Gisela von Arnim

[HANOVER, *February* 29, 1856.]

To begin with, and not by way of excuse, let me copy for you part of a letter which I wrote weeks ago, because it will show you how I have been beset by one disagreeable after the other this winter—and because it will tell you that you are always with me even when my pen is silent. It was written in the heat of the moment to comfort *myself*, but it remained unfinished, as do so many other things I undertake.

" I have just[2] been through a very bad time again —at the rehearsal of B.'s *Coriolanus* Overture. You

---

[1] Probably Marpurg's *Abhandlung von der Fuge* ("Treatise on the Fugue").
[2] February 8. See p. 117.

know that is one of my favourites; its waves of sound
strengthen the spirit, just as the wounds of the giants of
old were healed when they touched the earth.   How
I longed to hear that music, so passionate and simple
at the same time, so variable and yet so compact:
anger and tenderness, like day and night side by side,
the whole a tempestuous outpouring of the soul.
And at the very moment when one might have
called all that greatness to life one comes up against
the souls of tradesmen instead of artists—men who,
instead of longing to feel Beethoven's warmth in
their hearts, have no hearts at all, but at the most a
pair of scales filled to the brim with stupidity and
vanity which their tongues set swinging backwards
and forwards.   Matters went so far that several ill-
disposed members refused to obey me as musical
director, whereupon I laid down my baton with the
remark that I did not wish to be head of the orchestra
any longer.

"For years I have hoped to give these musicians
confidence in me by my behaviour towards them—I
never wanted to be their director, but their colleague,
who had taken over the work of conducting as they
had that of playing.   It is bitter to have to admit that
these were merely the chimeras of a tyro—that good-
will combined with uncompromising enthusiasm for
one's art cannot be understood by the people, who
appear to be accustomed only to cowardice and
arrogance.   After to-morrow's concert, which I am
bound to conduct so as not to cause the King any
inconvenience, I will not appear again with the
orchestra."

I had written so far.   Having made this resolution
I could not wait for the King to act with his usual

goodness and love of justice with regard to my affairs. I will tell you this much : The same day I requested an audience with the King (with the *knowledge* of my chief, Count Platen, on whom *alone* I could not depend, as he had probably been at the back of the matter, or had desired it, at any rate) ; the next day I explained to the King the difficulties which stood in the way of my retaining my position. He insisted on having full details—and as I had to give an exact report I was forced, against my will, to make a complaint, and to help to dictate to the King's secretary a letter to Count Platen which should satisfy *me*, and in which the disturber of the peace was most sharply reproved and commanded to attend the rehearsals in future, so as to give his sanction to me, before his creatures, as the only authority on musical matters.

I am sure I need not tell you how painful the whole business was to me ; I would far rather beat an accompaniment on a big drum made of gourds and jackal skins to the kaffirs' war-songs than make such a song about my own authority—but what could I do this time against the King's *energetically* expressed wishes ?

I have been interrupted by matters concerning the concert—to-morrow is our last concert but one. Accept these Hanoveriana meanwhile ; it was only for the sake of writing to you at last. . . .

You are the only one to whom I gave an exact account of the matter in the letter I did *not* send.

### *To Gisela von Arnim*

[HANOVER, *March* 15, 1856.]

. . . I did not go to Leipzig ; my arm, which had been somewhat overworked during the last few days, was really weakened by a chill, and this was (between ourselves) a welcome excuse for breaking my promise to go there.   Last winter was such an absolutely miserable one that for the time being I hate every disturbance, and most of all concert tours. Yesterday a horrible great Mecklenburg horse *bit* me in the arm as I was quietly taking pleasure in the blue blouse of a carman belonging to the team, because the man inside it looked so contented.   That's what happens to harmless contemplatives : along comes a vicious beast and attacks the unconscious victim! Luckily I had on a thick coat; I have only turned rather blue and red.   It is healing up already.   God keep you now in terrible Berlin!   Since Pfeil's audacity there has been horror upon horror!   I hope your friend from Bonn will help you to forget them somewhat. . . .

I played *Abendglocken* here the other day; I have seldom made such an impression on the Hanoverians, and I had to play it to the King again the next day, who himself got up a musical evening for that very purpose, and commanded it to be played again shortly.   Is it not astonishing ?

*From Herman Grimm*

[BERLIN, *April* 25, 1856.]

Dear Joachim—I am answering your letter[1] at once.   What struck me most in it was the impression the news has made on you.   To me (in spite of the lack of personal knowledge of him, and judging only by his music) Schumann's condition has followed such a natural course that I could only regard a cure by

[1] On Schumann's condition becoming worse, Joachim had obviously returned to his notion of the spring of 1854, a cure by magnetism ; it is not possible to date Grimm's letter as far back as 1854, because of the mention in it of the projected trip to Italy.

artificial or external means as the galvanising of a
spiritual corpse which is treated with indignity out of
a mistaken sense of duty.   Forgive the word ; I mean
it in the higher sense.   An organism which by the
furious rapidity of production rushes headlong to a
point at which it overreaches itself and collapses,
cannot, by any means, be restored to its former power.
Supposing that did happen.  What then ?  More work,
more rush, and a still more terrible end.   I think only
one thing could procure him absolute peace, that all
external things should, to a certain extent, adapt
themselves to the morbid ideas of his wounded
organism, but not that he should be tormented by his
consciousness being strung taut again.

Look at his music.  If there is any future for it, his
ever-increasing haste can be physically felt.   He is
riding at full speed up a mountain which he could
perhaps never climb if he went slowly.   Now he is at
the top, he becomes giddy, and there is no stopping
him.   I beg you not to torment yourself with hypo-
theses.   Szapary makes helpless muscles active, and
awakens dormant faculties, but he does not renew
withered limbs or disentangle mental threads that
have become so weak they would break if they were
stretched.   That is my opinion.

You know of course that after all this you ought to
go with me, if only for your own sake.   So decide
whether we are to meet here or at Dresden.   I should
like to leave here on the first of May, and I have
already procured my pass.  We will let the warm
sands of life breed new activity in us.   I am looking
forward to the blue sky there and the gentle waves in
the canals.   I mean to learn swimming there.

Good-bye, and send an early reply to your

HERMAN.

## To Gisela von Arnim

VENICE [*May* 18, 1856].

. . . We have been here since Thursday ; to-day is Sunday. Whilst I am writing to you Herman has gone to lunch with Count Portalez [Pourtalès], who was so kind and courteous as to invite me too, but after having lacked the presence of mind to say no to such an agreeable man, I have asked Herman to make my excuses. I am no good socially, and travelling makes no difference—I am the same, and my soul has its own burden, as you realised in Berlin! I hope God will soon grant me the peacefulness of being physically in my home and roaming in thought and imagination through strange lands ; there is a spirit of restlessness in me which can be calmed by work and by nothing else, and then I shall be cheerful and amiable again towards those around me. If I were not afraid of offending Herman, who is perhaps more touchy and sensitive to neglect than he would admit to himself, and if it did not mean breaking my word, I should be capable of deserting. I have practically ceased to imagine that I might be something more to Herman than an occasional, pleasant variation ; I feel that with my uncertain, and frequently taciturn, moods I must appear very dull compared with him, who grasps everything so lightly and eagerly. Whilst I am still forging Icarus wings to carry me to my destination, he has flown over it long ago, or else reached it by familiar marble steps! But what is the good of all this !

*To Gisela von Arnim*

[VENICE] *May* 19 [1856].

I began to write the enclosed letter to you yesterday—it was turning out so gloomy that I preferred to stop, and as the rising moon was shining beautifully, and shedding a soft shimmer of light on the dark, heaving waves in front of my rooms (we are right on the Grand Canal), I was tempted to take a gondola. I went to the Lido, about three-quarters of an hour away, on the sea. My heart, too, became lighter and freer every minute. I thought gratefully and calmly of all dear things, of you most of all; I determined to torment myself no longer with the reproaches for having undertaken the trip which have accompanied me like a refrain up to now. On the way here I asked Herman to wait for me for a few days in Vienna : I could not go so near to Pesth, on a pleasure trip, without visiting my parents, as my mother has been dangerously ill during this last year. I was rewarded by finding everything as I had hoped, my parents pleased by my surprise visit, my brothers and sister well and happy. It made me feel how far apart I am from them.

The scenery of Pesth and Ofen delighted me once more by the rare beauty of the contrasting shores, and the brilliant colours and vivacity of the Magyar people. I wished you could have been there; you too would have enjoyed this sight, both grand and individual as it is!

As I had travelled by night as usual, in order to have two full days in Pesth, I rested at Vienna after the tiring journeys. Count Flemming[1] was very hospitable to me, probably in memory of the Weimar

---

[1] A friend of the Arnim family, who married Gisela's sister in 1860.

days, of which I also was reminded by his pleasant
way of living and of playing the 'cello ; he had collected
together a lot of Italian instruments for my benefit, in
which of course I took the most polite interest, and
there really was one among them with a very fine
tone.   In the evening I heard the most beautiful and
charming Italian voice I have ever come across, as
Zerline in *Don Juan*.   The singer was called Borghi
Mamo[1]; if Mozart had ever been able to spirit his
music into a throat instead of writing it on music
paper, it would have sounded like that.   Delightful ;
not a breath too many, and yet so full and soft.
Indeed, the whole opera made a greater impression on
me than ever, in spite of the mediocre orchestra,
because the characters were alive, and particularly
because the freedom of movement was expressed by
the *rhythm* of the singing ; Germans often neglect
this point.   In this case you readily forgot that
much in it was not ideal enough, just because there
was a natural element in it all, which gave Mozart's
indestructible grace free play.   I never understood
Mozart's genius for opera writing so well before, and
kept thinking affectionately of him whilst I was in
Vienna.   I meant to write to you from Trieste, but my
box was lost, and I was so upset until I got it back
again, as it contained, among other things, manuscripts
of yours, Hafbur's, etc., that the most I could do was
to loiter about the harbour.   It had been kept by
mistake at a station on the way.

Venice impressed me as being gloomy at first.
Laugh at me !   I cannot help it.   I feel like a mole at
present, and the black masses of stone, the bleak
lagoons in bad weather, with the black gondolas and
we two silent fellows on them, formed inviting ground

---

[1] ? The name is written indistinctly.

for my burrowing thoughts. The whole town seemed to me like a monstrous robe of mourning for departed greatness. But now my impression is a different and a better one—since I have seen the active simple people, gliding past the old walls like many-coloured lizards, as though they had no other business in life than to amuse themselves, and were never weary of enjoying the soft breezes, and watching the lovely reflections of the moon in the lagoons. I will try and see everything in this spirit, until I start for Milan. . . .

### From Franz Liszt

WEYMAR, *July* 10, 1856.

These few words are just to remind you of my feeling of true, deep and admiring friendship for you, my dear Joachim. Even though others, more intimate with you, have tried to make you doubt this friendship, let their trouble have been in vain—and let us always remain true and faithful, as befits a couple of fellows like ourselves! Your viola pieces are *magnificent*; they soothe and refresh me. I wish I could have written them; but I am still more glad that they are by you. I have given a hearty salute to the "numerous kings of Hanover" who roam through them. Härtel will have sent my things or rather nothings to you in Hanover. Even if you do not care for them this shall not be an apple of discord in our friendship. "It is a grave fault," says Goethe, "when a man imagines himself to be more than he is and rates himself lower than his 'worth.'"[1] I wish to avoid this fault; and so my survey of what I have accomplished and may yet accomplish is very objective.

---

[1] "*Ein grosser Fehler, dass man sich mehr dünkt, als man ist und sich weniger schätzt, als man 'wert' ist.*"

When are we to meet again ?   Would you like me to come to Hanover at an earlier date, or are you soon coming to Weymar, where you have been expected since February?   I asked Herr von Beaulieu to write to you before I go to Vienna.   Now, *Sapperment*, if you do not yet know that I love you, may the cuckoo take your fiddle.   Apropos of the cuckoo (not the one in the Pastoral Symphony!), can you imagine that Cossmann has been so foolish as to fall out with me because Singer has been given the title of *Konzert-meister*!   Is that not a Lamento without a Trionfo! Excellent fellow and 'cellist, he has gone off to Baden-Baden without saying a word to me, having previously declared here that he would only return as *Konzert-meister*.   Amen.

May you have the best of good luck, dear friend. Write soon to your faithful          F. LISZT.


*From Clara Schumann*

BONN, *July* 28, 1856.

Dear Joachim—Only a few words!   I have been here with Johannes since yesterday.   We are staying at the *Deutsches Haus*, but we spent the day at Endenich.   I saw him yesterday.   I cannot speak of my grief, but I had some loving glances—these will accompany me through life!   And once he embraced me, he recognised me!   Pray to God that he may have a peaceful end—Richarz says it cannot be far off. I will not leave him again!   Oh, Joachim, what grief, what anguish, to see him again like this!   But—I would not forego the sight of him for anything in the world.   We are just going out there again!

Think of him and of your

CLARA SCHUMANN.

K

*To Gisela von Arnim*

BONN, *Wednesday* [*July* 30, 1856].

The day before yesterday Brahms telegraphed to me that Schumann was dangerously ill, and I came here yesterday. His wife was here; when we got to Endenich at 4.30 in the afternoon he had just passed away. On the last day he appears to have sunk softly and gradually to sleep. His face was gentle and peaceful; my last impression of the beloved master is grave but calm; his life was pure as few others have been.

Whilst my plans are uncertain I have ordered all letters from Heidelberg to be sent to *Hanover*. Your letter had not yet reached me; you will hear what I am going to do to-morrow. There is much to see to —this is just a line.

Your mother will be shocked by the news; you will know how to tell her.—Your friend,      J. J.


*To Franz Liszt*

DÜSSELDORF, *August* 2, 1856.

Dear Liszt—Frau Schumann has entrusted me with the solemn duty of informing her friends of her terrible loss—of Schumann's death. One of my first thoughts was that you, who stood in artistic and friendly relations with the departed master in the old days, would be particularly moved by the news—for even though fate, external and spiritual circumstances, had forced you to travel along different roads in life, even though you had mutually voiced this fact, yet I am sure there is no one who will have a clearer understanding of the full worth of the man who has gone from us, or who has the power and the wish to realise it more deeply, than you at this sad time.

I am sure you will be grieved that you were not able, as I was, to show the master's remains the last honours when he was buried at Bonn on Thursday. It would not have been in keeping with the composer's nature to publish the day of the burial in the papers for the benefit of his friends and admirers, for he always preferred to live in his own solemn and sacred thoughts; but many sympathisers followed the body to Bonn. It was carried to its resting-place by artists and lovers of art, and buried close to the earthly remains of Niebuhr and Schlegel.

Frau Schumann returned yesterday; the presence of her dear ones and of Brahms, whom Schumann loved as a son, is a comfort to this splendid woman, who even in her deepest grief is to me a noble example of strength and resignation. I shall probably stay in Düsseldorf for a few more days, and I count on receiving the letter from you promised me by Dr. Pohl, for which I thank you in anticipation, and to which I hope to send an early reply.—With sincere respect, JOSEPH JOACHIM.

*To Gisela von Arnim*

DÜSSELDORF, *August* 8, 1856.

. . . A few sympathetic words from you are sure to do Frau Schumann good; I know no one who can give comfort so tenderly and warmly as you, and she will feel that too. You must not imagine her as oppressed by sentimental grief; she has a healthy impulse to work and a warm love of music which will always raise her above ordinary people throughout her life. Schumann saw her again before his death;

although convulsed with agonised nerves, he appears to have smiled tenderly on her, as he used to do when he was at his best, a sign that he recognised her; although he repelled her at times, as he did every one else, he often made a movement as though to embrace her. That is a consoling memory to her when she thinks of his and her trials. Frau Schumann was on the best of terms with the doctors and Fräulein Reumont;[1] she had confidence in them, and I can only say that they showed every consideration without being in the least officious. Every one in Bonn was the same; the Mayor [Otto], Jahn, Groth, etc. I undertook most of the details, the burial, and letters to Schumann's friends; that was why I did not write to you again at once; I thought you would understand. Seeing to so many things helped me to get over many gloomy thoughts at the beginning. In spite of everything I realised, what I had previously imagined, and what one usually tells oneself by way of consolation, that a man had gone from the world with whom I could sympathise in the highest sense—who knew this, and who thought kindly of me. Through all resignation there runs, without our being aware of it, a thread, half desire, half hope—a secret something which we only miss when death comes with his grave, pitiless smile (I might almost call it) at the egoism of the individual when opposed to universal laws. The wise yet gentle expression which rests on the brows of the dead is remarkable; I noticed it in Mendelssohn too, the only person besides Schumann whom I have seen after death. I have much more to tell you about Schumann; his papers have revealed a great deal to me and shown me, too, a really great and beautiful side of his character. An extraordinary benevolence

[1] Nurse at Endenich.

side by side with the most obstinate pedantry ! There were the most elaborate drafts of every letter he wrote during his illness, even of the most unimportant little note—as though for works of art ; one could see the effort it had cost him to construct the shortest sentence, as, for instance, in his letter to your mother. Then again he had begun numerous complicated musical studies, and written them *correctly* ; for instance, the beginning of an arrangement of my *Henry IV.* Overture as a piano duet, which covered several pages. How it touched me to find this indication of his affectionate memory of me ! His wife promised, first of all, to give it to me ; but as it is the last thing Schumann wrote, she ought to keep it. . . . Brahms has recovered from his fall. He has an abundance of mental power. His mind is capable of grasping the sublimest as well as the tenderest conceptions. I leave in three days' time : I am quite well on the whole. . . .

### *To Georg Gottfried Gervinus*

BERLIN, *August* 27 [1856].

Honoured Professor—Since that last evening in Heidelberg, which I spent in such stimulating company, and my sudden departure immediately afterwards, many things, some of them sad, have happened to me. Instead of the much discussed water cure, I have covered a great deal of firm ground. Since then I have been in Bonn, Düsseldorf, and Hanover, and before returning to my official duties I am now in Berlin, from whence Dr. Chrysander will bring you this letter. In spite of having been so un-settled, what you told me that last delightful evening in Heidelberg has constantly recurred to me. The edition of Händel is a project I have very much at heart, and the more the publishers hesitate, the more urgent becomes the duty of those who take an intellectual interest in the undertaking to give voice, if possible by deeds, to their earnest desire for its realisation. The edition ought to be of double importance to German musicians now, as it will give them a chance of showing that they are just as willing to serve Händel and to comprehend him as were his great contemporaries. For this reason I am glad to be able to tell you, whose love for Händel is combined with real understanding of his worth, that I was not mistaken in saying confidently that many of my contemporaries would willingly devote their musical talents to the forwarding of the desired edition of Händel, by means of such work as lay in their power. All the colleagues to whom I have spoken regard the compilation of selections for the piano for the great project as a stimulating exercise, and a most welcome opportunity of studying the master's creations more deeply and with a more lively interest. From my more intimate friends, Johannes Brahms, Dietrich at Bonn, and Bargiel at Berlin, I have had a definite *consent* to set to work energetically. But there is no doubt that, besides those I have named, other capable men will join us in the work, who will voluntarily offer their time and capabilities for the purpose. If you think it would be in any way helpful, dear Professor, to repeat what I have just told you, please make any use of it which seems desirable to you. If there is anything more definite which I and my friends could do, I sincerely hope you will let me know. It would give me so much pleasure to have news in this way of you and your wife, to whom I owe so many delightful hours.—With sincerest respect,

JOSEPH JOACHIM.

A QUARTET AT BETTINA VON ARNIM'S.

Pastel (artist unknown).

*From Clara Schumann*

DÜSSELDORF, *September* 28, '56.

What on earth has become of you, dear Joachim, and what are you doing? Is there not room for one little corner in your thoughts for your other friends when you are staying with Bettina? I suppose it was absurdly arrogant of me, but I did think you would at least remember me on the 13th![1] We have just played your fine *Henry IV.* Overture on my two beautiful grand pianos, and we were once more all on fire; the flames of anger against the faithless one have been changed by your music into flames of enthusiasm! But please, please, write; we long so much for news of you! And Johannes would like so much to recommence the delightful musical correspondence. Do send him some studies again and that will make him work! When do you go back to Hanover? Are you going to play at Hamburg? Joh. has consented and will play the Concert-Allegro, and I suppose you will play the Phantasie? You two, his dearest friends, will surely be glad to assist worthily at this festival? Avé wrote in despair that you had sent no reply to three letters from him. . . .

. . . My nerves are in an extremely bad state. God knows what I shall be like in the winter (for I must leave soon). You would not believe how the thought of travelling upsets me, indeed you do not know how grief rages in me, so that there are times when the courage to go on living deserts me! He who has not been through it does not know what it means to bury his beloved. When you saw me at Bonn I was composed and calm to a degree I could never have believed possible, but I was entirely dominated

[1] Frau Schumann's birthday.

by the thought of *his* peace; all sorrow vanished in gratitude that God had released him, but that could not last, and now I feel my loss more bitterly every day. We visited his grave at the beginning and at the end of our tour—it was overgrown even after those few weeks! What a serious thing life is! Do you think of him too sometimes? Why not remember me too occasionally? Let me know soon when you will be in Hanover. I wonder if I shall see you there? How are things turning out there? Are they any easier for you yet? The best thing you could do would be to go away for good. It really hurts me to think of you back again in that hole. . . .

It makes me anxious to think that you are staying such a long time with the Arnims. Are you not exposing yourself to unnecessary pain? Are you not taking your heart for stronger than it is? You artists are divine only in your art, otherwise you are only human, better and nobler certainly than most, but more sensitive for that very reason. You wish to steel your heart, to renounce a love, but you are feeding it daily. Do not exact too much from yourself, lest that noble, generous heart should succumb. Do not be angry with me or laugh at me for speaking in this way; it comes from my anxiety for you. I should like to see you a truly happy man—you know I have your welfare at heart as though you were my own son; you know how highly I esteem the Arnims, but all the same, I wish you were not with them now. . . .

### *From Herman Grimm*

[BERLIN] *December* 23, 1856.

Dear Joachim—A thousand thanks for having gone to Celle for the burial of my play, and for having

written such a faithful account of the funeral rites.[1]
I hardly expected as much, and foresaw much worse
things, but as the offer was made to me I did not
want to refuse it altogether, and so I let things take
their course.   It will go no better at Hanover.   But
I hope my new *Rotrudis* will have a better fate at
Vienna.   Laube[2] has as good as accepted it.   At any
rate that is how I interpret his letter.   He asks for
certain alterations, to which I have agreed.

You know that Bettine has had another stroke.
I saw her yesterday evening.   Her right arm is still
helpless and her foot is very weak.   She is read aloud
to continuously.   There is a feebleness in her expression which I suppose I notice particularly, because
I only see her occasionally. . . .

I am at last working at my essay on Raphael and
Michael Angelo.   I am indeed half-way through.   I
am enjoying it very much.   I shall have it printed
in Brunswick.[3]   I can work very well at present, and
have many plans.   I hope things are going equally
well with you.   Work is the only true happiness on
earth.

Bargiel's Violin Duet[4] has found a brilliant critic
in Rellstab, and Wendt's Quartette almost an enthusiastic one.   At Bülow's concert recently I heard a
Trio of Schumann's,[5] the first thing by him which
has really made an impression on me.   Unfortunately
the instruments did not blend in the least.   Laub

---

[1] Does not appear to have been preserved.   The letter refers to the (unprinted)
comedy *Ein ewiges Geheimnis* (An Eternal Secret).

[2] At that time manager of the Burgtheater at Vienna.

[3] It appeared in the second volume of *Westermann's Magazine*, at Brunswick,
1859, and was later included in the *Essays*.

[4] At the second Chamber Music Soirée on December 9, played by A. Grünwald
and Robert Radecke.

[5] In D minor, at the second Schumann Trio Soirée, in the English Hall on
December 17.

played with a sentimental tenderness, Wohlers with a fine, rather meaningless tone, and Bülow with cold correctness. The three together were by no means inspiring, but one had an idea of the thing all the same.

To-morrow is Christmas, a day like all other days. I no longer have a suspicion of the feeling I used to have about it. I am going this evening to Lepsius to help decorate the tree for the children.

Rudolf caught cold on the journey and is in bed ill. He will probably leave us again soon, because, as lieutenant, he will have to join his company against the Swiss. They are to march on January 6. I can see nothing more in the whole business than miserable confusion.—Your                    HERMAN GR.

### From Franz Liszt

WEYMAR, *January* 9, 1857.

Honoured Friend—What a long time it is since I heard from you! You have been in the Tyrol, in Venice, in Heidelberg, and God knows where besides! I saw your father in Pesth and met several acquaintances of yours on the journey, but nobody was able to tell me all that I longed to hear about you, and since you left here a wall of dense mist seems to have come between us. Allow me to hope that it will not be so very long before the former sunshine beams on us again.

A friend who has become very dear to me, Hans von Bronsart, will call on you in the course of a few days. Permit me to recommend him to your kindness. He himself will bring you his best letter of recommendation in the shape of a Trio [1] which I like particularly. I think it may rank with the best music which has been written during the last few years, and I

---

[1] Op. 1 in G minor, published by Aibl in Munich.

am curious to know whether you will like it. Bronsart
has a very *distinguished* personality ; there is in him
a happy combination of firmness of character and
charming and graceful manners, and if you get to
know him better you are sure to grow fond of him.
At Altenburg and Weymar he had the honour of
being presented to the Grand Duchess Constantin and
of playing before her. She has also been gracious
enough to invite him to Hanover, where he will stay
for a few days, going from thence to Paris. Be so
kind as to introduce him to Wehner and your other
friends at Hanover. You may be sure that he will
not belie my recommendation.

I am still in ill health, and I am writing this letter
to you in bed, where I shall be obliged to get rid of
the remains of the illness I had at Zürich. Bronsart
will tell you the little there is to tell about Weymar
and your humble servant by word of mouth. The
day before yesterday at his farewell concert he
played his Trio with Singer and Cossmann, the piano
part of the Schumann Ballads which were declaimed
by Fräulein Seebach, and, in conclusion, my 2nd
Concerto.

I also had the Symphonic Poem, *Ce qu'on entend sur
la montagne*, performed ; I will shortly send you the
score of this (together with the three last of my
Symphonic Poems which have been published).

Goodbye, dearest friend, and remember your
faithful                                           F. LISZT.

Could you not manage to come here for a Court
concert in the middle of February? Try and arrange
that we may meet again soon. The memory of you
here is still so vivid that it is not so easy to stand
your forgetfulness.

*To Clara Schumann*

[HANOVER, *January* 15, 1857.]

Dear Frau Schumann—I have something very curious to tell you—I have been offered an engagement in London to commence on July 22 for 3 or 4 weeks, by the Surrey Gardens Company. A new hall has been built there which holds 7000 people, and I should have to bind myself to play there every evening—*the music to be chosen by me* ; for this I should receive £60 a *week*.

To be quite honest I am very much attracted by it ; but there is a drawback—*Jullien's* orchestra. On most evenings, certainly, only good music will be played, but on others there will be polkas. In spite of the attraction of £240 in one month I cannot make up my mind to do it, and I hope you will say I am right. I have debated with myself as to whether there were not a certain amount of artistic arrogance in my refusal of such a pecuniarily brilliant offer—but my original feeling against such an association with an undisguised charlatan and speculator triumphs over all arguments to the contrary. What relations can remain sacred to me in life if I cheapen my art by active association with a mountebank?

Write me a line about the matter, which I suppose Johannes will hear about too. — With affectionate greetings to you all,                    JOSEPH J.

. . . You will not laugh at me for writing to you on the subject (of Jullien). The Wehners[1] were so down on me for my arrogance and obstinacy when I

---

[1] Brahms replied (*Brahms-Joachim Correspondence*, vol. i. p. 156): "I join in saying that we agree entirely and emphatically with your doubts about Jullien. If you had not consulted the Wehners, you would not have consulted us." This letter has been *erroneously* placed in the summer of 1856.

told them about it quite innocently, that I felt I had to talk about it with some one who, even if they thought I was mistaken, would not misunderstand me.

### To his brother Heinrich

[HANOVER, *second half of January* 1857.]

I thank you with all my heart for the trouble you have taken on my behalf, on top of all your own affairs. I only got your letter on arriving here from Hamburg yesterday; that is the sole reason for the delay in my reply. I would gladly enter into such a profitable engagement as the one for the Beethoven and Mendelssohn concerts, if only that—confounded Jullien were not conducting them. It is disgusting that this chief of snobs should be mixed up in the project of the Surrey Gardens Directors, which is otherwise so praiseworthy in its attempt to popularise our great masters of music. But, once and for all, I cannot stand Jullien—although I manage to put up very well with St. Julien-Medoc occasionally, the fire in which is more genuine than in that of its name-sake. Do not take this for an artist's vanity or even for prudery; it is not the name (what's in a name?[1]), but the thing itself that disgusts me; for although I can *laugh* at the tricks of the composer of dances when it is a question of his polkas, *it makes me really angry* when the fellow, in his character as con-ductor, introduces his charlatanism into the works of Mozart and Beethoven, and this will be *inevitable.* A jackdaw cannot help stealing, and Jullien could *not* leave off being a humbug, even if he intended to do so. Why do not the directors appoint another conductor for the musical evenings at their hall?

---

[1] Written in English in the original.—TR.

That would necessarily be the first condition of any decent *professional musician,* myself among them. But as its fulfilment appears to be quite out of the question, I must ask you rather to say nothing at all on the subject if you meet Mr. Bowley, and simply to tell him that I thank him for his offer and pleasant visit (he was very charming and amusing), but that I had changed my plans and could not be in England at the end of July. But I shall gladly·come with Frau Schumann in May; if you can make a good engagement for me at the Musical Union or anywhere else where the choice of music rests with me, please do so, dear brother.

### *To Gisela von Arnim*

[HANOVER, *beginning of March* 1857.]

Bargiel writes that Stern wishes to produce my Overture at a concert at which compositions by Liszt and Berlioz are to be performed. I have no objection, for what I am most anxious about is that *you* should hear it. The unhealthy neighbourhood of Liszt's music will not endanger mine in your ears, so I shall not worry Stern with trifling objections from motives of artistic prudery. If ever I declare myself to be opposed to any participation in Liszt's musical endeavours, it must be in a more dignified manner than by such a feeble little protest which would make me appear afraid of the conductor with whom I was associated for so many years. I only hope the performance will not take place on March 19, for I have arranged to have my Overture played here in Hanover at the last concert, which falls on that day.

I have a peculiar feeling about Stern's praise of my things; I do not trust it altogether. If he really thought them so remarkable, he would not have allowed himself to be dissuaded for so long from producing one or other of my pieces, which are in his hands ; and moreover I cannot reconcile his respect for me with the fact that he has laid on one side without a word the Schubert compositions which I instrumentated and placed at his disposal.   That really has rather annoyed me, because I took the trouble to write my opinion of Schubert, and because his silence on the matter looks like an unmerited belittling of my dead favourite, whose work I would have so gladly prepared for the enjoyment of others, because I consider it one of his finest, and quite worthy of the title of Symphony, in spite of the modest word " Duo " by which he has described it.[1]

But that is all one to me if only you can manage to hear your Overture.   You write that that would brighten the whole winter for you.   Is that really true ? . . .

. . . To-day Frau Dirichlet sent a few charming words to accompany an engraving of Raphael's violinist.   She has such a shrewd, clear outlook that I cannot understand her friendliness towards me, as it is much more disinterested in her than in the other members of the Mendelssohn family.   Of course, you know the picture of the violinist !   Does he not look refined and proud, and yet charming ?   Raphael must have loved him dearly, too — the laurels on the bow are no mere convention—that is clear !   Where did you and Herman meet Frau Dirichlet ?   She mentions it in her letter.

I have read Oulibicheff's book on Beethoven. It contains many a shrewd and useful attack on Beethoven's spurious imitators, and on the arrogant

---

[1] The title of this work, which appeared after Schubert's death, probably originated with the publisher.  Cf. Brahms' *Correspondence*, vol. ii. p. 68.

commentators who put their own vain construction on that sublime and sacred life; but the Russian has no understanding for Beethoven's greatness, for the divine and ardent resignation which distinguished the proud, lonely victim through all his anguish, and which made of him the most touching martyr Providence has ever sent for the purification of the human race. Finally, his only standard in art is good taste, and whatever is pleasant and does not disturb one's enjoyment; the technical remarks on music in the book are as limited as they can be. Where will all this chatter about art lead us. "My soul bleeds when I see this race of owls crowding to the light." How soothing it is to think of you and your warm, upright heart. You only have to tap at truth's door, and it is joyfully opened to you. . . .

### To Herman Grimm

[HANOVER, *middle of April* 1857.]

Dear Herman—I must stick to my resolution not to go to Rome, in spite of the pleasure I had so vividly pictured myself enjoying with you. The journey would really be nothing but a distraction to me; I am not immersed, like you, in work which would render Rome the pleasantest place in the world to me. I will be quite honest with you; I feel that if I went there with you my interest in the things which occupy you, which we should see together, would take up too much of my mind. Really and truly, however delightful it may be to draw nourishment for the mind from all directions, and to widen it in every way, it would only be as a dilettante, after all, that I could enjoy wandering among these monuments with you. I should never be able to work in the sense I mean: to make a *technical study* of composition. St. Peter's dome, the *Loggias*, all that

sort of thing would whirl round in my head and
occupy my imagination, and yet I am not skilful
enough in composition to be able to convert this
into material for my work.   There is no music
there; I should be homesick for the strains of an
orchestra.   The Italian church music which would
interest me so much is not being played now either—
in short, I foresee that I should bore you horribly after
a time with my unsatisfied longings.   I am such a
barbarian that Bach is much more to my taste now
than any Italian sky, and even indeed than Correggio's
faces!   I think it will end in my staying on Hanoverian
ground, and wandering over Hanstein, Plesse and
Gleichen.[1]   I love the German ground on which Bach
and Beethoven grew up.   But you must believe, dear
Herman, that I could never for a moment be indifferent
to your invitation to join you; I know that there is in
your proofs of affection an atmosphere of love in which
they mature.   And I shall read every word you write
from Rome with interest, and enjoy it as though I
were with you; you must promise to write to me
from there.   I should like so much, too, to see you
at Göttingen again one day, if you pass through.   You
will write to me again I hope, and as soon as possible,
so that I may know that you do not put my refusal
down to "temper," or bear me a grudge for it.   I can
only be proud of the interest you take in me.   *Vale.*
—Your                                        J. J.

### From Franz Liszt

WEIMAR, *August* 19, 1857.

Honoured Friend—On the 3rd, 4th, and 5th of
September Weymar is celebrating Carl August's

---

[1] Castles in the neighbourhood of Göttingen.

L

Jubilee. The new musical Weymar is still so much *yours* by reason of many delightful memories that it would give us all, and me especially, real pleasure to see you again at our Festival. At the concert, which will take place on the 5th of September, and for which the orchestra will be considerably strengthened, my *Faust* Symphony, a new Symphonic Poem, *Die Ideale* (after Schiller), and the *Chorus of Artists*, together with several other similar things, will be performed.

If you can possibly come, do not fail us on this day, and *Kehr zurück, du kühner Sänger*[1] to your sincerely devoted friend,                                  F. LISZT.

### To Franz Liszt

GÖTTINGEN, *August* 27, 1857.

The continued goodness and confidence which you show me, great and courageous spirit, in including me in that community of friends who are dominated by your power, gives me a sense of shame for the lack of candour I have shown up to the present—a feeling which I am not now experiencing for the first time, and which would deeply humiliate me in my own eyes, if I were not at the same time consoled by the knowledge that this lack of candour, which contrasts so badly with my life at Weimar and your unchanging kindness, is not cowardice, but has its root rather in my best feelings. It is as though my humble self, however insignificant my mental power and energy may appear to you, yet had the power, by means of the intense love of truth and the real affection for you which you know are rooted in me, to turn into a thorn which I dared not use to wound you. But what is the good of hesitating any longer to tell you plainly

---

[1] "Return, bold singer" (*Tannhäuser*).—TR.

what I feel—my passive attitude towards your work would surely reveal it, thinly veiled, to you who are accustomed to meet with enthusiasm, and who know me to be capable of a genuine and active friendship. So I shall remain silent no longer on a subject which, I confess to you, your manly spirit had the right to demand to know long before. Your music is entirely antagonistic to me ; it contradicts everything with which the spirits of our great ones have nourished my mind from my earliest youth. If it were thinkable that I could ever be deprived of, that I should ever have to renounce all that I learnt to love and honour in their creations, all that I feel music to be, your strains would not fill one corner of the vast waste of nothingness. How, then, can I feel myself to be united in aim with those who, under the banner of your name and in the belief (I am speaking of the noblest among them) that they must join forces against the artists for the justification of their contemporaries, make it their life task to propagate your works by every means in their power? I must rather make up my mind to strive for that which I have marked out for myself, to separate myself more and more from them, and to work on my own responsibility, though it were never so quietly, for that which I know to be good, and which I consider to be my mission. I can be of no assistance to you, and I can no longer allow you to think that the aims for which you and your pupils are working are mine. I must therefore refuse your last kind invitation to take part in the festival at Weimar in honour of Carl August; I respect your character too highly to act hypocritically, and I revere the memory of the Prince, who lived with Goethe and Schiller and wished to rest with them, too much to be present out of curiosity.

Forgive me if I have given you a moment of sadness during your preparations for the Festival; I had to do it. Your awe-inspiring industry, the number of your followers, will soon console you, but when you think of this letter believe one thing of me : that I shall never cease to carry in my heart a grateful pupil's deep and faithful memory of all that you were to me, of the often undeserved praise you bestowed on me at Weimar, of all your divine gifts by which I strove to profit.          JOSEPH JOACHIM.

### From Clara Schumann

BERLIN, *October* 6, '57.

Dear Joachim—It gave me real pleasure to see your handwriting yesterday—it was as though your letter came to me from home, it made me weep. God knows how miserable I am here! I am still in a fearful muddle, although I have been putting things straight from morning till night for the last fortnight. I feel as though I were no longer *I*; there is not a note in me. Oh, this inner joylessness is terrible. Berlin seems to me such a dreadful place ; I feel like an exile here. . . .

Johannes wrote and told me of your magnificent playing at Bonn. I was with you both in spirit all the time. I shall never forget the Wednesday which I spent alone at Düsseldorf; it was one of the darkest days of my life. When Johannes left me in the morning my heart bled. On this day and on the following one when I left the place where I had settled, full of happy hopes, with my husband and children, alone, my husband in his grave, my friends at a distance (perhaps hardly thinking of me in the midst of delightful experiences), I lived over again the whole of the three

years of suffering, and arrived here physically and
mentally shattered. How much I regretted that I had
not ventured to ask you both to accompany me on the
Thursday as far as Hanover; but I had not the heart
to make you lose any part of the happy days you
spent together, and probably, under similar circumstances, I should again be unable to do so. . . .

. . . Do not be vexed with me, dear Joachim, for
talking so much about myself, but there is nobody to
whom I can lay bare my heart with so much confidence
as to you two, who will never misunderstand me. I
am sure you will understand what I mean when I tell
you that I suffer indescribably in being separated from
Johannes, although you will not be able to realise what
I am feeling. And yet is it not most natural that I
should love and esteem Johannes so much, after such
a long and intimate intercourse with him, during which
I have learned to know fully the riches of his heart
and mind? But I must stop. I will write to you
again soon. . . .

### *From Herman Grimm* [1]

BERLIN, *Wednesday evening* (*November* 11, 1857).

Dear Joachim—I came back here the evening
before last and found both your letters on my table :
the first with the photograph, the second in which you
ask whether we are to meet. This was before your
visit to Bonn.

On the 13th, whilst at Rome, I received a telegram
from Teplitz to say that Giesel was ill and wanted to
see me. Unfortunately I could only start on the 14th,
but then I travelled day and night and arrived in six

---

[1] This letter, contrary to Grimm's usual habit, is written in German characters,
and capital letters are employed.

days. I found the danger over. The illness consisted of a complete nervous exhaustion. At night she would wake up with beating heart and a vivid sense of fear. Added to this Bettine was in a state of mental and physical weakness, and Armgart laid up with nursing and solitude. We remained another fortnight at Teplitz, and then, at last, it was possible to travel. We arrived in Dresden the day after your last concert there and stayed two days. Now we are here again and I go *hinter den Zelten* every evening as usual. Giesel can see no one; she is giddy if she reads or is read to, but she is sleeping better at night and altogether there is a decided improvement, but how long it will be before she is well again no one can say. At times she herself despairs of it.

This is my news. I spent June in Rome, July in Florence, the first part of August in Naples, and the second part and the first fortnight of September with Cornelius in Albano; then I went to Rome and remained there another four weeks. I had intended making a slow return journey, touching at various towns, but that came to nothing. I found all my people here well.

Your letters call for an explanation from me as to our attitude towards one another for the future. You are quite right, we could not drift apart in silence, neither could we, when we met, hide the truth from one another by insincerities. The threefold friendship, as it then was, had become impossible to me. One or the other of us had to change his attitude towards G. I could not do more than say that I was ready to do this myself. And this I did. But even this step seemed to have been made in the sand and all traces of it vanished. At last I requested Giesel to break off all intercourse with you, and she has done so.

Dear friend, in acting in this way any thought of separation was far from me, and from us all three I think. Nothing can destroy a spiritual sympathy, and should a poisonous stream of hatred come between, the instinct which seeks an affinity would bridge it. We shall never be far from one another. I cannot say when it will be, but that we shall and must meet again seems to me natural and inevitable. When I forced on a final decision I was thinking as much of you as of myself. Fate has been cruel in alienating from me the one man of whom I feel that he understands the career I have set before me. For I cannot expect you to forget that I have taken from you that which had begun to be, or already was, the joy of your life. But I could not have done otherwise, and if you will forgive me for this, I will forgive you for having driven me to it.

So much for what lies behind us; these things seem to me to be finished and done with. Let us think of the future. My thoughts cannot move further than the next few days; I measure the steps she makes in progress, and try to avert everything that might hinder her. We often speak of you. You can believe that I love you. You know that Giesel does. But I could not stand by in silence and watch you spoiling each other's lives.

Please answer me. I will send you further news soon.—Your                                    HERMAN.


*From Clara Schumann*

MUNICH, *November* 27, '57.
*In the evening.*

My dear Joachim—Thank you so much for your delightful letter, which I put gaily into my pocket just as I was starting for Augsburg for a second concert, intending to answer it the same evening when I got there. Who would have thought what was to prevent me! Imagine, I had hardly arrived when I had such pain in my left arm that the next morning, after a fearful night, I had to cry off from the concert and come back here, to give up a second concert and several others here as well. After medical examination it proved to be rheumatic inflammation, brought on partly by over-exertion and partly by a chill. I have been (it is a week to-day since it began) more poorly than ever in my life before. I was, of course, incapable of doing anything, as I suffered uninterrupted pain and could not move. Nettchen[1] had to wait on me as though I were a little child. But the worst days of all were the two last! The day before yesterday I had such an attack of nervous pain that I thought I should die; for six hours I cried aloud in agony; it was as though some one were trying to tear the bones from my arms, neck and breast with red-hot irons. I never suffered such torments before; the doctor gave me opium, which relieved the pain, but I was in an absolutely exhausted condition the whole of yesterday, nearly all the time on the point of fainting. To-day I am better, however, although I still have my arm in a sling and cannot move it properly. So nothing can be decided about future concerts at present, but the fact remains that I have suffered great losses and that the inner conflict must certainly have equalled the outer one. On the morning of the day on which the attack began, I had had such a delightful rehearsal with the orchestra; I was to have played Robert's Concerto, but I suppose it was too much for me to have undertaken. I have never seen

---

[1] Fräulein Nettchen Yunge, her companion.

such enthusiasm in an orchestra as after this Concerto ; I felt it rising before it was half-way through, and I myself felt so inspired that I entirely forgot myself and all around me. Applause from the orchestra delights me more than any other, and especially when, as in this case, the work was undertaken almost reluctantly (Robert's music is still looked upon here as almost insurmountably difficult, but now I think the ice has been broken). The orchestra, moreover, is excellent, and Lachner a capable conductor, although he seems to me to have more understanding than poetry ; but at any rate he commands great respect.

There is no need to tell you what a magnificent town Munich is, what splendid art treasures it has, etc. You must know it. Unfortunately I have seen nothing like all there is to see, as I have been in my room for the last week.

How you made my mouth water with all the lovely commencements to the Quartettes! Yes, indeed, dear Joachim, if only we could all live in the same town— and we could do so really! . . . If you should make up your mind to come to Berlin later on we must play the Quartettes at my house ; that would be lovely. I know much too little in that way, and too little of the little I do know.

I heard Gisela's three tragedies talked about here the other day. Heyse (a man whom I think you would like) has them. I will try and get hold of them, but I fear I shall not understand them. Write and tell me something about them and how you like them. Can you be unbiassed ? I think so, because I always think that we are most strict towards those we love the most, just because we are always anxious that every-thing about our dear ones should be as beautiful as possible. Only the other day I realised most bitterly how much it hurts to find a defect in one whom we love supremely. That will perhaps explain to you my tears when playing Robert's Concerto, which you must have thought childish.[1] Are you considering about the last movement? How grateful I should be to you for that! If you have any special desire tell it to me and I will fulfil it for you if it lies in my power, when you have made a really fine last movement! Let me know what else you are working at, and whether you are going to be really happy now? . . .

### To Clara Schumann

[HANOVER] *December* 1 [1857].

Dear Frau Schumann—You have no idea how anxious I was, knowing that you were travelling about giving concerts, and having no news whatever of you; finally I wrote to Woldemar for your address, as I thought you could not have received the letter I wrote to you at Munich, but Wold. also was silent. And so you have been seriously ill? I always thought you would attempt too much if you were left to yourself. Your friends would almost have welcomed a little warning from above—but not that you should have had to suffer so much! Poor friend, what you must have gone through—existing all alone like that without music. It is terrible! Four years ago I went through a time like that here, just when I had taken up my new position as Konzertmeister. At the first rehearsal of Mendelssohn's Symphony, which was to be my first appearance, I conducted too energetically in my zeal, and for a fortnight I had not the strength to use

---

[1] Frau Schumann felt that the work was not on as high a plane as the rest of Robert's work. After mature consideration Joachim decided that he could not undertake to remodel the last movement, as Frau Schumann had desired.

my bow or a pen.   What a début, without friends and
without colleagues !   But it must have been still worse
for you, just when you were about to do so well for
your family.   You have been obliged, no doubt, to
use all that the concerts at Leipzig and Dresden
brought in, and will be forced during the next few
weeks to do what is so disagreeable to you.   But in
that case you will not forget, will you, what you have
often told me, that Johannes and I are the friends in
whom you have most confidence, and you will come
to one of us for the necessary advance for your Swiss
concert tour ?   How childishly delighted I should be
if my little capital, now in your hands, which I have
put by in obedience to your wise counsel, could be so
useful.   It would encourage me to be careful in the
future if my small savings could be of use to a friend ;
and I really ought to demand, in the interests of my
financial education, which you have begun so successfully, that, if you have any need of that kind, you
should not pass me by.   I am sure you will have a
good laugh over me !

The success of Schumann's Concerto with the
Munich orchestra was at any rate a gleam of sunshine
in the gloom of the sick-room !   I should not have
credited Lachner and his friends with such warm,
unprejudiced feeling, and it pleases me very much.
Last Saturday, at the second Quartette Soirée here,
Schumann's A minor Quartette, which I played, as well
as one of Haydn's and one of Beethoven's, also had
a friendly audience.   Many were quite exalted by the
warm musical flow which runs so unconstrainedly
through the work.   We soon noticed it, and played
with real love.

Next Saturday is the first subscription concert ;
Piatti, the 'cellist from London, is to play at it.   Be-

sides that, H.M. the King, when he was travelling, heard an Italian singer either at Schwerin or Strelitz, and has commanded that . . . Signora Fortunis [1] should be engaged for his first concert. She will sing fine stuff! And Piatti with his fantasias on *Linda* [2]— that will be a treat for the high and mighty ears: delicious! But I am firmly resolved to laugh the whole evening, and not to be annoyed. I know very well in my own mind what I shall do if the King does not leave my concerts alone! But I hope I shall be able to enjoy the orchestral pieces: Mendelssohn's A minor Symphony and Schubert's Overture to *Fierabras* have been chosen. Do you know the latter? There are very beautiful harmonies in it, a splendid introduction to the second theme, and major and minor alternate throughout in a very original way; it is genuinely characteristic of Schubert. Unfortunately it is too diffuse, and the wind instruments are too noisy here and there. I have already had a rehearsal of the 9th Symphony; it is to be performed, together with selections from *Orpheus*, in the theatre on the 19th, at the second concert. Heaven grant that nothing occurs to prevent it! It ought to be a memorable evening; Jaëll cannot come, so I have chosen for a solo a beautiful Concerto of Viotti's [3] which I have never played, and which I am practising with great enjoyment.

I must stop for to-day; I have written anything that came into my head. I think when one is away from home it is comforting to imagine you can hear a friend chatting away as though he were with you.

---

[1] Rather, de Fortuni. But she did not sing until the third concert, and then sang the "Cavatina" from *Lucia*, a Rondo from *Somnambula*, etc. Piatti played Molique's Concerto and some Fantasias on *Lucia*.

[2] Opera by Donizetti.

[3] Joachim, however, played Spohr's *Gesangsszene*.

To be continued shortly.    Let me hear soon that you are better, and give my sincerest regards to your nurse. —Your truly devoted            JOSEPH JOACHIM.

### From Hans von Bronsart

HANOVER [*about December* 13, 1857].
*Half-past one at night.*

Honoured Sir—Do not misunderstand my motives in sending you this letter instead of calling on you myself.  I must tell you first of all that it was one of the happiest moments of my life when I heard from you that you really take a kind and friendly interest in me, and that your reason for not answering my letters was not that you could only meet my request in a manner insulting or wounding to me.  There is no need to discuss what the reason may have been ; I gave up that hope long ago, and the cool manner in which the King received me to-day was not calculated to revive it.  I am telling you exactly how I feel about it.  It would have been a great and genuine happiness for me, you know, if I could have been comfortably settled so near to you, for in those few days my heart warmed to you with real affection, and although I had to admit that many of my aims would appear strange and unsatisfactory to you, yet I believed that you would recognise that they are, at bottom, akin to yours.  And you must believe this of me, too; I know of no more desirable lot here on earth than to strive unceasingly for the ennobling of my art, and I *will* accomplish something worth while, and I *will* continue to go forward until the last breath leaves my body.

Perhaps you can sympathise so much with my mood that you will understand how I come to be filled with an irresistible longing for Liszt, now that I am back again in my quiet room. I will be quite open with you: as a matter of fact Liszt wrote to me that I was not to make my visit to Hanover too short, more especially because of you; his words are: Joachim will always be a great artist and a fine spirit; [1] and how fervently I remembered these words when you were speaking to me so kindly and delightfully.

But I shall have no more peace until I am with Liszt again, with him who has taken me so lovingly to his heart, who comforted me so gently and affectionately when I confided to him what was making me sad, who inspired me with new courage and new confidence when I was on the verge of despairing of my powers. Oh, you must love him too, as a father, as I love him!

Now there is not a shadow between us, so allow me to hope that I may come and see you some time at Hanover, not "on business connected with the Court," and accept my thanks for having so kindly overlooked my touchiness.

Will you also be so good as to make my excuses to Fräulein Seebach and Fräulein v. d. Gabelentz for not being able to call on them as I had promised, owing to the fact that I am leaving in a few hours' time?

And now farewell; this time I shall ask you to test me and not to answer this letter. But will you allow me to write to you from time to time when my heart urges me to do so?

With sincere affection and esteem.—Yours,

HANS VON BRONSART.

---

[1] Quoted in French in the letter.—TR.

*From Clara Schumann*

MUNICH, *December 27, '57.*

. . . The day before yesterday I played Robert's Concerto here in the Odeon with great applause, and afterwards received from the orchestra a beautiful laurel wreath which I would, oh so gladly, have offered to him there and then, even if it were only to lay it on his grave. Indeed I had no lack of wreaths, but I did not receive one without thinking how many leaves belonged by right to you both, to you and Johannes, and if I could deck you as my heart and conscience dictates, nothing would be left for me at all. No one but myself knows what I owe to you; it is not possible, however, to put it into words, but I shall always feel it deeply. . . .

*To Clara Schumann*

[HANOVER, *January* 3, 1858.]

Dear Frau Schumann—How much there is to say in answer to your full, kind, and delightful letter. And yet I shall have to content myself to-day with saying what is absolutely necessary. There is not much time left before the last post. The day before yesterday, the first day of this year, I had really intended to make a good beginning by giving you the pleasure of a letter — but Johannes came in the afternoon, although that was delightful too. Unfortunately he left again after three hours and a half; he wanted to please his parents by going to them on that day — and his friend could raise no objections. But he was in splendid spirits, and I think we can flatter ourselves that, with his good sense and energy, he has laid a good foundation at Detmold for an independent existence. I was delighted with Johannes' remodelling of the first movement of the Concerto.[1] He has added many beautifully quiet connecting passages, which I am sure would please you also. The second theme, in particular, is broader and more satisfying. The whole thing seems to me almost *too* rich. But that is a good fault! All my hopes of obtaining something new and beautiful in music rest with my dear friend! The most recent artistic productions are terribly sterile.

Reinecke has sent a Violin Concerto—it sounds so ordinary, sometimes even so *clumsy*—I should never have expected such a thing from so experienced a composer.

What made you ask after Richard Würst? In case I forget the uninteresting man, I will tell you at once that I have known nothing of his work for some time. Years ago I heard a Quartette and an Overture of his, and they were just what a busy maker of music would put together from reminiscences of Spohr and Mendelssohn linked up with some colourless material of his own. I have heard little praise of his new Symphony from Stern and others, but rather lamentations because of its dullness. Stern came here for the 9th Symphony with his sister-in-law, Jenny Meyer, who also helped. I never heard the Orchestra play so well, or the choir, which was not numerous but very accurate, sing better. Only the solos left something to be desired. But it was fine, all the same, and you must write and tell me when you think of coming here, so that I may try and fix the second performance of the Symphony, which we intend to give, for that time; you *must* hear it played

[1] The D minor Concerto.

by this orchestra, and I *must* have the pleasure, for once, of knowing you to be in the audience when I am conducting it. Ah, why are there so few people capable of perceiving, even momentarily, the sublimity of Beethoven's intellect? It is so wonderful to believe without a doubt—and he does indeed raise us to the heights of pure devotion from the first note. It is all purity and strength!

And then one is expected to be patient when one hears fools quarrelling about it; whether the standpoint of the "last" Beethoven is not too "dizzy," and whether its influence is a healthy one. In his wanderings through the fresh mountain air, Beethoven certainly did not seek out morasses overgrown with thistles for human donkeys like these. But forgive my abusive words, I could not help them—when you come we will enjoy ourselves without such notes as these, and sing to a more joyful tune.

Dietrich has been here for several days, and often sings Schumann's songs to me, almost all of which he knows by heart. He wrote that "longing" had driven him here; but I do not think that means so very much with D.—although I may certainly be connected in his mind with pleasant memories of the time at Düsseldorf. He is a really good fellow, whose musical capabilities one is obliged to respect, especially when compared with those of the Hanoverian musicians. But his new Quartette is not sufficiently melodious to give lasting pleasure. Wehner produced *St. Paul* here yesterday, and conducted in such a way that a complete breakdown was only averted by the persistent marking of the first beat on the part of the gallant orchestra. I should never have believed that a conductor would have been able to cripple such splendid vocal and instrumental material in this

M

way. The King was delighted by the performance and has commanded another. If I do not give up my post altogether, I shall at any rate get leave to go to Rome. Do write there beforehand, and let me know the result of your enquiry. There would be no need to bind oneself until a few months before the time.

I hope you will keep me posted in your Swiss addresses; may Heaven once more bestow rich blessings upon your household. . . .

*From Clara Schumann*

STUTTGART, *March* 12, 1858.

Dear Joachim—And so, after six weeks without a line from you, I am writing to you again from here! Your silence hurt me, although I had expected as much because you were so anxious to know my Swiss addresses!

I found a note here from Johannes yesterday, when I got back from Switzerland, in which he tells me among other things that you are both waiting to have a rehearsal of his Concerto[1] until I come; I should like to know *as soon as possible exactly* when the rehearsal is to be, so that I may come to Hanover *before* going to Berlin. . . .

I am anxious about Johannes' Concerto because of the orchestra! Do you remember with what ill-will they accompanied Robert's Concerto that time—will Johannes be any less unfortunate? I should be so terribly grieved if he had to encounter opposition when his heart is full of the fresh warm feelings of a composer! . . .

In Geneva I had again to do absolutely nothing for a fortnight, because I had the same rheumatism in

[1] D minor Concerto.

my right arm which had previously attacked my left.
I sat there without anything to distract me, without a
friend, and I suffered greatly.   What pleasure a letter
from you would have given me!   I cannot quite get
over it however hard I try, although I suppose I would
have had no right to expect it if you yourself had not
roused such lively hopes in me.

Well, dear Joachim, here is an affectionate greeting.
I could wish you did not know so well that I am
always the same true friend to you: perhaps I
should hear oftener from you then, although not so
spontaneously as I do now.   So I suppose it will
always be the same with you and with me.—Your

CL. SCH.

*To Clara Schumann*

[HANOVER, *April* 15, 1858.]

Dear Frau Schumann—I have just got my London
address, which I am giving you at once : 23 Queen
Street, Mayfair.   It is at a baker's, so at any rate there
is not much danger of my starving!   Piccadilly is
near by, so that you may have an idea of the position.
To-morrow I am playing at Bremen for Sobolewsky ;[1]
I leave here on Tuesday 20th ; Reinecke's concert at
Barmen is on the 21st, and so I ought to arrive at
Mr. Follet's, Baker, 23 Queen Street, Mayfair, on
Friday evening, the 23rd.   Perhaps I shall find a note
from Dessauerstrasse awaiting me at the said baker's ;
that would be a kindly omen !   Was it not nice that
after I left we must have written to one another on
the same day?   I am wearing the pretty chain[2] as a
double memento of you and of Johannes.

[1] E. Sobolewsky, a pupil of Weber's, conductor of the orchestra at the Bremen
theatre 1854–58.   Died in America 1872.

[2] A steel watch-chain similar to one given by Frau Schumann to Brahms.

I am delighted, too, with the Fantasie[1] which you have given me again, and I hope to make great use of it. I am sorry to say I have not heard from Johannes again. Our Dublin friends want to engage me for a week from May 14. Besides Ella's four concerts, Pauer has hired me for two evenings. Well, we shall see how I like it, how they like me, and whether I can make plans ahead for next year. I am playing for the first time on the 27th; I think I shall write and say how it goes off. Yesterday was the birthday of our charming Queen. I had the pleasure of waking her with a *Kinderstück*, and she is really so good that I did it willingly! Countess Bernstorff will have written to you that the Queen will be pleased to write her name in your book of songs. I am so pleased that you wished her to do so. This will be my last letter before I go to England. Wish me a calm passage! Good-bye, dear Friend—from yours,

JOSEPH JOACHIM.

*To Clara Schumann*

[LONDON] *Saturday*, 15 [*May* 1858].

Dear Friend—I was just going to write to you when I got your message from Fräulein Krüger, so that I do not feel a bit as though the ocean were between us. It seems incredible that I should already have been here three weeks. The mass of impressions from the most beautiful music to the most boring of acquaintances, makes one forget at first that there are such things as weeks, months and time. But you have been through all that yourself! I have been to Manchester and Dublin too. Over there you were constantly remembered, now by Mrs. Robinson, now

[1] Schumann's.

by him (I stayed with the R.'s), now by me, at a concert or at breakfast or in the Park ; in short you are quite one of the household gods to these dear people, *who desire me to send you their love.*[1]   There is something very bright and charming about Dublin with its large gardens in the middle of squares, and the good-natured, almost importunate enthusiasm of the Irish individually, not of the public, which is rather stiff and provincial.   I can imagine that you found your stay there pleasant and restful, for, in spite of all its splendour, it is not to be denied that there is in London a sombre, oppressive atmosphere and a joyless activity. But there is certainly much splendour ; the Crystal Palace, the many important productions, the sharply-defined national spirit—in short, I do not regret one moment spent here in exchange for Hanover, and I have practically convinced myself that there are wiser things to do than to allow oneself to be annoyed by provincial folk day after day.   I only wish you were here and we could enjoy many things together, instead of my having to console myself with the thought of next year.   My reception here was a very warm one. It is to the credit of the English that they stick to their friends.   My playing at the Philharmonic resulted in my being engaged to play on the 24th for that Society.   I have only played once as yet at a concert of Ella's ; I am to play again on the 25th, with Rubinstein in the Kreutzer Sonata.   Besides that I shall play Beethoven's Septet there for the first time, which I am looking forward to.   On Thursday I am going to Manchester again where your friend Garcia will also sing ; I shall be very glad to make her acquaintance.   She has only just arrived, or else I would have called on her before for your sake.   I

[1] Written in English in the original.—TR.

have spoken to Miss Busby [1] but I have not heard her. But I have not yet been able to show any courtesy to Fräulein Hartmann,[2] although I was anxious to do so. I will send her tickets for Pauer's concert on Wednesday, and hope to have a few words with her there. We had a very good performance of Schumann's D minor Trio at P.'s first concert, with Piatti, who is a *fine* 'cellist. We had two rehearsals, and I think you would have liked to have heard us. We intend to practise the E♭ major Quartette with the piano, too ; I shall play the viola in that, and will take the opportunity of playing the *Märchenbilder*.

Look on this letter, dear Frau Schumann, merely as a stop-gap ; there is so much to tell you that I feel as though I had not begun. But let me hear from you *very* soon all the same. When are you going to Wiesbaden ? I am staying here, at any rate, until the end of June, as I have made engagements up to then. I shall be in Liverpool for a Philh. concert on June 1. I have to play at Court to-day (without any letters of recommendation, otherwise I should have felt ashamed, as Gretry and Playdi [Kreti and Pleti] often play there). I remembered Johannes on his birthday and obtained for him, through Chrysander's kindness, an unusually good portrait of Händel, but I did not write as I was travelling. But I will make up for it soon. . . .

*To Clara Schumann*

[LONDON] *Monday, July* 12 [1858].

Dear Frau Schumann—Your friend, Frau Townsend, gave me a very delightful afternoon yesterday, Sunday. I called on her on your account, and besides

---

[1] With whom Frau Schumann had stayed.
[2] The singer Mathilde Hartmann from Düsseldorf.

being rewarded with a very kind reception, I got your welcome letter with the enclosure of music, and indeed my surroundings reminded me so vividly of you that I am truly grateful to the good folk at Champion Hill. For we know, alas, that my silence often has no connection whatever with my thoughts of my dear friends! The enclosed note from your friend Pauline (for heaven's sake! that reminds me of another very different Pauline in Hanover![1]), whom I have almost arranged to meet with you at Pesth in November, will show you how much I have thought of you. What do you think of it? I am very anxious to know, as it depends on this whether I make a tour in the English provinces in the autumn or not. There is no need to tell you that I should prefer to go to my native Hungary *with* you—but if you did not care to go to Pesth my plans would be quite different. So please let me know soon; in any case I must stay here until the 21st as I have made an engagement at Exeter for that day. Otherwise I have no professional engagements, and I intend to enjoy London the magnificent during the next few weeks, and to write my friends many let——

The Goldschmidts,[2] to whose house I have not yet been, have just come to take me into the country to Roehampton, where they live. To be continued to-morrow.—Yours,                                  J. J.

*From Clara Schumann*

WIESBADEN, *July* 17, 1858.

Dear Joachim—Your letter has upset me very much; you expect me to make a decision, on which

---

[1] Pauline Viardot-Garcia ; the Pauline in Hanover is Frau Wehner.
[2] Otto Goldschmidt and his wife (Jenny Lind).

your decision again is dependent.   What am I to do?
The engagement which you have been offered must
be a very profitable one, or you would not think of
accepting it, for a first-rate artist does not readily
undertake such a tour unless it is going to bring in a
*great deal*?   I should do it certainly, because I have
to, but you? . . .

When I saw your writing, dear Joachim, I was
delighted, but I am not sure that it is not better to
have no letter at all rather than *half* a one, from
which one can gather nothing of all that one longs to
hear.   I know nothing, not when I shall see you
again, nor where, nor many other things!   Grimm
and Johannes and Woldemar are all asking after you
—I can tell them nothing.

I cannot get rid of the miserable feeling that you
have not thought so very much about your friends after
all, or you would not have neglected them like this.

In case the day should dawn on which you send
off the continuation of your letter, I shall be here until
the 23rd, "Dotzheimer Weg, No. 1ᶜ."

Thank you very much for the enclosure from
Pauline.   How splendidly she writes about you!
That gave me most pleasure.

I should like to go on writing to you, but I cannot
because I feel sad.   Farewell.   Where will you be on
the 24th?[1]—Yours,                                    CL. SCH.


### To Clara Schumann

[LONDON, *end of July* 1858.]

Dear Frau Schumann—I have made enquiries
about a tour through the provinces.   But it is not

---

[1] Frau Schumann means the 25th; Joachim kept his birthday on that date
until, in 1863, he saw from his birth certificate that he was born on June 28.

advisable for artists who have not previously appeared here *during the season* to undertake such a tour. It is just as well. You and I and Fräulein Viardot will meet at Pesth in the autumn. You will like this better, and it is what we agreed to do when we were in Hanover. The King must give me leave from the end of October to the end of November—I once gave up a year and a half for the sake of his concerts. So much for that! I do not think it very kind or trustful of you to suspect me of undertaking a tour for the sake of money which, for other reasons, no reputable artist would make. But I can refute this by telling you that Hallé, Piatti and your humble servant had intended to test the English people's sound and apparently increasing taste for chamber music (in the provinces too) and to see how it would repay the artists. As Hallé has experience in giving concerts in England he would have taken the practical arrangements in hand. I have had nothing to do with Beale and Mitchel,[1] hardly even seen either of them. In any case I thought you would know that under no circumstances would I have sacrificed anything as an artist for the sake of profit, and so I was not a little astounded when, in a moment of annoyance at my slackness in writing, you attributed all kind of "Oxford street business"[2] to me. Well! Well!!! Another time I would rather you abused me with the worst possible names and words, as, for example, MorenborstorftausendsapperlotStötteritzBombenGranatenelementkonzertmeister!!! The affair with Hallé and Piatti is of course at an end, and I am glad to be coming to Pesth again, not only on my own account but for my parents' sake. The good people seem to be very anxious for me to pay them a visit, and it is

---

[1] English concert agents.    [2] Written in English in the original.—Tr.

my duty to respect their wishes in their old age.  So you need not have the smallest scruple because I made it dependent on you whether I came to Vienna and Pesth in the autumn or in the spring of next year.  I only hope our concerts will be profitable.  I have nothing to complain of in that respect here.  I think, after expenses have been deducted, there will still be about £250 left over, and these I will either add to the 400 thalers you have or give to my brother.  I might have earned more if I had not refused all private engagements, which would certainly have brought me in over £100.  I refused other engagements, too, for instance three at the Crystal Palace for Kuhe, whom I dislike.  I refused these simply because I do not see why a foreigner should adapt himself to English bad customs.  However fine a place the Crystal Palace may be to visit, and however much respect I may feel for the English people for maintaining such a costly marvel at their own expense and without the help of the State—as a place for music it is monstrous, unless several thousands are singing and playing there.  To perform as a soloist in it has the same effect as announcing oneself to be the youngest in a swarm of gnats.  But never in my life have I so much regretted that I was not an organist as in this wonderful temple of glass.  To hear Johannes play there on one of the many beautiful organs, and particularly on the large one in the middle of the building, would be magnificent.  Indeed, Johannes must make the acquaintance of London, it would suit him there.  I like it so much that I am going to inspect my dear London a little, now that I can do so undisturbed by the season's turmoil, which is fortunately over.  Last week I went to the delightful Isle of Wight, where I saw the most beautiful sea coast I ever came across.   Did you ever go there?   I have also been to Exeter, Southampton, Salisbury, and Bath; I only played in the first of these.   But I saw marvellously beautiful churches there.   And various buildings and chapels and college gardens at Cambridge with Bennett.   He is at the seaside now with his wife and child.   I will write soon and tell you how much longer I am staying—I am not sure yet.   When are you all going to meet at Göttingen? Send good news of yourself soon to your faithfully devoted                                              J. J.

What was the 24th?   You ask me what I was doing on that day.

### To Clara Schumann

[HANOVER, *October* 17, 1858.]

Dear Frau Schumann—Your telegram seems to imply that you are not coming in the immediate future, at any rate.   The King's refusal, for, as I could only leave here for certain on the 10th and would have to be back here at the beginning of December, it is as good as a refusal, is most galling.   My parents had been looking forward to it so much!   And it is all so unnecessary; just because the Grand Duchess is coming here early in November, and there may possibly be some music one evening!   I considered it a mere matter of form to ask the King at all, and now he plays me this trick, after having taken no notice of me the whole time I have been here.   I believe he looked pretty black when Platen told him of my wish to go to Vienna.   He did not *require* me *now*, but I had to be here when the Grand Duchess came!   Well, it strengthens me in my resolution!   Had you engaged the halls yet? Could we not make up for it in March? I shall be *free* then.—Sincerely yours,

JOSEPH J.

*To Clara Schumann*

[HANOVER] *Thursday* [*October* 21, 1858].

Dear Frau Schumann—As soon as I got here Platen practically *gave* me leave, it only had to be referred to the King as a matter of form. I urged him to do so, but Platen can never get hold of His Majesty. And I had counted on speaking to the K. myself—I went to Herrenhausen, his country-seat, on purpose to report myself. I must have fallen into disfavour! It has this advantage, at any rate, that my feeling for the King does not bind me any more, and so I can give up my post before long. The reason why I do not send in my resignation on the spot is that I do not wish to *revenge* myself by leaving them in the lurch just at the beginning of the concerts. But at the beginning of January I shall simply write and tell Platen that I shall consider my contract cancelled in three months' time. So I shall not be free until *April*; and then we have to go to London, not Vienna. We should need a month or two for that, counting Pesth. It is really too tyrannical; the whole time I have been here nobody has troubled their heads about me, and just because the Grand Duchess might *perhaps* like a musical evening when she comes, I must give up my trip, which would not have interfered with my concerts at Hanover. . . .

I am delighted at the great success. How glad I was to hear of the applause Johannes' pieces received. —Always yours,

J. J.

*To Clara Schumann*

[HANOVER, *November* 1858.]

Dear Frau Schumann—The day before yesterday, the Court concert, to which Dreyschock was summoned from Prague by telegram (!), lasted from a quarter past nine to half-past one, and the numbers in the second part could not be played because it was getting *too late*! The whole thing was so badly arranged (Wehner) that I felt ashamed to be present, and I intend to ask an audience of the King to-day in order to tell him that I cannot, as Concertmeister, permit such things to occur. My title really makes me responsible to the outside artists, and I was there just as if I were a guest myself, the victim of the stupidity and bad taste of the programme manufacturers.

I hope to hear from you soon.—Yours sincerely,

J. J.

*To Julius Otto Grimm*

[HANOVER] *Sunday* 28 [*November* 1858].

Dear Grimm—I have sad news for you and your friends at Göttingen, which will excite your pity. Our poor Bach who has been with us and played with us so often and was so full of life has—ceased to be. He contracted a chill three weeks ago, which afterwards developed into a nervous fever. Finally I got a famous doctor to see him—but even this was in vain. This morning at half-past four he ceased to breathe. He had been unconscious all the last few days. The whole illness has shaken me very much, as you can well imagine. I was afraid you might be shocked by hearing the news through strangers, and that is why I am writing this note. Let me hear soon how you all are, either through your wife or yourself.—Yours,

J. J.

*From Clara Schumann*

VIENNA, *December* 9, [18]58.

For the last three days, dear Joachim, I have had a letter ready for you, but I could not bring myself to send it off, and, finally, to-day I tore it up—it was so sad that I was ashamed of showing you my weakness. But will this one be any better? I received your last letter just after my concert. Fortunately my brother had kept it back until then, for I was terribly upset by it. I was both glad and frightened to hear that you had gone to poor Bach's[1] assistance. If you were my son, I should say to you, in spite of all anxiety, You have acted rightly. Thank God, you are well, and full of energy.

And Frau Dirichlet's death has grieved me so much! Although I never felt much in sympathy with her, yet she seemed something precious to me as a legacy from the immortal Mendelssohn. So one after the other goes, and only memory is left to us! I have slept very little during the last few nights, and I often wonder whether you have joined your family, and why heaven should snatch away such vital people as Bach, and allow those to live who find the daily burden of life so heavy. Ah, if only I had gone to rest in his place!

Be thankful that you are not with me, for I am in a terribly sad frame of mind, so much so that my will is often quite powerless against it. I do give concerts, but with what inner torments! My health is being ruined by it. Just imagine, I cannot give a single concert at which I do not play one piece after the other in an agony of terror because my memory threatens to fail me, and this fear torments me for days beforehand.

[1] A promising pupil of Joachim's.

I have no strength left to fight against this state of things. At my last concert in Pesth I completely lost my head in two pieces, and my thoughts were so confused that I had to summon my last atom of strength to prevent myself from stopping altogether. After experiences like these you can imagine the state of mind I was in when I gave my concert here. After the first piece I had such a fit of crying that it was a long time before I was myself again. But I think it would be better if you were with me, apart from the artistic benefit; it would be balm to my heart, which is so terribly lonely. Ah, my dear Joachim, my art must soon come to an end, for even if my physical strength should suffice, my mind is weakened and my heart seems broken. If only I knew that I would find my Robert again! Do not be cross with me, dear Joachim, and continue to be kind to me, and to be the forbearing friend of my weakness. I know I ought to be stronger and prouder before you, but I know also that you are too generous to abuse the free confidence of a warm heart and to respect it less for this, even if it is a burden to you. But enough, I will speak of other things. First of all about Pesth.

Your people were all well. Your dear mother was very grieved at not seeing you, and so was Josephine. The former was wondering whether she could not visit you at Hanover in the spring. I spent an evening there and the whole family was present—I had to listen to a great deal of talk, but I did so patiently, because I kept thinking of you and of how well your parents meant it all. I saw your sister several times, and you and her Hermine were always the subjects of our conversations.

Good-bye, dear friend; remember your faithful

CL. SCH.

Write and tell me what progress your Concerto is making, and all about *yourself*!

### To Clara Schumann

[HANOVER, *middle of December* 1858.]

. . . I should think I did think of you during the Quartette the other day, and how I wished that you were there! Sometimes, on very rare evenings certainly, performances take place under a peculiarly lucky star; and that happened then. I have never played in quartettes before the public so unconstrainedly and with such feeling; I was not in the hall at all, but, particularly during Schumann's Quartette, face to face with the composer, and when we played the Variations I felt that I should like to penetrate to his very heart: the way the rich, lovely theme is woven in and out is so delightful. Those who played with me seemed to be feeling just the same, and it was *this* feeling that spoke to the heart of the public. That evening Sch.'s Quartette made more impression than anything else. Beethoven's C♯ minor is probably too deep and too full of gigantic power to be understood by many in the hall, even though they bowed humbly before the God of Music whose presence they felt. How many must have thought again of the noble poet, who had spoken to them so *humanly* and so consolingly in the previous piece, as of a glow of sunshine!

After the Quartette I had to go (my feet lighter than my heart) to the King at the palace; I was commanded to play a Duet with Blagrove[1] (two movements of something by Spohr), which was duly performed; afterwards the King was tactless enough to

[1] Henry G. Blagrove, born 1811, pupil of Spohr's. Died 1872.

invite *me* to play a solo instead of the guest Blagrove. Of course I had brought *nothing* with me, and let it go at that. To-morrow B. is playing at the theatre and I am to conduct his Kalliwoda and very own— Pegasus from the orchestra. He is a nice fellow, and I like the English better than I do their compositions. A horrible little man from Berlin, X., played before the King that evening, too. The Lord preserve us! Do you know him? I hope not. . . . My goodness, and they call that *music*! He looked like an over-fed Capuchin who had been fetched away from his half-finished pork sausage and who was swallowing down the accompanying gravy seasoned with many vulgar spices. Although his intonation was quite clean, I kept thinking that a waiter ought to bring him a serviette for his fingers instead of the batiste handkerchief with which he toyed as a man of breeding. I feel irritated with the excellent fellow, because he behaved as though I were in sympathy with the whole business. Wehner, who has just been to see me, says that the King has again countermanded the violoncello from Berlin for next Saturday. I suppose I shall have to play! I have been gossiping, and instead of turning over a new leaf, I must speak badly of another musician, at your command, for you told me to report on Herr Y. Unfortunately, I *cannot* give a good one. . . . The man has absolutely no taste and no musical or aesthetic culture. I did not know that his pupil, Fräulein Z., was supposed to have appeared with success, and *I do not believe it.* As it is a question of the education of a young lady in whom you take an interest, I feel I must give you my real opinion and warn you, otherwise I should not have talked about the man at such length. Let us talk of something pleasanter!

N

How kind and modest it is of Johannes to praise my Quartette movement. It cannot really satisfy him; it is not false modesty that prevents me from speaking well of it, and I hope that, one day, I shall produce a better one. . . .

Let me hear about you and your plans soon, dear, restless friend! I had good, or at any rate better, news of Bettine through Frau Detmold. If you see any of the family give them the warmest messages from me.—Yours,                    JOSEPH J.

### To his Parents

[HANOVER, *January* 11, 1859.]

My dear, kind Parents—I thank you very much for your congratulations, which I repay with the most affectionate good wishes to you and to dear Regi. I have nothing but good news to tell you since my last letter, although, I am sorry to say, I have not been able to do much work. Everything went off well at Leipzig; I met everywhere with kindness and sympathy for myself and my work. When I got back I had to see about the second concert here, which was *most* successful. I conducted an Overture of Mendelssohn's and Beethoven's Pastoral Symphony, and played a Concerto for two violins by Spohr with a member of our orchestra, Kömpel, who was Spohr's favourite pupil and a very fine violinist. The King was not there, for he is still ill, but the Queen, and the Duke of Altenb., etc., etc., were there. The King has given me a very charming proof that he continues to take an interest in me, and it has pleased me very much, because I thought his manner had been colder towards me for some time past. The day before yesterday he sent me the Guelphic Order (4th class), a little silver star, with the words "*Nec aspera terrent*" and the royal founder's name, Ernst August, on it, attached to a blue ribbon.    I do not set much store by external successes, but the thing has pleased me, because it is a sign that the King is well disposed towards me and is satisfied with my work, for I know he is very sparing with his Orders to artists.    But it is getting more and more difficult for me to resign!    My friend Brahms is staying with me at present for a few days ; I am growing to love him more and more, both as friend and artist, and I am continually and joyfully amazed at his enormous musical powers. . . .

### From Johannes Brahms

[LEIPZIG] *Friday morning* [*January* 28, 1859].

Dearest Friend—Although I am still quite dazed by the sublime delights with which my eyes and ears have been assailed for the last few days through the sight and sound of the wise men of our musical town, I will force this hard and pointed steel pen of Sahr's to relate to you how it came about that my Concerto has had here a brilliant and decisive—failure.

First of all I must say that it was really done very well ; I played far better than I did at Hanover, and the orchestra was excellent.

The first rehearsal excited no kind of feeling either in the performers or in the audience.    No audience at all came to the second, and not a performer moved a muscle of his face.

In the evening Cherubini's *Elisa* Overture was done, then an Ave Maria by him was sung softly, so I hoped that Pfund's[1] drums would be opportune.

---

[1] A famous performer on the kettle-drums in the Gewandhaus Orchestra.

The first and second movements were listened to without the slightest display of feeling. At the conclusion three pairs of hands were brought together very slowly, whereupon a perfectly distinct hissing from all sides forbade any such demonstration.

There is nothing more to say about this episode, for not a soul has said a word to me about the work! —with the exception of David, who took a great interest in it, and was very kind and took a lot of trouble about it. Neither Rietz nor Wenzel, Senff, Dreyschock, Grützmacher, Röntgen, have made even the most casual remark. I asked Sahr a few questions this morning and was pleased at his frankness.

This failure has made no impression whatever on me, and any feeling of depression I may have had vanished when I heard Haydn's C major Symphony and the *Ruinen von Athen*. In spite of everything the Concerto will meet with approval when I have improved its form, and the next one will be quite different.

I believe this is the best thing that could happen to one; it forces one to concentrate one's thoughts and increases one's courage. After all, I am only experimenting and feeling my way as yet. But the hissing was too much of a good thing, wasn't it?

Your letter, which I received at the hotel yesterday evening, was very soothing, and I did not feel in the least annoyed with Hermann, etc., who all drank with me in the most friendly manner and said not a word about the Concerto.

Frau Schumann, I am told here, is still in Vienna; I wish she could have been here! . . .

The faces here looked terribly solemn when I came from Hanover, after having been used to seeing yours. I am going to Hamburg on Monday. There is to be some interesting church music here on Sunday, and in the evening a performance of *Faust* at Frau Frege's.[1]

Please send me Hanover newspapers at Hamburg. I shall write again from there. . . .

## *To Clara Schumann*

[LONDON, *August* 26, 1859.]

Dear Frau Schumann—Otto Goldschmidt tells me that you suspect me of having kept a letter from Herr X.[2] through carelessness.   The suspicion is unfounded—I think I am fairly exact in *business* matters. Goldschm. had acquainted me with all the particulars of the American business by sending me the papers, and in order not to send these back again to G. at Wimblanden and so lose time, I had agreed with him to send you the letter from Scharfenberg (*and only that one*) *myself*; glad as I always am to correspond with you, I welcomed this arrangement. The letter from X. to Scharfenberg contains really *nothing* but what the latter has put more considerately and kindly.   The fact is I did not want to let you see (because it was unnecessary and would have cost postage besides) with what audacity and callousness a blatant speculator like this appraises us artists as though we were commercial goods, feeling thread after thread of our personality with his coarse fingers, as though we were a piece of cloth, and then, posing as a man of honour, falsely depreciating us.   The letter was so dull, besides being stupid, that I could not even see the matter in a humorous light.   It was

[1] Livia Frege, *née* Gerhardt, a singer and a friend of both Mendelssohn and Schumann.

[2] A well-known impresario who had proposed that Frau Schumann should make a tour in America.

the most ill-bred, revolting slave traffic! I thank my Maker that you are not going over there! Indeed, if impossibilities were possible, I would rather we, all the good musicians joined together, could produce, by our playing, castles and orchestras in the most beautiful surroundings, simply in order to be able to pay homage to Bach and Beethoven and play our favourites to one another! But that would be just as easy to achieve as that you, with your high artistic claims and your tastes, should be certain of obtaining 30,000 thalers in one year from an *entrepreneur*. So much for the letter from X. The . . . must not cause us to quarrel. As regards my journey to Ireland (the thought of an island in this heat is pleasant!), it will take place at the end of September. I shall be back in Hanover at the beginning of November; for how long I do not know; that depends upon how much good I can accomplish in connection with the concerts. I am glad that I shall bring back material gains from England—so as to have a few more thousand thalers' worth of independence of my post in Hanover. How I sympathise with what you must be going through now at Bonn! Only the day before yesterday some songs of Schumann's brought before me all the wealth of love and goodness in his beautiful nature. Treasures of pure feeling! What does his resting-place look like now? There is always to me a deep and moving melancholy about autumn—but not without a consoling transfiguration when the slanting rays fall on the many-coloured foliage. It is my favourite season— and I wish I had a knapsack on my back and were with Johannes on the banks of the Rhine. That is better than England after all!—Yours,

JOSEPH J.

*To Clara Schumann*

[HANOVER, *December* 31, 1859.]

Dear Frau Schumann—I should like you to receive
a few words from me on the first day of 1860, as a
good omen of my improvement as a correspondent.
My wishes are always the same, warm and sincere,
and the egotistic wish is included that you may
continue your kindness towards me and that I may
act so as to deserve it more and more. You know
these are not mere words, and it did not need the
warm comfortable floor covering provided by your
thoughtful kindness to make me feel grateful to you
now. But the sight of the lovely soft skin at my
feet gives me particular pleasure. I was here for
Christmas, and although I was not with those who
are nearer to my heart than any one on earth, yet I
was among pleasant, kindly people, at Kaulbach's.[1]
Fräulein Ney[2] was there, and I think my conjecture
will be justified! I like the girl because of her talent
and her charm, and I should be very sorry to hear
anything but good of her. I write this in reply to
your chaff and to the "queer stories." I was detained
here chiefly by my desire to get on with the remodelling of my Concerto,[3] and the first movement is in the
hands of the copyist, as it had to have a new score and
some fresh parts. If only I could finish it once and
for all! Soon perhaps! The grand piano is in the
next room, well looked after. Jaëll begged to be
allowed to play Schumann's D minor Sonata on it
with me; I imagine you would have no objection. I
want to hear the Hebrew Melodies again, too, because
I should like to add some new ones. Johannes has

[1] The painter, Friedrich Kaulbach, father of Fritz August von Kaulbach.
[2] Prominent sculptor.   Died 1908.          [3] Hungarian Concerto.

sent me the greater part of his Serenade instrumentated; most of it is just as though he had never had anything else to deal with but the orchestra. Well, he was born with it, of course! I am not in favour of an orchestral concert in Berlin; you cannot break fame across your knee. And a concert with doubtful receipts is a violent measure which we had better leave to the Weimar lot—do you not think so too? Artists ought to earn something by their work, not make a present of it to the public. The work will be performed at Hanover, Hamburg and Leipzig. I hope some one will publish it; the rest will follow. Perhaps there is another reason against it by which I am unconsciously influenced—I should like to be present, and I could not manage it this winter, because I should have no time. I expect you are looking forward to enjoying *Orpheus* to-morrow? We did *Fidelio* here a short time ago : the orchestra excellent, the singers moderate, time often bad. But all the same it stirred me to the depths, as it always does! But how isolated I am here as far as music is concerned! I followed Marschner's last son to the grave to-day.

I will write to Haakman in Holland about you. How about Brunswick?

When am I to have my green umbrella, and when is Fräulein Marie going to play to me? Remember me to her and to all the family, and write again soon, dear friend, to yours sincerely, J. J.

### From Clara Schumann

BERLIN, *January 2*, 1860.

Your lovely long letter gave me so much pleasure yesterday evening, dear Joachim, that it made the

close of a not very happy day quite gay. Even
though I know you to be my true friend, it is in the
nature of woman to long for an affectionate word
occasionally, and when it comes it does one good!

On Sylvester even I went to the *Midsummer
Night's Dream,* and when the ♪♫♫ ♫♪[1] came I was
firmly convinced that you must have been knocking
and that I should find you when I got home, and
Frau Gisela's remark that you had promised to come
here *one* day confirmed the idea. *A Midsummer
Night's Dream,* although only moderately well performed (especially the musical part under Taubert),
was enchanting! Such a play combined with such
music is surely the highest bliss!

Frau Gisela spared me an evening a few days ago.
Unfortunately Herman Grimm was not with her—it
was funny, she said he was not well and she had sent
him for a walk; he was afraid he would hear music
at my house, and that would have excited him too
much.   It is strange that people always think
musicians can only be happy when they are at their
music.   I spent the evening just with Frau Gisela
and Rudolf Grimm, without music, and yet I enjoyed
it.   The time went by quickly.

I thought you would be working hard at your
Concerto, and my present request is all the harder to
make, because it will rob you of a great deal of your
precious time.   I am sending you the Bach 'cello
Sonatas, and I would ask you to go through them
and tell me whether I can have them printed *just as
they are* . . . Schubert wants them as soon as
possible. . . .

As regards Johannes, dear Joachim, you did not
quite understand what I meant.   I have no wish to

[1] The rhythm of the Scherzo.

procure fame for him, but it seems to me such a simple matter that, when I am giving a concert here, he should produce his Serenade. That is not importuning the people; if I do it, it will be simply for the sake of the work, but if Johannes, on the other hand, tries to force a performance of the Serenade at Leipzig, that would be much more like breaking it over one's knee. He will certainly have to fight against ill-will there. Here he would have to conquer ignorance at the most, although I feel sure he would find a small public in sympathy with him. But, as far as the recognition and propagation of his work goes, Hamburg *is useless*. After Leipzig, Berlin is the most important. But I did hope you would have been there! Well, I will *force* nothing. Johannes is much too good and kind to me for that, so if *he does not care about it* I will let it alone. I suggested it to him because he himself wrote that *he would like to produce his Serenade as often as possible*. . . .

### From Robert Franz

HALLE, *January* 20, '60.

Best of Friends—Forgive me for troubling you with a twofold request. Last year the great C major Duo by Schubert, arranged for the orchestra by you, was performed at a Gewandhaus concert. As far as I am aware, the work has not been printed in this form since then, and so those who wish to make use of it must rely on your goodness. As we are giving a concert here in a few weeks' time, at which I should very much like to have it performed, I want to know whether you can and will be so good as to lend me the score and orchestra parts for a short time. I know quite well that this is really a large order ; but my love for the work and the confidence I place in you as a genuine artist give me the courage to overrule objections of that kind. I should be very grateful to you if you would let me know about this as soon as possible.

Out of this naturally arises an old wish of mine, namely, that I should one day have the pleasure of bringing your wonderful powers before the people of Halle. We shall not, it is true, be able to offer you anything like what your talents justify you in demanding. I shall not be able to go beyond 6 Friedrichsd'or, as the resources of the treasury here would not stand a greater strain. I am not dreaming of suggesting that you should come all the way from Hanover to Halle for the sake of such a bagatelle, but perhaps you could fit in my suggestion in connection with Leipzig, which you always visit once a year during the winter, and in that case you would perhaps not be obliged to refuse me at once. I need hardly tell you how fortunate I should consider myself if I could present to our public a piece of work like your Beethoven Concerto—let alone the pleasure of seeing you and talking to you again. The concert which I have in mind takes place on February 10 at the Berggesellschaft here.

Are you really not angry with me for asking so much? Will you excuse it because circumstances have obliged me to reckon on outside help? But I will say no more about it, and I am convinced that, if you are able, you will help me in one way or the other.— Begging you once more to send me an answer in two words as soon as possible, I am, with kindest regards, yours, Rob. Franz.

*From Clara Schumann*

VIENNA, *March* 3, 1860.

Here I am in the Emperors' city once more, and again without you, dear Joachim! And you are having such glorious music to-day, and I shall not be there![1] I wonder if you will think of me?

Well, otherwise things are going well with me here! My first concert was the day before yesterday. I had a magnificent reception. When I appeared the applause seemed as though it would never cease, so that I was really touched, which is saying a great deal for me, as you know what I think of the public. I have never given such good concerts here as these three; long before the day there was not a good seat to be had. That is pleasant! Unfortunately matters are very bad, pecuniarily; the value of money is so low here that one loses a third. But it is delightful to play here; one's power seems to increase incomprehensibly.

But I have not only thought of you with longing, dear friend, during the concerts, I have also remembered to do business for you with Spina. He will print your Duo this summer *with pleasure*—but I thought he might pay something for that pleasure, and so with that in mind I told him the work had been expensive and would not repay you so well as a solo piece, for example, and that your demands would not be exorbitant as you had already told me you would gladly take Schubert's *Works* published by him as *part* of your fee, and I thought you ought to ask at least enough to cover the cost of copying the score and parts, say 100 gulden, which will give you 50 thalers per cent

---

[1] The performance of Brahms' 1st Serenade took place on the 3rd at Hanover.

*at present.*  I know Robert would have done that, and I feel sure Spina will give it ;[1] or if you think that too much ask 60 gulden, the copying must have cost you that much, and I would tell Spina that in your place, because it could not possibly be regarded as a fee. He told me to ask you to send him the whole thing soon.  If you want me to do anything more in the matter, you know how willing I shall be.

I spoke to Herbeck[2] yesterday, too, about Johannes —he is going to have the Ave Maria and the Funeral Song performed at the first opportunity.  If I could only fix something up with Eckert[3] about the Serenades —I will try to at any rate.  Spina[4] is going to produce Schubert's Duo at one of the first concerts next winter ; he told me that as soon as I mentioned it.  If I only had the score of the Serenades, because of course every one who might produce them asks for that at once.

I do not think I shall go to Pesth ; things seem far too unsettled there.

I enclose an article by Hanslick on Liszt's *Prometheus* —it will interest you—it is really delightful to find that for once the public has its heart in the right place.  I wish I had been there, I should have wanted to join in their rejoicings.[5]

---

[1] He had no intention of doing so and postponed the printing for years, foolishly enough, for Joachim was afterwards asked for the work by various conductors who wished to produce it.  It was not published until 1872, by Spina's successor.

[2] Artistic director of the Society of the Friends of Music.

[3] *Kapellmeister* at the Vienna Court Theatre and conductor of the Philharmonic concerts.

[4] Probably written in error for Herbeck.

[5] See E. Hanslick, *Geschichte des Konzertwesens in Wien*, part 2, 1870, p. 200.  "The Society of the Friends of Music had arranged that Mozart's G minor Symphony should follow immediately after Liszt's *Prometheus*. . . . An unheard-of incident occurred.  After the first four bars of the well-known Symphony the entire audience broke into delighted applause."

A little time ago Eckert had Robert's D minor Symphony and Overture, Scherzo and Finale, played at the Philharmonic concerts, and both works excited the greatest enthusiasm—if only I could have been there! They are all delighted with the *Manfred* too. Why has it only come now! I always feel at once glad and sorrowful when I hear of it.

At one of the Society's concerts to-morrow I am to hear three choral songs, which I do not know yet, as Whistling laid them aside for years without printing them, and Arnold has only just published them. Herbeck is much impressed by them—I am looking forward to it. What a lot there is here to see and hear! To-morrow the *Ruins of Athens* (which I have never heard), on Monday *Midsummer Night's Dream*, Tuesday *Faust* (Mephisto—Lewinsky), and so on— something interesting for every day in the week. Well, I must have something to make up for missing the Serenades! I dare not think of it to-day, it upsets me so.

Please, dear Joachim, write and tell me about it and about everything else that concerns you—I love to hear anything from you.

I am just going to write to Johannes at Hamburg, as I am afraid my letter would not catch him at your house.

Good-bye.—Remember your faithful old friend,

CL. SCH.


*P.S.*—My second concert is on the 8th—my Trio !!!¹ —What do you think of my courage? (It is the first time I have played it in public, and I have only done so after being urged on all sides)—Beethoven's E major

¹ G minor, op. 17.

Sonata, etc.   The third is on the 15th—*Davidsbündler*, B minor Sonata, Clementi (perhaps), etc.

Good-bye once more !

### *From an unknown hand*

HANOVER, *March* 5 [1860].

Brahms' Serenade is a monstrosity, a caricature, a freak, which should never have been published, much less performed *here* ; we say here, whilst the piano concerto served up to us last winter still sticks in our throats !   It is inexcusable that such filth should have been offered to a public thirsting for good music. That was an hour—a fiendish torture that can never be forgotten.   Poor Mozart, poor Beethoven !   Did you look down upon us ?   What has become of you ! ! May we be spared grimaces of this kind in the future ! We all unite in bidding farewell to Herr Brahms and Herr K[onzert] M[eister] [?] : do not tax the patience of your audience too severely, and do not impose on them a taste for that which can only be the greatest torture to people with *sound* ears.

Accept the homage of all future admirers—but not that of the higher and better friends of music.

M. H.

### *To Clara Schumann*

[HANOVER, *circa March* 13, 1860.]

Dear Frau Schumann—As your last concert is on the 15th, this letter will reach you just in time to let you know how much I should like to be there. I am so delighted that my dear Viennese have been so charming to you ; it makes me long to join you in the Emperors' City.   Well, next autumn, please God !   But your last concert is sure to be followed by the last of all, and then by a farewell concert ; I can foresee that. Brahms will already have written to tell you about his Serenade and our time together last week. You know (or at any rate you ought to know without my having to tell you) that we missed you greatly as audience and sympathiser. The work has gained considerably by its new dress of metal and skin. The trumpets and drums sounded so fresh and triumphant in the first and last movements that one felt inclined to join in. And the Adagio, so full of beautiful melody and deep harmonies, often reminds one of the sound of the organ. Unfortunately, the orchestra could only rehearse it twice for two hours, but although the rendering was not altogether free enough to satisfy our ideals, because of the novelty and individuality of the work, yet it sounded *good* and *clear* all the same. The King and Queen and Hauptmann, who was here, were very pleased, and the public—rather amusing, to use no harsher word. It is the same old story: when the bare name does not compel attention and respect from the very beginning, people are inattentive or disconcerted, antagonistic or lazy. But if I stay on here I shall not give in! Besides, in spite of the denseness of the public, I am not afraid for Johannes. On Saturday it is my turn with my Magyarember Concerto. What luck shall I have? I am sorry you are not going to Pesth on account of my parents and sister. Otherwise the political feeling is probably too unfavourable to the musical. God grant it may be different next year, but whatever happens I am going there. I am very grateful to you for the news that Spina is prepared to print my arrangement of Schubert, and I must also bow to your diplomatic skill with regard to a "part of the fee." The 40 Rthlr. for "copying expenses" will certainly be very welcome; they will mean a few more mountains to climb in the summer. How I shall enjoy the free months this summer, and what good use I shall make of them! Chappell's will hear from me to-day that I am not going to London. I am terribly sick of parading on concert placards, and sorry as I am to give up London, I owe it to my spiritual and physical welfare. Do you know yet where you will spend the summer? Let me know soon, and also *when* you will fulfil your promise to the King to come here once more in the spring. There has been a good deal of music at the Court lately, twice on account of Hauptmann, and the King is " charmed " with his compositions. Be madly enthusiastic or nothing, seems to be the innocent motto of the dear royal couple. At the King's special request I played H.'s G. minor Sonata twice with *Wehner*! How much rather I would have heard your Trio instead! I recollect a Fugato in the last movement, and that once, at Frege's, Mendelssohn was much amused because I could not believe a woman could have composed anything so serious and scholarly! You will not escape your fate, and you will see that Trio and the Romances included in the royal repertoire. If only I could enclose in my letter my half-malicious, Bennett-like smile, so that you could join in, at the same time shaking your finger at my impertinence!

You will have heard from Johannes about the protest we concocted here against the Liszt clique. You will approve of it. There is much to be said against it from a worldly-wise point of view—but I am anxious to repeat openly, in a short, dry, and simple form, that which is only known by my intimate friends, so that I may, once and for all, clear myself

o

from the suspicion of cowardice. And I add the frivolous comment, what comes after that remains to be seen. On Saturday we are finishing up with

Beethoven's F major Symphony !

May *this* thought which sprang from the Emperors' City awaken the most joyful springtide thoughts in you! Good-bye for to-day; remember me kindly to Elise.—Yours,                    JOSEPH JOACHIM.

### To Robert Franz

*The 21st [March 1860], Bach's birthday.*

Dear Friend—After mature consideration it seems to me to be my duty, not only to make known to you the contents of the enclosed declaration before it is published, but also to urge you most earnestly to give your sanction to it by signing it. Incited by Berlioz' article, I, friend Brahms, and several others have lately discussed the evil influence exercised by the "New Germans," by their works and the way in which they propagate them by any and every means, not omitting the deceitful trick of fortifying themselves with the names of those who, for the good of art, praised be Apollo! have absolutely nothing in common with the "New Germans." We felt that we had been slack, if not actually cowardly, in not protesting long ago against those who, in their vanity and arrogance, regard everything great and sacred which the musical talent of our people has created up to now as dung for the rank, miserable weeds growing from *Liszt*[1]-like phantasias. The word *Liszt* is out, hard as I find it to connect this name, which

---

[1] A play on the name—*listig* meaning "cunning."

evokes memories of many a fine and admirable deed in the old days, with a public protest against an artistic clique; but, *Amicus Liszt, magis amica Musica.* The consequences of what he is doing, and which he must abide by, willy-nilly, have become too destructive. About three years ago, on the occasion of the Karl August Festival, to which I was invited, I contented myself with writing *privately* to him that I did not wish to attend it either from curiosity or hypocrisy, and that I could not go from any other motive—I found it hard enough to write this to a man older than myself who had often been so kind to me. But in spite of that I must, as guardian of the art which is dearest to me, and because of his destructive propaganda, join in the defensive outcry which has now penetrated to you also. Strengthen our protest with the weight of *your* name; that, more than anything else, would divert from their false ideal *those* misguided spirits who, through the cunning of the " New Germans," are mad enough to believe that you countenance this school, with which you have nothing whatever in common. I would much rather talk over the matter with you (unpractised in writing as I am); but I cannot possibly get away now : our last concert is on the 24th, and on the 27th, in accordance with *long-standing* promises, I have to play at Bremen and Hamburg. Kirchner, Grädener, Bargiel, Dietrich, Wüllner have consented, and I intend to write also to Gade, Rietz, and Hiller. I should like to ask Herr von Saran,[1] but I do not know his address. I have heard very favourable accounts of his things, and I hope I shall get hold of them soon and make

---

[1] August Friedrich Saran, born 1836 at Genthin. Published in 1875 *Robert Franz and German Folk and Church Songs.*

acquaintance with them. The fact that they have been praised in the *Brendel'sche Zeitung*, as I hear from a friend (for I only read the paper myself occasionally by chance), is just one of the crooked confusing manœuvres by which they make people believe that artists, who must condemn their aims, belong to their party.

As Saran's friend and teacher, will you be so good as to show him the declaration if he is staying at Halle? I have the pleasure to tell you, dear friend, that, encouraged by your sympathy with my arrangement of Schubert's Duo, I have offered it to Spina, who is going to print it. As soon as you can spare the score please send it to me, and if, when you heard it, you noticed anything which might be altered, be so kind as to tell me; it is more than four years now since I heard the work.

Looking forward with pleasure to hearing from you soon.—Yours most sincerely,

JOSEPH JOACHIM.

### From Robert Franz

HALLE, *March* 23, '60.

My very dear Friend—I hope you will not think me weak or even cowardly, if I take upon myself to stand aside from the protest you have told me about. I certainly think it is justified by the circumstances, and regard it really as an action taken in self-defence —but, in spite of this, personal reasons prevent me from severing myself publicly from L. Besides this, I hear that for some time past, in consequence of many bitter experiences, L. is as though crushed— surely a fresh blow would render his condition yet

more unhappy.   But sentimental considerations of
that kind would bear no weight if I could convince
myself that the " New Germans " were a serious and
lasting menace to art.   This or that vain weakling
will be enticed into their mad camp, it is true—that
kind of people can never be guided by regulations—
but are individuals like these any great loss to art ?
I scarcely think so!   Moreover, I am firmly convinced
that lying and deceit will never succeed in seriously
hindering the real progress of the universe.   Truth
and beauty only shine the more brightly by contrast !
Unless every indication is deceptive, we are nearer
the desired goal than ever before.   The " music of
the future " has found its place by reason of its own
poverty, and the only further use we have for it will
be to make the genuine music stand out more clearly.
Taking all this into consideration, I am sure you will
not be angry with me for my refusal, the more so as I
can hardly believe that I could be of any material help
in changing the present condition of things.   Besides,
my whole life is one continual protest against " Young
Weimar " — unprejudiced people must have been
convinced of that long ago without any statement
from me.

I was very pleased to hear that your arrangement
of Schubert's Duo is to be printed.   May I ask you
to let me keep the score a little longer ?   The copyist
has not quite finished—but I have urged him to finish
his job as quickly as possible.   But if you cannot
allow me any more time, you shall have it by return
with a few personal remarks.

Your kindly feeling for Saran gave me great
pleasure.   He has unusual talent which deserves to
be encouraged in every way.   He is in somewhat
poor circumstances, I am sorry to say—acting tem-

198 CORRESPONDENCE OF JOACHIM

porarily as schoolmaster at the orphanage here! I told him about your letter—but he will not take part in a public protest from motives of modesty which are quite justifiable.

In conclusion, I am very far from wishing to influence in any way the decision come to by you and the others; the Brendel clique deserved such a step twofold and threefold long ago. My attitude with regard to the matter is a purely personal one, and therefore quite unimportant. If I did not owe L. so much—he has always treated me in a generous and disinterested manner—it would be another matter, and I would, with the greatest pleasure in the world, help to hurl my ancient love, "the great Franz Brendel," back on to the dung-heap whence he has had the insolence to crawl.—With kindest regards, yours,                                        ROB. FRANZ.

### To Clara Schumann

[HANOVER, *April* 13, 1860.]

Dear Frau Schumann—Of course I will write to Chappell; I am only afraid it will not be much use. It is too much in his interest to act for artists who join in his undertakings *year after year* for him to take much trouble about the presentation of a stranger, however important. But it can do no harm, at any rate! And so you will probably pay the dear island folk another visit? Sometimes I feel positively home-sick for the fine old trees in the squares, and the variegated life and the peculiar feeling of isolation which comes over one in the midst of the turmoil and draws one to the parks. In short there is much that is glorious in dear, dear London! But I mean to stick to my resolution to work hard this summer and to go to

Weimar and Pesth in the autumn.   Meanwhile, I am
staying on here, but I have promised to play in
Düsseldorf at Whitsuntide.   If I were not tied here
next week by a promise to play at Hildesheim (for
old Heinemeyer), I think I would have looked you up
at Dresden.   To-morrow is the Queen's birthday and
the last Quartette concert.   We are playing Mozart's
E♭ major, Rob. Schum.'s A minor, and Beeth.'s C
minor.   If you are coming here, and let me know in
time, I should like to arrange to have the Hungarian
Concerto and perhaps the Schubert Duo played for
you; I should like to hear the latter (before sending
it to Spina); or Brahms' 2nd Serenade.   Of course,
I cannot promise it.

Remember me to friends at Dresden, especially
Rietz.—Yours,                                        J. J.

### From Clara Schumann

BERLIN, *April* 25, 1860.

Dear Joachim—I am *not* going to England; I feel
too overstrained, morally and physically—I will give
you the other reasons later on by word of mouth.   I
shall not see you before May—is there any chance of
a rehearsal then?   I hope, at any rate, to hear some
quartettes.   I found it hard to make up my mind
about England, but I am glad I shall be in Düsseldorf
for the Musical Festival.

Thank you very much for going at once to Count
Platen.   But what a strange business about the Court!
Are you in disfavour again?

Do not be alarmed at the fearful letter [1] enclosed,
but read it and then advise me.   I cannot go there to
celebrate a festival like that with people whom (as

---

[1] Invitation to the Schumann Festival at Zwickau, June 7–8.

a musician) I despise from the bottom of my soul. Shall I say just what I feel about it? How these Weimar folk do intrude wherever it is a question of boasting of Robert's friendship! If I only knew how to express myself concisely and to the point, but without harshness. Do you think my place is at a festival of this kind in any case? My feeling is that, as a woman, I would not fit in there, even if the Weimar folk were not taking part. Is it not a case of self-torment? How can I be indifferent to the matter? But for nothing in the world would I display my feelings on such an occasion! And so there are obstacles on every side. Shall I say this or that? Please advise me!

How is the declaration getting on? Could I not add my signature? Do I not also produce as well as reproduce? Then people would know what I thought and would not be always asking me.

Send back the letter *very soon* and your opinion. Do not be cross, dear friend, but the matter is too important for me to decide about it without any friendly advice.

I am staying here for another 8 or 10 days, and then I hope I shall see you.—With sincere regards, your faithful                                    CL. SCH.

### To Johannes Brahms

LEIPZIG, 15*th* [*May* 1860].

Dear Johannes—My violin was finished to-day, but I cannot resist the temptation to attend the rehearsal of the great D major Mass by L. v. B. to-morrow, and I shall not leave for Hanover until the evening. I am sorry I am not able to go to Hamburg, dearest friend, but my *fiddle* and my fingers require too much practice for the Musical Festival. If only you could come to Hanover with Frau Schumann! We must meet after the Musical Festival somewhere or other, even in Hamburg; because the company of other musicians does not lessen the longing for you! Yesterday, by the kindness of Frau Frege, I heard at her house a very good performance of the *St. John's Passion*; there is much that is very fine in it, and quite new to me. Dr. Härtel is in Genoa; but I said what there was to say about your things to his brother, and I think he is prepared to print one of your Serenades. But he did remark he would like to print some smaller things at the same time. Can you not offer him some songs? He was not so amenable with regard to the Concerto. I did not mention mine.[1] *I hope you will write to him soon.*

Rietz will join our protest[2] on condition that we wait for a definite provocation. He thinks this is sure to occur at the Schumann Festival at Zwickau; because he considers it absolutely necessary to chastise the people who so insolently claim Schumann as one of their company. He has promised to write to me about it before long, and he takes the matter *seriously*, although he was not convinced, at first, that any good would result from it. The gist of his objections is that the people in Weimar would only imagine we were attributing an importance to them which they could turn to their advantage. He says they are played out in any case! But Rietz will join in, as I said, on condition that the Schumann Festival at Zwickau is used as a pretext, and *that the blow is deferred until then.* Hauptmann, Lachner and Hiller

---

[1] Joachim offered Breitkopf and Härtel his "Hungarian" Concerto for 25 Louis-d'ors in a letter of August 23, 1860.

[2] For a full account of this protest see Fuller Maitland, *Brahms*, pp. 11 et seqq.—TR.

would also like to join in, in that case. I think that as we have delayed so long another three weeks will not matter. He would like some of the expressions to be made more forcible. I do not know Volkmann's and Franck's addresses.

Remember me to Frau Schumann, and write to Hanover, so that I need not wait for your reply. —Your                                          JOSEPH.

### To Herman Grimm

HANOVER, *Sunday* [*May* 20, 1860].

Dear Herman—I would much rather have gone with you through so many unknown towns, and as I am tied now, I wish you, at any rate, the best of humours and physical powers. I could hardly have come just now in any case, but I hope very much to see you both again when the Musical Festival is over. Will the drawings still be on view then?[1] I read about the worthy man's letter in your printed notice of his treasures; I shall be delighted if you give it to me to read, in Berlin. A recognition and an appreciation of your efforts gave me great and unexpected pleasure at Leipzig; it came from an old teacher of mine—not Klengel, whom I have probably mentioned to you sometimes, but a much older man, who has lived for the last twenty years almost like a hermit in the Observatory, correcting proofs all day long so as to be independent, and therefore descending to mankind at the most once a day, at dusk, when he could not work, for a walk. He used to be an ecclesiastic, but as his views did not altogether agree with those demanded

---

[1] Owing to the efforts of Herman Grimm and A. von Humboldt an exhibition was given at that time of drawings by Cornelius, who had almost been forgotten in Germany.

from the pulpit, he preferred independence to an appointment, although he not only has a liking for society, but was much sought after as a tenor with a beautiful voice and as a cultivated musician. On Mendelssohn's recommendation he took me as his pupil in Latin and Scripture history, and I used to climb up to him, actually and metaphorically, several times a week. When your name was mentioned casually, without knowing how intimate we are, this man broke out into the warmest praise of you, whose noble, refined, manly language (I am merely quoting) and deeply moral outlook, which he only knows from articles in the daily papers, had caused him to regard you as a personality of unusual significance. Was it not nice that I could show him your article on Cornelius, *which you had just sent me*, and could tell him how it was I understood his warmth of feeling so well? You must confess things still happen sometimes that make life worth living. I am glad you have read a favourable report of my Concerto. I have not seen a line about it yet, but I have had many kind things said to me; the nicest of all was from the orchestra here, which, contrary to its usual limited and divided opinion, broke into loud and delighted applause after the rehearsal. I must go to Herrenhausen now, to the poor, blind King. If you care to, let me know how you are enjoying yourself, and so give me a little share in your and your Apapa's trip. Write to me Poste restante, Düsseldorf. I am going there on Thursday. I will write from there to Gisel, to whom I send all messages, and tell her how I have got on. Fare as well as I wish for you.—Your                J. J.

*From Jenny Lind-Goldschmidt*

ARGYLE LODGE, *May* 24, 1860.

Dear Herr Joachim (without titles)—We were very glad to hear direct from you again, as otherwise we should have thought you had quite forgotten us and our last journey—during which you placed yourself under my motherly protection, all the same!! But I believe in a nature like yours—I *know* what it is like —and so whether you are silent or whether you speak we shall always have the same affection for you. Now I must tell you of my misfortunes—I have been to London twice this winter to hear music, and what a cruel fate was mine! To hear the Tartini Sonata (that is, *your* Sonata) and the Mendelssohn Concerto (likewise *your* Concerto, honourable director of concerts!) played by Herr X.! Bah, that went against the grain —and I will say no more now—except that every one of your notes resounds in my heart—and you do not make a single pause—or anything else that I do not feel and know was meant to be played thus and *only thus*. Yes, yes, you are gifted with a certain musical nobility, you bad violinist. Well, welcome to Sweden, if you decide to go there. . . . God be with you. —Yours sincerely, JENNY GOLDSCHMIDT.

*From Elisabeth Ney*

BERLIN, 4/6, 1860.

My dear and honoured Friend—Only something quite unusual could move me to do more than carry out my promise to write to you when I leave a town. The news has reached me for which I have been looking all these last few days: your work is brilliant,[1] it has once and for all ceased to be ephemeral, the people for whom you worked have accepted it with acclamation! How grateful I am to the people whose words sound as though they came from my own heart, and how I envy them their good fortune! When I heard it for the first time it was to me a great and wonderful event. Now I feel sure that, supported by the souls of all these people, you will fly even higher and cast a spell upon the spirit of immortality.

Enough. You need not reply, or thank me for my sympathy. You told me it was welcome to you, and it is the least that we can give you.

ELISABETH NEY.

I shall stay here for the summer. Write and tell me where you are.

### To Clara Schumann

[HANOVER] 13th [*June*, 1860].

Dear Frau Schumann—Unluckily, our wish to play together again at Herrenhausen has come to nothing. On the second day I called at Herr^sen, but did not see their Majesties; now I have just heard that the King went to Berlin yesterday. He remembered me in the *most* liberal manner on his birthday. An increase of salary to the extent of 1000 thalers, quite without asking for it, can only be called royal! A notification from the Minister of Finance informed me the day before yesterday that my salary had been doubled, without any further duties having been laid upon me. Yesterday I wrote a letter of thanks and—

[1] Refers to the Hungarian Concerto and its reception at Düsseldorf on the occasion of the Musical Festival on May 29.

did not give notice of my resignation. How long I shall stay I do not know, not longer than a fortnight in any case.[1] I shall go to Berlin for two days before that. I have not gone to Hamburg because I had to pay my respects after this mark of favour, and now it is too late, as the Goldschmidts sail for Stockholm on the 15th. I am to go through the Bach Sonatas[2] to-morrow with Lindner. Where am I to send the manuscript? I await your commands, and hope to have a few lines from you at any rate before you leave. . . .

*From Clara Schumann*

DÜSSELDORF, *June* 14, 1860.

It was a good thing, dear friend, that you did not tell me about your rise in salary in person, because I think I should have thrown my arms round your neck for sheer joy! Oh, it is splendid! I cannot tell you how glad I am! But you must not resign now—such a position, with 2000 thalers for 6 or 7 months, *such* an orchestra is not to be found again in the whole of Germany, and if you stay others will join you there. If you arrange that they appoint me there for 2000 thalers I will come, and then you would always have a decent accompaniment, at any rate. I have messages of congratulation from all around me. . . .

Please send the Bach Sonatas in my name (and with my thanks in anticipation) straight to Schubert at Leipzig—that is the quickest.

I am writing so badly, but I am so excited I cannot help it. There is no greater pleasure than when good fortune smiles on a dear friend—first the recognition of your glorious Concerto, then the 1000 thalers!

[1] Before going to Bonn for the summer.
[2] The 'cello Sonatas arranged by Schumann.

Prose treading on the heels of poetry, indeed, but life for an artist is made up of such changes. . . .

## To Clara Schumann

[BONN, *July* 5, 1860.]

Dear Frau Schumann—I have just been at Dr. Breusing's; the children were out, but he told me that the holidays only *begin* on the 15th. So your assumption must be based on a misunderstanding. But that holiday-time really suits you best, and when the children come to see me in a few days, as Dr. B. promised, I shall tell them how nice your home is. Yes, the place is really delightful,[1] from the little room in the valley with the Bach Suites, to the highest peak of the red rock, and I shall often think of it in future. We could not make up our minds to go straight by rail to the lonely study; so we only went as far as Bingen, and from there we *walked* to Bacharach, with knapsacks on our backs. We visited Sonneck on the way, and climbed up ladders and scaffolding to the very top of the tower! The castle is being rebuilt for the royal family. Although we were on the road at mid-day we did not suffer from the heat; there were light clouds in the sky, and a fresh sweet breeze came from the Rhine. There is nothing more delightful than to wander through woods and vineyards with a good, faithful comrade. I am hoping to enjoy my summer holiday thoroughly. This morning we had some music quite early; Dr. Becker[2] was leaving, and as we like him we wanted to give him a little pleasure before he went. I played Schumann's Phantasie and Johannes' many Fugues

[1] Cf. Litzmann, vol. ii. p. 181.
[2] The famous oculist of Heidelberg, who afterwards married Joachim's cousin.

from the *Wohltempiertes Klavier*, and I also played some things of Bach's. After that, and of course without an audience, we went through the accompaniment to the violoncello Sonatas[1] *together*. As I consider it my duty to be absolutely straightforward with you, I cannot, after having gone through the work several times, do otherwise than express the hope that you have given Schubert no absolute promise that they should be published. When I went over them in Hanover I marked several passages which I wanted to alter, and I hoped that Johannes would think I had been too scrupulous in my doubts about other passages—but our friend is in *absolute* accord with all my misgivings, indeed, with his quick brain and deep feeling for Bach he has convinced me that there are many un-Bachlike passages which I no longer wish to leave as they are! In short, I must really advise you seriously against publication, sad as it makes me to fulfil this duty to the beloved Master, whose works I regard with ever increasing respect and gratitude for their greatness. But just because the leaves in the laurel wreath of immortality woven for him by posterity are so thick and fresh, we must not be so weak as to add to it a withered leaf, instead of hiding it from the gaze of the musical world with watchful love. There is no need to tell Schubert " why "; with his commercial point of view, he does not deserve that we should lay bare to him our inmost feelings. You could simply write to him and say that on comparing it with the Bach MSS. at Berlin too many discrepancies were apparent, and that, considering the exactitude with which editions of Bach's works were now criticised, only Schumann himself could have decided what should or should not be

---

[1] Arranged by Schumann.

altered in consequence.   A man like that is always easily satisfied ! . . .

*From  Clara  Schumann*

KREUZNACH, *July* 8, 1860.

. . . Thank you, above all, for having gone through the Bach Sonatas again so conscientiously, and for having told me your opinion so honestly and yet so gently.   Your conscientiousness gives me new proof of your love and veneration for the dear one, as, indeed, the way in which you refer to him always does me good.

I agree with all you say and I will write to Schubert as you advised.   There will be a good deal of argument, I am sure, because he had already announced the publication.

*To  Clara  Schumann*

[HANOVER, *September* 24, 1860.]

Dear Frau Schumann—This time I was really rather anxious, because, up to now, your conscientious exactness has spoilt me.   Well, thank God, everything is all right !   I am looking forward to our music in Dresden, and I agree to everything, especially to the three different kinds of seats ; for although I think that in a large town full of visitors the attendance at our soirées would be big enough even at the higher price, I think it is our duty to make it possible for people of limited means to hear good music too. Teachers and small officials are often the most earnest part of the audience ! . . .

There is something in the idea of asking Rietz to play in a Trio.   But I must leave the decision to you,

P

as you have, no doubt, played with him more recently than I. I used to think his tone rather hard and his technique rather stiff; but he was certainly very reliable and a certain conscientiousness in ensemble playing made me like to play with him. . . .

My first orchestra rehearsal will take place next Friday. I am going to try the Overture, Scherzo and Finale at it, and I will think of you. Perhaps I shall go through the Schubert arrangement too, under Scholz' conductorship, so as to make sure of its effect on me, as *audience*, once more. Spina is a strange fellow; I wrote to him twelve days ago and have heard nothing yet. Perhaps he regrets having undertaken what he could not refuse you at the time. I played Schubert's Quintette for two viol., viola and two 'cellos yesterday. Much of it is beautiful, overflowing with feeling, and quite individual; and, unfortunately, the whole does not satisfy one! Irregular and with no feeling for beauty in the contrasts! What a pity it is that such a genius should never have fully developed! And yet one cannot help loving dear, good Schubert so much![1] How I am looking forward to Johannes' new things! I cannot grudge him the wonderful surprise he made of them for your birthday.[2] My friend far surpasses me in talent as in charming attentions; but if you remember that I have practically been abroad since my ninth year, far from my home, you will see in that some little excuse for my lack, not of appreciation of such tender thoughtfulness and not of the warmest good-will for my friends, but of the ability to put these attentions into practice. But I still have hopes that I shall improve. My belated but

[1] This Quintette, one of the finest of Schubert's instrumental works, was one of Joachim's favourite compositions in later years.
[2] With reference to this see Litzmann, vol. ii. p. 184.

hearty good wishes for your birthday.  You say nothing about the dear boys.  What about Frau Bendemann's suggestion?[1]  Am I still to write to Klengel?

In any case I hope you will let me know your address when you leave Mehlem.  I send you and Fräulein Marie very kindest regards, and am as always, your sincerely devoted            JOSEPH JOACHIM.

## From Clara Schumann

GODESBERG, *October* 11, 1860.

Dear Joachim—I have been hoping for the promised programme for some days.  Can you believe it, I cannot think of it at all without becoming quite nervous, so much so that I cannot play a single piece without sticking, simply at the thought of the public. What will happen at this rate!  Please make up the programme; I cannot. . . .

Many thanks for your advice, which I am glad to follow.  Bargheer is to play at all three soirées.  I quite understand your feeling about Berlin, although a man ought to conquer feelings of this kind, which are excused in the sensitive and also limited nature of a woman.  But it does me so much good to find sensitive feelings like these in a man!  But are you never going to play in Berlin again?  You must remember that as people's curiosity is satisfied by facts, the interest will soon die down (I mean the curiosity).  I shall be passing through Hanover at the end of next week.  Would it not be possible for me to hear Johannes' Sextet?  He wrote that he had sent it to you.

Are you playing at Leipzig on the 19th?  Johannes'

---

[1] That they should leave the school at Bonn.

2nd Serenade is to be performed there—and I am coming from Berlin. *But you must conduct it.* He will not go. . . . As always, yours sincerely,

CL. SCH.

## To Clara Schumann

[HANOVER, *October* 12, 1860.]

Dear Friend—It is nothing new to me that you have completely forgotten how to play the piano; I have heard that too often from you before, and I satisfied myself of the truth of it at Kreuznach, when you played the Bach Suites and the Beethoven Sonatas! That comes of walking over Eberburg and Rheingrafenstein instead of diligently practising finger exercises! And what on earth will happen when we play together; there are sure to be lots of mistakes in time! Incidentally the same thing happens to me at the beginning of *every* winter; I can never understand how I shall ever be able to stand in front of so many people without sinking through the ground with shame, if I think of it *beforehand.* And for that reason one must not think of it; it goes all right at the time, because the music makes one forget all that nonsense! And so we will only think of the programme. . . .

## To Theodor Avé-Lallemant

[HANOVER, *November* 18, 1860.]

My dear Avé—I was well advised in hesitating to telegraph to you yesterday. Assuming that I should be able to speak to H.M. the King myself at the concert, I hoped to be able to please you by going to Hamburg on the 4th. But as the King told me he was coming back to the town from Herrenhausen

on the 1st, and that he hoped to make up then for the
music he has missed from being absent and in mourning, as, moreover, just as I was going into the royal
box, Count Platen whispered to me that I was to apply
to the King myself for leave to go to Leipzig on the
26th, as he had not yet done so, there was nothing
for me to do but most regretfully to sacrifice my
Hamburg friends for *this time*.  Count Platen has the
amiable peculiarity of never liking to say " No " to me,
and then he has not the courage (courtier-like) to ask
the King for something which might cause a dawning
smile to vanish for a moment!  This is quite *entre
nous*!  We must seem like a lot of slaves to you
republicans? . . .

### From Clara Schumann

LEIPZIG, *December 7, 1860.*

Dear Joachim—What a pity I cannot be with you
to-morrow!  How I should like to sit there as an
enthusiastic listener!  And how I long for a quiet hour
with you!  My heart is so full on account of our dear
Johannes.  If ever I felt that you were both dear to
me, it was here.

I felt with you as deeply in your joy as I did with
Johannes in his sorrow—perhaps more than you did
yourselves.  My grief at Johannes' bad reception was
somewhat lessened by the evening at the Conservatoire, when nearly all the musicians had to
admit, after the Serenade, that it was beautiful.

Johannes left the Saturday after you did—he was
a little more cheerful during the last few days.

Gade's 3rd Symphony was good yesterday—a
violin Concerto (Dreyschock) by Rietz was unutterably
dreary !

*To Clara Schumann*

[HANOVER, *December* 12, 1860.]

Dear Frau Schumann—I wish I could have written out a more attractive programme for you than the following :

1. Overture by Scholz (MS.).
2. Concerto for violin by Paganini (Ole Bull).
3. Overture to *Euryanthe.*
4. Solo by Ole Bull.

———

5. C minor Symphony.

It is only partly owing to me that Ole Bull is playing. I wanted to get permission for him to give a concert in the *Theatre* and mentioned it to H.M. ; but the King would not hear of anything but that he should be invited for the concert, and although I imagined at first that Ole Bull himself would rather play in the theatre, and said so several times, etiquette did not permit me to oppose the King any longer, as it might have been interpreted as a kind of jealousy on my part. The Norwegian interests me more than I expected : he has remarkable power over his instrument, a very fine tone, and plenty of vitality. It is true I have only heard him play, in a room, fragments of some very beautiful little Norwegian folk-songs of the simplest description. . . . Yours,

JOSEPH J.

*To Herman Grimm*

[HANOVER, *about December* 22, 1860.]

Dear Herman—Ole Bull has been here over a week, and, as a man, I like him very much. We have several times discussed a two days' visit to Berlin to

see you both, and I think we shall carry it out.    But
I shall come without the Norwegian if he does not
make up his mind to it; I could manage it best at
the New Year.    Would the 1st suit you, or have you
too many engagements then?    I suppose I owe the
bottle of Cape wine and the charming Murillo to Ernst
Rudorff, who must have told you of my success![1]    I
was childishly delighted with the things, as I am with
everything that comes from my two friends.    The
article on Humboldt [2] reminded me vividly of our walk
in the Thiergarten last spring.    Your *Michelangelo*
seems to be becoming widely known; I have heard
all sorts of people speak of it with enthusiasm.    It
has made me take up Italian; I am reading and translating with a Signor Caggiati.    The little picture of
Ristori inside the Norwegian book may please Gisel—
and the book too, in spite of the bad translation.    Ole
Bull played at a concert the other day, and on Sunday
at Court together with Frau Schumann.    We may
hear him once more in the theatre.    I like his playing
better in a room than in public, because, in private, he
often selects very original Norwegian melodies.    His
tone is pleasantly soft and full of feeling.    Your parents
will have been very grieved at Dahlmann's death.    I
did not call on him in Bonn, as he was very ill then
and was not going into society.    I have been very
much bothered for the last week by a rheumatic
affection of the left hand; I could not take hold of
anything without pain; but, thank God, it is all right
again now.

With a thousand heartfelt greetings from yours,

J. J.

---

[1] At Leipzig.    Rudorff attended the Conservatoire there at that time.

[2] Alexander von Humboldt.    Died May 6, 1859.    The article is embodied in
Grimm's *Fünfzehn Essays*, 1874.

*To Clara Schumann*

[HANOVER] *December* 22 [1860].

Dear Frau Schumann—May the little book [1] which accompanies this note testify that you are in my thoughts now as always. I have only glanced through it, but Johannes, who has a copy, thinks very highly of it ; and to you, with your love of nature and the prospect of going to Norway, the pictures of the snow regions will be attractive and refreshing. Fräulein Marie could perhaps read *Joseph im Schnee* aloud to you. I have not read it yet, but I have often passed a pleasant hour reading Auerbach's peasant tales. I am going neither to Berlin nor to Düsseldorf, because, in consequence of an audience which I asked for in connection with the Kömpel affair, the King has commanded me and Count Platen to go to him on the second feast day, so that he may make the arrangements I had asked him to make. I am very glad that the scandalous calumnies which have been circulated with regard to my attitude towards Kömpel [2] will be practically refuted. I am very sorry I cannot go to Berlin because of Eugenie and Felix. I have thought out a plan for the little fiddler, who would have been *my godchild* if you had had your way,[3] which I hope you will allow me to carry out. I should like to give him my Guarnerius violin, on which I played in public for the first time in Leipzig, and which I have only ceased to use in public since I got the Stradivarius violin ten years ago. As soon as his little fingers are not " too short " he will have it altogether in his own

[1] Tschudi's *Animal Life in the Alps.*

[2] Reports arising from Kömpel's jealousy of Joachim. Kömpel afterwards became Konzertmeister at Weimar.

[3] Felix Schumann. Joachim could not be his godfather because he had not yet joined the Christian faith.

hands.   And I hope he will be my pupil by that time.
You must on no account say " No," because I am so
fond of the instrument I would never sell it; so my
only anxiety is that it should be used for a worthy
purpose, as I do not play on it now.   I count on seeing
you here in January, dear Frau Schumann; the King
says he means to ask us then to play the D minor
Sonata just for him and the Queen, without any other
audience.

### To Clara Schumann

[VIENNA, *February* 11, 1861.]

Dear Frau Schumann—I know you will be glad to
hear that all your prophecies about my visit to Vienna
have been fulfilled.   That is why I am just writing
this brief card.   I played Beethoven's Concerto, an
Adagio by Spohr, and Tartini, and although I was
nervous at first I was soon so spoilt that I felt quite
happy and at home.   I go to Pesth to-morrow; I return
here on the 15th and give the second concert on the
18th at 5 o'clock; I am going to play my own
Hungarian piece then.   My relations are very kind
and most considerate.   Lewinsky is a nice fellow, and
everything promises to turn out pleasantly.   Just this
hasty greeting for to-day.   I will write soon again!

J. J.

### From Bernhard Scholz

[HANOVER, *beginning of March* 1861.]

Dear Friend—The arrival of your letter cancelled
all the secret reproaches we had been aiming at you
until now, but even these were not very violent
because I could very well imagine that every minute
of your time has been taken up.

We are very glad you are coming back soon, and we have been counting the weeks of your absence. This time it is you who are disturbing the domestic peace! I will not believe that your wish to have the concert fixed for the 23rd points to your early departure again, because (1) you must help to celebrate my and Paula's (who, thank God, is still here) birthday; (2) you owe it to the King, now that he has dismissed Kömpel in disgrace, to give up some of your time to him; and thirdly, fourthly, fifthly, sixthly, etc., we cannot spare you so soon again. I am going about "*als wär's ein Stück von mir.*"[1]

How much I wanted to be present at your triumphs! We have been as happy as kings about them—and I should have liked to be at the performances you have heard and are going to hear. You will hear the great Mass at Aix-la-Chapelle, as you have been invited to go there; at any rate our friend Wüllner asked for your address for this purpose.

Nothing much has happened since you went away.

Kaulbach is still working at Paula's portrait, but it will only require one more sitting before it is finished. Marchesi has sung before the King. Ole Bull is giving a concert to-night in the theatre, and I do not think he will make his expenses out of it. But he said he *had* to give a concert, if only because people were intriguing against him to prevent it. I see nothing of him, thank God; he is positively repellent to me now.

Come back soon, and stay with us then for a bit! Hanover is a horrible place without you.

One more thing! My brother is always reminding

[1] "As though 'twere part of me." Quotation from a famous German song, *Der gute Kamerad.*

me about the fiddle! And my mother repeatedly asks me about it. If you should happen to come across a reasonable instrument (200-350 thalers), please keep an eye on it for the time being.—Kindest regards from yours,                               SCHOLZ.

Remember me to Dessoff and Gunz if you see them.

### To Clara Schumann

[HANOVER, *about May* 30, 1861.]

Dear Frau Schumann—I am sending my photographs, which ought to reach you before you leave for the baths, together with the friendliest greeting. I cannot find a copy of the position leaning against the "column" amongst those I have, so please accept these, until I can hunt up the photograph you want, and distribute them *ad libitum*. I will not forget Johannes. My head bears no more traces of the accident on the railway;[1] it appears to be hard enough to stand a good knock! I was very glad, after all, that you did not come to the birthday concert.[2] You would have been too irritated by the polite cads in kid gloves, from whom one did not expect any reverence for Händel and Beethoven, but who might have shown some respect for their royal mistress's choice instead of drowning not only the *pp* but even the *ff* in the Symphony with their chatter. I ended by regarding the whole affair as really comic. The King has asked me to conduct the Symphony once more before the holidays, so that he can enjoy it in peace. That

---

[1] The week before, near Gütersloh, the train in which Joachim was travelling was derailed ; but the only injury he received was that he was startled by his violin falling from the rack on to his head.

[2] In honour of the Queen's birthday.

means that my journey to Berlin is put off again for another week, because the King will probably command the orchestral music for Saturday. The Scholzes are going to Mainz on Saturday, too; he has asked for definite information with regard to the Niemann affair by that time, and has sent in his provisional resignation, should he have had no answer by then. I also stick to my decision that I will not let him go alone, if the King really puts a higher value on a good voice than on artistic probity! But I cannot believe that.

My best wishes for the baths, and please let me hear whether they are effective! Kindest regards to Fräulein Marie and the other members of the household from yours
J. J.

*P.S.*—The Queen has presented all those who took part in the concert, that is, Scholz, Stockhaus and myself, with pins. A very fine pearl, which I mean to wear.

### From Bernhard Scholz

HAMMERMÜHLE, *June* 10, 1861.

Dear Friend—Nothing has been decided yet! And I am strongly inclined to believe that, in spite of the royal promise, I shall not hear anything before the end of the term we fixed. It is the easiest way for His Majesty to get out of it, and to say afterwards, " Scholz would not wait for my decision ; I was well-disposed towards him, and would certainly have forced Niemann, etc."

I will let you know the outcome of the affair at once, whether it is determind by the King's decision or by his silence.

I went to see Herr von Guaita at Frankfort, and

my kind reception made me suspect that you had already written to him. If I was mistaken, please do so now, so that his good opinion may be increased to the superlative.   If the Frankfort business comes to anything I shall be adequately compensated in *one* respect—and yet how sorry I shall be to leave Hanover and—and you!   It was so pleasant and would have become pleasanter still.   Do you *still* think I have no cause to hate a man from my heart who can ruin a delightful future for me out of sheer malice?   I am growing bitter about it and will stop.

We are enjoying our life here, we are well, the children are doing splendidly, and I should have every reason to be quite happy if I did not keep remembering this unfortunate business.   That is what annoys me most of all, that it has put me out of humour for weeks and continues to do so.   The only thing about it that gives me pleasure is the revenge we shall take on the King.   That is one good thing, and I shall be revenged on N. too, in one way or another, of that I am certain.   I have not been and am not yet able to do any work; I keep thinking of my Requiem, but things will have to be more settled before I can collect myself.

I fill up my time with walking, driving, shooting, etc. ; our beautiful country offers so many means of enjoyment!   Come and see me and all of us soon! Perhaps I shall not see you any more next winter!

Write again soon ; I need it badly!

Paula and all my family send kind regards.   What a welcome you would receive here!

My wife sends a thousand greetings, as I do also. —Your faithful                                    SCHOLZ.

*From Clara Schumann*

SPA, *June* 12, 1861.

. . . The neighbourhood is charming whichever way one goes, lovely woods everywhere. How you and Johannes would like it! I only wish I could enjoy it with some degree of cheerfulness! But melancholy always overcomes me ; the more beautiful Nature is, the more deeply I feel my sorrow at not being able to enjoy it with him, my beloved husband. Oh, dear friend, what is the whole of Nature in her laughing mood to me, compared to one dear, loving glance from him! It is only in pleasant, stimulating society that these thoughts do not gain the upper hand—and then I can enjoy the other lovely things around me! . . .

I am very glad I did not go to Hanover for the concert, it would have made me so angry! You were certainly wise to look at it from the funny side, but it would have been rather *tragi*-comic as far as my purse was concerned.

I wonder if you are in Berlin? or if Johannes is with you? or you with him at Hamburg? What is really going to happen this summer?

Please write *soon* and fully, dear friend ; remember what pleasure it gives me. My address is, Spa en Belgique, Palais de Westminster Nro. 9A. But do not imagine I am living in a real palace—they call every little house here palace or hôtel, and every room in which one can turn round, salon.

What has happened about Scholz? Nothing definite, I suppose. I think I shall feel quite sad when you are no longer at Hanover—where shall we look for you then!

Well, dear Joachim, my very kindest regards, and think of your faithful friend          CL. SCH.

Canone per tonos a 4.                                    J. B.[1]

Tö - ne, lin - dern - der Klang, Du   kannst nicht neh - men die

Schmer - zen      A - ber die Tö - ne viel - leicht

mil - dern die lei - den - de Brust.

The Canon I told you about the other day—it is
so lovely.

## From Frau Scholz

HAMMERMÜHLE, *June* 14, 1861.

If I knew what was to my advantage, dear Master,
I would quietly wait until you were at Hanover or
at some place where you were doomed to be bored
occasionally like every one else, and would greet
every letter with welcoming eyes.   But I am so
grateful to you for having been so considerate to us
that I feel I must write to Berlin and tell you so at
once.   As I am writing a terrible storm has arisen,
and the great acacias close to my window are shaking
their heads so emphatically that I have quite lost

---

[1] Canon at a fourth below.                      J. BRAHMS.

etc.

countenance. I believe they strongly disapprove of my continuing; and I know now of what they are thinking: "*P.S. (For your wife)*"[1] is really not the nicest way for some one to write to some one else's wife; and not the most likely to evoke a reply—but the contents of this "*P.S. (for your wife)*" were so charming—some one else's wife *must* reply to it. I really do not know how to thank you for having actually gone to our house.

After your last letter my husband wrote to Kaulbach and begged him to remind His Majesty to send word *direct*; but, early this morning, before this letter reached H[anover], three telegrams came, one from Kaulbach, one from the theatre management, and a later one from Herr Lex, all to the same effect: that His Majesty would command N[iemann] to sing under S., whose resignation has therefore not been accepted. We were very glad, because to lose (1) you and (2) the rest of Hanover was not a pleasant prospect for us. Now we can enjoy our quiet country life in peace and freedom from anxiety. My husband sends his kindest regards; he is taking a little trip up the Rhine with his mother and sisters, where they are to meet young Streckers. I cannot be long away from home yet, and so, apart from Mainz and Wiesbaden, have been here all the time. And the children repay me for it; their cheeks are so fat and rosy it is a pleasure to see them; Hennie finds her chief pleasure in being with the cows.

Your *Adam Bede* is lying on my writing-table, rejoicing in its beautiful binding; up to date not a soul knows whether it has a beautiful interior. But I will try and find out as soon as a whole regiment

---

[1] Joachim had added a note for Frau Scholz to his letter to her husband.

of little coats and frocks, which owe their origin to the quiet here, have grown from my needle, and are clothing the plump, rosy limbs of their owners. A good third is finished, and I am stitching bravely on towards my *Adam Bede*.

Dear Joachim! I am so fond of you, and I should envy any one else from my heart for being all day with the daughter of Bettina, who must be like her wonderful mother in many respects. I should be frightened to death of Herman Grimm, for if he is really cleverer than you (which, between ourselves, I do not believe for a moment) other people would not be able to face him at all.

My husband begs to be excused this time. You might write to *me* sometimes now, and *long* letters.

Bernhard, Henni, and Paula send their love, and I am, sincerely yours,

Luise Scholz.

### To Frau Scholz

[Hanover, *about June* 24, 1861.]

Dear Friend — I am really grieved that poor Bernhard had to be disturbed at his summer residence with telegraphic messages! I hope you do not need my assurance that I am quite innocent in the matter, however much I may rejoice at seeing him again so unexpectedly. As a matter of fact, when I heard that B. was threatened with this bolt from the blue sky of royal favour, I let it be understood that, if His Majesty desired, I would play for once with Wehner! That seems to have borne no fruit. It is very annoying to have to give up a lovely town in republican Switzerland for the sake of a Russian Grand Duke! But after the latest royal decision we must not be too particular, and

Q

it is really very well meant although it seems clumsy and inconsiderate. But we will keep our highly treasonable opinion to ourselves ; other opinions must fade before our proper respect for this new blossom from the cornucopia of royal favour, the more so as many an interrupted tenor cadence is being circulated among the public. "But that can't damage us,"[1] as Rabe says. I have only been back from Berlin two days. I had a very delightful time ; I stayed at the Schumann's, of whom, however, only the youngest, Felix and Eugenie, two charming children, were there ; Frau Schumann herself is at Spa. But I spent most of my time with my friends the Grimms, and enjoyed myself so much that I cannot think of any special occasion which stands out above the others. We talked, made music, went together to see nice people and good pictures, drove, and yet it was not all these things which made my visit so pleasant! And it is a poor description to call it the good genius which always accompanies true friends in the shape of the consciousness of understanding and being understood. The best part of the intercourse between friends, as in a work of art, cannot be explained. One delightful visitor from the outside world came to me in the midst of my happy time in Berlin, for which I ought to have begun by thanking you most sincerely, before I told you anything else, and that was your dear, kind, vivacious letter! I seemed to see you all in the large room, you called up such a vivid picture of your happy, united existence. How grateful I am to fate for decreeing that you and Bernhard should continue to be near me! I think we shall often laugh at the memory of this curious drama with a happy

---

[1] *Thut uns aber weiter keinen Abbruch.* Joachim's servant Rabe had used this expression on hearing Ole Bull, the violinist.

ending.   I read your letter to the Grimms, who have
heard a great deal from me about my new friends.   I
hope the acacias are not *shaking* their heads this time,
but nodding them in gentle approval.

Hermann G. is coming to pay me a visit in the
autumn ; then you will see that, in your lack of faith,
you have overestimated me.   Bernhardus will tell you
about my plans for the summer, which are still unsettled.   Contrary to my habit I have chattered a lot,
and ought to stop !  My kindest regards to your parents,
parents-in-law, sisters-in-law, and all whom you love
and who remember me—Yours most sincerely,

J. JOACHIM.

A kiss to Henni and the boy.

## To Hans von Bronsart

HANOVER, *September* 30 [1861].

Dear Bronsart—Your letter came whilst I was
travelling in Switzerland, and only reached me when
I got back again after having been all over Switzerland.   If you have noticed the absence of a reply from
me, which I hardly think likely, during your stay in
Danzig, please accept the above circumstance as the
excuse.   I wish you happiness on your marriage,[1] with
all my heart, and may the kindly fate which has
united you in life and in art unite all good things and
bestow them upon you !  I shall always take the
greatest interest in your career.   If only the rumour
which caused you, dear Bronsart, to congratulate me
were not a false one !  But—unfortunately I am not
of those of whom Schiller and Beethoven were inspired
to sing :

[1] Bronsart married Ingeborg Starck, a pianist and composer.—TR.

My consolation is that both singers were able to rejoice *without envy*, although they themselves had had no share in this happiness! Sch. was not yet married, B. never married.

Thank you for what you tell me about your Leipzig plans. Feeling as I do a real respect for your self-sacrificing zeal and high ideals, it would have been a great pleasure to me to help you in carrying out what you propose—but many things stand in the way, of which I owe it to your honesty as a colleague to speak openly. First of all, I must confess that the idea of representing at one concert the group of artists who appear to you to be Schumannesque does not seem to me a very happy one. Either the compositions are really so similar that the arrangement would be justified from a critical point of view, and in that case I think there would be a certain monotony which would not have anything to excuse it (commemoration, illustration to lectures, etc.). Or else, the classification is an arbitrary one—and that would do away with any attraction it might have as a kind of "historical" record. Malicious people might even accuse the two living composers, who are not very widely known as yet, of making use of their warm personal relations with the famous dead in order to insinuate themselves into programmes in which they would not otherwise appear. As far as I, personally, am concerned, I must admit that the idea of forcing myself and my efforts, whilst I am still alive, within the orbit of such a famous name, gives me a feeling of almost physical fear. What I have produced is unfortunately not worth any one's while to classify! But if my compositions have ever been inspired by love for our great models, I should certainly attribute this good fortune to other masters no less than to the glorious Schumann.

I have not yet mentioned your proposal to Brahms; we do not happen to have corresponded very much lately. But I believe his feelings on the matter would not be dissimilar to mine. It is easier for me to pass judgment on my friend's works, which far surpass mine in number and in value, than on my own efforts. And so I feel bound to say that I often feel as though the ideal after which his fine intellect strives is rather that of the master of form as opposed to mannerism, the great Sebastian on the one hand, and Schubert's folk music on the other, than Schumann's deep, noble and delightful subjectivity, which he undoubtedly reveres with love and gratitude as few others do.

But to what lengths have I been led by a simple answer to a suggestion for a concert! Forgive the digression, which will have kept you only too long from pleasanter matters! Please give my sincerest regards to your wife. I look forward with pleasure to seeing her and enjoying her playing again. I count for certain on hearing from you when your wife is passing through here. Then perhaps I can make more definite arrangements with her, if it is only at the station. In any case I shall speak to Count Platen beforehand about it. The concert dates are not fixed yet, but the middle of December would probably fit in best.

And now, do not be angry with me for my refusal, behind which is concealed no party feelings or other trivial motives. I wish we could play together amicably and to our mutual enjoyment, as we used to do in Hanover, instead of squabbling by letter; that would be more sensible! Is there no prospect of it? A few friendly words, dear Bronsart, would give great pleasure to your sincerely devoted

JOSEPH JOACHIM.

*To Clara Schumann*

[HANOVER, *October* 15, 1861.]

Dear Friend—I was introduced to young Spohr[1] at your house by Laub, who thinks very highly of him. His technique is excellent, and it is only a pity that the poor young man makes such a miserable impression with his sickly, overgrown appearance. I really cannot say how he gives lessons; you know yourself that a man can play very well without having any talent as a teacher, and vice versa! Although I should love to help Lixchen to find a master, I cannot take the responsibility of advising on the matter. Do you know Wendt in Bellevue-Strasse? I credit him with a certain pedagogic cleverness, and even though he does not play like a virtuoso himself, I think he would have an agreeable way of making a little chap keen on playing and of bringing him on. I should be almost inclined to advise that he should be tried for six months.

And now I have a request to make, namely, that you will let me know as soon as possible whether you can play at our second concert on November 30. The first is on November 16, and I must start them by playing then, so that Platen may not think I am drawing my salary for nothing. But if you could *not* play for us at the second concert, I should have a reason for putting off *my* performance until the second concert. That could be arranged. Platen agreed warmly to the suggestion that you should be invited. When are you going to Hamburg? Are you passing through here by any chance in time for our 2nd Quartette on Saturday? I wrote a long letter to Johannes to-day

[1] Afterwards conductor of the Royal Orchestra at Berlin; no relation to L. Spohr.

and sent back his quartettes[1] which I enjoyed very much. I hope we shall soon *hear* them. The disagreeables I mentioned the other day must have been physical. But if I complained of Hanover, the theme is one which always produces discomfort from time to time, even although nothing special is referred to. I have better news from the Grimms.

Remember me to them when you get there, and also to all your dear children.—Yours,     JOSEPH J.

### To Clara Schumann

[HANOVER, *October* 19, 1861.]

. . . I am in good spirits because I have a pleasant commission to carry out. It ought really to be done with much ceremony, but my pen will not be restrained and insists on coming straight to the point. It is this, I am to ask you (in the names of the *King* and *Queen*) whether you would care to undertake to give the princesses piano lessons for six months from December 1 of this year or from January 1862. Their Majesties are most anxious that you should, and to make it possible suggest: 1st, free residence, 2nd, a salary of 2000 thalers. If you should wish for two or three days' leave from time to time, so as to give concerts in the neighbourhood, no objection would be raised. On your side it would be understood that you would play at their Majesties' private soirées. The idea originated with the Queen, who told me a fortnight ago how glad she would be if the princesses' good musical abilities could be developed by you. I have heard more of the matter since then from Fräulein v. d. Gabelentz, and to-day, through the same channel, I was definitely *commissioned* to approach you. For

[1] Piano Quartettes, op. 25 and 26.

this reason please be so good as to word your reply so that I can show it to Frl. v. d. Gtz., who takes the greatest interest in the matter.

I need hardly tell you with what suspense I await your decision.  Do not delay too long, dear friend.—Yours,

J. J.

### From Clara Schumann

HAMBURG, *November* 3, 1861.

Dear Joachim—Before I mention anything else I must press your hand once more for having given us such great pleasure by coming here.  I only realised when you had gone that I had not thanked you nearly enough—you always avoid such things so charmingly, and yet it is such a pleasure to express them.

The enclosed is, to my own grief, a letter of refusal. But I realise more and more clearly that I cannot accept such a post *now*.  I still feel the power in me—whether luckily for me or not I hardly know—to work in public, and so I should feel discontented in a position of that kind.  You know all the larger reasons.  It has been very difficult for me to come to this decision in view of the fact that I could have been with you for some time.  How many delightful hours I should have enjoyed with you, and what glorious music I should have heard!  But I do not renounce the hope that a kindly fate will bring us all together one day—I will seek strength by clinging to that.

Read the enclosed letter, and if you approve of it, send it; but if you find anything to object to in it, let me know. . . .

*From Clara Schumann*

LEIPZIG, *December* 15, 1861.
*In the evening.*

Dear Joachim—I must just write to you to-day ; I know you will rejoice with me.   I was most successful yesterday with Johannes' Var., and they received enthusiastic applause, recalls, etc.   The people with whom I spoke had to admit, at any rate, that they are "interesting," although I found, as I always do, that the professional musicians are the most difficult to approach—they cannot rejoice impartially in the fact that some one is writing good stuff again ; they hardly care to admit that there is anything in it !   I could cite instances, but I will keep them to tell you by word of mouth.   At all events they all have at least respect for these Var.; the rest will follow later.   Meanwhile I am delighted that it should be so.

The Mozart concert the other day went off very well, much better than I had expected, except that R[einecke] had the misfortune not to come in with the orchestra after the Cadenza, which brought me very roughly to earth.   The rest went very well, but I could not feel happy any more.   I had the great pleasure of hearing my Robert's songs for mixed voices, which R. has rehearsed charmingly, and which delighted the audience.   The *Zigeunerleben* with Grädener's instrumentation sounded splendid—I could hardly believe it was the same thing I had heard in Cologne, when it all sounded as dull as possible.

I saw the Röntgens, dear artistic people, to-day, and I am expecting them this evening, when we are to have some music.   Unfortunately he is very much out of health at present, but he played so beautifully at the Gewandhaus the other day that everybody still speaks of it with enthusiasm, to my great delight. If only he could be where he deserves to be! I am glad he is giving up the theatre—it goes against the grain too much with him.

Now that I see once more how matters stand here, I am very glad after all that you are not here. You only have one person to deal with in H. at any rate, and here you would have several who would drive any one to distraction. I shall be quite miserable now if you give up your post, and I still think you could spend the whole of your five months' leave in work somewhere else, could earn something between times during the winter, and would have no need of England or of any one else. I suppose it is stupid of me to return to this subject again, but it is so often in my thoughts!

The Röntgens have just come. I am to send you their kindest regards, and to say that your room is always ready for you.

Marie wrote to me the other day about Laub's playing of your Concerto; I had better write it down: "You could tell that he had studied it with the greatest love and devotion, but he lacks all the qualities which make Joachim's playing so delightful, so sympathetic, and so superlatively beautiful. His tone has neither the grace nor the soul, and you can imagine my feelings when I had to listen to Laub's playing of this magnificent Concerto; although his technique was really masterly, one felt that he had not mastered it."

*D. 16.*

I could not finish yesterday, as I did not like to keep the Röntgens waiting too long. We played Robert's D minor Sonata, and Röntgen's delicate, soulful playing gave me real pleasure. I could grow very fond of both of them, and I wish I could live in the same town with them ; the wife would be such a friend as I have always wished to have, an eager, artistic nature, and at the same time a loving wife and a splendid mother. I think her heart is big enough to hold everything, and strong too. I am going to see them again to-morrow—I wish I could do so oftener but, as you know, I cannot call a single minute my own here.

So good-bye, dear, good Joachim. Let me hear from you soon. A thousand greetings from yours,

CLARA SCH.

## To Th. Avé-Lallemant

[HANOVER, *middle of February* 1862.]

Dear Avé—It was a great pleasure to us both[1] to get your letter, and we are much interested in what you say about the *Josua*. The performance at Aix-la-Chapelle was most impressive too, but I do not know who did the orchestration.[2] Perhaps nowhere is intellectual greatness, combined with descriptive powers of an intensely sensuous nature, presented with such simplicity as in Händel's works. In the passage where everything begins to quiver and sway, you feel, with a shudder of fear, that you are not safe in your own seat! There could hardly be a greater contrast than the work I am practising for the next concert at Count Platen's request : Berlioz' Scherzo, *Fee Mab*! Everything in this is for effect. But I think I shall enjoy studying it, all the same. . . .

[1] Brahms and Joachim.　　　　　　[2] Julius Rietz.

*To Clara Schumann*

[LONDON] *March* 6 [1862].

Dear Frau Schumann — Since I parted from Johannes on the 24th of last month [1] I suppose I am cut off from all chance of hearing from you unless I specially beg you to write. I have no idea where or how you are living! Hiller told me you were at Karlsruhe and that you would be there for a few days. I read in the papers that you are expected in *Paris!* You told me once, in the winter, that you would like to go with me to see the London Exhibition. Shall I speak to Ella, Chappel, Bennett, etc., and tell them you are coming for the season *for certain?* Otherwise it will, of course, be very difficult to fix up engagements.

But, in any case, please let me have news of you and yours very soon. Is Julchen better again? I hear the poor child has been really ill. I am very well now that I have got over a horrible crossing. I do not regret having come over here; my little room is very comfortable, with a fine Broadwood in it, and Rabe's [2] comic, friendly face has accompanied me. My address is: 40 St. James's Place, St. James's Street. I saw Miss Busby the other day, and the Lehmanns, [3] at whose house I am to dine with *Dickens* next Tuesday. But I could only give very unsatisfactory answers to the 1000 questions with regard to Mme. Sch. put by them and many others. Please avail yourself soon of my address, so that things may be different, and I need not blush when people ask after you, as though we had quarrelled. That is not

---

[1] At Hanover, when he went to Cologne and on February 25 played his Hungarian Concerto at the Gesellschafts-Konzert there.

[2] Joachim's servant.          [3] Rudolf Lehmann.

as it should be. I want to tell you about Gade[1] and other news from Hanover, and so I hope to hear from you before long whither I am to direct my thoughts. It is unsatisfactory to launch letters into space without any definite goal, as I daresay you have experienced too.

Schuberth has asked me for permission to print my arrangement of the *Abendlied*. I consented on condition that he does not advertise it and simply prints in small letters, in brackets, on the title page of the piece: "Arranged for the violin, etc., by J. Joachim." Do you agree to this? Schuberth is waiting for an answer, so you *must* write a line soon.

Goodbye for the present!—Yours most devotedly,

JOSEPH JOACHIM.

### To Bernhard Scholz

[LONDON, *March* 13, 1862.]

Dear Scholz—It is more than a fortnight since I left Hanover and I have done a great deal since then, but, alas, I have had absolutely no news of my friends over there. I suppose you are revelling in fancy-dress and other balls? Or are you composing? Or are you away? Or do you sleep[2] until later than 8 o'clock? I am having a very good time; I am playing a great deal, in fact the other evening I procured a wraith for myself, as I had promised to play at St. James's and the Hanover Square Rooms at the same time! Seriously, I drove to and fro twice so as to fulfil my obligation, as you will see from the enclosed programme. I played my own Concerto yesterday evening. The second and last movements

[1] Gade had called on Joachim at Hanover in the middle of February and had there made the acquaintance of Brahms and his Piano Quartette.

[2] A reference to Mendelssohn's *Elijah*.

went very well, but the first was not sufficiently rehearsed.   But the audience was very kind, most of
the musicians in London were amongst the 2000 who
were present, I am glad to say.   People treat me
here as though I were an old friend, with sympathy
and cordiality, and that is always pleasant.   The only
thing which stands in the way of faultless performances
here is lack of time.   The capabilities of the orchestras
of several societies are unusually good.   And our (or
rather your) Hanoverian orchestra could not *read*
better.   But it remains at that, unless the members of
the orchestra get to know certain things by heart
through repeated performances.   I heard Mendelssohn's
*Lobgesang* the other day at Exeter Hall.   The chorus
was very steady and powerful, but had no delicacy.
*Israel* is to be performed there to-morrow.   It has
entered into the very flesh and blood of the people
here and it will be very fine, I hope.   I suppose you
are in the midst of rehearsals of that work.   I am to
hear Dickens read to-night.   I made his acquaintance
at dinner the day before yesterday, and I was delighted
with his vigorous, unaffected manner; a contrast to
my neighbour on my right, who was none other than
*Bulwer*.   What would I not have given for your wife's
album?   *There was an occasion ! ! !* [1]   B. is pedantic,
vain and affected, not uninteresting, of course, with
*haut goût blasé*.   Dear friend forgive this scrawl, but
if I do not send these hasty lines I run the risk of not
writing at all and of not hearing from any of you in
consequence.

Remember me to Miss Henny and Buba and all
my friends, Nicola, Brinkmann, Kaulbach, Eyertts.

I have not had a word from the King ; I call it
discourteous.—Yours sincerely,                      J. J.

---

[1] Written in English in the original.—TR.

Rabe's[1] tongue is beginning to be loosened; he croaks English, which does not make him any less amusing.    He is on the broad grin because I have told him I am writing to the Scholzes.

## To Clara Schumann

[LONDON] *the 20th* [*March* 1862].

Dear Frau Schumann—I have rarely been so taken aback as I was by the confirmation from you of your arrival in Paris; because neither Johannes nor I had taken the reports in the newspapers seriously.    I am very curious already as to what kind of a success you will have to tell me about.    The Parisians are said to be very experienced critics of virtuoso playing, and so you will have enthusiastic audiences at any rate.    It must be very pleasant for you, besides, to see something of Frau Erard and Frau Viardot. Please remember me to both these ladies.    I should like to see the Louvre and some of the smaller theatres again myself.    I was rather too young twelve years ago to appreciate Paris properly.

Your first concert there, of which I hope to have news before long, must be to-day; I suppose your plans will largely be based on that.    What you say about London so far sounds, alas, as though there were little chance of my welcoming you here!    Meanwhile, as soon as I got your letter I spoke to Chappell's, Ella and Bennett.    Unless you have *definitely* decided to come to London, it is quite impossible to get engagements, however gladly they would be offered to you, no doubt, if you were sure of coming.    I could only arrange about six engagements for you for certain, to start with, with the Musical Union, the

1 *Rabe* means "raven."

Popular Concerts, and the old Philharmonic. The new one and the Musical Society of London would probably follow suit, and no doubt many others besides; but you cannot possibly expect all the people who give concerts to hold a meeting so as to get together a round number of engagements and offer them to you. It would have been rather different if you had already promised at the beginning of winter to spend the season here.

Whether the latter will be "brilliant" does not seem certain, but it will certainly be an interesting time, and I am looking forward to the stimulus which the Exhibition will bring in its train. As you are so near you ought, in any case, to come over with Fräulein Marie for a fortnight in May and see the Exhibition; the Benzons, who have just returned, would be delighted to put you up, I have no doubt. At any rate that is what her brother, Lehmann, thinks. I do not know the Benzons myself but I have got their address . . . so as to make enquiries on your behalf. My Concerto really was a success at the Musical Society this time, at least the two last movements, which were well accompanied, but one or two little mistakes occurred in the first movement.

I can tell you nothing about Hanover as yet; the King has not replied to my request for leave.

### To Clara Schumann

[LONDON, *April* 1, 1862.]

Dear Frau Schumann—You will be surprised when I tell you that I am going to Hanover from May 21 to 30th, so as to conduct a concert there in honour of the King's birthday on the 27th! The Queen entreated me, through Fräulein v. d. Gabelentz, so kindly

and urgently not to spoil her notion of "surprising"
the King in this way, that I could not possibly have
been so ungallant as to say "No"; although I know
that by doing this I shall bring down on my head all
sorts of unpleasant explanations with regard to my
application for a two years' leave. But I intend to
remain firm, the more so as even the thought of the
little town with all its formalities makes me shudder.
But this business of the surprise is between ourselves.

I am very well; you know how much at home I
feel here, and my only and constant regret is that the
dark side of the life here has not been made bearable
to you, as to me, by the conjunction of happy memories!
I should so like to advise you strongly to come here
in any case; but I must not do so because it would be
too selfish of me! I have talked to the elder Broadwood,[1] too, and he also is of the opinion that it is still
uncertain whether the effect of the Exhibition on the
concerts will be favourable or unfavourable. He
hopes very much that you will come, and is genuinely
interested, but he says every foreign artist must run a
certain risk unless he comes regularly every year. I
think Ella has written to you himself. Chappell's
would engage you for two of the " Popular Concerts,"
and for others if these concerts are continued weekly,
as will probably be the case. I hope the name
" Popular Concerts " will not alarm you ; it arises from
the fact that some seats are sold at a shilling, so as to
enable those who are not well off to attend. Only the
very best Chamber music is played, from the latest
Beethoven to the earliest Haydn, before an audience
of over 2000, and here Apollo certainly sheds his
golden rays over just and unjust alike! How nice of
the Parisians to be so grateful to you, and to under-

[1] The piano manufacturer.

R

stand you! Yes, music played with reverence is a power; the better the works of the great masters of Vienna are understood by the artists and played with conviction, the more widely will music be diffused. It attracts the amateurs, and thus these ripples circle further and further into the sensibilities of mankind. I realise this here when I compare the present with ten years ago. Even though there is a certain amount of affectation about it in individual cases! How is Johannes? I cannot correspond regularly here with the best will in the world, but I will write to him in a day or two. The Benzons were in Paris at the same time as you and did not know that you were there.

At Marie Benecke's [1] the other day (the 28th) we celebrated what would have been the Mendelssohns' silver wedding by playing three of his quartettes. I was strangely and deeply impressed, and my heart was warmed through and through by many a luminous passage in these works, which, as I thought of him, seemed to me to be part of his fine and pure humanity.

Good-bye, dear Frau Schumann! Remember me to Fräulein Marie; and think of my sincere devotion if you feel inclined to be vexed with me sometimes.

J. J.

### To Frau Marie Benecke

[LONDON, *April* 8, 1862.]

Dear Frau Benecke—I was genuinely grieved to hear that neither you nor your husband are coming with me to Manchester. It would have been too charming if we could have changed the "professional" journey into a pleasure trip! The other day I wandered in vain through the Crystal Palace trying to

---

[1] Felix Mendelssohn's eldest daughter, who married Victor Benecke.

meet you; but I must not fail to congratulate you, although somewhat late, on the success of your protégé,[1] who has the good fortune to be introduced into the musical world as your godchild.    Much in Sullivan's music attracted me.    Strength and originality will no doubt increase with the years (seeing that the young man has such a grasp of the subject and such skill in handling his material) and produce delightful work.

With kindest regards to Herr Benecke.—I am, Yours very sincerely,      JOSEPH JOACHIM.

### From Clara Schumann

PARIS, *April* 9, '62.

Dear Friend—Your delightful letter would have been answered sooner, but I have been fearfully busy and am really quite worn out now.    I have to play every night this week, and the Soirées in the small rooms at such a high temperature are more tiring than all the concerts put together.    I am now able to tell you about my last concert and the one at the Conservatoire. Everything went off very well at the Conservatoire, and there was a perfect storm of applause after the Beethoven Concerto.    Yesterday was quite satisfactory, too.    I played Robert's Quartette, and Armingaud's Quartette accompanied me beautifully.    It strikes me as remarkable that Maurin's Quartette is much more highly thought of here, and it is surely not a very hopeful sign as regards taste; in my opinion it is not to be compared to Armingaud's.    Maurin delights in violent contrasts, he either draws out the notes or else he suddenly saws away on a few notes, without the least comprehension of the music, until it is horrible to

---

[1] Arthur Sullivan, then twenty years of age, was the first to hold the Mendelssohn scholarship.

listen to! I think Armingaud's Quartette is so full of feeling, but people tell me that is only when they are playing with me. At any rate, Armingaud and Lalo (viola) are cultivated musicians, whilst Maurin is really stupid. But this is for your ear alone. I am being very cautious here, and catch myself exercising a diplomacy which surprises me. But it is only too necessary, for the gossip here is as bad as in any little town. . . .

### To Clara Schumann

LONDON, *April* 15, 1862.

Dear Frau Schumann—So you have decided not to come! Sorry as I am *personally* I am consoled to a certain extent by the thought that you would have had to face a great deal of fatigue if you had come to the Exhibition. A great many acquaintances have come together already, and some very pleasant ones : Karl Mendelssohn[1] whom I have just seen. In an hour's time Marie's friend, Helene Figdor,[2] will be arriving with her father and brother. But to come to the most important matter ; your protégé.[3]

If you think it is absolutely *necessary* to his happiness that he should leave Paris now and come here, I will of course do all I can to help him to carry out his plans. But I would just point out that the Exhibition season will be a very exciting one for a young man, and likely to distract him from his studies. If he goes everywhere and does everything (or at least a great deal) it will cost a lot ; and, on the other hand, to live in London and think of nothing but one's studies, whilst other people are seeing

[1] Felix Mendelssohn's son, a well-known historian. Died 1897.
[2] Joachim's cousin, engaged to the oculist O. Becker of Heidelberg.
[3] The violinist Rose, who was studying in Paris at that time.

interesting things and enjoying themselves, would
have depressed me very much as a young man.
Added to this, *my* time is very much taken up, not
only by concerts, but also by a host of friends and
acquaintances from various places ; relations, artists
from *Vienna*, Scholz (in June), etc., for whom I
suppose I shall have to procure as many tickets as I
can.   Take all this into consideration and remember,
too, that hearing music is not everything !   If, after
this, you still think young Rose ought to come here,
I will, as I said, do all in my power to help him.   I
cannot advise him.   I know nothing of the young
man's talent or character, and I should not like to
take upon myself the responsibility of having caused
him to take this step.

Shall I suggest that you should come to Hanover
for May 26 ?   I am sure the King could not have
a surprise that would give him more pleasure ; and
the Queen only did not think of you because she
was too diffident, of that I am convinced.   Are you
going to the Cologne Festival ?   If so you could
combine the two ; you did not seem disinclined to
do so !   I am rejoicing with you in spirit over all
the good fortune which is falling to your lot !

With kindest regards to you and Fräulein Marie,

JOSEPH J.

### From Bernhard Scholz

HANOVER, *April* 16, 1862.

Dear, dear Friend—How glad we were to get
your letter !   It came at breakfast-time to-day, was
greeted with cries of joy, and its cheering effects will
last for a long time.   It was high time, too, because
the temperature here is low, in more than one respect.

I am counting the days until your return. We want to make the most of your short stay; the only pity is that my dear wife will not be able to enjoy much of your company just then. I am looking forward tremendously to our time together in London, too; when I first heard that you were coming back so soon, I was quite alarmed because I thought you did not intend to return to Old England, and that I should be in London without you. So now my pleasure is twofold.

Platen knows nothing, as yet, of your return; I will tell him at once, or else he will think me a conspirator. I do not believe he was the originator of that questionable article, but I think he and Fischer have intrigued together, and that your return will be very displeasing to both of them. . . .

If you are writing to Fräulein Gabelentz about the concert tell her *too* that you want *my* help and not F.'s, otherwise the disagreeable fellow will be mixed up in it after all; but if my help is requested from high quarters direct, Platen will not dare to drag in F.

The question of leave is sure to be settled reasonably; the only bad thing about it up to now has been that you did not approach the King in person, P. spoilt it all, and now there is the added pity that your stay here will be too short to arrange for you to discuss the matter properly with the King. Meanwhile, he is anything but annoyed with you, he spoke of you to Stockhausen and myself the other day with the greatest kindness. As for the Queen, she is really grieved about the matter; she is a good woman and he is . . . a King! *Ayez pitié! Misericordia!!* Think what you will of my representations, reproaches and suggestions with regard to your application for

leave, but do not forget for a moment that I am
your sincere friend.  We will *talk* over the matter
when once you are here.

Have you no orders with regard to the concert?
What wind instruments do you want?   All the firsts?
Shall I speak to Platen about it?   Or will you write
to him yourself?

Are *you* writing to Stockhausen?   Or shall I?

Remember me to your brother.   Tell Rabe I
hope he is looking after you well and keeping an
eye on you, and that I am coming to inspect matters
before long.

A thousand greetings across the sea (*via* Ostende)
from yours,                                    Scholz.


### From Clara Schumann

PARIS, *April* 27, 1862.   *Sunday.*

Dear Joachim—The bearer of this, Herr Rose,
longs so ardently to have at any rate one *interview*
with you that he has decided to go to London for a
few days and discuss plans for the future with you,
as he realises quite well that nothing can be done
at present.   I need not ask you to receive him
kindly, as you would do that in any case.

After much persuasion I gave a fourth concert
this week which went off very well, Stockhausen sang
beautifully, and Madame Viardot played Robert's
Variations for two pianos with me delightfully.   But
what has pleased me more than anything is that I
have inspired respect for Johannes in people here,
that is, in the best people.   Most of them spoke
contemptuously of him, but they either knew nothing
of his, or else only the Serenades or one or other of
the Sonatas, which they did not understand.   You

can imagine how this upset me, so the other day
I invited a few musicians to come to see me, so
that I might play them *nothing but* Brahms. It was
rather difficult, at first, to arouse their interest, but
they warmed up with the Sextette, and finally, after
the Variations, they were fairly alight, and Szarvady,
in particular, begged me to play them again before
a larger number of people. So to-night I am giving
a little Soirée for artists *only*, first Robert's Trio in
D minor, then Johannes' Variations, and then I hope
Stockhausen will sing some of Johannes' songs.
The German Choral Society is going to do the
*Harfenlieder.* This makes me feel happy the live-
long day, more especially as it was extremely difficult
to carry the matter through 'in the midst of such a
lot of tiring work, and with such limited time. I
could not even practise the Variations.

I was delighted to hear that you played Johannes'
Sextette not long ago. Heller wrote enthusiastically
to Damke about it. So we have each done our
share. You know I never like to force the works
of those I care for on any one, but I could not help
it in this case, it was like a burden on my heart day
after day! . . .

Goodbye, dear friend. All good wishes from your
faithful                                    CL. SCH.

### To Otto Goldschmidt

[LONDON, *probably the summer of* 1862.]

Dear Goldschmidt—On returning to my rooms
after a concert I found the enclosed envelope containing fifteen guineas. I do not understand this at
all! You must recollect that we agreed that my
services at the concert for the lady artists were not

offered for money but in aid of the good cause. I have never been accustomed to receive money when I have played for a philanthropic object, and I do not wish to begin to do so in England. You must have forgotten to tell the committee of the F. A. Society this, and I hope you will realise that, as friend and artist, you owe it to me to make good this oversight. —Yours sincerely, JOSEPH JOACHIM.

### To Otto Goldschmidt

[LONDON, *summer of* 1862.]

Dear Goldschmidt—I have been in Manchester, and I will ask you to accept this excuse for not having answered your letter sooner. I count absolutely on your returning the fee intended for me to the Committee of the F. A. Society—the ladies owe me nothing. At your request, on behalf of the Society, I took part in the concert, on the *clear understanding* that I was giving my services for this good object (which was, from what you told me, to enable the lady artists to continue to exhibit their work, which they would not otherwise be able to do in the future) and not for the money which you have been so good as to offer me. If the ladies of the Committee could not or would not accept my services on those terms, if they did not wish to permit me to follow your wife's noble example, I ought to have been told so *before* the concert; in that case, of course, I and my music would have ceased to intrude.

The unpleasant incident of having received a fee for my services cannot, of course, spoil my pleasure in the memory of having played with you and your wife. It will always be a delight to me to prove this to you by deeds!—Yours sincerely, JOSEPH JOACHIM.

*From Stephen Heller*

PARIS, *June* 8, 1862.

Dear Joachim—I should have written to you from Paris in any case, even if I had not had a special reason for doing so, which I will tell you presently. Since I have been in Paris I have often thought of your idea of spending part of the summer here and determined to write frankly to you about it. Paris seems to me very comfortable, pleasant and charming. It is not so grand as London, but it is gayer, and the people look neither so taken up with making money and succeeding nor so insolently rich as so many of both classes (the working [artists] and the leisure classes) look in London. All the same, I think the *good* Englishman is more cordial, honest and sincere, but, the ignorant, unpleasant Englishman, on the other hand, is far below any Frenchmen of the same species ; you never meet one of the latter so lacking in all graciousness and *bonhomie* as are certain bizarre and aggravating Englishmen. Besides the quiet sincerity and unpretentious manners of the *Guten im Lande,*[1] I miss all that rich green which you get in the parks and squares and gardens. The heat is intense and I dread July and August. My new lodging is pretty and cool and comfortable. The only drawback is a piano mistress who lives on the 4th floor, and gives lessons the whole day long ; her satanic pupils destroy all one's pleasure in music. I cannot hear it much in my study, but in my bedroom I am roused from the sweetest dreams of Beethoven by miserable strumming.

And now for my request. My friend Berthold

---

[1] The good men of the country.

Damcke is going with his wife at the end of June to
Hanover, his native town, to spend a month there
with his 80-year old mother.    Many years ago he
played the 'cello in the orchestra there, and afterwards
for 12 years in St. Petersburg, where he gave lessons
in composition and harmony and was very intimate
with Rubinstein and Henselt.    Now he is settled in
Paris, where he gives lessons and is very highly
thought of.    He would like to take the opportunity
of being in Hanover to play his Trio or his Sonata for
piano and violoncello before the King, who saw him
years ago and gave him a gold medal in return for
a dedication.    What do you think?    Is he likely to be
granted the favour of playing something before the
King?    And could you give him a letter to some
influential person which might be of use to him?
You can recommend the Trio and the 'cello Sonata as
excellent and scholarly works on my responsibility.
They have been played at concerts here by Mme.
Viardot - Garcia herself, and most appreciatively
received.    Both these works are far above the
*Veillée*, which you know, and have been accepted
here.
      You know enough.    I know you too well to doubt
for a moment your willingness to help my friend.    If
you care to write a letter, send it to me.    I miss you
very much, dear Joachim, and the thought of our last
intimate talk gives me a kind of melancholy pleasure.
I count my closer acquaintance with you as one of the
gains of my trip to England.    I hope your thoughts
of me are equally kind.
      Good-bye.    May you delight many more by your
rare talent!—Yours very sincerely,
                                    STEPHEN HELLER.

*From Clara Schumann*

MÜNSTER AM STEIN, *July* 1, 1862.

Dear Joachim—I see quite well that I shall not hear from you for a long time, unless I write to you again and beg you please to remember your German friend sometimes! I have been hoping for a letter from week to week, especially on the 8th of June, when I thought you would think of my Robert and so of me, but in vain! It is indeed hard to have no news of those dear to one, except through the newspapers, and you ought to bear that in mind sometimes, dear friend!—

I take it for granted that you are still delighting the ears of the English, but it would give me twice as much pleasure to hear it from you, and besides I should hear other things as well: for instance, when you intend to return to us? What your plans are for the summer? When you have to go back to Hanover? I heard quite by chance the other day that the King has secured you once more. I realised then how egotistic I can be, because, although I was half sorry for many reasons, yet I was more glad than sorry. The thought of you living always in England was too melancholy. Rose wrote me a long letter six weeks ago full of enthusiasm for you, and I was delighted to hear how cordial you had been to the warm-hearted fellow—although I know quite well you would have done just the same without my recommendation. Yet I must thank you. Perhaps I had something to do with your having received him so cordially *from the first*, after all. I hope very much that he will go to you in Hanover in the winter—I could not imagine anything better for him.

So far I can give a good account of myself, although I had grave trouble when I was in Berlin in

May, and I am still anxious, especially on Julie's
account. I must do all I can this summer to make
her stronger. I have come, as you see, to Münster
am Stein, with her and Marie and Eugenie, for treatment. It is delightful here. You must remember
Ebernburg and Rheingrafenstein? I can see the
latter from my balcony right in front of me. Fräulein
Leser is here too, and so we are a cosy family party.
After the Musical Festival at Cologne Johannes,
[Albert] Dietrich and Woldemar came here. The
last named is spending the whole of his holidays
(until July 14) here; Johannes and Dietrich spent a
fortnight here and lived right in the country in a house
at the foot of Ebernburg. They liked it so much that
they were very loth to go. Johannes regretted that
he had not brought any real work with him so as not
to loaf about, which he cannot stand for long, as you
know. They all left the day before yesterday (Herr
von Sahr had joined them) for a walking tour in the
Palatinate; they have had very bad weather, I am sorry
to say, and here it is more like autumn than summer.

   Johannes sent me a little time ago — only fancy
how surprised I was — the first movement of a
Symphony [1] with this bold opening :

etc.

---

[1] The beginning of the 1st Symphony in C minor, which appeared in 1877.

That is rather tough, certainly, but I soon got used to it. The movement is full of wonderfully beautiful passages, and the motives are handled in the masterly fashion which he is making more and more his own. It is all interwoven in such an interesting way, and yet it goes with such a swing that it might have all been poured forth in the first moment of inspiration; one can enjoy every note of it without being reminded of the work there is in it. He has succeeded in making another splendid transition from the second part back again to the first. Besides this he sent me *Magelonenlieder*, some of which I like very much, others not so much. I suppose you know his Variations for four hands on Robert's last theme? Those, again, are magnificent! When he came here himself and played all this and many things besides, as well as playing with me the D minor Quartette, C major Quintette and Octette of Schubert's several times, I was very happy.

Who knows at what busy moment you will receive this letter, so I will cut it short!

Only this one word more about myself. I shall be here until July 18 and then, after staying for a few days with the Schroedters at Karlsruhe, I am going straight to the Rigi, where I shall stay until the end of August. I may take a trip through the Bernese Oberland, during which I shall be sure to think of you very often and *wish* a great many things, and after that I do not yet know what I shall do.

Woldemar, who was not at all well—in fact I feel really anxious about him—wishes to be remembered to you. You dare not let him see you think him ill. The air here is doing him a lot of good, too, if only he had not to go back into the traces so soon!

*From Stephen Heller*

PARIS, *July* 3, 1862.

Dear Joachim—. . . Carry out your resolution to play here this winter. You will be satisfied. You will find Damcke a cultured, intellectual man, and his wife a woman of unusual charm and goodness. You will like them and be at ease with them.

I sometimes read the third column of the *Times* to see if the concerts are still continuing. I always see your name and Hallé's, and I feel as though I must put on a white tie and go to St. James's Hall! Whoever went with you two joined in your music! The realm of white ties no longer exists for me; I go about like a ragamuffin here and rejoice in my shabbiness: old coats, old straw hats, wide trousers adorn my waistcoatless body, and an English servant would refuse to announce me.

Goodbye; take a rest, shake off all Full Dress (both mental and physical) and give a friendly thought to yours very sincerely,          STEPHEN HELLER.

*To Herman Grimm*

[LONDON] *Tuesday, the* 15*th* [ *July* 1862].

Dear Herman—Be so good as to let me know whether I am to send the rest of the M[ichel] A[ngelo] MS. to Freiburg, " Poste Restante." I am afraid of trusting the manuscript to the post without being sure it will come straight into your hands. I am beginning to take breath, and I shall never bind myself again to play at so many concerts in succession. I am going to spend a few months in the country not far from London, and I am looking forward to it. Last week I spent two days in Dickens's house, near Rochester, an hour's railway journey.  You and Gisel would enjoy being there ; the house stands on Gadshill, where Falstaff's knavery, of jovial memory, took place.  As soon as I am assured with my own eyes (by means of your handwriting) of your presence at Freiburg, I will write more.—Always yours,        JOSEPH J.

### From H. W. Ernst

NICE, *July* 17, 1862.

Dearest Friend—I have already requestedChorley,[1] Hallé and Chappell to express my thanks generally to all those who have been so kind and sympathetic to me.[2]

You are in the first rank of these, so let me embrace you warmly and give you a brother's thanks for your brotherly conduct.

You honoured me, too, in this, and I cannot tell you how happy it has made me to realise that your friendly action has not lessened your reputation as an artist.  But as no pleasure is complete in this world, I still feel the deepest regret that I have not heard myself through *you* : who knows if this pleasure will ever be mine, and my regret is all the greater when I think that this strength-giving source was close to me in Vienna, but that the modern law-giver of violin-playing refused to wave his magic wand.  You have shown, too, that you are a greater magician than your illustrious predecessor, for you have worked the wonder of causing my mouth to water *here* when you wielded your magic bow in *London*.  Write to me

---

[1] Writer on music.  Contributor to the *Athenaeum*.

[2] On June 23 a Monday Popular Concert had been given for the benefit of Ernst, who was suffering from an incurable illness.  At this concert Joachim, Laub, Molique and Piatti played a string quartette by Ernst, whose *Elegie* was also played by Joachim.

soon, as your brother promised. Nothing gives me comfort or courage save the conviction that those for whom my heart has always been, and still is, full of love and admiration have not grown indifferent towards me. I have been rather better again for the last few days. I have less pain, and the weather is so glorious that I can go on with my sea bathing without interruption. I hope I shall obtain some relief and sufficient strength, at any rate, to enable me to get through the winter fairly well. Not a thing has been found out about the robbery at our house; but the probability of its having been done by our servant seems more and more evident, now that it is too late. She left us nearly a month ago, however, and the police do not seem anxious to start a fresh enquiry. Apropos of this robbery, I forgot to reply to the charming and intelligent Heinrich's (I do not mean myself but your Heinrich) remark that it just proved how well and soundly I slept. My answer to that is that such a thing could never happen to a child of fortune like himself, that it takes an unlucky wretch like me to be awake the whole night until a quarter past four and then, when the thief was presumably growing impatient, to turn over and fall asleep from sheer weariness and pain— and allow his watch and other valuables to be stolen from his bed-table before his very behind. If it was a professional thief it was probably lucky that I did not turn round and face him at the moment. I can laugh over it now, because in life all unpleasant impressions grow weaker, thank God, but I can assure you that I did not have a moment's peace during the night for a week after this unfortunate occurrence. As all this is addressed more to your brother than to yourself, I will send him word to be more charitable next time something like this happens (and I hope it will fall to

S

his lot and not mine) and *Goimel zu benschen*[1] for this time (I expect he will know what that means).

I entreat you, once more, to write to me, and if you have composed anything new send it to me, together with your Concerto in D minor, which you promised me in Vienna.

God be with you. Your faithful, affectionate and admiring friend and brother, H. W. ERNST.

As you are sure to see the Klingemanns and the Horsleys, remember me very kindly to them. My wife sends her kindest regards to you and your brother, and says you are to tell the latter that she considered he owed it to his friendship for us to have sung *Wilikens* at the concert in the masterly style we admire so much—*il vous aurait certainement tous enfoncés.*

## To Clara Schumann

[LONDON] *July* 18 [1862].

Dear Frau Schumann—One stage of your journey to Switzerland must be passed, whilst I am still held fast in the midst of London by those fetters which the season throws over all who give themselves up to it, *nolens volens*! I have undertaken to play here again on the 28th and 29th, and then I am free, thank Heaven, as I have refused all offers to tour in the provinces. My plan is to go into the country somewhere quite near London, to Norwood perhaps, and stay there for some time, so as to work and also to acquire a better knowledge of London's art treasures

---

[1] *Gaumel*, or *gomel benschen*, is an expression used by German Jews and means a short prayer of thanksgiving for having been saved from danger or restored from a serious illness. A prayer of this kind was recited by those who had been cured or saved after the invocation to Thora, and the congregation joined in the responses.

and of the Exhibition. I long to go to Switzerland again, it is true, where I enjoyed myself so much last year—but I dread moving from place to place so much, it would end in making me restless. I am so well that I have no need of change or mountain air, however much I should like to hear the thunder of the avalanches again! Johannes is getting on well at Ham, so Heins, who saw him before he left Hamburg, assures me. I am delighted with what you tell me of his Symphony. If I could only see it, but I am afraid he would hardly like to send it over here. But I will try and persuade him. When I think of the pleasure it would give me to rehearse Johannes' Symphony and to be the first to produce it, I must confess I feel very much inclined to accept the King's suggestion, which was that I should take my two years' leave, the only condition being that I should *continue to draw* my salary, and, in return, conduct six concerts each year (the dates to be chosen by me). I know you will advise me to accept! . . . Always yours,                                               JOSEPH J.

### From Bernhard Scholz

HANOVER, *August* 26, 1862.

My dear Friend—I got back to Hanover two days ago, and here I am without wife and children (whom I shall only allow to return after the move is successfully accomplished), without Joachim—without even Brinkmann, who is still away, so that I feel as lonely and deserted as Adam in Paradise before Eve was created, except that Hanover is by no means a Paradise, and that I would far rather meet the beasts of Paradise than many an obnoxious countenance here.

Is that not grist to your mill?—I can see you

grinning maliciously at my being so ill at ease here. But it is an evil mood, a touch of home-sickness of which I ought to be ashamed, and which I am sure I shall soon overcome. If I look ahead things appear more promising. I can see pleasant evenings with my wife, with Joachim, and many a good friend, of whom I have already seen several—I will only mention Papa Nicola, who asks to be remembered to you.

Come back to us soon, dear, dear friend; we will do lots of work together—and I must confess it is high time I did work, for I have not touched a pen the whole summer. I have no ideas—I feel discouraged, and I do not think I shall write anything again until I have heard my Requiem; then perhaps I shall recover some confidence in myself and my talent—if I have any at all. I am looking forward all the more to what you will have to show, for your remarks gave me hopes of something big from you. We will produce it splendidly for you; only come back very, very soon!

My dear wife and the three children are particularly well and jolly, and the country life suits them. Henni is beginning to talk better, Dickerchen is a darling little chap, burnt so brown that his skin is darker than his hair—and your little godchild thriving excellently. He will come into contact with a hostile world in a day or two for the first time, *i.e.* he will be vaccinated.

How I long for my family, although I have been away so short a time! But I hope the separation will soon be at an end; I think I shall be moving into my new quarters next week.

Fräulein Weis stayed near us during her holidays and spent a good deal of time at Hammermühle. We think her a delightful and excellent girl. You know for yourself how talented she is. I am anxious to help her to get on. Operatic singing alone is not enough ; she must also go in for Oratorio, for which she has a marked talent. She intends to learn French this winter ; I should rather advise her to study *English*, a language more suitable to her purpose, as she is not likely to go to France, but will, I hope, certainly go to England by and bye. Would it not be possible to bring her out in England, some time during a London season, under your ægis and, possibly, with introductions from Hanover ? She works hard and has greatly improved this summer in depth of expression in singing. I think it would be worth your while, and a pleasure too, to help on a girl who stands so far above the general run of so-called artistes. What do you think ? Shall she study English or French ?

Write and let me know soon, and do not forget to send my wife the letter you promised ; she is very jealous in this respect, as you know !

Last of all, best love. Eyertt, Grün, and Lindner's wife wish to be remembered to you.—Think sometimes of your                                    SCHOLZ.


### To Clara Schumann

LONDON, *August* 26 [1862].

Dear Frau Schumann—I have not written a word to one of my friends for the last month—and they have not missed anything by it, because it takes some time to regain one's old delight in art after the prosaic business of all the performances of the season. I made a few trips in the neighbourhood of London—the last one was to Hastings-on-Sea. I liked it so much that I am going there to-morrow for several—perhaps six—weeks. I cannot give you my address there yet—

I want to find rooms near the sea; but if you send me a line, care of Herr Victor Benecke, he will forward it to me.   He is Mendelssohn's son-in-law, and you will readily understand that I think all the more of him for that; Marie Mendels. has become an excellent housewife, and so clever and charming besides that you see her parents in her.   Karl and Lili impressed me very favourably too, and I hope to be able to say the same of Paul, whose acquaintance I am to make before long at his sister's house, as he is to pay her a visit at Hastings.   So you see I shall not lack society, even if I do not have that of my lady musica.   But when we meet again in October I hope to bring with me some sheets of music to show that the last-named lady was, after all, my dearest companion.[1]

Perhaps I shall be able to invite you to Hanover for Brahms' Symphony at the end of October.   I have sent some of my things there in advance by Rabe, who returned *via* Bremen to-day.   I am looking forward to the six concerts at the end of the year, which, I fancy, will be the last of my work in Hanover. Give my greetings to the glorious Rigi, which, I am sure, has strengthened and refreshed you.   Remember me very kindly to Fräulein Marie and Julie.   My birthday present will occupy a proud position among its fellows.   Very many thanks from yours most sincerely,        JOSEPH JOACHIM.

### From *Herman Grimm*

MONTREUX, *August 29*, 1862.

Dear Joachim—We arrived here yesterday in the rain, and to-day heavy clouds are hanging over the

---

[1] At that time he was writing the G major Concerto.   When it was published twenty years later, a well-known musical journal stated that it consisted merely of a collection of phrases from the Concertos by Brahms and Bruch !

mountains and sea. We found your letter here, enclosing your excellent portrait, and immortalising Rabe's personality (of which the contents princi- pally consisted). Rabe will live. I shall write Michel Angelo's life and Joachim will write Rabe's. I shall dedicate my book to you; you will dedicate yours to me. I must confess that when I found Rabe still dominating the fourth page of your letter I felt rather depressed. Did you mean to punish me in this way for my ingratitude? Dear friend, I did not write to you because I was glad to have the poems and there was no urgent necessity to write. But as to our daily discussions whether we should not send you a pressing invitation to join us (perhaps you would have done so), that is another matter altogether. In spite of the good effects of the trip, Giesel has been very poorly, low-spirited, and often scarcely in a fit state to see the most casual acquaintances.

And we have often talked about Rome. You could not go to Florence, it is too cold and dry and rheumaticky. But Rome would be the place for you. There you would be able to fill all the gaps in your existence. The only thing that prevented us from suggesting it was the consideration that, in Giesel's present weak state, we should see so little of one another. But try and go, as we mean to try. But the poor, tragic, warrior saint with his generous nature, who is rushing on his fate,[1] makes us still hesitate about going. For if there are disturbances in Rome I cannot take Giesel there. In this case we intend to go to a place in the Riviera near Genoa.

My book will keep me here until October 15.

[1] The volunteer army raised by Garibaldi against Papal Rome was, however, scattered on the same day on which this letter was written.

Twenty sheets of it are printed and ten to twelve are still to be done, of which only the last six remain to be written here.    To-day I had to *absolve* no less than three proof sheets.    I find that the excessive concentration which has been required of me during the last two months for the sake of this work is more exhausting than any other kind of exertion.    It is like toothache. One goes through strange countries and among strange peoples, and one shakes off all impressions as though they were drops of rain.    But so much shaking ends in making one dizzy.    I went to the station just now ; my box of books has arrived.    But I must have a quiet room before I can begin.    Our present room looks on the market - place, and right underneath women are washing clothes all day long, and their tongues are used more diligently than the soap. Added to this I have a bad cold.    We have been most unlucky in that respect this year.    It would be nice to hire a little sunshine now and then, just as one can hire the lights in a theatre.    It was so cold, latterly, at Heinrichbad that we could hardly get warm between the thin wooden walls.

Good-bye, and work hard at your violin Concerto, to which we are both looking forward, I expect you know how much.    Your last Concerto was for me my sole musical experience—to have seen something emerge which did not exist before and which now is.

Giesel sends many thanks for the picture, which is sticking in our mirror.    I hope you will soon write me a few lines, but not with the raven's plume.—Your

HERMAN.

[Postscript in Gisela Grimm's handwriting.]

Your picture just came in time for my birthday, which is to-morrow, and I shall be able to add to it

some figs, myrtles, and roses picked in the open air.
You would like it here, everything is grander, the trees
and flowers taller and more abundant than at home,
and the people seem more historic as well as the
houses and gardens. Herman amused me so last night
—in the patriarchal dining-room he looked just like a
child in a strange postchaise whom some one had
suddenly taken on his knee; which would have been
extraordinary if one did not know him. There were
old men there with white hair, who looked as though
they were about to bless one, and youths with ringlets.
But how lovely the high mountains look stretching
round the lake—everything is different, just as slender
as steep, as luxuriant as strong; one does not often see
so much of Italy in Switzerland. Your portrait is
good, but you might have given your mouth a nicer
expression; it is the way you pout sometimes. My
little picture of Joachim is nicer—he has gone from us
too. I am surprised at your thinking my letter as
charming as usual. Because I am so fond of you I
am always open and sometimes very harsh with you,
but then I have nothing to say against you behind
your back; that is what you prefer, I imagine? May
you prosper—the more people I see the more I congratulate myself that we three know and love one
another. I am afraid I cannot find any one to join us,
Emerson perhaps, if I knew him better—this is not
false pride, it only comes from the thought that our
ideals are pure and disinterested, and so when I am
sitting silently amongst people I am often blissfully
happy when I think of our acquaintanceship, in the
truest sense of the word. I cannot write much. I
have been ill very often. Herman is done up too,
after working, whilst travelling, in uncomfortable, noisy
rooms, and looking after an invalid at night. But

things will be better now. Here is another picture of me. —Your                                                    G.

Herman has teased you about your account of Rabe, but I liked it, only you might have added something about yourself. . . .

### To Herman Grimm

HASTINGS, *September* 20 [1862].

Dear Herman—I would have written at once to tell you how grateful I am to you both for your dear letters if I had not been taken up just then by an unhappy event (in my family at Pesth). My second sister, with whom I stayed when last I was in Hungary, suddenly returned from a watering-place very ill, and died that evening. It is a cruel blow for my parents, who have not lost one of their children within my memory. You see they are over seventy; they would like to see more of Heinrich, my brother in London, and myself, and they wanted us to go home at once. In short, as you may imagine, the whole affair has moved me very much. But it would hardly have been practicable for me to rush over to Pesth just now; it is several days' journey from here, and after all one is not exactly a sea-gull to soar into the air and go where inclination drives at a moment's notice. I need a time of rest and quiet after my busy summer in London, so as to come, at last, to a decision with regard to where I am to live in the future. *What* my decision will be as regards Hanover, I cannot yet say; it depends rather on what I hear in the course of the next week or so. The only thing I am sure about is that I shall not retain my post, because I do not like the place well enough to be able to tolerate the prospect of spending my life there. Please tell

Gisel that all she says about Hanover seems to me absolutely just and right and as clear and characteristic as the picture of herself which she has sent me. I was delighted to find that you took such an interest in Garibaldi, too, and that our feelings about him were exactly similar. But matters seem more unfavourable than ever to your visit to Rome ! I think Napoleon intends to assert his supremacy as long as he can by pitting the passions of the Papal and Italian parties against one another. I am curious to know how matters will stand by the middle of October, and what your movements will be when you have completed Part II.[1] Can I do anything more for you in London ? I am going there in a week's time and shall stay with my brother. I am sorry to say I did not get the little house here I told you about. My present rooms are very pleasant but rather noisy sometimes with passers-by and unexpected street music. It will be something to remember all my life that I have lived for a time by the sea, which surges outside my window. My Concerto is growing and I feel inclined for other work.

I hope you or Gisel will send me a line soon, if only to let me know how you both are ; your last letter made me rather uneasy.—Always yours,

JOSEPH J.

## To T. Avé-Lallemant

41 PALL MALL, LONDON, *September* 27 [1862].

My dear, good Avé—You are the same good fellow as you always were ; instead of reproaching me for not writing, you forward my letter to Brahms and write a friendly letter to me. That is truly

---

[1] Of *Michel Angelo*.

Christian and good. Well, you need have no fear that I am becoming too anglicised; although I would rather be here than in *Hanover*, not a day passes on which I do not call down blessings upon the German heart and the German mind! But it is all in vain; in spite of this I shall remain here another three months, after having come back here the day before yesterday from the sea, where I spent my time bathing (swimming), walking and collecting material for work. London is practically deserted by "society" now, but to live once more in a big city, with no reason to fear the demands of the public, is just what I like. If only Johannes were here too it would be nicer still. He never writes to me, but he is bound to get on wherever he is, and I would give something to see the looks of astonishment and wonder cast at him by the men (and the women more particularly) of Vienna. But I cannot go in for any more journeys and distractions at present. I am so sorry, too, not to be able to carry out your suggestion with regard to Frau Schumann's concerts. But I honestly believe that the people of Hamburg would just as soon go to a concert without me, and that it will make no pecuniary difference, at any rate. I will not fiddle for you again until I have produced a new violin concerto, be it good or bad. I have played the old things often enough for you. I am not going to Hanover before the New Year, and then only to put my things together. But *please do not mention this*; everything gets into the *Signale* or some paper of that kind at once, and the King does not know yet. If you have news of Johannes pass it on to me; I am afraid I shall not hear direct from him at all. Rose is a fine fellow. I believe Fräulein X. plays well, but when I knew her (without hearing her play) she was very affected—one of those people who think they can learn to play "classical" music "classically" just in passing, as people like you to display Rococo goods as a rule.   Y. is a brilliant, "elegant" performer ;  I mean the kind of elegance which does not imply refinement.   I did not like him He makes a great impression wherever he goes. Remember me to your family and do not forget your                                JOSEPH JOACHIM.

## To Bernhard Scholz

LONDON, *September* 28 [1862].

My dear Bernhardus—I can hardly give you and your dear wife any idea of how hard it is for me to tell you, of all people, something which I may not keep to myself any longer.   I have given up my appointment at Hanover, and I am writing the news to Count Platen by this post.   The fact is no one should allow himself to be forced to do what is against his nature. You dear, good friends, all of you, would not forgive yourselves later on if you bound me so closely with roses and brambles that I could not loosen the strands when I longed for freedom.   That is what would have happened if I had given in to the King's gracious persuasion for a year, and yet another year—without any of the warmth of real gratitude, simply in a moment of weakness and emotion, when my own experience told me it could not last.   The royal enthusiasm for art is not rooted nearly so deeply in Georg of Hanover as is republicanism in Georg Joseph Joachim.   As a courtier I have put up long enough with graciousness and patronage, thus sinning against my nature ;  and no real happiness is to be found except in adjusting the conditions of one's life to one's convictions.   I could continue to expatiate on this theme, in jest and in earnest, for ever—but I will not do so. I will only add that I know very well many people will consider me a—Hedemann![1] I am by no means indifferent to this, but I shall have to bear it. I cannot speak of the Quartette and the orchestra, and of certain dear friends old and young —it makes me too sad. I expect I shall stay here until the end of the year; I have refreshed body and mind at the seaside, and I hope to do a lot of work. I shall come and take away my things from you in January, and if Napoleon the Horrible and Garibaldi the Great and Good permit, I shall go to Rome, or to the south at any rate! But these plans are all in the air. Heinrich, with whom I am staying at present, is in Paris, but is coming back to-morrow, and will be agreeably surprised, I hope, by my decision. I am sorry to say I lost a dear sister three weeks ago, and I was more especially distressed by this at the thought of my parents. Klingemann[2] died here suddenly, too, a double loss to me now. Keep me in your hearts and kiss both the children. JOSEPH JOACHIM.

## From Bernhard Scholz

HANOVER, *October* 6, 1862.

My dear Friend—Your letter has made your friends here very sad, and we have not yet reconciled ourselves to losing you for good and all.

We will not discuss the necessity of the step you are taking; after all, that is for you to decide.

But I must point out to you that your behaviour with regard to the King is not right, and that

---

[1] A general and marshal in the King's service. Shortly before this he had been placed under arrest for extensive embezzlement, but succeeded in escaping. He was however recaptured and committed to prison.

[2] Mendelssohn's friend.

it would be painful in the extreme to me if you took your departure in any but the most dignified manner.   You cannot say the King refused you leave; on the contrary, he consented to it, and at the time you promised to carry out his wishes with regard to a short stay here during the winter.   Do not say that you did not say " Yes "; at any rate you did not say " No," and you allowed the King (and us) to believe that you had accepted the King's suggestion, and that you would come back here, if only for a few weeks. You said as much afterwards to Prince Georg, and, after all he has conceded to you, the King is justified in expecting you to come.

And now, just when we thought you were returning, your letter to Platen arrives, in which you absolve yourself from your obligations, and do not even observe the formality of giving six months' notice, but.wish to be free from the first of June.

All this does not seem at all right to me; it is not unlike a breach of contract with the King, and it will be very generally regarded as such.   Either you should have declined the King's proposals altogether in the spring, or you ought to come back now. There is no other alternative.

Or if you have felt more strongly than ever lately that you cannot remain here—very well, then come now, have the courage to state this personally to the King himself, and give due and formal notice of the termination of the contract.

You owe so much to the King and to yourself!

All your friends here are of the same opinion.   If we must lose you, we should at least like to feel that no *just* reproach can be made against you.

As regards the Platen business, which is the chief cause of your leaving, it is getting so bad that I shall be obliged to enlighten the King on the subject before long. If you were only here—a lot could be done just now; the seed is gradually ripening. I believe we could lay the foundations of better conditions, and I shall discourse to the King on the relations between you and Platen so as to give ample grounds for your decision. I shall tell the King that if musical and theatrical affairs continue to be conducted in this way no decent artist will be able to stand it here.

You have my deepest sympathy in your sad losses; but the way of life is strewn with such.

Come what may, we shall remain the same old friends. After all, your time in Hanover has brought you many a true friend, and that is something.

My dear wife joins me in kindest regards to yourself and your brother Heinrich. Make up your mind quickly! Count Platen is away and the King will not be officially informed of your letter until Thursday or Friday.—Yours as ever,

SCHOLZ.

### To Bernhard Scholz

[LONDON, *about October* 8, 1862.]

My dear Scholz—If anything could make me feel how much I am giving up with my post at Hanover it would be your faithful care that I should get away from Hanover without giving a false impression of my character. I thank you for your kind and open letter, for the sake of which I am writing a few lines to Platen, which, although they contain nothing new as to my resolve, will make it impossible even for *him* so to represent my former communication as though I wished to break my contract, if the King should consider it desirable that it should be fulfilled. But, first

of all, I must correct a mistake of yours ; by my contract a three months' notice only is required on either
side, not a six months' notice. It was only in the
financial interests of the management (and also because
it would be disagreeable to me to pocket money I had
not earned) that I wrote to Count Platen and suggested
(*not demanded*) that to "*simplify matters*," instead of
taking the three months' notice, our contract should
end in June. Of course, I took for granted, too, that
the King, in his impulsive, uncompromising way,
would not want to hear another note of mine as soon
as he knew I was determined to go. My supple-
mentary letter to Count Platen to-day is to tell him
that I am, of course, prepared to conduct the six or
eight concerts during the months from January onwards, *should the King still wish me to do so before I
leave his service* (which appears to me very unlikely).
If, on my behalf, you will explain to him by word of
mouth also the difference between a "*suggestion*" made
to "*simplify*" matters for both parties and a breach
of contract, it might not be a bad thing. Perhaps it
would help him to comprehend if you told him that
my proposal was not to *my* advantage. I can understand very well how intercourse with our chief is
gradually becoming intolerable to you. We have
wasted our breath often enough on the subject of
this cavalier ; but even if you succeeded in bringing
some too barefaced misdeed before the King's notice, it
would depend on a mere chance whether any good
would result from it. So long as kings regard the
care of the arts as a court appointment (to provide
for otherwise unemployable noblemen) things must
be as they are. The King and Queen know Platen's
character to a certain extent, and they cannot bear
his airs and graces ; they even believe that if he could

T

embitter any pleasure of theirs, he would do so—and yet they have kept him in attendance on them and marked him out for favours for the last ten years.

The only way to put a spoke in Platen's wheel, if it is possible at all, would be by evading the authority conferred on him by the King—by "intrigue." But I will not discuss this page, one of many others from the chapter on court favouritism at Hanover, any longer; only, do consider the matter again before coming to the conclusion that it is worth your while to plunge your *honest self* into a fight with Platen. Thank God, *you*, at any rate, know why you must insist on an assured position, in which you can make the influence of your fine nature felt : Louise and Henni and Richard, that other music, which is yet one with all the desires and aspirations of your songs ! Consider yourself fortunate, my friend ; but, for that very reason, do not be hard on one who would live at peace with his soul, and wishes to "serve" no worldly power if he can avoid it.

I have undertaken (for the sum of £20) to play quartettes and other chamber music every Monday up to Christmas. I hope, later on, to pass through Hanover on my way to Italy, either to conduct my farewell concerts, or simply to put my affairs in order. I live up four flights of stairs, peaceful and solitary, although in one of the busiest streets : 40 Pall Mall. As I do not have to make any great preparations for my quartette playing with Piatti, and as it is a congenial way of earning a living, I am looking forward to a pleasant winter, so far as outside matters are concerned. Apropos ! If Fräulein Weis carries out her plan and practises singing in English diligently, she is sure of obtaining a good position here in Oratorio singing. But of course she would have to study pronunciation, mannerisms, and expression on the spot. With her talent I should think it would be easy for her to acquire the necessary knowledge quickly. Remember me to her and to all my friends : the Brinkmanns, Nicola, Unruhs, Eyertts, etc. I need not send a special message to your wife.—Yours,

J. J.

Let me know how Kaulbach is ; whether there has been an addition to his family.   He is sure not to write to me again.

### To Clara Schumann

[LONDON] *October* 14 [1862].

Dear Frau Schumann—Scholz sent me your first letter yesterday, and your second, of October 8, arrived to-day.   You can have no idea what pleasure they both gave me.   I had really quite firmly made up my mind, and pictured it in my imagination in the crudest of colours, that you and Johannes (of whom I have only heard indirectly through Avé at Hamburg) had given me up altogether.   To make this comprehensible I must tell you that I wrote to Johannes from Hastings asking him to let me know as soon as possible (at the *latest* in a week's time) whether he would like to rehearse and conduct his Symphony for the first time in Hanover.   I told him I was very anxious to know this *before* I went to Hanover.   In case he replied "Yes," my intention was to go there and only to give up my appointment definitely *after the concerts were over*.   But no answer came whatever.   What more natural than to fancy he was seriously annoyed with me and had no wish to make use of my friendly assistance in getting a hearing for his work ?   And so, as my chief motive for conducting the concerts at Hanover no longer existed, I decided to terminate my contract from here so as to avoid the painful explanations by word of mouth which would have been inevitable if I had done so on the spot.  In spite of all the comforts of the appointment, the discomfort of living in a town in which one cannot feel absolutely at home, and *my antipathy for courts in general*, had destroyed all feeling of harmony and put me out of humour for too long a time.  It was very difficult to trample in this way on so many delicate and generous signs of favour on the part of the royal couple, but it had to be done.  I hope to turn my freedom to good account; otherwise the thought of the orchestra I am leaving would always rise up to reproach me.  I shall remain here until the end of the year.  I like London much better now than in the season.  I am to play in quartette in public every Monday, but otherwise I am living, on my fourth floor, for my music alone.  If, in spite of giving notice, I am summoned to Hanover for the eight concerts, I shall, of course, have to obey, for the last time, in January.  But I do not think this is likely; the King will be too angry.  Scholz says in his letter to-day that there is a parcel there for me from Brahms from Vienna.  I have asked him, of course, to send it on here at once.  Hurrah! perhaps it is the Quintette! I know nothing about the Symphony yet; it may be that after all.

I was very much surprised at your decision to set up house in Baden.  I am so delighted to think you will have all your dear ones round you at last that this weighs with me more than any other consideration. But I know the neighbourhood so little that I cannot exactly feel pleased or otherwise.  You must not think I shall always remain in England.  I know the dark side of an artist's life there too well, even though I like the life in many ways. Excuse these hasty lines. I did not want to keep you waiting for news. With a hundred greetings to you and yours.—Yours,

JOSEPH J.

### To Bernhard Scholz

[LONDON, *about October* 23, 1862.]

Dear Friend—As, up to the present, I have neither received the manuscript from Brahms which I begged you to send on at once, nor had any news of the fate of a letter to the King addressed by me through you to "his gracious majesty" (and which I posted *myself*), I am rather uneasy about these two matters, which are of importance to me. Have my communications not reached you? Please write a line by return! You mention a parcel of letters for me, but I have seen nothing of that either. I have, however, had a letter from Count Platen. I shall, of course, have to go to Hanover and drain to the dregs the cup of my bondage to the Guelphs. I had just begun to settle down here for the winter, and to think with delight of travelling in Italy in the spring. . . . Well, I am quite cured of my gratitude. But it is quite impossible for me to leave here before the first week in December, and I cannot go then without suffering financially, which is, of course, a secondary consideration. I counted too positively on the King being proud enough to say, "The fellow may go to the devil," or generous enough not to spoil something for me on which, as he must see, I had set my heart. I think a more refined nature would have acted in that way. But I will not run away. How is Kaulbach's wife?

My kindest regards, as always, to your dear wife. From yours, JOSEPH J.

*To Frau M. Benecke*

[LONDON] *Thursday* [*October* 23, 1862].

Dear Frau Benecke—The symphony which your dear mother showed me, under the title of Reformation Symphony, was not in the original manuscript. I can recall the big book in a green binding, with very large notes on rather stiff paper, as though it were lying before me now. The writing was quite different from Mendelssohn's, and I should be inclined to ascribe it to a conscientious copyist. I remember quite clearly that I read the Symphony through in your dear father's little study in Königsstrasse; but I do not know whether it was in December 1847 or early in '48. I did not refer to the *original* manuscript in speaking to your husband; I have a dim recollection of Rietz in Dresden mentioning it to me, but I can only swear to my recollections of the time in Leipzig, which, because of the place and your mother's kindness, later experiences have failed to wipe from my memory.

I am hoping to see you and Herr Benecke to-day, and am yours very truly, JOSEPH J.


*From Clara Schumann*

FRANKFORT A/M., *November* 10, 1862.

Dear Joachim—Do not be angry with me for not answering your two letters before, but I have been fearfully busy again for the last eight weeks. Your first letter with the news that you were going to remain in London made me so sad that, if I had answered it at once, my letter would have contained nothing but lamentations. But the good news followed soon after, and I cannot help being glad for my own sake, although I am sorry enough for yours, that you have to stay on

another winter under such unpleasant conditions. But
I must frankly confess I do not think you have acted
rightly. You ought to have said " No " definitely in
May ; I am sure that would not have been so wounding to the Queen as your present behaviour. Besides,
I believe that when you are once back there again
things will settle down, and I hope you will find
Hanover easier to bear than you imagine now you are
in London.

Your last letter reached me on November 1 ; but I
was glad you were not there in person, for, in spite of
the utmost goodwill on all sides, the performance was
*very mediocre*, and I should have been really sorry if
you of all people had heard the *Faust* for the first time
performed like that. I should so much like you to
hear it done as perfectly as possible, because then I
know you would *have* to admire it, and think it even
grander than you imagined. But I am very grieved
to hear that you are actually leaving London on
December 4,[1] and not a few days earlier so that you
could have come to Leipzig *before* going to Hanover !

You have, no doubt, heard from Johannes himself
how very much he likes Vienna, which was to be
expected. He is remaining there through the winter.
I suppose you have had his Quintette by now? He
is to play it, or rather to have it played at Hellmesberger's at the end of this month. I should like to
hear you play that one day! I expect you know that
Johannes is playing his G minor Quartette in Hellmesberger's Quartette to-morrow.

I cannot tell you how horrified I was at Mad.
Bennett's death ; I had no idea she was ill! I feel so
sorry for poor Bennett. What a loss for him, she was
such a sweet woman ! Please tell him how deeply I

[1] Schumann's *Faust* was to be performed at Leipzig on the 4th.

feel with him and his children in their sorrow. Express my heartfelt sympathy to Frau Klingemann also; that was another death which grieved me! So one goes after the other—if only one need not remain behind so long oneself! . . .

Goodbye, dear Joachim. Have a good journey and bring back the same good heart as ever to yours sincerely,                    CLARA SCHUMANN.


### To Herman Grimm

[LONDON] *November* 13 [1862].

My dear Herman—If you only knew how sad I feel in writing to you at Rome, instead of going there myself! As they will not hear of my suggestion in Hanover (to consider the contract as terminated from June) I have to go there at the beginning of December to serve another six months. I thought my contract provided for a three months' notice, but that was a blissful dream. I was so sure that the King would be either proud and angry, or (because I asked for two years without a salary) kind and yielding, that I undertook engagements here until the end of the year, so as to be able to go to you in January. . . . Dependence on circumstances may call forth heroic qualities; the sadder they are the more satisfaction we may derive from bearing them bravely. But it is very hard to forgive ourselves for having voluntarily given any one such power over us that he can wreck our most justifiable hopes, although necessity does not force him to do so. I have passed some feverish nights, during which, as I lay awake, I had an almost physical sensation of bondage—I shook the bars of my iron bed as though they were chains. I suppose you are not likely to know yet how long you will stay in Rome. Hardly until June! Even if you did, that would be the worst season, and you would have to leave then. I did not want to beg for "mercy." Besides, I have told no one the reason why I was so anxious to be free this year. It would be misunderstood.

A day or two ago Th. v. Bunsen brought me messages from you from Berlin, and told me of the death of Count Oriola;[1] the news must have upset Gisel very much. Does the Roman climate suit you both? Could you write to me here once more before the 9th of December, dear Herman? The fog was so thick here yesterday that you could not see from one gas lamp to the other. In the evening, on my way back from a friend's house, I had to turn into an hotel for the night! But it has not been as bad as that for several years. Otherwise, I like being here very much. All around you, you see people occupied with the most varied interests, even if they are not always the highest, and the absence of an atmosphere of petty Court intrigue is very soothing to me. I met one of your Spangenbergs casually at a concert the other day. I could not think of his name at first, although his face was familiar. He has made no use of my address up to the present. His news of you both was stale. If you make the acquaintance of the American sculptor, Story, write and tell me what you think of him and his daughter. They are relations of Maclellan's and friends of Emerson. . . . He showed me an excellent statuette of Beethoven, which you will look at, perhaps, for my sake. His " Cleopatra " and a " Sibylle " in marble made a sensation at the Exhibition. They seem to me dignified and out of the common, but intelligent and cultured rather than deep or animated. Will you two dear people send me

---

[1] The husband of Gisela's sister Maxes.

refreshment sometimes in my time of durance and continue to think kindly of your old                J. J.

### From B. Molique

30 HARRINGTON SQUARE, N.W., *December* 2, 1862.

My dear friend Joachim—Accept my sincerest thanks for the pleasure which your magnificent playing gave me last night.   I would have come to you this morning to thank you for the care and trouble you have taken with my Quartette, but unfortunately I have caught cold and have to remain at home again for a few days.   It will grieve me to hear you next Monday for the last time and to know that you are going away, for I must confess to you that you have made yourself indispensable to me as a violinist.   I shall never listen to S. Bach again unless you come back to London and I am still alive, because I shall not let the impression your playing has made upon me be spoilt by any one else.   God be with you.—Your sincere friend,                            B. MOLIQUE.

### From Clara Schumann

BERLIN, *December* 19, 1862.

My dear Joachim—At last, at last, there is a letter from you [1] from Germany again !   It was sent on to me from Breslau this morning, and I am answering it at once.   On the Saturday, when you conducted again for the first time, you were in my mind the whole evening and I felt for you in your painful position with all my heart, and I am very glad now to hear that the King, at any rate, has been wise enough to make matters more agreeable for you, outwardly.   Pretence or not, it is better so.

---

[1] This letter cannot be traced.

Your decision not to come to me at Christmas makes me doubly sad now I know that I was mistaken in concluding you would not ask for leave under *any* circumstances. You cannot take it ill that, as an old friend, I too would have liked to have been an exception in your eyes. But I realise that you were doing a great service to Scholz[1] at the same time, and besides, your stay here would not be very satisfactory, since you would miss your dear friends.[2]

Do you know we have not seen one another for nearly a year! It may not have seemed so long to you with your varied life, but *I* have felt it deeply and cannot think without pain on how our dearest friends can be separated from us by outward circumstances. But it is still sadder when this happens because of an inner separation, as with Johannes. I really could not wish for his presence here at Christmas, because when he was here a year ago, and again in the summer at Kreuznach (where he came quite of his own accord), he made life with him almost unbearable ; and added to this he hurt me deeply this summer in the same way that he hurt you, and about the very same Quintette. I received it just as I was starting on a tour in the Bernese Oberland. Knowing I should not have a minute to spare on a tour like that, and that I should not find a piano on which to play the Quintette, and being nervous besides of carrying such a valuable manuscript about in my trunk, I left it with my things at Lucerne. But I came back in four days' time, studied it very carefully and wrote to him most warmly about it ; whilst I was away I had written to tell him I had received it, etc., etc. (out of consideration for him

[1] By his presence at the performance of the *Requiem* at Cologne, at which Fräulein Weis sang the contralto solos.
[2] The Grimms.

and for fear he should be expecting to hear). Meanwhile I got, in answer to this note, a letter from him
saying he had not known I travelled with so little
luggage nowadays, that a few scraps of music paper
would not have overburdened me, and that I knew,
besides, how he disliked letting his manuscripts out of
his hands for any length of time, etc. That was a
heart-breaking blow; if ever a reproach was unjust it
was this one. Well, you have felt all this too, but you
are a man and get over such things, but my heart
bleeds whenever I think of it—and of all my years of
devotion to his work! But the Quintette is beautiful
—I have it with me now and will bring it to you, for
surely I shall see you again now. I told the King the
other day that I should come again at the beginning of
January, but I expect you will not like that, because of
the playing at Court? At any rate I shall arrange
matters so that I can hear the concert on the 3rd.
Could you not play me a Symphony of my husband's
and the F minor Beethoven on Sunday morning?

I think it is very hard that I shall not be able to
hear the *Faust*, but I shall probably be in Paris at
that time. In spite of the fatigue I would make the
journey from thence to Hanover, but the expenses are
too great.

I will say good-bye now, although I should like to
ask you so many more questions. I feel so upset,
your letter to-day has made me sad, I hardly know
why, and yet I do know! It is simply that my heart
always beats the same for you! I wish I could press
your hand in welcome!—Yours, CL. SCH.

## *To Clara Schumann*

[HANOVER, *January* 29, 1863.]

Dear Frau Schumann—I have just written to your
sister Clementine[1] in London, to send her a letter of
introduction to Hallé; but that does not appease my
desire to hear from you! I do not suppose I shall
hear how you are getting on unless I ask? Count
Platen told me you played at Cologne the day before
yesterday when he was there. But as I have never
been on a friendly footing with him as regards
aesthetic matters, I do not know whether he heard
you, although with any one else that would have been
clear from his bare account of it! How did Woldemar's
Psalm go?[2] I should like to hear something about
that too, and I hope you will write and tell me.
Yesterday evening, at the Singing Academy, we had
the first rehearsal of the chorus for *Faust.* It will be
a troublesome business; I had no idea how hard the
work would be with these amateurs. Each of the four
voices of the Chorus has to learn the notes separately,
as though it were the a b c, and it makes me positively
giddy to think that some soul must be put into it
within six or eight weeks. Stockhausen is helping us
by being at Kolmar! According to his *second* promise
he ought to be here the day after to-morrow; we shall
see what telegrams he sends! But, all the same, I
am looking forward to hearing him in *Faust* and wish
he were here now.

I think you will be glad to know the final decision
about the Hanover business. *You,* especially, will
think it satisfactory. After a two hours' audience the

---

[1] Clementine Bargiel, Clara Schumann's step-sister.

[2] On January 27 Frau Schumann played Beethoven's E♭ major Concerto at
Cologne, and Bargiel conducted his XIII. Psalm.

King suggested that I should only live in Hanover for four months and regard my stay there as a kind of interlude, so as not to give up my connection with him and the orchestra. Besides this, at two out of the eight concerts some big choral work should be performed under my direction, and other improvements for the Institute, etc., etc. In short, I have not been able to resist the really touching foresight with which the King has met my views. Instead of being angry with me for giving notice, he disarmed me by the remark that, so far as he and the Queen were concerned, all pleasure in their favourite art would be gone if I went away for good. That is real generosity, and although, as regards politics, there is much in his character which I think crooked, I must confess his manner to me in private was almost that of a fatherly friend. He said we had concluded a new *contract*,[1] so that I should not feel burdened by a mere favour in staying away from Hanover so long, and could enjoy my freedom. They wanted to bind me for *life*, but that I declined.

Last week I had a most stimulating and delightful visit from the poet Björnsjerne Björnson, a Norwegian, whose vigorous and poetical writings are the expression of his fine personality. I think I once lent you and Fräulein Marie his *Arne* to read. Please be kind to him, for my sake first of all; you will soon be glad to see him for his own sake. One does not often come across such true, deep natures! With kindest regards to Fräulein Marie.—Yours,

JOSEPH JOACHIM.

---

[1] The new contract was signed on March 1.

*To Th. Avé-Lallemant*

HANOVER, *January* 31 [1863].

Dear Avé—If I waited until I could tell you
whether I can come to you at the end of April, it
would be too long before I thanked you for your kind
letter.   I have half, or rather three-quarters of an idea
that I may go to Rome at the end of March, spend
Easter there, then go to Florence, and perhaps later to
Naples !. But it will not be definitely settled until the
end of February.   I shall be free at the end of March,
for my new contract, which the King himself offered
me after I had given the management notice, only
binds me to remain in Hanover *four months in the year*
(my salary to be retained).   The King was so delightfully sympathetic, so anxious for my welfare, and
repeated so often that neither he nor the least
member of the orchestra could spare me after having
been accustomed for ten years to the thought of
having me here, that I should have been absolutely
heartless if it had made no impression upon me.   And
it is really a blessing for me that it has turned out
like this.   Think of my independence from the toil of
daily concerts and the scope I shall have for my best
powers !  Because, besides this, I stipulated in the
new contract for two productions of choral works,
regular orchestra rehearsals and greater independence
in deciding the programme.   Well, more about all
this by word of mouth ; because of course you are
coming to the performance of *Faust* about the middle
of March ?  Stockhausen is to sing Faust.   Whether he
will give much assistance in rehearsing it remains to
be seen. . . .  Meanwhile Scholz and I have had the
first rehearsal of the Singing Academy, and the
Cathedral Choir is to be added to that.   Scholz, who

in his relations with me is the most unselfish of friends,
had all along intended that I should have the pleasure
of conducting the thing, as he knows how intimate I
am with the Schumanns.  We are to share the mental
work of getting it up, of which I am glad, as Scholz is
a thorough musician and a fine fellow.  But it will
give us a lot of trouble ; the second part is very difficult
and the material is *very* amateurish !—What am I to
say of your plan with regard to Stockhausen.  You
know I have the greatest respect for Stockhausen's
talent as a singer, and he is possibly the best musician
of all the singers ; but, when it is a question of the
choice between him and Johannes as head of a musical
institute, my limited musical understanding cannot
grasp why the former should be chosen !  Simply as
a *man* on whom one can rely I have the highest
opinion of Johannes' capability and character !  There
is nothing he could not grasp and conquer with his
steadfastness of purpose.  You know that as well as I
do.  And if all of you, in the Committee and Orchestra,
had treated him with love and confidence (as you, as
his friend, *always* did in private) instead of domineer-
ingly and suspiciously, you would have cured his
nature of its harshness ; instead of which, his patriotic
love for Hamburg (which is touchingly childlike) has
made him more and more bitter at seeing himself set
aside (for some one greatly inferior to him in talent and
character).  It would make me too sad if I thought
of how his nearest countrymen have given up their
chance of making him gentler and more contented,
and the productions of his genius more accessible.
I should like to give the Committee a moral hiding
(and a physical one too !) for having left you and your
views in the lurch.  The insult to Johannes will
not be forgotten in the history of art.  But, " Basta."

We are once more heartily in agreement in our
admiration for the contralto, Fräulein Weis, dear Avé!
I think her voice alone tells you what a deep, pure
nature dwells in the young girl, who lost her father
when she was only eighteen, and later, tending the
death-beds of her mother and sister, remained in the
great imperial city free from any trace of the wild
theatrical life around her.   Here again true love of
art has been a real gift from heaven, and I think, with
her sincerity and earnestness, she will attain to yet
higher things, to the consolation of herself and of
others.   And modesty and ambition go hand in hand
in this case, as they should do!—But here I am on
the third sheet!  Just one more question, how did
Rose get on?   Give him my kindest regards and
your own dear ones also.   Do not let them forget me.

Yours very sincerely,                    Joseph J.

### From Clara Schumann

Düsseldorf, *February* 2, 1863.

Dear Joachim—You were quite right in supposing
I should be delighted to hear that your affairs at
Hanover have been happily settled at last.   Now you
will be in Germany sometimes, at any rate—if only you
would never go to England again!

The King has behaved well, one might almost say
generously, if he had not stood to gain so much
himself.   Your news has delighted all to whom I have
told it, as yesterday at the Hillers', who send their
kindest regards.   You were quite right not to enter
into a contract binding you for life—a man of thirty-
two should never fetter himself like that.

I enjoyed my few days in Cologne.   I am sorry it
happened to be Count Platen who heard the E♭ major

U

Concerto that evening. Some one else might have given you a very good account of it, for all the musicians seemed very pleased, and, most important of all, I feel myself that I play it better than ever. Woldemar's Psalm went off very well. The first movements are really very fine, even if they are not original, but, unfortunately, the last chorus is so long and monotonous that it obviously spoils the effect of the whole. But you know Woldemar—he will not see it, although every one told him so. However, he seems to me to have made great progress, although I must stick to my opinion that whether there is one such work more or less in the world is not of the slightest importance and that it will soon be counted among the forgotten ones. But I was touched when I saw his joy as a composer. I have never seen him in such a state of happy excitement. . . .

They are very busy here over the Musical Festival. Only think, they wrote and asked the Lind if she would sing, and she replied at once that she would sing gratis if they would let her husband conduct the Festival! What boundless, grasping ambition! She cannot love her husband at all, to force him upon people in this way. How unwomanly of her and unmanly of him!—But guess of whom they are thinking besides, of Wagner! The Musical Festivals here in Düsseldorf are becoming more and more commercial; the original artistic aim is being pushed quite into the background.

### To Frau Klingemann at Bonn

[HANOVER, *February* 16, 1863.]

Dear Frau Klingemann—Only something quite extraordinary could make me treat the enclosed sheets with less care than their contents and your kindness in sending them deserve.

Have you guessed anything from this preamble? I must write it down in any case, because the sound of it is so glorious. A few days ago[1] I

became engaged!

And so you must forgive me if I only write a few lines. I cannot describe my fiancée or my happiness. I hope you will get to know her on the Rhine this summer. She is a singer, an Austrian, the daughter of an official, an orphan, with a wonderfully expressive contralto voice and great dramatic talent, but she means to sacrifice even her profession to domestic happiness, for which she is an enthusiast. Her name is Schneeweiss (Weis on the stage).

And now good-bye! I am going to write to Miss Sophy[2] too; she will be surprised. I never believed myself that I should ever be engaged! I hope Lenchen will soon be quite well again.—Yours very sincerely,                    JOSEPH JOACHIM.

### To Clara Schumann

[HANOVER, *February* 18, 1863.]

My dear Frau Schumann—It would grieve me if you had from some one else the first intimation of something which will change my whole life; and so I must tell you, however briefly, of the great happiness which has come to me. Now for it! I am engaged to Fräulein Weis. Her real name is Schneeweiss, and as she is giving up the stage I ought not to have introduced my fiancée to you by her professional name! But you know her already.

---

[1] On February 11.

[2] Miss Sophy Horsley, daughter of the artist, who was a friend of Joachim's and Frau Schumann's. Cp. J. C. Horsley, *Recollections of a Royal Academician.*

And yet you do not know her; because in your presence she was so shy and ill at ease, as befitted a really modest girl, however great her gifts, when confronted with the perfect mistress of her art whom she has long revered. Only yesterday when, before she started for Leipzig, I asked her whether she sent you any messages, my fiancée replied: "Yes, but dare I do so, to so great an artist?" But I reassured her by telling her that in our case you always thought *first* of the friends and then of the artists, or at any rate did not separate them. I was right, was I not? And so I am sending you and Fräulein Marie our very sincerest greetings from full hearts, and I hope that you will both respond very soon, so that we can have the pleasure of your sympathy during this wonderful time. We have only been engaged a few days, and at first we intended to say nothing about it in Hanover—but, as I should only have been able to see my dear Ursi at the Scholz's in that case, it would have been too difficult a game of hide-and-seek! And so I am sending the joyful news out into the sweet spring, like the bright sunshine which has not failed us since the day of our engagement. Let us hear from you soon, dear friend!—Yours, as always,                JOSEPH JOACHIM.

*P.S.*—On reading my letter over, it seems so different from the cry of joy I wanted to send you— it is as though I were still too breathless to speak! But the chief thing is there.

### To Johannes Brahms

[HANOVER, *middle of February* 1863.]

My dear Johannes—This is a large sheet—but there will not be much on it; but, short as it is, it is worth your while to read it. You must make the acquaintance of *my fiancée* soon, dearest friend! I am engaged, yes, yes, yes, thrice blessed word. My Ursi's surname is Schneeweiss, she comes from Styria, and has a contralto voice which you only need to hear in order to know the depth and purity of her nature. And now, do not expect me to rave to you about her charm and beauty, her goodness and lightheartedness, and about everything which is making me happier hour by hour! And do not run away with the usual notions which are unfortunately connected with the life in our operatic circles, dear Johannes, when you hear that my fiancée has been on the stage since her sixteenth year (she is now twenty-three); you will see no trace of it—her mind and her appearance have remained so simple and refined. I am unspeakably happy. And now a word as to our plans for meeting again, because you must not imagine that my new love has deprived me of the power to care for those who have occupied my heart hitherto. If I can persuade the King to release my Ursi (who has a two years' contract here) from the theatre by the end of March, we shall be married then and go to Italy. If that is not possible, I shall have to wait until June, when Platen has promised to release her, and then we shall probably be married somewhere on the Rhine and go to Switzerland. In any case, we must meet somewhere; I can hardly wait in patience for the time when you will learn to love my Ursi ("Fräulein Amalie Weiss" on the stage). Good-bye, dear old Johannes.—Your

JOSEPH.

*P.S.*—I have not been engaged a week, and, although I am making no secret of it, you need not mention it unless you are questioned. I have not written to tell my people yet.

If my fiancée were not in Leipzig, from whence she is returning on Friday, she would send her kind regards. Her photographs are all dreadfully bad. We are going to have another taken, together, and then you shall have one.

### From Clara Schumann

LYONS, *February* 22, 1863.

My dear Friend—All that the heart can feel at the happiness of a beloved friend I felt when I read your letter. I wept long over it—there is a joy which comprises so much that it turns into melancholy. If I could only express what I feel, what I wish for you both! May you have such happiness as my Robert and I enjoyed—I cannot wish you anything better. And how delighted I am at your choice! From the first moment I saw your fiancée I liked her so much. I hope the time will come when she will recognise in her husband's friend a friend of her own. Do your best to this end, dear Joachim, and let me go on being your intimate friend; you know how, for years past, your friendship has formed a part of my inner life, and so it will always be. When are you going to be married? Surely in the spring, in the lovely month of May? And then I suppose you will go to Rome? And when you come back you will remember me and pay me a visit in Baden with your dear wife? Oh, I am so glad that you too will know the highest joy life can give!

You would have had my answer sooner, but, as you see, I am at Lyons, and only got your letter yesterday evening before the concert here. It was a bad thing for me, because I could think of nothing else but you.

I enclose a few lines to your dear fiancée, whom I love already.  I hope, through her, to hear something of you again before long.  Please, do not leave me so dreadfully long without news now; remember how much you are in my thoughts and that I want to know all about you.  How I envy the Scholzes, who can show themselves your friends by deed now, whilst I must be far away, and yet have a prior right!  You may call this feminine weakness, but there it is and I cannot help it.

You may be sure that Marie joins with me in the sincerest good wishes.

Good-bye now.  When you are with your fiancée think sometimes of her who will always remain—Your truest friend,                    CL. SCH.

If only I could see you in your happiness!

### From Johannes Brahms

[VIENNA] *February* [24] 1863.

You lucky fellow!

What more can I write, unless I add a few more exclamations of the same kind!  My wishes would sound almost too solemn if I were to write them down.

No one will feel with you in your happiness as I do, more particularly as your letter came upon me when I was in a dark mood.

The whole time I have been here I have not ceased to wonder whether, since I must guard against dreams of another kind, I had not better experience and enjoy everything with one exception, or whether I should make sure of one thing, that is, go home and let all the rest slide.

And then you turn up and boldly pluck the ripest and most beautiful apple in Paradise for yourself.

What better can I wish than that everything will turn out as lovely and good as the fact is in itself lovely and good and desirable. With the addition of the beautiful snow-white [schneeweiss] heart of the apple, and the fine young apple trees, and more apples, and more apple trees, etc., *in infinitum.*

Such is my sincerest wish, and I shall look forward to the time when I can come and see you and, as I have already done at the house of many a faithless friend, bend over a cradle and forget everything in the contemplation of the laughing baby face.

Remember me very kindly to your fiancée.

The name sounds like a fairy tale, and at first I did not know whether you were giving me your pet name for her, or her real name.

That is another reason why I ought to go to my home in the north. Otherwise, when shall I see you in your happiness?—Always yours, JOHANNES.

### *From Herman Grimm*

ROME, *February* 26, 1863.

Dearest Joachim—You can imagine how your letter surprised and delighted us. What a good thing that you have escaped the cruel loneliness to which you have been condemned up to now. I will say nothing more than that we wish you happiness with all our hearts. Giesel would not merely say it through me if writing were not still too fatiguing an undertaking for her. Thank heaven she has been a little better lately.

Dear Joachim you write of coming, of your hope of really being here for Easter; you have even allowed hints of this to appear in the papers. To

begin with, I have no doubt that instead of being
married in four weeks' time you will not have got so
far in eight weeks, for these things always take a long
time, and secondly, it will not do because of Giesel.
If you had come alone we had assumed that we, you
and I, would have gone round together during the day
and you would sometimes spend the evening with us.
But if your wife comes with you such an arrangement would not be possible.   Giesel would overtire
herself, perhaps without realising that she was doing
so, and the slightest thing which would put her back
must be avoided until she is quite well again.   So let
us all meet somewhere in Germany in the summer;
I think that is the most sensible plan.

Now good-bye.   Let us hear from you from time
to time, and let us know how things are progressing
to their happy end.—Your                HERMAN.

Hüpeden sends messages and rejoices in the name
of the town of Hanover.

My heartiest congratulations to you and your
fiancée.                                    GISELA.

### To Eduard Möller at Bremen

[HANOVER] *February* 26 [1863].

Dear Friend—Many thanks for your kind invitation, but still more for your sympathy and consideration.   Much as I should like to appear with my fiancée
at a concert before the (I hope I may say) friendly
musical public of Bremen, I think it would be better
if I came alone this time.   I should have the feeling
(and I know you will not disagree with me) that we
were not appealing solely to the artistic interest of the
public, and I dislike nothing so much as mixing private
emotions and feelings with public affairs!   So be con-

tent with me alone; you probably only thought of it owing to a misconception of Hiller's, to whom I may have said that I thought of coming to hear the " Passion Music " at Cologne. But the management at Bremen must not misunderstand me if I decline with thanks the invitation to my fiancée (who is at present in Hamburg); as my wife, I hope she will not give up her music, and I am sure, later on, she will sing nowhere with greater pleasure than at Bremen, with which I have long had such happy relations. . . . I approve of the Beethoven Concerto; Kreutzer's Adagio and Rondo might be the second piece! Remember me to all your dear ones.—Affectionately and respectfully yours, JOSEPH JOACHIM.

### To Herman Grimm

[HANOVER] *Saturday, March* 14 [1863].

Dear Herman—I must ask you to do me a service which I think you can easily carry out, as, probably, the influence of the Prussian embassy (or, through Hüpeden, of the Hanoverian embassy) is yours to command. My colleague Scholz, the only musical friend I had here, is going to Rome in a few days. He is, of course, anxious to hear the music in the Pope's chapel on Good Friday and Easter Sunday. But he fears he will miss the ceremonies unless steps are taken beforehand to secure him the necessary tickets. Hence my request to you to obtain a permit for Scholz, so that he may have a good place from which to see the solemnities, if you can do so without too much trouble. Scholz will have enough tact not to bother you if you would rather be left to yourselves; but you may possibly like to listen to the music in the company of an intelligent professional. Scholz has

studied early Italian music a good deal and is altogether
one of the best of my younger colleagues. He
produced a Requiem of his own not long ago, much
of which I liked very much. I am sorry to say you
were only too right when you prophesied that the
arrangements for my marriage would not go through
so quickly! I shall be glad if I am able to meet you
in May in Switzerland or somewhere! But I have
one pleasure in store : the King has paid me the
honour of appointing me to rehearse and conduct the
*Orpheus* (for the Queen's birthday on April 14). It
will be my fiancée's last part. I shall not promise to
write, but I will do so. Good-bye to you and dear
Gisel from                                        J. J.

## *From Bernhard Scholz*

[ROME] *April* 4, 1863.

You dear friends, if you have thought of me half
as often as I have of you, in spite of all the new
impressions I am receiving, I shall be content ; but
you will be forgiven if that has not been the case, for
it is folly to make the smallest demand of this kind on
engaged people. But as it is hard, all the same, to
get used to the idea that those you love only bear you
in mind occasionally, I will act the tyrant for a bit,
and by sending you this letter extort for myself the
pleasure of making you think, if only for a few minutes,
of your old bear.

First of all I must tell you, dear friend, that your
friends have received me most kindly, and we get on
so well that I am with them every day. I consider it
a great good fortune to have found them here, and I
only hope they will not think my frequent visits a bother.
They certainly invite me to come most cordially, and

so I hope the liking is not all on one side. I am sorry to say I shall soon be deprived of this pleasure, as the Grimms have decided to leave on the 15th.

I cannot tell you all the beautiful things I have seen and enjoyed already—as a matter of fact, up to now, I have really *seen* more than I have enjoyed. There is such a tremendous lot to master that you only begin to enjoy them calmly when you have been everywhere and can go back to the places, pictures, sculptures or buildings which especially appealed to you; I foresee inexhaustible pleasures during my stay here.

Rome is immensely rich, above all, in magnificent antiquities. How often, dear Ursi, when I looked at these I have thought of you and wished you could have obtained your model for your *Orpheus* here. A descriptive artist can learn nowhere as much as he can here, where the antiques stand as everlasting examples of the artistic representation of nature in all her simplicity. *How much* you could learn here! When this letter reaches you the performance of *Orpheus* will be near at hand; you will be much in my thoughts that evening, and I shall turn in my thumbs for you, as I did vigorously on the evening of Palm Sunday. I am very sorry I cannot see your *Orpheus*—I had been looking forward to it during the whole winter. But you will do it again for me another time—won't you? I saw Rienzi's house yesterday, but, thank God, you were not lying under the ruins. They would not let me go into the palace of " Orsini and his band "; probably the porter smelt a rat and feared I was a friend of yours. I shall look out for you at Colonna.

Luise tells me you did the *Faust* beautifully, and I am delighted to hear it, because, to be quite honest, I was a little anxious about it, as you, dear friend, are

not at all used to working with amateurs.    That makes
the success of the performance all the greater.

I am surprised to find that good music is beginning
to gain a footing here in Rome.    There are some
very good Chamber music concerts being given.    The
other day I saw the following programme advertised :

   1. Quartette by Mozart.
   2. Quartette by Haydn.
   3. *Kreutzer* Sonata by Beethoven.

And again on another evening :  Quartette by
Cherubini, Quintette by Schumann.

Schumann in Rome!   What do you think of *that* ?
After these signs of improvement I was all the more
horrified at the absolute collapse of the Papal choir.
They sing perfectly appallingly.    Their intonation is
false, their voices are quite untrained, they phrase and
punctuate as though they were singing, say, the
Prologue to the *Midsummer Night's Dream*—in short,
it is horrible torture, and I have given myself a
dispensation from ever hearing them again.    They
even go the length of improving Palestrina by adding
turns, mordents and shakes—even the most abominable
tremolo, to which a revolting eunuch gives vent with
the greatest complacency.    It would be ridiculous if it
were not infuriating.

And now good-bye for to-day, and let me hear
before long that you are alive and love me.    That will
give *great* pleasure to your old      BEAR.

### From Bernhard Scholz

ROME, *April* 30, 1863.

. . . I saw Liszt in the street the other day in the
company of a priest.    His manner was humble, and he
was continually smiling politely and obsequiously. . . .

Six concerts of classical vocal music were given here this winter under his auspices, at which Palestrina, Bach, Händel, Curschmann, Mendelssohn, Mozart— and Liszt were sung. He moves much in clerical circles. . . .

### From Bernhard Scholz

ROME, *May* 5, 1863.

You shall not wait long for an answer, my dear friend. Your letter was such an agreeable surprise that I have seized my pen at once to thank you for it. You need not be afraid lest what gives you pleasure to write will bore me; on the contrary, I like to hear all you can have to say on the subject of your happiness. I have a great weakness for your Ursi, too, and my pleasure at the sight of *your* writing has made me realise again how fond I am of *you*.

Luise had already told me of the successful performance of the *Orpheus.* I suppose *Fidelio*[1] will be over too by this time. I am very sorry indeed to have missed these two performance of your fiancée's, because these were the very parts I studied with her most carefully, and all the miserable winter through I was looking forward to them and hoping they would compensate me for the many worries of my profession. It may sound bad that I, who am enjoying such wonderful things here, should complain—but I had set my heart on it. When I think of next winter and the pleasures incidental to my calling, I shudder. I cannot imagine, now, how I shall bear it, and I really do not think I shall be able to bear it for long. After all, as you rightly pointed out, it cannot really be my vocation to collaborate with Platen in amusing the lieutenants

---

[1] Farewell performance of Joachim's fiancée.

AMALIE JOACHIM.

Bust by Elisabeth Ney, 1867.

in the front row of the stalls.   Ought I to separate myself from my people and heap trouble and anxiety on myself, simply for the sake of work which I can only regard as absurd and contemptible ?   I have had dreams of being able to do something better.   Olle and I wanted to reform the German theatre.   She has chosen the better part, and I too long to shake off this burden which is robbing me of all courage and vitality.

But no more of this !   Let the future bring what it may, the immediate present is lovely and delightful.

If man were not forced, unhappily, to be *strenuous* I should never be able to move from here out of sheer enjoyment of the place.   But we happen to be made so that we cannot cease to strive, and the pleasure of accomplishing anything becomes all the greater because of the days of preparation and struggling and learning.   I hope to be able to show you something presentable when I see you again.   I hope you will be industrious, too.

I am to tell you a lot about the Grimms : that must be confined to the impression they made upon me, because we did not really *do* much together, as they have to lead a very retired life on her account. At first I went to see them chiefly in the evening, until 9.30, the official hour ; afterwards these evening visits excited Frau Grimm too much and she only saw her friends in the morning at breakfast.   Then they always went for a short drive, after lunch Frau Gisela went to sleep ; and Herman Grimm carried out this régime, so far as his wife's restless nature would permit, with the most anxious care.   Indeed, I sincerely admired the love and consideration and never-failing care with which he looked after her.   It is certainly no easy task, for he has to guard her rigidly against stimulating amusements of any kind, because otherwise she cannot sleep, and at the same time contrive to occupy her mind so that she may not be bored. Then he has to perform all the little loving services of domestic life which a wife generally does for her husband ; he makes tea and coffee, boils eggs, keeps house, and is in short indefatigable. How often I told myself, that, compared with him, I was a perfect horror of egoism and disagreeableness ! Altogether, he is an excellent fellow, and intellectual and charming as well, and I liked him better and better. His manner towards me was very friendly too, and before he went away he lent me Goethe's *Italienische Reise* for an indefinite period.

Frau Gisela is a remarkable woman, wonderfully lively and gifted, and with a heart like Bettina's, so that she must always please and do good to those she meets. But she is not free from a certain kind of vanity—a complaisant enjoyment of her peculiarities. It seems to me she feels obliged to act as spiritual guide and counsellor to some sensitive man who is to become capable of enjoying and appreciating beauty through her alone. And just as she prided herself on having " mothered " you in the old days, so it seemed to please her to be the first to disclose the wonders of Rome to *me*, a pleasure of which I did not like to deprive her, and which was really of use to me occasionally. Her efforts were better rewarded in the case of a young Swiss called Lutz, a very eager, receptive fellow, a lawyer, who, until then, had not troubled much about art, and to whom her refined and cultured guidance was the greatest benefit.

To be quite open, I must add that she is sometimes too naïve for her age, so that I could not altogether believe in her *naïveté*.

But with all this her excellent qualities outweigh

everything else, and I think her ill-health accounted
for many of her peculiarities—so that I am very glad
to have made her acquaintance.  She is really very
much to be pitied, full of vitality and interested in all
ideas as she is, and condemned to renounce all stimulating pleasures.  She met here with that which she
will have to encounter wherever she goes; people
judge her very hardly as a rule ; they say that if she
did not occupy herself so much with things which
excited her nerves and if she paid more attention to
those more suitable to her as a woman, she would not
be such an invalid.  Then, of course, I stand up for
her, and I am sometimes hard pressed. . . . I hope
she will be better further north than here ; the Roman
climate did not agree with her at all.  It suits me very
well now, and I can run round for four hours in the
hottest time of the day without suffering any great
inconvenience.  Yesterday, for instance, I went along
the Via Appia as far as Casale Rotondo, 6 miles
beyond the gates, and in spite of the dust and the
burning sun I thoroughly enjoyed the marvellous
road.  The Campagna is really too lovely!  Through
it one begins to understand the landscapes in the
pictures by Raphael and his predecessors, as, on the
other hand, these pictures teach one how to look at
the Campagna.  A remarkable purity and clearness
of outline, the distinctness with which the formation of
the country stands out, covered by no confusing
wealth of vegetation but only with lovely, isolated
trees, or small groups of trees—all this gives the
Campagna its peculiar character of simplicity and
clearness.  The quiet lines of the aqueducts which
traverse it increase this impression, and the bare hills
in the background, with their rounded sides and
crevasses clearly outlined, tone in to perfection with

the composition of the foreground and middle distance. The brilliant sunshine and the transparent atmosphere make everything, however far away, seem quite clear and distinct. How different it is at home on the Rhine! Not that the country is not just as beautiful, or more beautiful, but it is as different from this one as German from Italian art, and this comparison is the clearest proof of the close connection between art and nature, in *true* works of art, that is to say.

I made a very interesting excursion the other day to the Prima Porta, where they have been excavating recently at a Villa of Livia's. They have already found a very fine statue of Augustus, and they hope to make even more valuable discoveries. Besides this, the place is beautifully situated and affords a magnificent view of the undulating Campagna, of which it is practically the central point.

The shepherd's life in the great plains is wonderful too. These nomads make themselves at home in the ruins of former greatness or in crumbling monuments, and have put up their miserable little stone huts between mighty columns, so as to live there for a few months in the year. Horses, cattle and sheep graze all round; it is like coming across a bit of the Old Testament. Things are quite settled down in Rome and the surrounding district, but Naples is said to be in a bad way. Of course the reports are exaggerated. It will not prevent me from going there, but makes things less pleasant.

Good-bye, dear people, for to-day. Reward my prompt answer with the like. Kindest regards to you, and think kindly of your                    BERNHARD.

## To Clara Schumann

[HANOVER] *May* 26 [1863].

Dear Frau Schumann—It is a long time since your delightful visit, and I do not think this mutual silence should continue.  Are you still in the midst of the cares of settling in ?  Are you already comfortably installed at No. 14 Unterbeuern ?  Are you playing and reading and going for walks with your dear girls and boys?  I am so curious to see your house and I wish there were a photograph of it.  You know ours, but, unhappily, it is still empty.  I have been waiting for the last ten days for permission from the magistrates in Pesth to have the banns called in church, because they say they can do nothing in the case of an Austrian subject.  Let them go to —— Schindler,[1] all these boring, pompous idiots and *Slowcoaches.*  It will be at least another fortnight before we can drive to the church with the Kaulbachs, Brinckmanns, and Frau Detmold (if she is still here).  Johannes said he would probably come too ; you can imagine how pleased I should be if he did.  He was here for three days, and was very charming and sympathetic.  He heard the *Orpheus,* and I was able to have his Quintette[2] played for him.  It is a great pity that the general effect of this piece, in spite of so much that is remarkable in it, should be unsatisfactory, and I was glad that Johannes, on hearing it himself, wished to alter it.  A man of his strong character cannot accept anything on hearsay. I will, of course, let you know the day fixed for our

---

[1] The egregious "ami de Beethoven," who, as critic on the *Niederrheinische Musikzeitung,* had scoffed at Joachim as an interpreter of Beethoven's Quartettes, and finally, in the number of April 4, had ridiculed his Hungarian Concerto.

[2] The F minor Quintette, which was originally written for stringed instruments and then transformed into a Sonata for four hands, in which form, however, Brahms did not care for it.

wedding, dear Frau Schumann, so that you may think of us whilst we are in church. If you were only not so far away! If you are calling on Franz Lachner in the near future, do not say "No" to his request.[1] I have accepted, and I should like to begin the season with the good omen of playing with you. My fiancée means to write to you herself, and sends sincerest regards meanwhile.—Yours,     J. JOACHIM.

### To Th. Avé-Lallemant

[HANOVER, *June* 5, 1863.]

My dear Avé—We have just decided after much uncertainty that the wedding is to be on Wednesday at 11 o'clock. If you were not so tied to your home because of your wife and child, I might perhaps have had the pleasure of seeing you here; because, of course, there is no need for me to tell you that you are cordially invited by me and my fiancée.

I am like a man who, for the first time since childhood and after years of wandering, is to know what it feels like to have a home! At 5 o'clock on Wednesday we are to go through Nürnberg to Salzburg, and later on to my people. So much is settled for the moment. Will you be so good as to convey the enclosed note to Johannes the elder? Remember me to the younger and to all your family, especially your dear wife.

Snow-white is calling me, and sends her kindest regards to you all.—Always yours sincerely,

JOSEPH JOACHIM.

---

[1] An invitation to the Musical Festival at Munich in September, in which Joachim took part.

*From Bernhard Scholz to Ursi and Joachim on their wedding day.*

ROME, *June* 7, 1863.

You dear friends, I cannot remain so very far from you both on your wedding day.

I cannot look into your eyes or press your hands, but at any rate this will bring you a greeting and a relic from Rome—a leaf from Tasso's oak in the garden of S. Onofrio, which I picked whilst thinking of you.

May your cup, my friend, be filled to the brim with happiness, as his was filled with sorrow! I can think of nothing more to wish you, my dear sister, for, from now onwards, his happiness is yours—yes, you yourself should constitute his happiness. Love one another and love your friends, more especially him who loves you both best of all.

Let me have the pleasure of a few words from you soon, to say where you are, so that we may be in touch with one another. . . .

Good-bye for to-day. I must not detain you long on such a day. Give one another a good kiss for me! All blessings on you both!—Your faithful

BERNHARD.

*From Clara Schumann*

LICHTENTHAL 14, BADEN, *June* 8, 1863.

My good, dear Joachim—So it has come at last, the longed-for day which is to bring you the greatest happiness of your life, and I cannot be with you even to press your hand! Such happiness is hard to express in words, and indeed it is sufficient to know it and realise it with you. Oh, I should certainly have come, the distance would not have frightened me, but a reason which I do not like to explain because of its prosaic nature made it impossible! You did not tell me the hour of the wedding. I shall imagine it is 12 o'clock; I shall not be able to think of anything but you the whole day.

I received your dear Ursi's charming letter and thank her very much for it, but she alarmed me by the remark that she was looking forward to our meeting in—Munich. Have you given up all idea of paying me a visit here in the course of the summer? I should be extremely sorry if that were so, for I, and all of us, were looking forward to it with such pleasure! Write to me soon from wherever you set up your tents so that I may find you in my thoughts.

You were to have had a trifle from me before now for the new house, but the move took up so much of our time that we (I and my children) have only just been able to begin working at it. Meanwhile, take the good-will for the deed.

I suppose you received my last letter?

The sincerest wishes for you both from us all.

I am with you in spirit and with my whole heart.— Yours as always, CLARA SCH.

*From Bernhard Scholz*

HAMMERMÜHLE, *July* 27, 1863.

My dear Friend—I had heard nothing of you for so long that I was longing for news of you both. And yesterday I had a letter from your dear Ursi at last; now I know where to send my thoughts so as to find you in spirit. I can imagine how charming your little house in the lovely Salzburg country is, with its garden and pond, and I sincerely hope that your dear wife will soon be quite well and strong again so that you may be able to enjoy all the beauty around you free from all anxieties.

I have been here for the last fortnight, and my mind is still full of visions of all that I saw so short a time ago. I saw wonderful and beautiful things, and when I came home my wife and child were well and merry, and that was best of all. I have to go back to Hanover again on the 20th of August. I cannot tell you how I dread the work there. I have been far from all these vulgarities, and I am positively afraid of seeing those beloved faces again. If you were only going to be there from the very beginning there would be *something* for me to look forward to! I do not think I can stand the theatre, or this one at any rate, much longer ; art is treated altogether too disgracefully there. Sometimes I think it would be better if I settled on my own heritage and ploughed my land ; at any rate, I should not then be obliged to assist in heaping indignities on the art I love ; for it is questionable whether my services are of any benefit either to my art or to myself. I often feel as though every note I write were a sin against the Holy Ghost and actively evil. The goal I wish to attain is so distant, so distant, that I shall never reach it. And so I go on wrestling helplessly—for what? And my dependence on the Court and its corrupt environment oppresses me. Here I should be a free man ! How different your position is, and how much pleasanter ! How many hearts are rejoiced by you, how many eyes shine with a brighter light when you have played ! You are made welcome by all good men, you can *see the blessing of your work* every day—after all, that alone constitutes true happiness. Do not imagine that I am labouring under any false modesty, or that I am smarting under a lack of public recognition.  Far from it!  When I compare myself with others, I am not modest.  I would credit few people, hardly one, with more powers than myself; little as I am satisfied with my work, I should be just as dissatisfied with the work of any one else.  I make an exception of your Concerto and a good many things by Brahms.  But if I were satisfied with myself I would not care a hang for recognition from the public.  The only piece I do not regret having composed is the Requiem—and even that has great weaknesses which I do not conceal from myself.  But enough, I ought not to say all this to you, and yet —in whom could I confide so frankly if not in you, the only one of my friends who can really understand my point of view?

I still have nearly four weeks of freedom ; I mean to enjoy them, it is so lovely on the Rhine!  And the country folk are so fine!  Last Sunday—tell this to Olle — we were on the plateau and the beautiful country of my birth lay before me.  Italy is more magnificent, but the cords which vibrate at the sight of home, of a beloved home with which all our youthful recollections are connected, are more powerful than any others.  The holy city of Rome has a similar effect on one—because it is a work of art created centuries ago. It impresses one like a true tragedy, at once purifying and elevating ; God grant that I may be able to go there once again!

And now, my dear fellow, if you cannot manage to come here whilst we are still here, do not leave us alone in Hanover for long.  I need you both there too much. . . .

*From Björnstjerne Björnson*

CHRISTIANIA, *November* 2, 1863.

Dear Joachim—I must really send you my photograph! I live here now and have it all my own way, the people are at my beck and call, but I have plenty of time to myself. I am just writing *Maria Stuart* in two plays. The first, *Henrik Dearnley*, in three long acts, is finished, and I have just begun the second, *Bothwell*; it will be in five acts. My previous work has not yet been translated; the Baroness had a fancy for something else, and I am quite indifferent. But I shall always send you whatever is translated, only I never make any effort myself to have my works translated. So it is possible that nothing more will be turned into German, for I am only writing plays, and they are not on sale at the booksellers.

I may not write long letters, I have taken a vow. Just look at my small notepaper! It is like having small rooms, so that one is excused from giving large parties.

Music here is practically at a standstill; that is, executive music, for national compositions are just beginning, and they are a delight to me. Our violinists are beginning to play Bethoven and Bach (in imitation of you). But I fear their four strings are like a very small stream; when the floods of Bethoven and Bach come down they overflow the banks—the stream is not wide enough.

A young Norwegian, Böhen, is coming to hear you and have a talk with you. He wishes me to recommend him. I cannot do so, first because your time is so limited, and secondly because he is not sufficiently educated, in the higher sense (technically he is). But people think a lot of him here, so please do all you can; all Christiania is expectant! Remember me to the conductor and his wife. Could I not have a small photograph of your wife's piquant face, and of the large-eyed Frau Kapellmeisterin? Do not forget me, all of you, I am such a polar bear, and sometimes I feel freezing cold, and long to be in the warmth instead of roaming about over the ice in the moonlight! Remember me to your wife and to Brinckmann and his wife.—Yours, BJÖRNST. BJÖRNSON.

My brother is going to the Polytechnic School at Hanover!

### To Julius Stockhausen

[HANOVER, *January* 24, 1864.]

. . . Things have got to such a pass in Schleswig H. that one has to put a powerful brake on one's thoughts on the subject—for matters are so uncertain at present that one does not know whether to wish Prussia defeat or victory. I am inclined to the former, because then there would be something for us to do. My violin will not be ready until Monday; I cannot play on any other, as I found out yesterday in the Aula. Although I had borrowed a Stradivarius with a sweet tone, I could play neither so softly nor so loudly as on my *own.—Semper fideliter*,

JOSEPH JOACHIM.

### To Ernst Rudorff in Hamburg

HANOVER, *the* 16*th* [*March* 1864].

Dear Herr Rudorff—First of all, many thanks for your letter, which showed confidence in me and requires no apologies; was it not on behalf of Rose, in whose progress I, too, take the liveliest interest? In spite of my trip to Leipzig I would have answered you before now, if I had been able to come to any definite conclusion—but I am really in some doubt as to what is best for him. It is quite true it would be better for his future if he had the stimulus of a visit to London now and then, instead of giving lessons at Hamburg year in year out. But, with all his undeniable talent, has he, so far, got the stuff in him to hold his own among the prominent musicians who all compete for engagements in London during the season? You and your friends in Hamburg who have observed him closely can really answer this better than I, who have not heard him since, eighteen months ago, he played a few short, disconnected movements to me in my room. The fact that he has been playing seconds very well lately is not sufficient for the present purpose. If I must really advise, I shall have to hear friend Rose play again here at my leisure, for several days at least. Recommendations are of no use unless it is possible to call attention with absolute conviction to powers which afterwards make their way on their own merits. If Rose imagines he can *go on studying* whilst getting to know people during the rush of the London season, I think he is under an illusion. Concentration is required for that, and the interest of zealous and loving friends, if God should bestow such a rare favour.

Your opinion coincides with my experience—but *how far* it applies to Rose I could only decide if he thought it worth while to give me full knowledge of his capacity. He will always be welcome here for his own sake!

It is a real pleasure to me to know that you still like to think of my visit to Hamburg;[1] *I* owe to it

[1] On February 19 Joachim had played his Hungarian Concerto in public at Hamburg; the previous evening, at Avé's house, he had played Rudorff's Sextette in A major, op. 5.

my faith in one more sincere and genuine artist, who aims at the highest with all his might. . . .

*To Clara Schumann*

[HANOVER] *the 20th [April,* 1864].

Dear Frau Schumann—In the first rush of my boundless delight at receiving your dear letter, I wanted to write to you at once from Cologne where I played the day after, but I could not manage it at the Hillers'. Afterwards, when I came back here I had a *very* bad cold for a few days—and so my thanks will reach you much later than they should or than I intended. Yes, you have been very far away for ever so long, and I am particularly sorry, for artistic reasons, that you are still at such a distance, because next week I am to hear my new Concerto[1] with the orchestra. You and Johannes used always to be present at experiments like these. I need not speak of the pleasure and stimulus I gained by it—I will just say : If only you could be here! I have lain fallow, as a composer, for so long that I am really glad to have completed something, and I am beginning to look forward again with pleasure instead of with melancholy to the thought of composing. I am not yet satisfied with the first movement—and I should have valued your fine judgment so highly. Let us hope for another time! Shall I see you at Aachen?[2] It is stupid not to have invited you too ; I expect they are afraid of the expense of two soloists, and the violin is more the instrument for large halls than the piano! My Ursi was asked to sing contralto, but unfortunately (or rather fortunately, because of the reason!) she cannot go. She will have to take great care of herself

---

[1] In G major.        [2] At the Lower Rhine Musical Festival.

until the autumn, when we look forward to a great and happy change in our household.   And so from Aachen I am going alone to London for five weeks—in my present circumstances I must not lose the 2000 thalers which are practically assured to me by engagements over there.   Then we are thinking of taking a house in the Harz or near Thüringen in July ; we cannot go far.   I wish the stern doctor would allow us a trip to Baden, *Vederemo.*   I had the delightful surprise at Cologne of meeting the Bendemanns and Julie.   I cannot make up my mind to say " Fräulein Julie " except to her personally.   She looked very well and seems happy with the Bendemanns.   She enjoyed the music, and has probably told you about it.   I enclose a few lines from my wife which I have not read ; she never allows me to read what she has written.   Is it not cruel of her?   Now I shall be scolded for having complained ! . . .

### *To Bernhard Scholz*

[HANOVER, *beginning of August* 1864.]

Dear Scholz—We have thought of you so often during the last few days that you must have had a continuous singing in your ears.   Brahms was here, and then Grimm came (the one from Münster) and I went with these two to Göttingen where, in spite of the worst possible weather, we made two lovely excursions to the Gleichen and the Plesse.   I was away for a day and a half, without Ursi, who, however, is occupied with all sorts of needlework nowadays, and thinks more of the future musician than of the present one !   I had hardly got back when Dietrich came to see me, and the two of us together again missed you very heartily.   D. is going to his relations in Saxony for his convalescence; the dear, dreamy fellow has quite recovered from his sad condition— but, unhappily, one cannot banish all fear of a relapse, one sees what a nervous and excitable creature he is. It does one good to think of a nature like Brahms', fortified by its healthy egoism, in spite of all his devotion to the beautiful. He has given up his post as director of the choir, so as to live entirely for composing; for however much the rehearsing and producing in the company of real music lovers stimulated him, he was equally distracted and worried by the search for cheap soloists, piquant novelties, etc., etc. He is particularly sorry that, in giving up the post, he will have to leave his wish with regard to your Requiem unfulfilled; and he asked me to tell you so. You have fairly wallowed in artistic and natural beauty these holidays! I found little to stimulate me in England, with the exception of some magnificent pictures. My life seemed to consist of a never-ending rush from one concert to the other. It seems all the quieter here; nearly everybody is away. I shall do nothing in my unpleasant affair[1] until Platen comes back; but I am determined to let no kind of consideration keep me here if Grün is not appointed *sans phrase*.

Well, you are soon coming back too, and I am looking forward to it already!—Always your most sincere friend,  JOSEPH J.

### To Count Platen

HANOVER, *August* 23, 1864.

In accordance with your Excellency's wish I am writing to you with reference to the conversation

---

[1] Moser ii. 124.

concerning Herr Grün, which I had with your Excellency before the beginning of the holidays.   I can say with absolute truth that since then I have thought the matter over frequently and conscientiously, as your Excellency recommended—without, however, being able to regard it in any other light.

I could not possibly forget (and I beg to lay great stress on this) that Herr Grün was engaged on behalf of the management *through me*, with the express understanding that he should eventually succeed to the post then occupied by Herr Kömpel.   If Herr Grün, in spite of his excellent services and fidelity to duty, acknowledged by all his superiors, and after years of patient waiting, is not to be promoted after I have called attention to the matter, *because he is a Jew*, and if, for this reason, the promises made by me on behalf of a higher authority are not fulfilled, then, according to my idea of honour and duty, I shall have no alternative but to justify myself by retiring from my appointment at the same time as Herr Grün.   If I remained in my present position after the rejection of Herr Grün I should never be able to get over the purely personal feeling that because I had become a member of the Christian Church I had gained worldly advantage and had obtained a privileged position in the Royal Hanoverian Orchestra, whilst others of my race were forced into humiliating situations. . . .

### To Clara Schumann

[HANOVER] *August* 24 [1864].

Dear Frau Schumann—I am writing at once so that my letter may catch you before you start on your wanderings through the dear old places, and not follow round after you hopelessly.   You would have heard from me again sooner than this if your last note had not made me hope for further news. I thought you were on tour through Switzerland *with* Johannes; your references to both were so vague and hasty. I am glad you are in that beautiful clear atmosphere which I enjoyed so much with you three years ago, whilst here, alas, for a long time we have had nothing but cold and rain and storm, such as I have never known before during the summer. It is dreadfully depressing to see this Hanoverian sky! To come to your questions, I will answer the last one first of all. I have just sent a letter to the management in which I have said that, if Herr Grün is not promoted to be *Kammermusikus* (as he was promised on high authority at his engagement), I shall leave when Grün does. They cannot ignore it, because I concluded by saying that I had expressed my intention *before* September 1 in accordance with the contract, so that I might not be bound in that way. You shall hear as soon as I have any news. I must confess that just at present, after I have just settled down, and before I know where I shall go, the idea of giving up my post is not agreeable to me; meanwhile I shall be at liberty to remain in my present house, even if I give up my post, until I have found a home I like better. Herr Grove became one of the dearest of my English friends in London. He is secretary to the Crystal Palace, but that is merely for a living. In competent learned circles he is considered the greatest English authority on the geography of the ancients. He is therefore a distinguished scholar, and he has, at the same time, so true and deep a love of art, such a German absorption in music, that a visit to his simple, hospitable home is delightful. He seemed to me, with his wife and children, like a German colonist in England, although none of them can speak German. For instance, he is an ardent admirer of Schumann, and wherever anything of Schumann's is being played, there he is with a company of believers, and joins with them in clapping until he is worn out! So, if you have not yet sent him your picture, you can do so now without misgiving; he deserves it in every way. And what he writes about the propagation of Schumann's music is quite true. I was not able to play any of Schumann's Quartettes in public, because at Ella's Matinées, for which I was engaged, a Sonata (A minor) and Quintette had already been arranged for. They would not do at the Popular Concerts yet; Schumann's intellect is too exclusively of the German romantic type for the *general* public in England. He will only penetrate to the masses through individuals. I am sending back Grove's letter. I cannot write any more to-day, but I shall say more about your plan for an English season in a few days. You will, of course, leave instructions for your letters to be forwarded if you leave the Rigi before then. You have considered my Concerto in the kindest light; I hope the one I have in my mind now will be better. . . .

### To Clara Schumann

[HANOVER, *beginning of September*, 1864.]

Dear Frau Schumann—I hope you are happily with your dear ones, and that you have been favoured with better weather than we have had! It is really very hard for me to answer your questions about England, and I will begin by telling you how *I* got on. For six weeks I literally led a slave's life, and yet the result was only about £330 gross. If I had accepted engagements at private houses I might have

Y

made £400. And yet a violinist's chances are better than a pianist's. The people who have the arrangement of the concerts in their hands *must* keep in with Hallé, Pauer, and Mrs. Davison, because they need them throughout the whole year, whereas the London violinists are less pretentious. (The resident pianists, because they give lessons, are more closely connected with society, with ladies who give musical evenings, etc., and therefore have an influence over all sorts of musical *commerce*. *C'est partout comme chez nous !*) But if you intend to go to London for several seasons *in succession*, I should certainly advise you to do so; but it is not worth while to go for *one* season. However, I can give you no better advice than to ask Mr. Grove for his opinion; he is independent enough not to be obliged to consider the pianists over there, and yet his tastes and position as secretary make him thoroughly conversant with all the circumstances. Whether I shall go to London again depends on the King's decision with regard to Grün. But in any case I would not do again what I did last time; *i.e.* I should only bind myself for certain concerts and raise my fee in each case, or I should make the *experiment* of giving some concerts myself, in which, of course, there is some risk. I think there is something inartistic in playing at *any and every* concert. I will let you know the King's decision as soon as I know it myself. I am sending you, for now, the enclosed letter from Platen.[1] How delighted I should be if there were any prospect of our once more spending some time together in the same town! *Let me know your plans for the winter as soon as possible.* Herr Ullmann has repeatedly made me offers for concert tours—I too have control of the *programme and advertising*—and

---

[1] Not traced.

he would try and secure you also. But it was not possible to agree to it! Good means cannot sanctify evil ends!! Rather black bread from a clean platter than cakes from the dishes of a money-changer!!! I am sure you think as I do. All sorts of changes are taking place in my home so that the young citizen of the world may be worthily received. You will have word at once. The only other pleasant thing I can tell you about Hanover is that I am filling the first half of the first concert with *Manfred*, and the second with the Ninth, and that I hope to see you here for it. Is Johannes still with you? At any rate, I am sending back the Sonata in duet form, which, as a composition, I liked almost without exception. But I should like to hear it played by you both, so as to know what it *sounds* like. Is it always clear enough, with its full harmonies and intermingling of the parts? I understand too little about the piano to trust myself to form an opinion without hearing it. . . .

*To Clara Schumann*

[HANOVER] *September* 12 [1864].

Dear Frau Schumann—To-day, the 13th, is a red-letter day to us, your birthday, and we all send you our good wishes in a particularly joyful mood! For yesterday was a birthday too, and the little Joachim has shown his good taste in choosing the prelude to such an eventful day in the history of music for his happy entry into the world. He is a fine boy and seems pleased with himself, and his cry of joy caused his mother to forget all the seventeen terrible hours (from midnight until five o'clock in the afternoon!).

Ursi is quite well—I have just seen her break-

fast off milk and rusks. We both send our love !—
Yours, JOACHIM.

Is Johannes still in Baden? If so, this letter is for
him also.

## From Clara Schumann

BADEN-BADEN, *September* 15, 1864.

My dear Joachim—What a surprise that was !
We had just heard Johannes' Quartette, and we were
feeling worked up when the letter came—a real
musicians' cry of joy rang through our room.
Splendid ! and a son too. How glad I am for you !
Accept the congratulations of all of us (including
Fräulein Leser and Junghés). May all good spirits
protect the little citizen of the world ! I am told to
send you the enclosed cards. Johannes is writing to
you himself.

I am so glad your dear wife has got through it all
so well—they are indeed cruel hours, and yet nothing
is more easily forgotten. Please let me know soon
again (only in a few words) how Ursi and her little
one are getting on. But *when* was he born? Your
letter begins, "To-day, the 13th," but it is dated
"September 12." I imagine his birthday is the 12th
(our wedding day)?

We had a very happy day with Johannes on the
13th, and drank dear Joachim's health so loudly that
he must have heard it, but it was meant for two of
them ! ! !

Johannes gave me a delightful surprise in the
shape of a photograph of my little house, which I will
send you as soon as I have another copy.

This letter must go off this morning, so I will tell
you more about myself another time.

Good-bye, dear people! A thousand good wishes
from your old                          CL. SCHUMANN.

## To Clara Schumann

[HANOVER, *February* 3, 1865.]

Dear Frau Schumann—The sad news is indeed
true! My dear father was seventy-six years of age.
For the last few years the winter has always affected
him, but he picked up again very quickly. You can
imagine what a blow the news was to me after the
last concert; my wife had known the whole day on
the 21st, and had to get me to the concert and let
me conduct and play without telling me.

Poor darling! On top of this blow there have
been the ugliest calumnies about me in the papers.[1]
I foresaw this filth, but I am more hurt and upset
by it than I would have believed. I had an audience
of an hour and a half with the King, who tried to
dissuade me from my decision with all sorts of
cajolings; but I remained firm. More about this
by word of mouth. We did not go to Hamburg;
I telegraphed to say I could not go, as I could not
bring myself to play at a concert feeling as I did.

*Manfred* has again been put off, but for the last
time! It is to be on the 25th. Write and tell me
as soon as possible whether you can and will play
for certain. I go to London on March 1.

I shall only now have leisure to read the Sextette;[2]
you can imagine how I am longing to have a closer
knowledge of it. The Adagio looks lovely and
typical of Johannes.

With our kindest regards, and in the hope that
your hand will soon be all right.—Yours,      J. J.

---

[1] With regard to the Grün affair.      [2] Brahms' 2nd, in G major.

Perhaps you and our friends will be interested in the announcement of a paper which is taking *my* side in the Grün matter. My enemies had published that I wanted to introduce a pupil here *à tout prix*, that I had ignored the talent in the orchestra for his sake, and that the management had only said it could not be done on religious grounds so as to be able to refuse my urgent demands! etc., etc.

### From Clara Schumann

COLOGNE, *February* 8, 1865.

Dear Joachim—How grieved I am at all you had to tell me in your last letter! But do not let yourself be affected by these base people; a man so universally looked up to as you are cannot be injured by them; just think of Mendelssohn and all he had to go through! No one knows anything about it now; people read these things one day and forget them the next.

Are you absolutely determined to leave Hanover?

You have to mourn the loss of your father, and now Johannes has lost his mother. I expect he wrote and told you this, and that he is now in Hamburg. He had looked forward with dread to this sorrow for a long time, and it is a terrible loss for poor Elise.[1] I have no idea what will become of her, and I feel very anxious about it.

I cannot possibly decide to-day whether I can play for you on the 25th, but I will write as soon as I can. I have only been allowed to move my hand again since yesterday, after nearly four weeks. I am to begin to play a little again at the beginning of next week—I positively dread it, as you can imagine,

---

[1] Brahms' sister.

because up to now I have felt as though I could never play again.

Are you going to give *Manfred* with Richard Pohl's arrangement? Levi produced it the other day, only making partial use of Pohl's arrangement, and yet he had to employ three additional actors. They say the performance was magnificent. He had the final chorus sung at the back of the hall in another room, accompanied by the organ. Could you not manage that with a harmonium?

I must say good-bye for to-day. Remember me, please, to your people when you write to Pesth, and assure them of my warm sympathy. Kindest regards to dear Ursi and to you from us both.—Faithfully yours,

CL. SCHUMANN.

### *From Ernst Rudorff*

BERLIN, *February 25,* 1865.

Dear Herr Joachim—You have been through so much lately, such grave and sad experiences which must have moved you deeply, and then again such annoying and burdensome experiences which touched quite a different side of your nature, that it seems almost impertinent of me to write to you now, when your mind and heart are taken up with more important things. But I feel I must say a few words to express to you my heartfelt sympathy, of which, I hope, you have no doubt, and also to send you a farewell greeting before you go to England. I daresay you think it rather childish to regard a journey to England as such an event; but it is not only that. I had hoped—as matters stood with me at Christmas—that my course would not lie so very far from you, and that when I was in Brunswick I should be able to give myself the pleasure of frequently seeing you and hearing music at your house. I feel now as though matters had not fallen out well in this respect, and so I wish to thank you once more for all the beautiful and memorable impressions both in the way of friendship and music which you have always accorded me. Everything will be treasured up in my memory, the *Eroica*, the *Wasserträger* evening on which I first had the pleasure of hearing and enjoying such magnificent music in your company, and then the last days, the Beethoven Festival and the Quartettes on the Sunday morning. . . .

I am very anxious to know what will happen to you, whether you will really leave Hanover, or remain after all. If you could only put the orchestra in your pocket, so that we merely had to go somewhere else to hear the Ninth Symphony under your conductorship, it would be all right, but it is sad to think that you cannot keep the orchestra, and that it cannot keep you!

I suppose Frau Schumann is playing with you to-day, and I hope she can do so with a perfectly sound hand. She wrote to some one the other day about the possibility of playing here, and I wish her a grateful public that is really worthy of her; but whether my wish will have any effect is doubtful with the people of Berlin. Singing is so much more popular, and then it became the fashion to hear Stockhausen, if only because his concerts were so very expensive. This seems a hard saying, but it is true, nevertheless, I am sorry to say. On the other hand, Frau Schumann is neither new nor pretentious enough for people, and so I am not altogether easy in my mind about the attendance at her concerts. Perhaps you have heard from her

about what happened in Brunswick, and so I will
spare myself the weary task of giving you an account
of it by writing.   I have quite settled down here,
see fewer people, and am working fairly hard.
Schubert's F minor Phantasy[1] is not quite finished
yet.   I should so much have liked to send it to you
for your opinion, but your journey to England makes
it impossible.   My time is entirely taken up at
present by a concert which is to take place in the
middle of March.   Frau Jachmann-Wagner is to
sing the whole of the *Orpheus* for the Gustav-Adolf
Society; I am to rehearse and conduct it, and
this is at the same time a great pleasure and a great
anxiety.   You have no idea how hard it is to root
out an improvised chorus, a day for the rehearsals,
a room which happens to be free on that day, and
a time for the general rehearsal at which the Liebig
orchestra and all the other people are disengaged—
or rather you have a very good idea, because you
know such things, by experience, better than I do.
It has just occurred to me that Herr Scholz might
be able to lend me some copies of the chorus belonging to the theatre ; we have not sufficient, and I am
delighted at the idea, because the Gustav-Adolf is
too stingy to give out any more money for extra
copies.   So I shall write a line to him at once, which
I shall *not* enclose, as it is sure to reach him in
Hanover without any further address.

  And now good-bye for the present, and kindest
regards to you and your wife.   I am sorry I cannot
yet ask to be remembered to the little nameless one,
but it would not amuse him very much!—Yours, as
always, very sincerely,

                              ERNST RUDORFF.

[1] Op. 103, for four hands.   Rudorff arranged it for orchestra.

Have you tried Brahms' new Sextette? Frau Schumann gave it to me for a very short time, and I could only look at the first movement, but that seemed to me to be full of intellect and individuality.

*From Bernhard Scholz*

HANOVER, *April* 7, '65.

Dear Jo.—Your letter to Pinelli is in his hands by now; I sent it on to him yesterday. What news have I for you up to now?—Restlessness, anxiety, plans, thoughts! Yes, now I have a lot to tell you!

1. With Ursi's help my Soirée at Hanover went off well; I have distinctly gained confidence, and I hope it will go on improving.

2. I have resigned, and I think I am pretty certain to be in Florence or Rome next winter.

3. I went to see Schorse and had a long talk with him. He saw all my reasons for leaving, and regretted the miserable business with Platen : he said he would get rid of him if only he knew whom to put in his place. I must tell you that Schorse is firmly convinced that, now the Grün matter has been settled, you ought to come back here. He said you told him just before you left that if the matter were settled in a manner honourable to Grün, you would remain. I remarked that that ought to have happened whilst you were here, and that it was settled rather late in the day, to which he replied that he had been ill, and that the matter had certainly been delayed *at first* through Platen's fault. You know my opinion of the guilt and consequent responsibility of *both* these noble gentlemen ; but you are in the wrong now in *one* respect. You are shifting your quarrel with the King on to a different ground from that which you maintained here.

You said *here* to me and your friends, and to the King, that you regarded the matter as an abuse of your pledged word, and you stated positively that, if Grün expressed himself satisfied, you would retract your resignation.

You know I am fairly hard to please, but I think Grün has every reason to be satisfied. He has got everything, or more than you promised him at first. He is *Kammervirtuos*, just as Kömpel was, he has the same salary as the latter, he is *appointed for life* with *certainty of a pension* (that is the point on which everything turned), and the King told him and me that, if not *legally*, at any rate *morally*, as a Christian he considers himself bound to indemnify Grün for the *crying injustice* [*sic*] practised against him. That is all one can ask from a king. He can surely be allowed his little subterfuge of having kept back the title of *Kammermusikus*, for it has no further value. The *real* business has turned out very well indeed, so far as Grün is concerned. What you *can* say is: "Too late!" But that is all, and it would suffice certainly. But you owe it to yourself and to the whole affair to continue to be dignified and correct, and not to change your standpoint at the last minute. That is what I think. You could make one other representation : that you felt it would be derogatory to your honour to serve under a chief who has shown so plainly that he wishes to get rid of you. But your *course* of action must not be open to criticism. That is how it appears to me, anyhow, and I entreat you not to let your wishes or dislikes lead you to abandon the right and just course. . . .

Are you going to the Musical Festival at Mainz ? We could put up you and your wife and child. The Festival is in July ; but you ought to let us know soon.

You can imagine what a mental struggle I went through before I resigned. At last, when I was feeling absolutely ill and miserable, I dared to take the *salto mortale*, supported by my parents' approval. . . .

### *To Luise Scholz*

[LONDON, *towards end of June* 1865.]

Dear Louise—It would be a bad omen if the first 28th of June,[1] since fate has threatened to tear us so far apart, should pass without a greeting. And so lazy Jo is writing you this note to remind you, by the sincerest good wishes, that he is in the world, and has, therefore, been born also! How are you both and what are your plans? I suppose the first thing will be the Musical Festival, and I wish I could be with you to fill my ears with song and my mouth with Mainz beer. But Ursi's condition makes this impossible, unfortunately, and we are going to the seaside in a week's time. . . . After I left Hanover I wrote to Prinz Georg and Lex that I had never concealed the fact that I was going for *two* reasons, one being the unfulfilled conditions, and the other the impossibility, as a baptised Jew, of remaining at the head of an institution in which members of my race occupied a humiliating position. There is only one answer to this—that it is a matter of taste, but my taste happens to be like that. Is Pinelli on the Rhine? Please ask the Bear, for whom this note is intended as well as for you, to let me know. I have more time now, and I should like to write a word of consolation to the dear fellow for having to give up his lessons with me. I feel like that Sultan (or barber?) who thought he had dipped his head into the water for a

---

[1] Frau Scholz' and Joachim's birthday.

moment, and on looking up saw how many years must have passed meanwhile.   What a lot of changes took place whilst I vanished into the whirlpool of the season!

Dear Louise and dear B., do not let us lose the point of view we have always had, and let us cling fast to the unchanging sympathy between us!—Yours,

JOSEPH JOACHIM.

### *To Bernard Cracroft* [1]

WHITBY, *July* 23 [1865].

My dear Cracroft—I have heard nothing from you since you were so good as to send me Goschen's very interesting speech on the University Bill.[2]   Unfortunately my time in London was so taken up, not only by my own affairs but also by my wife's continued ill-health, that I could see nothing of my friends, and I hurried secretly out of London, almost as though I were a bankrupt.   We have been in Whitby for the last fortnight, and I am glad to say my wife is much better.   The air is beautifully pure and bracing, and has blown away from me too the real fatigue I felt after the season, so that I am longing for music again, and should like to play you all sorts of concertos and quartettes, if Upper Davies Street were not so terribly far away.

I suppose you are immersed in politics, and are thoroughly enjoying the Liberals' triumphant victory. I always forget whether you are a Cambridge or an Oxford man [*sic*].   As the latter, you would feel Gladstone's[3] rejection.   But *I* must say that I like to

---

[1] A stockbroker and writer on political subjects, and a friend of Joachim's for many years.

[2] In Parliament on June 20, with reference to the founding of Catholic Universities for Ireland.

[3] At the election in July Gladstone, who had represented Oxford hitherto, failed to win his seat.

think of Gladstone's genius working unfettered. And besides the country will realise with shame how far intolerance can lead even the most cultured! Let me have a line from you soon to say how and where you are; and especially whether I should have any chance of meeting you in London in the middle of August. I shall be passing through London about that time with my wife and child, and shall stay there for a day or two before I start for France and Germany. I should be delighted to see you again before I go, because I shall not come back to London again before February 1866. My wife is reading your book very industriously, and sends her kindest regards.—Always yours very sincerely,                JOSEPH.

### From *Amalie Joachim* to *Clara Schumann*

[HANOVER, *December* 30, 1865.]

Dearest Frau Schumann—Jo has to go to a concert, although only to listen—and I am making use of the blank space to thank you very much for your beautiful present. You have of course forestalled me again, and written to thank me in a way I really do not deserve. It was such a pleasure to me to work the trifle for you! We had a very happy feast-day—although far from all our friends. But I had Jo, and Putzi was very sweet, too. Unhappily, the merry time has passed so quickly—and now the grave time is before us! God knows what the New Year will bring! Many changes for us, that is certain. You may be sure Jo and I wish you a very happy one. I hope that we shall be near you again some time in the course of it!

. . . Jo just told me he wanted to tell you about Bargiel and Brahms. I was particularly sorry that

Brahms again failed to come.   I am firmly convinced
he did not come on my account; not that I am in
his way—I am not so vain as to think that—but
he thinks he takes Jo away from me, and that I
resent it.   If Brahms only knew how gladly I give
Jo up to his friends—and how pleased I am that he
should remain intimate with you and your mutual
friends—and should see you often!   I am so sorry
for Jo, buried here in dull Hanover, by the side of an
unskilful housewife, who shows him only too often how
badly and unpractically she keeps house, and yet does
not suffice him in other directions, as an artist—still
less stimulate and inspire him!   So I am really
grateful to you and his old, true friends if you keep in
touch with him and take no account of me—please
believe this, dearest Frau Schumann!   And it would
have been delightful if Brahms had kept his promise,
and I would have thanked him for every hour during
which he took my Jo away from me!

Jo[1] is going to the subscription concerts for the
first time to-day.   *Athalie* and a Symphony of Haydn's
are to be done, and—only think, dear Frau Schumann,
who has just interrupted me!?   Brahms has just come.
Is that not splendid!   I am so delighted—although
he says he must go away again to-morrow!   Good-bye
—and think kindly during the new year of yours
very sincerely,                              URSI.

### To Clara Schumann

HANOVER, *January* 27 [1866].

Dear Frau Schumann—Perhaps you have already
heard of the happy arrival of a second little boy; but,
in any case, I must write you a few words myself, and

---

[1] Joachim occupied no appointment at that time.

add that Ursi is quite well again after causing me serious anxiety last night. Towards evening she began to wander and in her fever she got into a state of mind for fear anything should have happened to her piano on its way through the post, etc., etc. I ran straight to the doctor, who reassured me, and, thank God, she is much better to-day. She suffered more than the first time, poor darling. But the little boy is very vigorous, and seems to me even prettier than his little brother. I was able to express my joy over the happy event in music the next day, on the evening of the 25th, at the *Marktkirche*. Brahms was there and displayed more kindness and sympathy than he usually shows (I do not mean than he *has*). I played the Beethoven Cavatina from op. 130, the *Abendlied*, the Adagio from Bach's Violin Concerto, and the first movement from Bach's G major Sonata (piano and violin). They say the music sounds beautiful in the church; there ought to be more music for violin and organ, and I hope Johannes has been persuaded to write some. Besides that the church choir sang some lovely old things by Michl. Bach, Hasler, Praetorius, etc., etc. . . . Very sincerely yours,                                   JOSEPH J.

### *To his brother Heinrich in London*

[HANOVER, *about April* 15, 1866.]

Dear Heinrich—I ought to have written long ago, but it is so easy to find excuses for not sitting down to write letters ! . . . The two boys are very jolly. The younger was baptised last Saturday and is called Giselher Bernhard Herman, after Scholz and the Grimms in Berlin. . . . I have been to Court two evenings to play. The King behaves as though everything were as before, and this affects me painfully,

for I have by no means made up my mind to stay
here! I played the other day with the orchestra at
the Court at Bückeburg (an hour by train), where the
Prince did the honours very graciously, and this week
I gave a concert here with the pianist Tausig, so
that I am the richer by 40 louis-d'or. . . . Tausig
gave a badly attended concert here alone, at which I
heard him. I was so struck and delighted by his
wonderful playing that I begged him to give another
concert here, and placed myself at his disposal for it.
But he is so proud that he would only accept my offer
on condition we gave the concert together. He has
a right to be proud in the best sense of the word—at
any rate, he is the greatest pianist playing in public
at present. He has a richness and charm of attack,
a varied repertoire, an absence of all charlatanism—
in short, an almost uncanny perfection for a man only
twenty-four years of age. I am still struck "all of a
heap"! Davison will open her eyes and rejoice that a
*man* has come to London (for he has just gone there)
who can give points to Hallé and Pauer. You must
hear Tausig! . . .

### To Clara Schumann

[HANOVER] *Saturday the* 19*th* [*May* 1866].

. . . I owe it to my enforced stay in Hanover that
I am now going to *remain* there! Stockhausen will
have told you about it. As I had told the King before
I went away that my chief reason for resigning was
that I would never again work under Count Platen,
and as he now tells me that " Platen is no longer
manager, and that, to avoid further misunderstandings,
I could arrange everything with him direct," and as
he also offered to change the concert season at Hanover

z

to the months of October, November, December, and January, and discounted all my objections, I was obliged to give in at last.   Who knows but that the war may not make any move to other towns in the autumn impossible—and so I shall turn my thoughts to the splendid orchestra and the lovely garden which we are to have in October, and to the couple of charming garden rooms (which can be heated!) which will always be ready for you and Marie, and instead of brooding over what might have been at Berlin or Vienna, I will be contented.   And I must confess that whenever I went to a concert last winter I felt very miserable at the sight of all that fine talent falling into other hands.   What immense pleasure you have given me in sending me the letters.[1]   I really thought I had lost them, as I had looked for them in vain, but I did not like to tell you; you have always been such an unimpeachable authority as regards method.   But now, of course, the exception only proves the rule! . . .

### To Clara Schumann

[HANOVER] 15th [June 1866].

Dear Frau Schumann—We are still in Hanover, and not from political reasons, but, I am sorry to say, we are detained here because my wife is suffering from an acute attack of rheumatism.   She can only drag herself about very painfully with the help of a stick. Is it not doubly distressing after the illness she has just been through?   I can hardly speak of it, and even the events which are rending Germany can hardly distract me from the thought of my Ursi.   There is no danger, but the pain may drag on for weeks, and it

---

[1] Robert Schumann's to Joachim, which the latter had given to Frau Schumann some time previously.

takes all her courage from her! If circumstances permit we intend to go to Creuznach so soon as my wife can travel. After all, any place would be uncomfortable! They say here that the Prussian troops are coming to take possession of Hanover; that may happen soon, at any rate, and the terrible part of it is that nobody wishes to throw himself unconditionally into the arms of either Prussia or Austria! A horrible chaos will descend upon Germany, I am sure! The Court is still here, and yesterday evening at 8 o'clock I was at Herrenhausen with the Goldschmidts and played for the royal party *en petit comité*. I really thought we should be countermanded after the news came from Frankfort — but perhaps the King felt the need of the distraction. Who knows if perhaps that was not the last time that we should play in that room, so I said sadly to myself. I am prepared for *anything*! Jenny Lind was in pretty good voice, and her bright animated nature still exercises its charm over me. You and I have long realised that she strives much more after effect now. She spent a week in the hotel here with a cold before she could keep her promise to sing at Court. She left to-day at mid-day. She was, of course, quite ready to carry out your wish on behalf of the charming princess,[1] and said she would undertake much more unpleasant tasks *for you*! She was still full of enthusiasm for your playing at Düsseldorf, and altogether " nice," and I was sorry to see her go. Console me with a line soon. I shall write as soon as I have anything definite to tell you. . . .

[1] For an autograph.

### To Bernhard Scholz

HANOVER, *June* 22, 1866.

Dear Scholzes—We have been detained here, first because we were waiting for the Goldschmidts, and afterwards because Ursi had an attack of rheumatism which she has not yet got over, and then, on the 15th, the fatal confusion broke loose. Now, here we are, trying to make up our minds where to go. We do not want to go too far from home because of the possibility of billeting, etc. Edel[1] suggested Harzburg to-day, which also has salt-water baths and is on neutral ground (*i.e.* Brunswick). I hope we shall be able to tell you in detail before long about the internal and external excitement of the last few days. We expect hourly to hear of the surrender or extermination of the Hanoverian army; God grant it is the former! You know that the King is with his troops at Göttingen. The Queen and the two princesses are here. I spoke to her yesterday in the Herrenhäuser Allée; she is calm and self-possessed, and bears her misfortunes with dignity. Apart from this, you probably know as much through the papers as we do, that is precious little.—Yours,

URSI AND JO. JO.

### To Clara Schumann

HANOVER, *June* 26 [1866].

Dear Frau Schumann—Many thanks for your kind and sympathetic letter, the warmth of which did me and my wife good. It took nearly a week to reach us! The war will have shifted close to your Lichtenthal, which is usually so peaceful; at any rate

---

[1] Joachim's friend and doctor.

the excitement in the little states which are split into parties for and against Prussia must be very great. Everything else has sunk into the background for me, compared with our own trouble.   My wife's condition has not yet improved; the poor dear suffers the greatest agony, and can only move from one room to the other with the help of two people; she cannot move her right hand without acute pain—it is really dreadful to see her sufferings.   There can be no question of change of air at present; and at any rate our house is not the cause of it, as a violent form of rheumatism is said to be prevalent here just now.   As it has taken the form of the so-called "flying" gout with my wife, the doctor thinks it may take a sudden turn for the better, and then we shall leave at once; but we shall not go to Kreuznach, but to Harzburg, where there are also salt-water baths (although they do not contain iodine and are not so good as at Kreuznach).   We are afraid of going so far from home at such a time, and Kreuznach is in such a bad position at the corner of Prussia and Bavaria!   I can always get from Harzburg to Hanover in three hours, and it is prettily situated.   It is no good making any plans, but I hope to see you in a few months' time when things are quieter.   If only my poor, tormented wife were better.   I can think of nothing else.   Stockhausen was here yesterday; he met his brother from Leipzig and is going on to Kreuznach.   A single man can risk it; he is sure to look you up if he can get through.   Give all your dear children our love, and take greetings yourself from my Ursi and your devoted friend,                     JOSEPH JOACHIM.

*P.S.*—You will have enough of politics in the newspapers.   The Queen is still here in the country, which is overridden by Prussians, as a private lady, with the two princesses; the King is said to have managed to creep into Bavaria through Thüringen with a part of the Hanoverian force.[1]

### To Otto Goldschmidt

HANOVER, *July* 5 [1866].

Dear Goldschmidt—Some exciting times have gone over our heads since that memorable 14th June at Herrenhausen! Accept my sincere thanks, dear Otto, for your kind care for us, and also for your promise to give us a proof of your friendship in London. I cannot, of course, make any plans at present; my contract binds me to wait so long as there is any possibility of the King requiring my services. You know from many a talk with me, what I think about Hanover—I should never regret having to give up my appointment for my *own* sake, but I will not make use of the misfortunes of the royal house to free myself. Nobody can foretell what will happen here. The Queen is here with her two daughters; I met the royal ladies the other day in the Allée and talked with them. They seem calm, but they still hope that the good will prevail. The Queen's dignified bearing is praised by all, by the Prussians also; she intends to remain here unless she is driven from Hanover by force. You will know as much through the English papers about the battle of Langensalza and the bravery of the Hanoverian soldiers as we do. But how uselessly all those heroes' blood was spilt—how blinded the King must have been, or how faithless the allies! Time will show us

[1] This he did not succeed in doing. The letter was written on the day of the battle of Langensalza.

which it was.    Let us hope the Prussians' brilliant victories in Bohemia will soon lead to peace. . . .

*To Bernhard Scholz*

HARZBURG, *August 28th,* 1866.

My dear Scholz—That is a fine letter of yours : you are full of hope and are going to Berlin, and we shall see one another at the end of September at any rate, because we are going back to Hanover about the 20th of next month.    My Ursi is beginning to get quite well; she has been taking the baths since the day before yesterday, as her cold and rheumatism left her both at the same time.    The children could not be better than in this bracing mountain air. . . . As regards our future place of abode, all that is settled at present is that we shall remain in Hanover *this* winter, as it is absolutely necessary for my wife to spend the winter quietly in our new, comfortable house after her long and painful illness.    I shall make use of my right to regard my appointment as annulled (as I had it definitely stated in my new contract " subject to further alterations to be agreed upon with His Majesty ").    I have been asked to play in Paris this winter six times during a month to be chosen by me (I shall take November), and besides that to spend six to eight weeks in England from the middle of January, and I feel inclined to do both.    Who knows how matters will develop as regards art in Hanover, and whether the people would not regard a sort of sinecure like mine as a burden, if I tried to insist on it.    If I could be there the whole winter and take over the Singing Academy as well as the Orchestra, it would be different! But I cannot take up an appointment which would bind me like that at present; in four or five years perhaps, and then it would be nice if it could be in a place where I could have stimulating musical intercourse with you! I think I shall end by choosing Berlin for my headquarters and home, as soon as the lease of my new house has run out. . . .

### To his Wife

ZÜRICH, *October* 29 [1866].

. . . Ah, if only I were a bird, or, better still, an electric spark; in spite of Brahms I would really rather be with you. But I have to go to Winterthur now, where we are giving a concert this evening. Brahms went on by an earlier train, says he is going to *practise*, believe it who may! He makes a new resolution to do so every day. I am curious to see how he gets on this week at the four concerts; the other day at Schaffhausen his playing got freer and finer with every piece, but, all the same, it is not the same Brahms whom we know at home. Adieu. I must still my raging hunger at the table d'hôte; they have dinner here at 12.30. Then I have an hour's journey to Winterthur, and return to-morrow morning. I hope to see your dear writing at Winterthur. From now onwards address only to Basel, which we shall reach on the 3rd; we shall probably give concerts there and at Mühlhausen (on the way to Paris). I have only just begun to write all that I want to tell you, but I must stop. . . .

### To his Wife at Hamburg

BASEL, *6th* [*November* 1866].

I have just crossed the Rhine in the ferry and climbed a little way up the mountains. It was a lovely afternoon, but there was a mist, so that the Alps were not visible.   But I could see the Schwarz-wald and Vosges mountains.   That alone would be thought extraordinarily beautiful country in Germany. The atmosphere here is positively enchanting, and so is the Rhine with its swift course and unadulter-ated blueness.   Brahms, Riggenbachs, Bargheer the younger, Bernoulli, etc., came with me, all charm-ing people with whom you would have got on very well.   We are *not* giving a concert here, after all ; there is too much going on this week, not to speak of the noisy fair, with its booths in front of the concert hall, some of the rooms in which have been let for a monkey-show, a giantess, and all sorts of things like that, so that on Sunday at the subscription concert I could hear the double basses and big drums from below quite plainly during the *piano* passages.   And then some of our friends said they would so much regret it for the good name of the people of Basel if our concert were not so well attended as we have been accustomed to expect—and we knew how to take this hint !   Now every one is saying what a pity it is we are not playing, but we do not mean to be misled.   No one should give a concert unless urged to do so.   But we are giving one at Mühlhausen on the 10th, and I go to Paris from there.   There has been a lot of telegraph-ing about Brussels.   They would have offered any-thing if I would have gone there on the 17th instead of to Paris.   But Pasdeloup cannot do without me on the 18th (his *concerts populaires*).   I am sorry, because the festivities are sure to be jolly at Brussels.[1]   You have had the *Peri* rehearsal by now ; you must give me a detailed account of it.   I am going to Bülow's Chamber Music Soirée now ; I am curious to know

[1] At the Coronation of Leopold II.

what sort of player he has become after all these years. They say that, up to yesterday, he had only got about twenty subscribers for the three soirées.  He is not a great favourite here, except at the Merian-Genasts, who flatter and pay court to him; he appears to be the same old uncompromising partisan that he used to be.  There is something touching in the way in which he sacrifices himself to Liszt and Wagner; it is a pity his good qualities cannot find a better channel for his enthusiasm.  We still avoid one another.  Brahms sends his kind regards to you. . . .

### To his Wife

MÜHLHAUSEN [*November* 11, 1866].

How are you?  I long so much to see your writing; well, now you must write to Avenue Montagne 29.[1]  I am just going to start; Bülow is sitting with me in the café of the hotel.  He came on here with his pupils, and as we met in a narrow passage and were just passing one another (as at Basel) he suddenly turned round and threw himself on my neck. That sounds comic.  But the warmth of feeling shown by the little polemical, political, God-knows-what-all fellow, really did me good.  When one has spent a happy period of one's youth with a man, something always clings to one's heart, and it is well that it should be so.  The concert here was *very* full, and our reception enthusiastic.

But now about Hamburg!  Write and tell me very soon.  Brahms and Bülow send kind regards. I shall not go to Uncle Bernhard's until to-morrow morning.  I shall arrive too late, and I have not let him know I am coming. . . . Your        Jo.

[1] The house of Joachim's uncle, Bernhard Figdor.

## To his Wife

[PARIS] 15*th* [*November* 1866].

Yesterday I had your dear letter at last! Bernhard came to town[1] and stayed for the rehearsal for the Athenée Concert in the evening—the people were very animated, they really enjoy listening, and that is very pleasant. But the first night is not until *next* Wednesday; something has gone wrong with the lighting! I am just going to move from the hotel to Szarvady's, because the Figdors are not coming back to town until next week, and I do not like to practise in the hotel; besides, I have a very dark room, for which I am paying 10 francs a day *without* attendance! The Szarvadys were so pressing that I had no choice but to accept. They are most sympathetic. But now for the chief reason why I am writing to you in such a hurry. Of course you are at liberty to stay in Hamburg as long as you think fit. . . . Stockhausen has always proved to be of use to you, but do not overtire my dear voice.

## To his Wife at Hamburg

SOISY, *Sunday* [*November* 18, 1866].

I came out here yesterday and helped to celebrate Cornelia's[2] birthday, and now I am going back to town to hear Pasdeloup's concert, because it is important that I should know the place before I play there myself next Sunday. I keep expecting to meet you here at every step; your dear person makes even this place holy, although it has not got much in common with you really. The life here is the same as ever. Although the individuals are so nice and

---

[1] Joachim had found that the Figdors were at their country house at Soisy.
[2] Frau Figdor.

pleasant—Mimi (who is turning out really charming
and is much quieter), my aunt with her talent for being
a delightful housewife, the Fumagalli as attractive as
ever—I could not stand it here for long.   There is
a lack of any common bond between us, there is no
feeling of pleasure and true intellectual satisfaction.
I accompanied the Fumagalli in a few things yesterday,
which she sang very well on the whole.   My uncle
had the tact not to ask me to play in the evening
(when there was a big dinner for the *élite* of the
neighbourhood and several attachés), which was nice
of him.   The Szarvadys did not come with me, so there
would have been no one to play my accompaniments.
. . . I have had a gay time of it up to now, and have
been to the theatre three nights running.   The acting
at even the smallest theatre is so perfect that it is
really a great temptation; I am dreadfully sorry that
you cannot enjoy it too.   The night before last I
heard *Alcestis* at the big Opera House.   You could
tell from the whole performance and particularly from
the solo singers, who were not otherwise remarkable,
that Berlioz had rehearsed the thing—certain accentua-
tions in the declamation, and the heightening of effect
in the scenes were striking, although Berlioz did not
conduct the Opera himself.   The material of the chorus
and orchestra ought to have been capable of the highest
excellence, but there again we have the shallowness of
the French people.   The orchestra played without any
zest, the chorus amused themselves by talking and
laughing and gaping during the most serious scenes,
simply because the audience showed no particular
interest either.   The house was three-parts empty, and
that made the performers dull.   I could have beaten
them to put a little life into them, the damned fellows,
—they could have rendered every part of it so beauti-

fully, and for the most part they might just as well
have been asleep. It was only as it got nearer the
ballet that the seats began to fill with people who
disturbed one by their entrance, and by the end of the
*Alcestis* act (*they did not do the last one at all!*) the
house looked brilliant and was quite full. You should
have heard with what fire and gusto the fellows rendered
the piquant ballet music ; but I did not stay until the
end, although I must say it made a certain sensuous
and stimulating impression on me. . . .

## To his Wife at Hamburg

[PARIS] *Wednesday* [*November* 21, 1866].

You will have had my consent [1] and a later letter
from me by now. I am very glad you are able to
carry out your wish at last, and I am anxious to see
the results. But be sure not to overstrain your chest ;
people have sometimes told me that Garcia and Stockhausen are inclined to overtax the voice. I know
nothing about it, but I thought I would give you the
hint. The fault I have sometimes had to find with
your singing is that it had not enough rhythmical pre-
cision—that you sometimes lingered too long on a note
or a syllable, not from choice, but because you could
not help it. Most violinists do the same thing in bowing, so that their rendering of a phrase is determined
by their technical skill and not by their intellectual
conception of it. I imagine your faulty pronunciation
is due to this too, because, otherwise, no one has more
feeling for fine and characteristic declamation than you.
Stockhausen is sure to help you to use the right
methods, so as to enable you to give full expression to
your feeling for what is right. The notices delighted

[1] To study with Stockhausen at Hamburg for a few weeks.

me, because they proved what an impression you must have made. But I have never come across so much stupidity and impotent vulgarity as in the attacks on Stockhausen which you enclosed. May he be able to protect himself from his friends as easily as he can from the harm his assailants think to inflict on him! And Böie's[1] powers as a musician are obviously not as great as his talent for idiocy and tactlessness. Good Lord! what a specimen! The fellow wounds himself at every lunge, and thinks he sees his opponent's blood when he has scratched himself! I start off to-day, at last, at the *inauguration de la salle*. I am playing again on Friday, and on Sunday for Pasdeloup in the Grand Cirque. You have no idea what warmth of feeling the orchestra has for my playing; when I took the Mendelssohn Concerto through yesterday for next Sunday (with about 100 musicians in the hall of the Conservatoire where they have the rehearsals) their applause lasted for some minutes after each movement, and these are the same fellows who, at the slightest delay, stamp their feet with impatience. I only hope I shall come up to their expectations when I play in public, and that I shall not make such a stupid mistake again as I did in the Conservatoire to start off with. There is something really impressive in the *sight* of the *concerts populaires* at the Cirque—with about 5000 people, from academicians to labourers, sitting crowded together, listening, judging, believing and enjoying. And what an outburst of sympathy there is after a movement of Haydn's or Mendelssohn's, which they insist on hearing twice over, as they did last Sunday, because they refuse to move until they do! You would enjoy that too, and I am burning to play there, God knows, not from vainglory, but I delight in making

---

[1] Violinist at Hamburg.

people love the beautiful.    Considering the size of the
place, it is not at all bad for sound ; at any rate it is
clear and distinct, even if the *fortes* do not make
sufficient effect.    My arm warns me to stop ; I have
a good string on my fiddle.    The Szarvadys send
kindest regards.    I like being with them very much,
and I am staying until Monday.    The Figdors are
coming back to town to-day or to-morrow.    The address
is not Avenue *Montagne*, but *Montaigne*, after the
great essayist, next to Molière my favourite French
writer. . . .

## *To his Wife*

[PARIS] *Monday* [*November* 26, 1866].

Dear Child—I had to promise Szarvady to tell
you from him that I had the greatest success yesterday
which has occurred up to the present in the Cirque
at Pasdeloup's concerts.    It was really a magnificent
experience, and you would have liked to have been
there, as my reception was even warmer than at the
Conservatoire.    So the ice is broken as regards the
public, which was represented by 5000 members.
The slightest applause reaches the performer like a
kind of earthquake, it almost alarms one.    I was in
good form, but the physical exertion is great in such
an unusually large hall.    At the end of the concert
(after the Overture) many voices called for me again—
*Joaschehng*—and I had to go and make my bow again.
So now I have told you all about it.    I expect I shall
play oftener than was originally arranged.    Now I must
go and stay with Uncle ; I am sorry, I felt so much at
home at the Szarvadys'.    They have a jewel of an old
*Miss Black*.[1]    They are doing Haydn's *Seasons* (in
French) at the Athénée to-day ; I must go and hear it.

[1] The name of the Joachims' nursery governess.

## To his Wife at Hamburg

[PARIS] 29 AVENUE MONTAIGNE,
*Thursday* [*November* 29, 1866].

I do not enjoy being here as much as at the Szarvadys', where there are children (two boys of nine and ten
and a little girl of four!).    And here, as you know, they
play mediocre Italian music, and in spite of my affection
I cannot bring myself to sympathise with that.    We
are going to the Théâtre Français to-day, the "Burgtheater" of Paris, for my sake.    How you would enjoy
it!    I have not been since *Alcestis.*    Were you glad
to hear of my success?    I have a sort of feeling that I
have broken a lance for German methods, and rejoice
in my victory.    If I can only continue to fight well!
Next Sunday I am playing Viotti's A minor Concerto [1]
(Brahms' favourite piece) at Pasdeloup's ; to-morrow, at
the Athenée, Mendelssohn's Concerto and Beethoven's
Romance in F major and the *Abendlied.*    The agents
for these concerts thought I had to play as often as
they wished me to, and as, luckily, my letter turned up
in which six times is definitely stated, they tried to
persuade me not to count in the inauguration—I was
so angry that I would concede nothing.    They are a
pack of money-grubbers! . . .

## To his Wife at Hamburg

[PARIS, *December* 6, 1866.]

You relieved me of great anxiety yesterday—I was
just going to telegraph.    Thank God, you are all well.
I am glad you are studying so hard ; we can discuss
later on how you can show your gratitude to your
teacher.    If you happen to see an engraving which is

[1] Cp. A. Pougin's *Viotti et l'école moderne de violon*, p. 122.

not "at the Stockhausens'," make a note of it.   When
are you going to Hanover?   You have not answered
*several* questions; please do so soon.   I have really had
a great success here—the big Opera House (Monsieur
Perrin) asked me to play there six times; they say that
has not happened since Paganini's time.   Tell the
Stockhausens this.   I did *not* accept, because I do not
want to give up the few quiet days with you.   How I
am looking forward to this inward and outward peace,
my child and my children!   I am playing at the Athenée
to-morrow, on Sunday for Pasdeloup, next week at the
Athenée again, on the 15th at Bordeaux, on the 18th
on the way *home* at Roubaix, and on the 20th in
Höltystrasse with Putz and Hermänni.   *Financially*
things were stupidly managed to begin with—but I
shall have about 10,000 to 11,000 francs from the *whole*
tour.   Perhaps we can make up for it another time!
Will you come here with me in the middle of April?

Rossini asks to be remembered to you; *she* came
herself to invite me to dinner on Sunday.   He had
said to her, "*Amène-moi Joachim*," as I had only left
my card once.   The fellow has such a fine, fox-like
face!   I told him you were working hard, so as to be
able to sing to him.

*To Theodor Avé-Lallemant*

45 LEINSTER SQ., BAYSWATER,
LONDON, 18. 2 [1867].

Dear Avé—I was very sorry to be obliged to send
you a refusal this year.   But perhaps it is just as well
that the Hamburg public should feed on Auer as
*Auerhahn*[1] for once, instead of *toujours perdrix*!   I
expected you at Hanover about Christmas-time, but you

---

[1] A play on the name of Auer.  *Auerhahn* means "blackcock."—TR.

never came! Now I shall be in the West so long that I do not know when we shall meet again. I shall be in England until the end of March, working hard, but I shall at least have the satisfaction of knowing that I am really making something worth while for my family. If only there were not this long separation! I shall be in Paris and the French provinces for April and part of May. I am to give four quartettes in Paris, to which I am looking forward; appreciation of German music is on the increase—a cheering reflection. I can understand your distress at Stockhausen's departure. It is a pity he loses patience so soon; he might have attained to something great before long, and the future would have had much in store for him, but I cannot judge of his action without knowing his reasons. I suppose, judging by the Philharmonic's antecedents, it is no good hoping that you will rouse yourselves now and offer a fitting appointment to the *greatest musician of our day* (I know what I am saying), to Johannes Brahms of Hamburg. A certain amount of suffering and lack of appreciation seem to be essential to the development of great minds, and perhaps the committee of the Philharmonic Society even consider it their patriarchal duty (we have a sufficient number of rulers whose worthy example we can follow!) to bring a patriotic sacrifice to Brahms' future by self-denial.

Do not take it for inquisitiveness if I ask you to tell me how you are thinking of filling the post. I am not thinking of it for myself, but an excellent musician and a friend of mine[1] wishes for the appointment, and I should like to know whether his application would stand any chance. You can count on my keeping the matter strictly to myself. If you write soon, which please do, I hope you will let me know how you and

[1] Albert Dietrich.

your dear ones are, to whom I send sincerest regards.
—In great haste, but always yours sincerely,

JOSEPH J.

## To his Wife

[LONDON] *early Monday morning* [*February* 25, 1867].

. . . I always enjoy the pop. concerts very much.
They are always packed, and I have to play something extra every time; the London public is very
faithful. We have a different kind of programme each
time, the day before yesterday it was Beethoven's C
major Quintette and Schubert's B major Trio; to-day
Mendelssohn's A minor Quartette and Schubert's
*Forellen* Quintette, which I have only played once in
my life. I think my playing must appeal to people
because I am thinking so much of you, my dearest,
at all the particularly beautiful passages! I am going
to give Brahms' Sextette soon, and Frau Schumann's
A major Quartette.

. . . The Goldschmidts have gone to Cannes;
they suggested that I should lunch with them here at
their hotel before they left, but I was just on my way
here, unfortunately. I am sorry, for your sake, because
I know you would have liked to hear something of
the Lind at first hand. I have hardly seen any friends
except Deutsch,[1] Straus,[2] and Elly's[3] parents, whom I
have been to see. I spend most of my time travelling! To-morrow I am off again to Bath, Clifton,
and Torquay, and shall not be back until Friday.
Follow me on the map with your finger. This
time I am going through lovely country. It really

---

[1] Emanuel Deutsch, Semitic scholar, assistant in the department of printed
books at the British Museum. Died 1873, at the age of 44. See *Dic. Nat. Biog.*

[2] Ludwig Straus, a member of Joachim's Quartette in London.

[3] Wife of his brother Heinrich and daughter of the composer, Henry Smart.

is dreadful that we should be separated from one another like this for weeks and months. But I have the consolation of knowing I am making this sacrifice for you, and that it is not in vain. The 7000 thalers I shall make here will enable me all the sooner to take an appointment which will suit me and you and the children, and to be separated from you less and less. So let us take courage for the two or three years during which we may have to be apart for months at a time. Think how horrible it would be if we had to cling to an appointment *à tout prix*! It would be awful to have to live under uncomfortable conditions, and perhaps spend one's life grovelling (to use a harsh word)! I had an offer from St. Petersburg to-day to settle there as professor at the Conservatoire and as conductor at the concerts. We shall not think of accepting, shall we? Our boys must not grow up Slavs. I do not know why, but I hate the very thought of it!

Next Sunday I have to go into the country to Sir Anthony Rothschild. I have avoided making his acquaintance for years; but on Friday I met the old gentleman at Sir Alex. Cockburn's,[1] and (strange to say) I liked him so much that I accepted. His daughter had already written to me. . . .

## To his Wife

LONDON, *Wednesday* [*Spring*], 1867.

. . . I have sat for the painter Watts for several hours, for the third time, and I shall have to do so twice again; but I am consoled by the thought that it

---

[1] The Lord Chief Justice. See Edmund Yates's *Recollections* (vol. ii. p. 136, 2nd ed.) with reference to Sir Alexander Cockburn's interest in music and his relations with Joachim.

will be a real work of art. At any rate, the portraits
by him of Tennyson and others which I have seen
are excellent as regards conception and colour. He
is painting me playing the violin. Watts belongs to
the number of artists, particularly rare in England,
who only live for their progress, and for whom the
public (in the sense of *dependence* on it) does not exist
at all. And so, in the midst of numerous ambitious
designs, of which his studio is full and which he is
carrying out *con amore* just as inspiration dictates, he
has begun to form a gallery of those heads which
appeal to him, and I am glad he has repeatedly asked
me to sit to him. I think he will exhibit my portrait.
He has promised to paint your head too. If you
knew how often all sorts of good, clever people wish
you were here, and how often I have to tell them
about you, I think you would love England. And
next year you must come over and show people what
Oratorio singing means (even without "tradition").
If you want to add your mite to our independence, I
do not see why we should tour separately. It is
wretched. Isn't it? Sometimes I think we might
take a furnished house with a garden here for a few
years instead of being in Hanover. You could sing in
more Oratorios in England than anywhere else. I
believe there is a splendid contralto part in *Jephtha* ;[1]
I do *not* mean the one from Bremen. Lord Dudley
made me promise the other day to grant a request of
his, and then it turned out that I was to tell him of
something you really wanted so that he could give
you the pleasure of having it. I must do so, but I do
not know what to say. How would it be if I told him
we were *both* very fond of photographs of works of art,

---

[1] By Händel. Joachim's friend, Reinthaler, conductor of the Bremen
orchestra, had also written an Oratorio of that name.

or engravings, and then he would have a wide choice and could give as much as he liked, and it would not be so embarrassing to me as jewellery or something of that kind? I am playing at his house for the third time to-morrow; but he had not the courage to ask me again himself, and Hallé had to come to me to find out whether I would refuse or not. The poor man only has a yearly income of £500,000—about three million thalers! So he can very well help to fill our portfolios and decorate our walls. I am very glad you have redeemed my promise to the *Warteschule*. Of course you must give the concert in *your* name; nobody would go for the sake of the other one. The programme is very good, worthy of the wife of a concert director and a grass widow. I have seen nothing of Frau Schumann during the whole of this fortnight; she has been in Edinburgh, and always in some other place than where I was working. We are both going to Frau Sartoris' to-night. Frau Schumann is staying until the beginning of April, *perhaps* she will be engaged to play in Paris at the Athenée. . . .

### To his Wife

[LONDON] *Saturday* [*Spring* 1867].

It is so mild to-day that a fire makes the room too warm. Regular spring thoughts have come to me in the land of fogs, and in the first piece I shall play

comes in, which I know you could trill beautifully! How pretty our garden must be! Are all sorts of green spikes showing by now? Or are you still in

¹ Trio of the Minuette from Mozart's E♭ major Quintette.

the depths of winter? I hope not. But the time is
coming nearer, thank God, when we shall be able to
be together undisturbed. And then comes the question
of the trip to Vienna. Are we really to start on the
tramp again in the spring? I think I shall have done
with France by the middle of May, and then our
garden will be at its best. I am very loth to give up
the time with you and the children, and quartettes
and Scottish songs, etc., *at home*. How shall we
manage it? What do you think of all this? Will you
and the children go to Vienna without me at the
end of April or beginning of May, and I come and
fetch you? Shall we put the whole thing off until
August or September, leave the children with Omama
and go together for a week or a fortnight to Mark,
Steyer, Marburg? . . .

I went to the Museum the day before yesterday
and saw many wonders of civilisation and pre-civilisa-
tion. A day like that gives one a better idea of
history and mankind than years of study in the school-
room, or even at school, and our children must grow
up in surroundings like these. Such enduring greatness, so far removed from petty aims, will be a
protection to them if they learn to understand it
rightly, and we will make every effort to prepare them
for this. What a fine and happy life may still be
before us. . . .

I have engaged Piatti for the second quartette in
Paris for 200 francs for the evening. That is dirt
cheap, but as Chappell has engaged him *altogether* for
several years I am dealing with the latter and have
no scruples. Chappell thinks he will get other engagements in Paris, and is doing it to oblige me. . . . I
was in the Houses of Parliament yesterday evening
from 5 to 9, in the Commons and the Lords; two

M.P.'s very kindly acted as my ciceroni. I was much impressed; there is something magnificent about the buildings, as though matters of world-wide significance were settled there! Gladstone, Stanley, and others spoke about Greece, in favour of the Turks really; the Christians practise atrocities just as much as the Mohammedans. . . .

### *To Bernard Cracroft* [1]

[LONDON] [*April* 1867 ?]

Friday I shall be in the country.

You tell me you have been practising a little with Wilhelmj, and you say "with my pupil." I wish he were; but I have even only heard him *once* in Leipsic, when his master David made him play to me, to show me his wonderful ability for everything connected with the mecanisme of violin playing. I long to meet him again and to see how his talent has grown. His tone was superb than [*sic*].

I don't know how to thank you for the brotherly manner in which you look upon what I have been doing in my art. I know that we sympathise in the love for it thoroughly—and you confide in me, my dear Cracroft, that at least I shall not step backward instead of "vorwärts." That is the principal thing; but I wish my travels were over and I could work. I do it for my two boys, who are in Hannover, else they would send all kind messages for you with my best love. Write again to yours affectly.,

JOSEPH JOACHIM.

[1] This letter was written in English by Joachim.—TR.

*From Bernhard Scholz*

BERLIN, *April* 8, 1867.

Dear Jo—You may have seen in the papers that I started a scheme this winter for concerts in Berlin corresponding to the subscription concerts at Hanover, and the concerts at Cologne, Leipzig, etc., a scheme for the production of classical and modern orchestral and choral music, as well as of first-rate soloists.   The three orchestral concerts which I organised have met with such approval that a committee is being formed to support me in continuing the undertaking next winter. It is proposed to combine chamber music concerts with the orchestral concerts; the Berlin public is to be offered the *best* at moderate prices (our ultimate aim is the organisation of *concerts populaires*), and we should like to start off very *brilliantly* next autumn.

That is why I want to know whether you will assist us at our first orchestral and our first chamber music concerts.   According to present arrangements, the concerts will take place every other Saturday.   We shall begin in the latter half of October. . . .

I hope your interdict on Berlin will be removed next winter.   *In any case* please let me hear *by return.* Luise and I join in sending our love.—Yours,

BERNH. SCHOLZ.

*To Bernhard Scholz*

HANOVER, 24*th* [*April* 1867].

My dear Scholz—You may take for granted that an undertaking like yours in Berlin has all my sympathy, quite apart from our personal relations.   I ought and could have written to tell you so long ago—but I wanted to give you a definite answer, and that I could not do whilst I was so unsettled. Unfortunately, I am no nearer a definite answer now, if, as you ask me, I am to arrange the details; I must discuss the matter with you first when we meet, as we cannot fail to do this summer! So, with regard to your concerts, I will only say that I have no reason for avoiding Berlin next winter, and that, therefore, I gladly consent to assisting at them. I even think I can arrange for your first concert, but cannot fix that irrevocably, as yet. Your programmes are magnificent! I hear from Kaulbach and Lazar that you are going to Hammermühle before long. We are going to spend the greater part of the summer in our really charming garden. We have planned a trip to Switzerland, as we have promised to assist at the Swiss Musical Festival, which begins at Zurich on July 13. We are bound to meet then at Hammermühle or somewhere; because I will not revenge myself on you bad people for arranging to go to Cassel *via* Halle and not *via* Hanover, although I feel it. Is it really true? . . .

### To his Wife

VIENNA, 20*th* [*June* 1867].
*To-day is Corpus Christi.*

I arrived here yesterday evening at 8.30 after continuous travelling. . . . I saw mother, who was asleep, and of course we did not wake her; but one of the three maids who take turns at her bedside declared that when she heard the carriage wheels she said, " That is my Joseph." I went to her this morning at half-past eight. She was very calm, but I think she was glad to see me, although she hardly ever expresses pleasure. She is perfectly conscious to-day; she is very much wasted, but her face is flushed. She asked after you and the children, and why I did not come before straight from Paris. Otherwise she hardly makes a sound, except groans of pain occasionally, and every four or five minutes she asks for a drink of water. She will not eat anything; they force her to take a few drops of soup every now and then, or half a biscuit soaked in Tokay. She is quite apathetic—and yet the end may not be for several weeks. Ah, dear child, why must this poor soul go on existing, to the torment of herself and others. It seems so cruel to sit there and feel one's health and strength as a kind of reproach. I give her water to drink and keep the flies away with some green branches—but what love can my poor mother feel now; she is too weak.[1]  I thank Heaven you are not here to see her.—Your          JOSEPH.

### To Clara Schumann

[HANOVER, *July* 17, 1867.]

Dear Frau Schumann—It seems to me that a mere singing in one's ears is not always enough, and that a few lines, however unmusical they may look, are indispensable links to friends who live far apart! You told Ursi you were sorry I had not passed through Baden on my return from Vienna—but I should have been able to stay such a short time and I should have been so gloomy, because, added to other things, I knew that my wife was ill. I had given up the Zurich Musical Festival for that reason, even before I knew how dangerously ill my poor mother was. She suffered terribly before the end—and to look on helplessly when those we love are suffering torments is, I suppose, the saddest thing in life. Brahms was a great comfort to me; he was so good and sympathetic

[1] She died a few days later, and was buried on the 28th in the Waehringer Cemetery.

and devoted all his time to me whilst I was at Vienna. He only played once, and then nothing of his own, I am sorry to say ; but he promised to send me some *string quartettes*, which have not come up to the present. Do you know them ? I expect you miss Brahms very much ; it would be a great boon to me, too, to have such a richly creative, musical mind close at hand. But meanwhile we are having a lot of music, for us at least ; the other day the four of us had a delightful Schumann Festival all to ourselves, of which the following is the programme :

1. A minor Sonata (Frau von Bronsart and I).
2. *Frauenliebe und Leben* (my wife and H. von Bronsart).
3. Études Symph. (Frau v. B.).
4. *Die Märchenbilder* (H. v. B. and I).
5. Three Duets for Soprano and Contralto (Frau v. B. and Ursi).
6. Carnaval (H. v. B.).

You will see from this that the Prussians have appointed a far more musical manager than the Hanoverians. He is very much in earnest, and socially, too, I like them both, so that we often meet. The Bronsarts are remaining here the whole summer like ourselves. Our charming garden makes this bearable ; I wish you could see the two little rascals busying themselves there. A few days ago I went to Marienburg to see Queen Marie. As I had unfortunately been engaged every time she asked me, when I heard that she was leaving I asked if I might come. Any evidence of sympathy pleases her, and she was particularly touched because, among other favourite pieces of hers, I had brought *your* Romances. I had to tell her all about you and your children repeatedly. She is a kind and really noble woman, and has resigned herself to her fate without thought of revenge ; she only laments that she has to leave the country and the little estate which she had cared for so lovingly down to the smallest detail. The house is really charming, and the situation, although there is nothing grand about it, is lovely. You would like it. It is still uncertain when she will have to go—but as the king is so misguided in his policy and in his arrogance, she will probably have to leave for good before long. There are sad rumours of his behaviour in Vienna. . . .

## To his Wife

[BERLIN] *Sunday afternoon* [*October* 20, 1867].

Is it not too bad that I have not yet written to you? But my time has been so taken up! Scholz was at the station and we went to the Hotel Wales; but it is not very nice there, and as Herman and Gisel have told me repeatedly, by word of mouth and by letter, that I could come to them (and they have plenty of room), I shall probably go there to-morrow. She said she wished it for his sake so that he should not begin to work again and overtire himself, and he told me it would give her so much pleasure that I must come. So I think I shall be doing right to go there; don't you? The concert[1] went off very well on the whole, but the pitch was unbearably high and the heat was intense. It was full, and after the Chaconne a girl from the chorus handed me a laurel wreath, of which I enclose a leaf. Scholz conducted with great energy and has the orchestra well in hand, although the tone leaves much to be desired and the intonation is not clear. We went and had drinks after the concert: the Scholzes, the painter Menzel with wife,[2] Dilthey, Julian

[1] The first Philharmonic concert under Bernhard Scholz, on the 19th.
[2] Menzel was not married at that time, possibly the lady was his sister, Frau Krigar.

Schmidt and wife, Hey, etc. I dined with the Scholzes yesterday and to-day; they have a very nice circle of clever young men, and *live* very comfortably. We could certainly get a very nice house for 600 thalers; they are all comfortably and practically planned. Everybody is pleased to hear we are going to settle here. . . .

### To his Wife

[BERLIN] *Tuesday,* 5 *in the afternoon.*
[*October* 22, 1867.]

I am to send you messages from the Radeckes, where I and the Scholzes have just dined, and where I am now going to hear Scholz's Trio. It was a delightful party. I am sure you will like the Radeckes; I am so looking forward to hunting for a house here with you! The Radeckes live in the middle of the town, they have a splendid garden attached to the house, which in its turn is next to a princely park, so that they have the freshest air, and pay 350 thalers for 7 rooms! It is not at all so dreadfully dear here . . . ! The poor bear is in the wars; he has offended the press by being stingy with tickets. It is not his fault, as he had nothing to do with the business arrangements—but all the critics (Gumprecht as well) are killing the concert by silence. X, who was really acting for the Committee of the Philharmonic concerts, only sent *one* ticket to an important critic (who is married). He sent it back, and by way of excuse they wrote and told him that if Gumprecht (who is blind) and Kossak (who is lame) had not *had* to have two tickets to go to it at all, they also would only have received one! Of course the man who complained has made the most indiscreet use of this and all the fat is in the fire! Poor Scholz takes the matter very much to heart.  I am looking forward to seeing Bletz [1] and will meet him at the station to-morrow.  I suppose you have found the Hungarian Concerto and sent it off!

## To his Wife

[VIENNA] *Friday* [*November* 22, 1867].

I am so busy all the time (with quartette rehearsals nearly every day just now, as well) that you must be indulgent, but you must have got my longer letter just after you sent off yours.  To-morrow is my 6th concert (with the programme to arrange, which is a very difficult matter, journeys, rehearsals, etc.).  On Sunday I am going with Brahms to Brünn, a little nearer to you.  It will only take up one day and will probably bring in about 200 fl. for each of us.  At the Redoutensaal there was only 880 fl. profit, *over* 700 fl. in expenses!  But they hope it will turn out better on the 22nd of December; the hall was not free before that.

The quartettes give me great musical pleasure; Kässmeyer is much better than the 2nd fiddle Eyertt, Hilpert is very good, and Röver, although he has less tone than Lindner, has more power of expression; I think it will go very well.  I will send the Programme later.  My visit to the Queen was very pleasant, only the King,[2] the children, an old Princess Esterházy (the daughter-in-law of Haydn's princess), Herr von Stock[hausen][3] and Countess Bremer.  We were there from 7 to 11.  The Queen wished to be remembered *most* kindly to you; she said she was

[1] The baritone, Bletzacher, from Hanover.

[2] King Georg of Hanover, who after the catastrophe of 1866 settled at Hietzing near Vienna.

[3] Formerly Hanoverian Ambassador at Vienna, the father of Frau von Herzogenberg.

quite well except for being so home-sick. I could see that she was. The King does not know we are going to Berlin; Stockh. told me he had not the courage to tell him. He is very much aged but very pleasant, and he said gravely, but without violence, that although he knew enough of his neighbours (as he was brought up in Berlin) not to expect any good of them, he had not expected this attack from the present king of Prussia, whom he had always considered an honest, well-meaning man. But, he said, God could not permit this injustice to continue, and he would bear the short separation from his beloved Hanover with courage. It was a terribly painful moment for me, and when he had finished I replied that God recognises His faithful servants by the firmness of their trust in Him in misfortune! What else could I say? Poor people! Do not forget, dear child, to send me the Guelphic Order in its case; the King felt the other day at the place where it ought to have been; contrary to etiquette, I had only been able hastily to fasten on a blue ribbon. I thought I ought to be careful not to show any "lack of disrespect." [1] . . .

### To his Wife

[VIENNA] *Sunday* [*December* 1, 1867].

. . . My wrist is better in spite of playing; I was really afraid it would upset all my plans. Now I shall stay quietly here this week, until Friday at any rate; then I shall probably go to Pesth. I have my second quartette concert on Thursday, so I have to rehearse for it every day. The first, on Thursday, went very well; but of course wise folk consider that

[1] A favourite expression of Joachim—"*Mangel an Nichtachtung*"—arising from a story about some one who was indignant at "such lack of disrespect."

Hellmesberger's quartette is finer and more perfect, because they play together all the year round. Well, let them! Besides this, it gives me a great deal of bother, and the 1000 fl. clear profit for the three evenings will not be a very great *pecuniary* compensation for the many, many hours I am spending; it was not *crowded*, but they hope the next one will be better. It is still uncertain whether I shall get permission to give my concert at the Redoutensaal on December 22. For the time being the police have forbidden it because of the feast days! But I have appealed to the consistorial court, and the magistrate Kornhäusel, to whom I spoke, hopes to put it through. He is a member of the Archbishop's Council, a very cultured, pleasant man of the world in a priest's coat, who told me it was a foregone conclusion that nothing would be performed at my concerts which would not be in keeping with the feast days; my aims guaranteed this, *vederemo*! I went to see the King again yesterday . . . both times I drove out with Brahms at 7 o'clock, we remained with them until half-past eleven, and then had to go to an hotel here for dinner, besides paying 7 gulden for the carriage. I should think it mean to mention this if it were not well known that there are 60 horses in the royal stables. The Queen and Princess Marie send you their kindest regards, they mentioned it several times and looked so kindly that it was really genuine. Your little parcel with the Order only arrived to-day, so it was too late. And not a line with it—you naughty child! It is a great misfortune for us to have to exist apart like this—instead of enjoying our life and *true* work together. If only you were all here! I have just had my only absolute pleasure, when the three first movements of Brahms' Requiem were played, although imperfectly, at the

2 B

*Gesellschafts* concert. The music is on an equally high plane with the whole idea, with a depth of feeling, and a loftiness and originality of conception which stamps Brahms for me as a great man, so that I shall never grumble at the trivial things I do not like in him. Oh, Uzzi, if only I could produce the work as I feel it and you could listen! Where and when will that be?! I should like Bronsart to hear it and admire it as I do! Then perhaps he would rehearse it at leisure during the summer months and produce it next autumn. Who knows how long Brahms will have to wait before he hears it played as it ought to be played. The audience listened sympathetically—a compact little party showed reverence and *enthusiasm*; a few cads who hissed met with no success, Brahms was loudly called for, and the applause kept on although it took him five minutes to come from the hall up the steps into the orchestra. Some of Schubert's music is charmingly pretty and gracefully popular. The performance was excellent, Herbeck knows how to interpret with delicacy and energy. A first-rate conductor who took trouble only with Schubert. Like everywhere else, there are not enough rehearsals here. . . .

### To his Wife

[VIENNA] *18th* [*December* 1867].

I am starting early on the 23rd, and please, God, I shall lunch with you all on the 24th; but perhaps it would be better to put off the presents until the 25th and then we can decorate the tree together on the 24th. How I am looking forward to it! Do just what you prefer about this. It is most unfortunate that the 22nd was the only possible day left! . . .

They are trying hard here to reorganise the

management of the Conservatoire and to arrange so that they can offer *me* a decent salary as Director. The appointment would provide me with sufficient authority to give me considerable influence. *I do not think* anything will come of it, and I have told people so who have questioned me, but I said at the same time, that I should consider it my duty to accept a *permanent* post which would give me a fine scope in musical matters. The re-election is on Saturday, and Schelle, Dumba, and others are trying to influence it to this end. But as I said we can move to Berlin with easy minds. Something could be done with the talents and the *public* here ; but then again I have become so very North German, and I hate these polite, obsequious people, of whom hardly one ever has the courage to live up to his convictions. The North Germans are simpler and more thorough, although they are less impressionable and have not the same *joie de vivre*. They get at the root of things sooner. Well, we shall soon be able to talk about this and many other things. . . . I do not know what to send to Frau Schumann, but take the Guarneri from among my violins, have it carefully packed and insured with Riechers'[1] assistance and send it, through the Grimms, to Felix Schumann. I always intended to give it to my ideal godchild. You can write that at the same time, if you agree to it. . . .

### From Carl Ferdinand Pohl[2]

VIENNA, *February* 15, 1868.

Dear Sir—I was delighted to read in the *Times* that you were once more in England. Do not be

---

[1] A first-rate violin maker, who moved later to Berlin.

[2] Archivist to the *Gesellschaft der Musikfreunde* (Society of the Friends of Music), born September 6, 1819. His *Mozart und Haydn in London* had

alarmed if I venture to lay siege to your goodness without any preliminaries. I will put my request briefly. When I said good-bye to you that morning, I felt very sad. I shall always remember your words, "If I can ever do anything for Papa Haydn." And so I will come at once to "business."

1. There must be, in the private possession of people in England, autographs of Haydn of all kinds, and some letters cannot yet have been brought to light. Please ask about Haydn very often, particularly in the chief provincial towns, and if you should find any music in Haydn's handwriting make a note of the first bar and the *date*, which is nearly always on it. If any one wishes to correspond direct with me, my address is :

F. POHL, Musik-Verein, Wien (Austria).

2. If you get the opportunity do mention my *Mozart und Haydn in London* sometimes (particularly in *Scotland*, in Liverpool and Manchester). Pauer wrote that the booksellers Williams & Norgate told him the book had a fairly good sale. There is no idea of an English translation at present. In the face of the almost incredible fact that a translation of Jahn's Mozart (2nd edition) was refused, I have no cause to grumble yet, even though the book must have more interest for England, and the Englishman will find nowhere else a history of her societies and musical celebrities, quite apart from Mozart and Haydn, which, like the whole book, is put together from authentic sources.

3. Stir up Chappell or some other Croesus to undertake a two-volume Universal Musical Diction-

---

appeared in 1867. He died in 1890, having completed his *Life of Haydn*, the first volume of which appeared in 1875.

ary.[1]   The last work of this nature appeared in the year
1824!!, a miserable production.   I have mentioned
this point in my Introduction to my book, because it
is a scandal that English people should have to go
to foreign books for any information with regard to
musical events during the last fifty years. . . . In the
present condition of music in England a work of this
kind, which was not too extensive, should be in the
possession of every decent family, I cannot imagine
there would be any risk in the undertaking.

4. You tried the violin Frau Polzelli[2] wants to sell
when you were in Pesth.   A friend of mine, a son of
Benesch of the royal orchestra, would like to buy it.
The lady asks 1000 F.   With much more hesitation
than I had over my other requests, I venture to ask
you to spare me a few minutes of your valuable time
in which to write and tell me whether you would
advise the purchase of the violin.

I have got into correspondence with this lady.   She
was very hard at first, but I have appealed to her
widow's heart and succeeded in softening her.   She
sent me copies of seven letters from Haydn, and the
portrait of her late husband.   It was notorious that
Haydn had no very violent affection for his wife; and
these letters confirm this.   "*La mia moglie, questa bestia
infernale*" are the very unflattering nicknames by
which he mentions her.   But the widow has many
other letters which are of so "delicate" a nature that
she will not let them out of her hands.   But she has
generously allowed me to look at these tender out-
pourings of our good Papa Haydn.   Dr. Härtel of
Leipzig has sent me everything relating to Haydn

---

[1] Grove's *Dictionary of Music* only began to appear in 1879.   Possibly
Pohl's introduction to his *Mozart und Haydn* added a stimulus to the undertaking.
Pohl wrote the article on Haydn in the *Dictionary*.

[2] Her husband was a pupil of Haydn's, who had been her mother's lover.

(notices, catalogues, valuable notes). Also Haydn's last Mass, composed 1801, in autograph, which was bought in Paris and which he has sent for me to look at.

I am fairly wading in work; but Haydn interrupts much of my breadwinning work, as it is to be printed in the autumn.

Please give my kindest regards to Pauer, Grove, Manns, Sullivan, the Brit. Museum, Cryst. Palace and the whole of London.

Our Conservatoire is writhing under plans for re-organisation. I have little hope of the result. There are many heads but no head; the chief one is absent. There is only one who could fill that position and he is far from here "across the channel." God be with you!—Yours sincerely,                                  F. POHL.

### To his Wife

[LONDON] *Sunday evening* [*March* 1, 1868].

. . . Yesterday evening after the concert I was to have gone to Sartoris, and to-day into the country to the Rothschilds but I have refused both. I think the latter had asked various people to meet me, among others Mrs. Gladstone, Benedict tells me. I am sorry for this as I might have got to know him in that way; but it will not hurt the R.s. What do you say to a baptised Jew and an author being Prime Minister of England? It is fine that such a thing is possible. Edel is sure to be delighted. . . . And so you are to go on the stage again?[1] With all Bronsart's good-will things are not managed on the stage at Hanover in such a way that I should care to see you there!

---

[1] Frau Joachim had been asked privately whether she would appear again in some classical operas.

Where is the audience I would think really worthy of you? No, the three little ones have too great need of you, not to speak of myself. Am I not right!! Eh?!!! . . .

## To Theodor Avé-Lallemant

45 LEINSTER SQUARE, BAYSWATER,
LONDON, *March 11th* [1868].

Dear Avé—How much anxiety and how much joy we have had since the receipt of your letter! We have been marvellously watched over by Providence. You will have heard that our little girl is well, and since then she has been better than ever before, I have had no less than five letters from my wife. Accept my heartfelt thanks for your affectionate thought of us. I am sure the prayers of warm-hearted friends bring a blessing, and although I do not believe that individual requests are heard up above (forgive me!) yet I feel that the gentle atmosphere of sympathy is a protection to me in the midst of my rush of concerts. The thought of a true friend is like an anchor in deep waters.

You want me to come to you on April 9. I shall be very reluctant to leave home again, but I must, of course! I suggest that I should play Bach's A minor Concerto and Bruch's Concerto. The first takes about twelve, the second twenty minutes. But I am sorry to say I must mention one thing more which I find very difficult to say. I think that, as I never give any concerts of my own at Hamburg simply because I always play at the Philharmonic, the Society might scrape together a higher fee. Would it be very painful to you to tell the committee I require 30 Friedr's-d'or? You know I am not grasping, but that I have chosen the life of a public performer instead of private study (*not* the better part!), not for *myself* but for the future of my family! Tell me your honest opinion. I am glad you are all well and send my kindest regards.— Yours, JOSEPH JOACHIM.

### To his Wife

[LONDON, *end of March* 1868.]

No one could have been luckier than I, in the crossing.[1] The sea was so well disposed, only the tops of the waves were ruffled, and it looked magnificent. Seagulls were flying round about and once a large snow-white one with three smaller ones flew round the ship as though they were you and the little ones keeping guard over me. I lunched contentedly on a mutton chop and drank Bordeaux to all your healths. My courage for the sake of you dear people was well rewarded.

I could not manage to write from Dublin, the concerts required many rehearsals, with two Irishmen! and a German 'cellist, Elsner, who comes from Frankfort and is very good. He has lived for years past in Dublin with his wife and child. It is a beautiful town, the only pity is that one sees so much poverty, drunkenness, and shameless dirt about. England has much of this on her conscience, and she is beginning to realise it. But the republican Fenianism is imported from America and has no future in the Emerald Isle, which really seems feudally inclined, enjoys display, and would gladly indulge its aristocracy, if its self-love were fostered and the people were treated kindly. I saw no sign of excitement or rebellion; that sort of thing always sounds worse at a distance than it proves to be

[1] From Dublin to England.

on a closer inspection. I am very much taken with your notion about Potsdam, but the house (which we should have to see first) sounds too small. Six rooms and two tiny rooms is not enough for us! We could rent a few rooms somewhere in Berlin if we wanted to go away from Potsdam for a few days, and were not absolutely obliged to take a three months' trip *every* summer. . . .

### To T. Avé-Lallemant

HANOVER, *August 11th* [1868].

. . . Fräulein Agnes Zimmermann is a first-rate pianist, indeed, an *artist*, and I wish her the success she deserves in Germany with all my heart; she finds it very difficult to make her way in gigantic London. I played the Kreutzer Sonata with her in public in London and was delighted with her performance, but still more with her knowledge of old music and her interest in modern music. She has also composed some very charming things, and a piano and violin sonata dedicated to me will shortly be published, which has, at any rate, many good points. If I were a Concert Director I would speak for her. . . . She is the right kind of musician. . . .

### To his Wife

[LONDON, *middle of January* 1869.]

. . . Has anything been settled for Radecke and Scholz with regard to the theatre? Eckert must have begun work by now. Does the new broom sweep clean? He will find plenty to sweep away as far as Opera is concerned! He sent a Violoncello Concerto to Piatti, through Benedict, which I am curious to hear.

We are having very good performances here. Bach's A minor Concerto yesterday, with only a two-part accompaniment, which I think is the best arrangement for it. We had to repeat the last movement. And we also had to repeat a movement in the Mendelssohn Quartette. Young Dr. Brentano,[1] who came to see me in the green room to my great pleasure, could not sufficiently express his surprise at the much greater enthusiasm and attention of the public here compared with the German public. But all is not gold that glitters. The people here are so yielding and uncritical towards any intellectual authority, and are therefore easily led; but on the whole, the things which make a lasting impression on us sink in deeper. I would not exchange England for Germany. I did not beg for the bassoon at the Rothschilds after all; I find it very hard to show them, of all people, that I recognise money as a power. However, it was very pleasant there, manners and society of the finest (Cockburn, some Lords with pretty daughters, Mrs. Senior, the blonde with the charming voice, who had come from Paris), fine weather, and a long walk over hills and through woods. Yesterday, to make up for this, we had a fog thick enough to cut. It has been warm all the time. . . .

### To his Wife

LONDON, *Tuesday* [*February*], 1869.

I could not write to you yesterday, after all; a very long rehearsal made it necessary for me to rest my arm. As soon as I feel any fatigue or inflammation in it I take great care, with satisfactory results up to the present. Unfortunately, the second violin and the viola are not capable of playing Beethoven's last

---

[1] The economist Lujo Brentano.

Quartette; in spite of all the rehearsals one cannot
rely on them. That brings my love of music and my
love for my fellow-men into painful conflict. Both
men have played with the quartette for years, and
it would, of course, do them serious harm if they
were turned off. They are fathers of families, and
they are, at any rate, very hard-working and willing.
What is to be done? With Piatti as 'cellist it might
be so fine, and the public has deserved the best one
can give them. After all, it is not a small thing
that 2000 people should come reverently to hear
Beethoven's last Quartette. Frau Schumann played
splendidly yesterday. I thoroughly enjoyed Haydn's
Trio with the Hungarian Finale. Only think, the
other day a Mr. Russell (cousin of the Earl) gave me
a stick which old Haydn had used for years as a
support, and which came to Mr. Russell through a
friend of Haydn's. Wasn't that nice? We ought to
be able to teach the children to keep time with that!
If only I were really with you all; in spite of the
spoiling I get I can hardly bear it. . . .

## To his Wife at Salzburg

[BERLIN, *June* 15, 1869.]

I was so glad to get your good news. I hope to
be able to join you at the end of next week, for, as
matters are at present, the individual sections can be
organised without any general consultations. That is
the best way of protecting oneself against Taubert's
importunities. A consultation with Chrysander, Kiel,
Stockhausen, and Rudorff, such as I wished for, is not
possible just yet. Stockhausen leaves to-day. I am
going to give the Minister a plan of the lessons (in
writing), wait for an answer from the 'cellist Müller,

and then leave.  I have something very nice to tell you : my appointment is not only for life, but the *full* salary is to be retained, so that even if I should become unable to work (which heaven forbid!) I should always draw 2000 thalers.  Under these circumstances the appointment is an excellent one from a financial standpoint also.  Think how long it would have taken me to make a capital of 40,000 thalers by playing at concerts!  So when we two are little old people we shall be able to live in peace and spend our capital on the children, eh, old woman! Meanwhile we are " jolly fine " people. . . . I engaged De Ahna to-day as assistant teacher for 400 thalers, for which he is to give eight lessons a week.  You see how taken up I am with my school.  I have had to pay seventeen visits to the senators, and I am sweating over my report, in which Herman is helping me.

Good-bye for to-day.  May all the mountain spirits protect my dear ones !                    J. J.

### To his Wife at Salzburg

[BERLIN] *Sunday morning [June* 20, 1869].

I hope to join you this week ; I do not think I have ever looked forward so much to anything.  And I expect you are imagining that I am having a very good time here!  But, latterly, I have spent two nights in the train, from Wednesday to Thursday and from Friday to Saturday, at Bergedorf and Hamburg, but I made a good catch in the last-named town, and the day and a half with Chrysander was worth some fatigue.  The catch is the 'cellist Wilhelm Müller, whom I have engaged for a year to begin with.  I thought that if I merely wrote to him difficulties would arise because of his brothers at Rostock, who would

also want to be appointed, so I made a rendezvous
with him at Hamburg, where the *coup* was successful.
That is a weight off my heart—Müller and De Ahna
are very capable fellows, and we are fixed up for the
first year.   Moreover, a talented 'cello pupil, Hausmann,
is assured to me by this.   You have no idea how
many little unpleasantnesses and embarrassments one
has to put up with.   De Swert and Ehrlich, etc.,
have already besieged me in the character of place-
hunters.   I shall have to acquire a thicker skin!   God
grant that Rudorff will accept in reply to another
letter from me with enclosure from Frau von Mühler ;
I really do not know what to do about the piano.
Chrysander is burning with enthusiasm for our undertaking and means to support it in his paper, because
he hopes great things of it.   He gave me valuable
hints about some of the Berlin people (Grell, Beller-
mann, etc.), and he will do anything in his power to
help matters on in the future.   He leads a strangely
isolated life—farmer, music printer, and scholar.
Happily, he has a very nice wife and charming
children, whom I met for the first time.   In the
morning he mows his own hay, feeds the cows and
goats, looks after the vines in the conservatories, etc.,
etc. . . .

### From Ernst Rudorff

Cologne, *Saturday, July* 31, 1869.

Dear Herr Joachim—I ought to have thanked you
long ago for your letter and answered your questions ;
but, for one thing, I could not find the time, and for
the other I was waiting for a report on the personal
character of Herr X., so as to decide whether he
should be proposed or not.   I have now received this
report, and I think he had better be left out of con-

sideration. So I wrote to Reinecke yesterday to find out from him the whereabouts of young Grieg. Do you not think he would be a very suitable and delightful person ? He was at the Leipzig Conservatoire with me, he is about five years younger than I, and even then he was very capable. At any rate, he has a refined and musical nature (you must at least have heard of his things), and I imagine his piano-playing is good too. I know practically nothing of Herr Barth ; I only have a vague impression that some one told me he was one of those who beat the drums for the musicians of the future, but I may be mistaken. . . .

Now, as regards the entrance examination, I would venture to suggest an alteration. It seems to me that to allow a fortnight before the beginning of the term for the preliminary examination is in the interests neither of the teachers, who have to be at their posts every day, nor of the pupils, who will not know what to do with themselves in Berlin such a long time beforehand. We always settle this in one day before beginning of the term. And all those, including Königslöw, with whom I have discussed it, consider this to be the most practical way. If, therefore, I may make a suggestion, it is that you should fix the entrance examination for the 27th and possibly the 28th of September (Monday and Tuesday) ; then the time-table could be settled by Friday, and distributed on that day, that is, on October 1, among the pupils, at the opening of the school. Forgive me for interfering in these matters. You may be guided by other considerations, but I just wanted to let you know what the custom is at other places. Applications will, of course, have to be made beforehand in writing. I shall not fix any special test for my class—I imagine that can be decided on the spot. I shall be disobedient enough not to come back to Berlin as early as you will, and perhaps you will think that is the only reason why I wish to change the time for the entrance examination. But that is not so! If my presence is not absolutely necessary I should like to remain quietly at work in the country a little longer, as I am tied here until August 20, and, as you can imagine, I am overwhelmed by all kinds of business now that I am giving up my post here. I have one more request to make, namely, that you should drop the " Herr " in addressing me.

### From Hermann Levi

CARLSRUHE, *September* 12, 1869.

Dear Friend—I did not know the date of the wedding[1] myself, and I had to write to Frau Schumann; that is why my answer was delayed. I have just had her letter, in which she says she has written to you herself. Frau Schumann will have told you in her letter that she was rather put out by your behaviour when you were at Baden.[2] She gave me the whole history with such passionate emotion that all my representations to the contrary were in vain. I am telling you this so as to beg you to come to Baden in spite of the postponement of the wedding—if it is not too much out of your way ; a few friendly words from you will set matters right again. Frau Schumann has been in a very nervous state lately, and needs the support of her friends more than ever.

Have you seen the eleventh volume of Varnhagen's[3]

---

[1] Julie Schumann's.

[2] Obviously because Joachim had gone to Baden on purpose to try to persuade Brahms to accept an appointment on the staff of the new school.

[3] K. A. Varnhagen von Ense, *Tagebücher*, in 15 vols.—TR.

Diary? Objectionable as it is to see a man of his standing occupied with gossip of this kind, yet it is amusing to listen to him. This volume will be specially interesting to you because it describes a period and a society in which you yourself moved in the year '54. One cannot but respect the energy and thoroughness of Bettina's character! His remarks on p. 161 about Rahel's and Bettina's relations to Goethe are admirable. What a lot you have seen and experienced, and why do you not let your tongue go sometimes, you close fellow? I did not know you actually knew Varnhagen. Do not be put out by page 127.[1] I am sure Bettina was right. I think, in judging the person referred to, your heart has ruled your understanding. You value the friend more highly than you do the author?

### From Clara Schumann

BADEN, *September* 23, 1869.

Dear Joachim—I cannot wait until I see you to thank you for your delightful letter to me and Julie which so warmed my heart. I had to stretch out my hand to you at once, and Julie will do so very soon from Turin, where she will be in eight or ten days' time. The tender thought you had given to your present was a charming surprise—I will say nothing here on the subject of your having sent one at all, since I only wish to express my pleasure and gratitude.

The wedding took place yesterday, and although my grief at the separation was very bitter, the happiness which enveloped them both softened it somewhat. But only a mother's heart can know how hard it is to

---

[1] The reference to Herman Grimm in which Bettina is said to have called him "vanity personified" actually occurs on p. 128 of the *Tagebücher*.—TR.

give up a child for good—I knew I should feel it, but I felt it a thousand times more than I had imagined.

You will have heard from Rudorff that I have sent in my Eugenie's name as a candidate for the Music School, but unfortunately she cannot begin in October, as the family with whom she is to board cannot have her before October 10. I may trust to your kindness in arranging for her to be admitted later, may I not?

You are just about to move, and you will both be very busy, I expect; if only one could help at such times!

With sincerest regards to you and your dear wife. —Always yours sincerely, CLARA SCH.

Love from every one here.

## *To his Wife*

[LONDON] *Saturday* [*February* 5 *or* 12, 1870].

. . . I stayed with Hallé in Manchester. Madame Norman Neruda came to the concert; I like her very much, and I think you would too. Her playing is more to my taste than that of any other contemporary —unspoilt, pure and musical. The poor lady has been travelling about since October, playing in public in the provinces nearly every day, and she will continue to do so until the end of March, but then she will make £1800 clear profit. Wilhelmj is travelling about the country too, but his playing seems to be deteriorating, and from all I can hear he must be a childish fellow. It is a great pity. . . .

2 C

*To Dr. Franz Egger [1] in Vienna*

BERLIN, *May* 21, 1870.

Dear Sir—In the name of the Committee for the Beethoven Festival, you have honoured me with an invitation to take part in it, for which I beg to offer you my sincerest thanks.

To my great regret, however, I am unable to avail myself of your invitation. I would have made some other engagement my excuse, had it not seemed to be my duty to speak the truth because of the many eminent men, several of whom I may call my personal friends, who are also included in this invitation. Let me, therefore, frankly admit that I would have come if I could have been certain that I could take my share in it freely and happily. If, for instance, one of the local directors [2] in Vienna had been entrusted with the conductorship, I should certainly not have questioned whether I was in sympathy with this or that name, but I should have gone as a pilgrim to the sacred spot, identified myself with it all, and have been filled only with the desire to contribute the best that is in me.

But the concerts have been entrusted to the conductorship of two foreign artists, the heads of the new German school, and although I admit that it would not have been possible to find more famous names, I cannot conscientiously conceal from myself the fact that they destroy my vision of Beethoven as a great, sublime yet simple spirit, whose unassuming majesty has gradually conquered the world.

[1] Chairman of the Committee for the celebration of Beethoven's centenary.

[2] "Just as Beethoven's genius shed its rays in various directions," so the "great masters whose aims were in various directions" were to unite at the Festival. Franz Lachner was to conduct *Fidelio*, Liszt the *Missa solemnis*, Wagner the Ninth Symphony, and Joachim, with Laub, Hellmesberger and Popper, was to "execute the proposed quartette."

Since it would be impossible for me, under these circumstances, to participate heart and soul in the Festival, I feel sure I shall be acting in accordance with the wishes of the Committee in absenting myself, so that the harmony of the centenary may be undisturbed.

With the expression of my sincerest regret I beg to remain, respectfully and sincerely yours,

JOSEPH JOACHIM.

### To Johannes Brahms

BERLIN, EICHENALLEE NR. 8, *May 24th* [1870].

Dear Johannes—I have just written to the Committee of the Beethoven Festival refusing to take part in it. It is enough to make one blush—men like Grillparzer and Karrajahn[1] at the head of artistic and scientific circles in Vienna, men who know right well Beethoven's unique and sacred significance—and Abbé Liszt is chosen by them to conduct the *Missa solemnis*! The worship of Rossini during Beethoven's lifetime, which is said to have embittered him, is nothing compared to this flippant comedy. I hope you never imagined I should do anything but absent myself, if you happen to have heard of the invitation. I found it hard to be moderate, and had to tone down my letter to the Committee three times. But even in its final milder form the statement remains plain, that for me, personally, the mention of those two famous men destroys my vision of Beethoven as a sublime yet simple spirit, whose unassuming majesty has gradually conquered the world, and that I therefore do not intend to go, so as not to disturb the harmony of the Festival.

[1] Theodor Georg von Karajan, well-known author of the monograph, "J. Haydn in London, 1791 and 1792."

I thought it right to tell you this. But I should like to know your *exact address*, because Herman Grimm gave me a volume of poems (by Candidus) for you some time ago; he thought you might like to set some of them to music as they are very original and full of feeling. You shall have them as soon as you write to me. How are you, my dear fellow? Have you been creating any more glorious things? I was absolutely delighted with your Rhapsodie, and your earlier works, as for example the B major Sextette which we played last Sunday, have not lost their charm for me either. I felt as though memories of precious days were speaking in my very soul. My wife delighted in it too. What are you doing this summer? We are taking part in the Festival at Aix-la-Chapelle, then I am coming back, and I shall probably spend my holidays, from the middle of July to the beginning of September in Thüringen with my wife and children. From there I shall take a three weeks' trip to Ammergau and the Alps. Are we likely to meet? Good-bye, and write a line to your faithful

JOSEPH J.

### From Clara Schumann

BADEN, *June* 13, 1870.

Dear Joachim—I am turning to you to ask you to advise me. I have had an invitation from the Vienna Beethoven Committee (signed by Herbeck). I feel as you do—the idea of a Beethoven Festival with Liszt and Wagner oppresses me, but how am I to get out of it? I, as a *woman*, cannot act as you did and say what I think, it would seem too arrogant if I, a woman, were to address men in this way, so I must invent a lie! But what shall it be, seeing I want to go to Vienna again in the autumn? I do not suppose you will be able to advise me, but tell me at any rate *whether you think I am right to refuse?*   But please let me know at once, because they are waiting for a reply.   Ask your dear wife to send me a line if you are too busy. . . .

### To Clara Schumann

[BERLIN, *June* 15, 1870.]

Dear Frau Schumann—Many thanks for showing such confidence in me ; I am seizing a free moment to tell you that, in my honest opinion, you should on no account take part in a concert at which Wagner is conducting.   *You* cannot ignore the contemptuous way in which he speaks of what is sacred to you.   The fact that you are a lady seems to me to have nothing to do with it, or rather it should be all the more reason for you to keep away from it.   Besides, as far as art is concerned you are " man enough."   I should simply tell Herbeck that I wished to have particulars of the entire programme before binding myself, and then either consent or refuse.

I imagine that what is painful to me, artistically, cannot be a matter of indifference to you.   And I do not like your having been approached by Herbeck and not by the Committee.   He is one of Liszt's *intriguants* on account of the influence enjoyed by that faction, and he will try to cover the snub they received from me by getting you to join them. . . .

### To Theodor Avé-Lallemant

[BERLIN, *beginning of July* 1870.]

Dear Avé—The Beethoven Festival will take place here on and after December 16, and of course includes the Mass in D, the Ninth, *Fidelio, Egmont,* an

orchestral concert and chamber music. The Committee has only met once and will not do so again
until August 2, when the details are to be discussed.
Happily, I shall no longer be here by that time, but
in Salzburg in the same house as last year. I must
confess that I only became a member of the Committee
because I think it would be wrong not to contribute
my share here; but (between ourselves) I cannot feel
any enthusiasm over co-operating with Taubert, Dorn,
Stern, etc. Unfortunately I am not to be allowed
to enjoy myself in my own way for a few days with
Brahms, Frau Schumann, and a good orchestra. I
shall have to contribute my mite of chamber music
and, probably, the Violin Concerto. I cannot possibly
accept your delightful invitation to Hamburg; the
Festivals here and at Bonn will take up more than
their due share of my time from my school duties as it
is. But write to Frau Schumann, who I hope will be
able to go. I think you have heard of the trouble she
is in over her eldest boy, who has come hopelessly to
grief and is in an asylum. Poor Ludwig, there was
something so gentle and refined in his character; the
poor boy is being punished so undeservedly. Who
can solve a problem like this? . . .

### To his Wife

[MUNICH [1]] 15*th* [*July* 1870].

Thank you for the good news. If only the political
news were not so bad! You do not mention the
threatening storm clouds which the insolent and
thoughtless Gauls are invoking. I can hardly think

---

[1] Frau Joachim had remained in Berlin with her second son, who had contracted measles, whilst the other children had been taken by their father as far as
Munich on their way to Salzburg.

of anything else, and if it were not for you I should
certainly fight in the war which seems unavoidable
now. They too obviously mean to insult us. It is a
blessing we have a man like Bismarck at the head of
affairs ; I feel that I am a *German*, not an Austrian.
Berg is sure to keep you *au fait* ; Saldern sees to it
here that I have news, through the embassy. My
one consolation is that the way to Vienna is sure to
be open to you, even if the French should render
Bavaria unsafe within the next fortnight, which I do
not think likely, although I am prepared for defeat *to
begin with*. I have no fear of the ultimate result ; the
sense of right and my faith in the mission of the
German people to spread its learning abroad will
sustain me.

The *Rheingold* did not teach me anything new
about Wagner ; it is really almost boring with its
eternal mystery and elaboration. Even Brahms was
forced to agree with me, although he likes to pose as
an admirer of Wagner. I am pinning my hopes on
the *Valkyrie*. Brahms is at Ammergau. Ise and Levi
are not here. . . .

### To Clara Schumann

SALZBURG, *August* 13 [1870].

Dear Frau Schumann—I should very much like
to have some news of you in these unsettled times ; I
often think anxiously of you, so near to the seat of
war. But all the same it is a joy to me to know that
our beloved Germany is safe from attack. How
magnificently our army has behaved under the Crown
Prince! But whereabouts is your Ferdinand? Have
you had news of him? I know you are large-minded
enough to see him go to fight for his country without

regret; but, all the same, your tender maternal heart must sometimes beat anxiously, and your friends feel with you. Write a line to me if you can and say how you all are. If I had not been detained here owing to the children having measles, whilst my wife was looking after little Hermann in Berlin, I should either be close to the seat of war or else back in Berlin. One longs to share to the full in these great times! At first we had a very sad time because communication with Prussia was so uncertain. My wife often had no letter from me for a week, although I wrote to her every day, and *vice versâ*. At last, on the 2nd, she came here with the boy *via* Breslau—Vienna. Since then we have had the worst possible weather, rain varying in degree from mists to downpours! The poor, convalescent children have to remain indoors (but they seem quite well again), and yesterday for fear our troubles should come to an end, our youngest little girl, who we hoped had been spared, sickened for measles!

### *From Ernst Rudorff*

LAUENSTEIN, NR. ELZE, HANOVER, *August* 15, 1870.

Dear Friend—If you have had my last letter I suppose you think of me as working at some hospital, and I must lose no time in disabusing you of this idea. After having waited for three weeks for a definite decision, I had a reply from Cologne yesterday declining my offer, with the remark that only trained nurses who had had at least a fortnight's experience in a hospital could be accepted. Of course there is no time now for me to prepare myself in this way, and besides I gather from the refusal that they do not require any more. And so the plan I had set my heart on for so long has come to a sad end, and I am just where I was three weeks ago.   The suspense is almost unbearable sometimes ; day and night one's only desire is that the next decisive engagement may result in complete victory for us.   If the luck turns now, God knows what the end may be.

I read in the *Signal* yesterday that there is a great unofficial gathering of musicians at Salzburg, including Brahms, and that the latter has accepted the appointment at Vienna.   Remember me very kindly to him, and if you happen to be writing tell me what new things of his you have seen.

I have often wondered lately whether we ought not to make use of this opportunity to declare war against France in the artistic sphere also, more especially on Herr Offenbach's muse.   I read a work on *Art in Everyday Life*[1] the other day, which was very charming in parts, and it has brought me seriously to the conclusion that bad, demoralising art should be prevented from entering into the lives of the people. Perhaps you will laugh at me for my unpractical notions, but an attempt ought surely to be made, either by the formation of a society or in some other way, to obtain influence in a matter of such tremendous importance.

And now good-bye for to-day !   Any news which is not connected with political affairs seems so out of place, and yet it is no use writing newspaper articles, we read enough of those as it is. . . .

### To his Wife

[LONDON, *February* 17, 1871.]

It is a week to-day since I came here, and I have done a great deal in the time !   I returned from

---

[1] By Emil Frommel.

Liverpool yesterday, where I was kept very hard at it because Piatti was ill, and as we had another 'cellist we were obliged to have a rehearsal just before the concert (from 6.30 to 8). The programme was unreasonably long, too. Quintette by Onslow, Quartette by Schumann, Romance by Beethoven with extras, and Schubert's *Forellen* Quintette with five movements, for my share alone, not to mention the choral items and Frau Schumann's solo! I entered a protest against a programme like that for the future. Onslow's Quintette, which was very much the vogue twenty years ago, is very dull, and its pathos is frenchified and affected, in spite of some good passages. I travelled with Frau Schumann and she told me of the success of your Frankfort concert; I congratulate you on your magnificent takings, and I am glad you were in such good voice and that you were paid the honours which are due to you. I only hope it will not have been too much for you! Elise writes most enthusiastically of you. How did *she* get on? I need not give you an account of *my* reception, as Heinrich has sent you the *Pall Mall* and the *Times*. But I must tell you of an amusing incident last Saturday when I went to the matinée and tried to get away unnoticed before the last Trio; but they recognised me from the gallery, one or two people called out my name, and the whole audience began to applaud, whilst I slunk away with my tail between my legs. The Berlin public is not yet on such a friendly footing with me. . . .

Admirers of Bismarck have a good deal to put up with here—they will have to get used in time to his greatness and to Germany's. It is really nothing but jealousy because we have dared to attain to an important position by our own efforts without the permission of the Allies. They have respect for Moltke's faultless

method and its successful results, but they think we
ought to turn our backs modestly on Paris now, so as
to spare the feelings of the French.    The devil take
them and their wishy-washy talk!!    The French
fellows are already beginning to say that Paris was
never conquered by the Prussians, that nothing but
hunger forced them to give in—as though the boasters
had made even *one* successful sortie.    However, I
fancy the majority in Bordeaux will be sensible, and
that peace, sweet peace, will come with the spring.
Thank God Belfort has at last capitulated also. . . .

## *To his Wife*

[LONDON] *Thursday morning* [*March* 2, 1871].

. . . There is a lot of nonsense being talked here
about the terms of peace.    They say we ought to have
turned the French from thoughts of revenge by our
generosity, and a lot more stuff of this kind, which, in
my opinion, is in very bad taste!    It was simply a
question as to whether we should make such easy
terms that they would be able to take revenge *very*
soon, or whether we should make such demands that
they would be harmless for a considerable time.    The
latter seems to me beyond doubt the right course, so
long live Bismarck.    I often feel annoyed when I hear
political discussions.    But Elly is a true German. . . .

## *To his Wife*

[BERLIN, *November* 1871.]

. . . In the evening, after our conference, I was
invited to the Princess's, without music.    Keudell went
too.    I rather dreaded it, but it was very pleasant.    I
chatted nearly the whole evening with Marie Bismarck ;
she is very simple and merry, and took possession of

me at once, as though I were an old acquaintance. I was glad of this, because it was a sure sign that I had not made a *faux pas* and that the Chancellor simply has too much to do to remember everything. She hoped her father would come in, and I was looking forward to seeing him—but a conference with Archbishop Ketteler which he had to hold that evening lasted too long, and at 11 o'clock he sent word asking to be excused. I strongly suspect that the conference with Ketteler was a ruse. You may be sure he does not care much for the great ladies in political circles! The Princess's condition is very serious, unhappily. She is literally tortured by her nerves, has fainting attacks, terrible noises in her ears, and spends most of her time in bed without getting any rest. I feel deeply for the poor lady. I am to give you young Prince Bismarck's very kindest regards. . . . There were about a dozen people there altogether, among them the Princess's brother, a Prince Hohenlohe, and *Treitschke*. Also a young Count Roon, who impressed me very favourably as a soldier of genuine culture and great simplicity. We are to play quartettes at the Princess's before long. I interviewed Schaeff about free tickets to-day. I have secured some (for money) for some friends, too, for the Keudells, the Richters, etc., six for you. Only think, the other day *Moltke* wanted to go to our quartette concert and could not get a ticket! Frau von Keudell told me this and promised to tell him from me that in future I would have a seat specially made for him if he thought of honouring us again! What a pity!! It would have been such a pleasure to play for him in return for what he has done! He is said to like music, and the Keudells are going to invite him so that I can play to him. I hope you will be there too then. . . .

### *To his Wife in Vienna*

[BERLIN] *Tuesday 19th* [*November* 1872].

. . . I heard Wilhelmj on Sunday, and, after my first impression of him, I was very disappointed. I had not expected such vacuity—even in the recit. of Beethoven's A minor Quartette he had not grasped the *superficial* effects to any marked degree, not to speak of putting any real life into it. And added to this he has bad technical habits which are not even his own, but derived from *David*; but he has an oily voluptuous way of bringing out a magnificent tone from his violin.

And now read the notices! It was not full (500 thalers net receipts with tickets at 1½ thalers). He played the *Abendlied* in D major instead of in the soft D♭ an octave lower on the G string, and *without* altering the accompaniment in the upper part. Perfectly idiotic——

One ought really only to play for oneself and a few friends. . . .

### *To his Wife*

*Sunday* [*December* 1, 1872].

I have just enjoyed something which would arouse the envy of a good many people, even yours and Brahms', because such things are not to be had in Vienna! I had a quarter of an hour's drive with Moltke in a little, two-seated carriage, as he was so kind as to offer me a lift from the conference on the concert to my house. I intended to enjoy the honour bareheaded, but he looked up and asked me whether my hat touched the roof of the carriage. The old gentleman was very cordial in his calm, majestic way.

He hoped you would be back again in time for the concert (which will probably be on the 15th, as Hülsen offered the theatre and the singers for a Sunday), as you would be a great help, etc., etc. I did not want to go to the conference at Frau von Pommer-Esche's house, which was only attended by "grandees," and I will give you my reasons in detail some time, but Herr von Burt came and called for me after all. I expect I shall have to play the Beethoven Concerto (under Eckert's conductorship), and I should like you to sing the *Alcestis* or something equally lovely. I shall really be rather glad the matter takes up so little of my time, because the rehearsals for the school concerts and the quartettes, etc., are coming on. I am delighted to hear your second concert was such a success; I hope it will be one crescendo until the *Saul*. . . .

## *To his Wife*

[LONDON] *Tuesday 18th [February* 1873].

. . . I played well on Saturday and yesterday evening, my strings were good and I was in the right mood. Brahms' Serenade was almost perfect and had an excellent reception. I felt as though I were back once more in the early days at Hanover when he wrote it and everything spoke to us of Beethoven and Schubert. A good deal of myself crept into the instrumentation and moved me with its recollections of former intimacies. I suppose he has got beyond such weaknesses as these! By the way, I must write to him about the Festival. It is not Frau Schumann who objects to his Requiem at the Schumann Festival, but the Committee came to me behind Frau Schumann's back, as they would rather have something shorter by Brahms, and the *Peri*. But I am going to insist

on the Requiem for the first day and make them change
their opinion.   The *Peri* has been done too often, and
the solemn and powerful Symphony in C major will
fit in splendidly with the Requiem. . . . I shall enquire
everywhere for a nurse.   But if I really do find one
who unites in herself all the qualities you require—
good speech, cheerful temper, youth, reliability, good
manners at table, and keeping the nursery clean—we
had better fix on her as a wife for Rudorff and lament
that Putzi is not old enough to take her for himself.
Poor Rudorff! I must write a line to him.[1] . . .

### To his Wife

[LONDON] *Monday* [*April* 7, 1873].

 . . . The day before yesterday I dined with Cockburn.   Afterwards, without a word having been said
to me, the Duke of Edinburgh came in, as he wished
to hear me play in a room.   He plays the violin
himself.   It was quite an informal affair, and I was
glad that Elly and Heinrich were there, as it was something of an event for them.   The Duke's manners were
very good, not without a touch of English shyness,
which is so often taken for arrogance. . . .

### From Clara Schumann

14 HYDE PARK GATE, W., *April* 10, 1873.

My dear Joachim—I was very sorry we were
interrupted yesterday when you were saying good-bye ;
I wanted so much to talk to you about Bonn.   I wanted
to tell you that the more I think about it the more I
would prefer that you should do Brahms' Requiem
instead of the *Peri*.   The *Peri* is so well known to all

---

[1] Rudorff had lost his father on February 15.

musicians and music lovers, and if you have not got an *exceptional* singer for the part of the *Peri* (I know of none myself) the work must suffer. Apart from the fact that the Requiem would make an extremely interesting item, it would be doubly appropriate because Brahms was so intimate with my husband during his lifetime, and even at that time my husband singled him out as a man on whom our highest hopes for the future might be fixed.

I can see no possible objection to the Requiem, unless it were the possibility of Brahms composing something specially for the Festival. But that he cannot do, he tells me, because he cannot find a suitable text. I am sure the Committee will make no difficulties if you tell them that I, as well as you, particularly wish the Requiem to be performed. *There is plenty of time to rehearse it.*

Please let me hear soon how the matter stands. . . .

### From Hermann Levi

CARLSRUHE, *June* 27, 1873.

Dear Joachim—If I had not been so rushed yesterday in Baden, I would have added my birthday wishes to Frau Schumann's. She will have told you how we toasted you and wished you every possible good fortune. Indeed, the conversation was chiefly about you and the Festival and Brahms. I cannot get over the fact that just now, when the Memorial Festival is recalling the old, happy days together, the very people who ought to be united are being separated by all kinds of trifling misunderstandings. And I think each one ought to do what lies in his power to soften and forget his grievances. Of course Brahms is put out again because he learnt of the omission of the Requiem from the programme through the news-papers (at least, so I imagine; he has said nothing to me about it). Frau Schumann knew nothing about it either, and could give me no reason for it. I am not a good mediator and do not want to go into details, but I could not help giving Frau Schumann a lecture or two on her behaviour towards Brahms, and I wish you had been there to hear some of them. She showed me a letter from Brahms which I was expected to con-sider inconsiderate, cold and unkind, which, with the best will in the world, I was not able to do. He is just himself; either he was not worthy of your friend-ship ten years ago, or else he is just as worthy of it now. I admit he is not capable of taking the first step himself; from what I know of him he is much more likely calmly to await a sign from you and Frau Schumann. I cannot entertain the idea that the cool-ness is permanent, and something must be done about it on your side. Will you not write to him now in a friendly, pleasant way, and just explain why you are not giving the Requiem? Forgive me for meddling in affairs which do not concern me, or which I do not rightly understand, but the fact that all is not as it could and ought to be between you weighs on my mind continually, and I would give a great deal to be able to help to put matters straight. . . .

### From Johannes Brahms

[MUNICH—TUTZING] *June* 1873.

Dear Joachim—I see from the newspapers that my Requiem is not going to be performed at Bonn, and what annoyed me still more, I heard that you justified your action on the grounds of a letter from me.

I am supposed to have written diplomatically and

2 D

not to have made it clear whether the performance would please me or not.

If my letter really made this impression, I should, naturally, have preferred that you should write and tell me so, or ask me a second question, for I think I gave a lucid reply to the first. It is easy to attribute all sorts of motives to a man who is not keen on answering and explaining. So you say I wrote *diplomatically*? I certainly said *nothing* on a good many subjects which I had very much at heart—and on the matter as a whole. But that was not diplomacy, merely my dislike of letter-writing. I suppose I ought to have said all that was in my mind in this case; how I wished to put all doubts and—misunderstandings on one side so as to cast no shadow on the memory of that excellent man and artist, and so that the Festival should be justified by the manner in which it was carried out.

But I write too impatiently and reluctantly about even the most important things to have said all this, and for this very reason it was hardly likely I should write a diplomatic letter.

I think I am clear-headed enough all the same to know *what* I write, and, if only for this reason, I should be very annoyed if that letter of mine were different to what I now believe it to be. Moreover, I do not think it would need any especially friendly eye to read it aright. We had discussed the matter long before; in your letter you only asked me which of us should conduct, and I only replied that I would agree to whatever you wished and decided to do. I told you at the time that I considered it desirable, not to say necessary, to introduce another name. If I had been organising the Festival I should probably have done Cherubini's Requiem, or something like that, at the end. Of course a performance of this kind is an honour to a living artist under any circumstances, but it is the kind of honour with regard to which one would rather remain silent, or which one might even refuse out of a genuine feeling of modesty.   I have no idea whether you credit me with such modesty.   At any rate modesty so easily looks foolish that it prefers to remain silent—as I did.   But if, in this case, you had considered the matter quite *simply* you would have known how completely and inevitably such a work as the Requiem belonged to Schumann, so much so that, in my heart of hearts, it seemed to me a matter of course that it should be sung for him.

I should find it very difficult to be more explicit on this subject—if it were expected of me.   Now I feel that I am miles apart from those who usually sympathise with me—but do we not make a hard and fast line, as a rule, between men and artists?   A heavy stone has fallen once more on the better side—but my garrulity will not add anything to its weight!

I must not write any more.   You must believe me when I confess that I had really intended to write quite a cheerful letter to you to the effect that I had never believed the performance would come off, because the Committee did not wish it, and that "the Herr Director was a very polite fellow."   I should be sorry if you took offence at this, but it is what I prefer to believe.

Is it owing to an increasing melancholy, or simply to my dislike of writing, that my letter has taken such a different tone?   At any rate, if my previous letter did not prove it, this will show you that I am no letter writer.   But, short or long, I am quite ready to believe that, with the best will in the world, there is not much good to be got out of it—and that it would not be difficult to put a good deal more into it.

Do not do that, treat it gingerly. In spite of all its confusion, this was intended to evoke a reassuring reply. I have so little cause to expect this that I am not even ending with a note of interrogation.—Yours,

J. Brahms.

*To Johannes Brahms*

[Berlin] *July* 7, 1873.

Dear Brahms—You write that I have justified myself for having given up the idea of doing *your* Requiem at the Schumann Festival at the last minute, after having been so enthusiastic about it, on the grounds of a letter from you. I have, however, *expressly* stated that, after a more careful consideration of the works by Schumann which are to be performed, it seemed to me impossible to cram a work which needs so much study into the two rehearsals and two days of the Festival, and that I would rather give up my pet scheme than give a faulty performance. *Nobody has read another word from me about it*, and, besides my wife, only one person, an intimate friend of yours and mine, has heard me say that your letter and your whole behaviour had, unfortunately, given me the impression that you did not enter heart and soul into the business, and would probably prefer not to have your name mentioned in connection with it. It is often very difficult to get over an impression of this sort! But let us be quite frank. For the last few years, whenever we have met, I have always felt that your manner towards me was not what it used to be, although I gladly credit you with having made an effort several times to make it so. There may be fifty reasons for this, and I am very far from saying that I may not partly be in fault. No doubt I have disappointed many

of the hopes you set on my development, and have
been more indolent than you liked in many respects,
and no doubt I have been more sparing than was
necessary with evidences of my genuine liking for you
—good Lord, what accusations can an honest man not
make against himself! What more natural than for
me to imagine that you regarded our old intimacy,
which I felt so warmly just in connection with our
relation to Schumann, as something embarrassing
rather than desirable, but that you could not bring
yourself to say so. You require so much energy for
your work that I can understand your not always considering it worth while to make your feelings clear, and
preferring to let things take their course. But in this
matter I considered it my duty not to deceive myself,
and so the enthusiasm with which I originally intended
to put the work through, in spite of many difficulties,
evaporated. You wanted a reassuring answer. I
wonder if this is one? I should be really grieved if
you were hurt, because your work is not to be done at
the Festival, and yet it would almost be a consolation
to me.—Always yours sincerely,          JOSEPH J.

### From Clara Schumann

BADEN, *July* 8, 1873.

    . . . The Brahms affair is very distressing! I had
a letter from him on the same day with regard to a
matter which concerns me very deeply—just the same
indifferent tone. I have not yet made up my mind
whether I shall answer it or not. I do not think the
letter to you is so very bad, merely cold. I fancy he
would really have liked to conduct, and was perhaps
offended because he was not definitely invited to do so
*by the Committee*, and I think he is justified in this. I

am extremely sorry that matters have turned out so that he is to take no part whatever in the Festival. I wonder if he will come to it? If he stays away he will be blamed, and if he comes I am afraid he will be in a bad temper, and then he will be blamed for that. He is in an awkward position now, and it might all have been so different. But there is nothing to be done now. . . .

### From Clara Schumann

BADEN, *August* 3, 1873.

. . . If only nothing interferes with the Festival! I am feeling the heat so much this year that I cannot imagine how I shall ever play in the warm hall. Indeed, the nearer the Festival comes the more my fear increases that something will happen to prevent it. The thought of the Festival, the idea that *I* and the children are to enjoy it *together*, and that I am to have the joy of taking part in it as a performer (in ten years' time that will not be possible), and many other reflections besides, have so exalted me and have filled my heart with such tremulous happiness, that I live in terror lest I shall not be there after all. You know how easy it is for sombre thoughts to spoil my pleasure. I suppose it is old age—the result of having gone through and of still enduring so much. I was deeply grieved at David's death—all the memories of my youth awoke in me. . . .

### From Clara Schumann

BADEN, *August* 29, 1873.

Dear Joachim—Not a day has passed since the time in Bonn on which I have not often thought grate-

fully of you, but I could not write because I found
plenty to do here and have had a great many visitors.

I have been going through my manuscript cupboard in the hopes of finding something to send you in
memory of the days which were made so sacred and
doubly memorable to me owing to your presence.    I
should have liked best of all to send you a symphony,
but, alas, there are no more left, not even the *Manfred*
Overture, and so there remains nothing but the
*Nachtlied.*  You said you would like to have it ; and it
made a deep impression on me, too.    Accept it, please,
and when you look at it think sometimes of your old
friend.  We are still living in the memory of those
days, but when I came back here I was overwhelmed
by all the sad thoughts which I had resolutely kept in
the background at Bonn.    Now I feel as though my
artistic career came to an end at this Festival, as
happily and peacefully as possible, but still—I cannot
tell you all I have been feeling, my heart is in a continuous ebb and flow of joy and sorrow !  When you
and all the public showed so much love for me, I could
have wept aloud, in spite of all the joy which filled my
heart, at the thought that all this love and veneration
for him was being poured out over me, whilst he lay
out there in the churchyard !   It is so hard not to have
the consolation of faith at such moments !  But my
heart is full of gratitude for what has been granted to
me and because the children have been permitted to
see their father's memory so glorified, more especially
by his brother artists who were so dear to him and
whom he revered so deeply, as we do also.

Johannes gave me a few happy days here by way
of an extra festival and brought some lovely things
with him.   Two string quartettes which seem to me of
the greatest importance, several marvellous songs, and

the Variations which you know and which I think *very* beautiful. He was very charming, too, and that made the time pass delightfully.

I wonder how you are now? I wish you were coming with us to the mountains—I am sure it would have done you just as much good as the sea, and would have been more stimulating for the mind. Have you got over all the hard work? And how is the dear songstress who sang so beautifully?

I have one request to make. Please impress on the Committee at Bonn to be sure not to choose a monument without our and Bendemann's consent! It so often happens that the best intentions are frustrated by stupidity, and that would be dreadful. For instance, there are Kietz and Donndorf at Dresden (pupils of Rietschel) who did the Uhland memorial, which is said to be first-rate, and they have our medallion to do as well. We have given a lot of thought to the stone which is there now. The gentlemen of the Committee told me it ought to remain. But, however acceptable that might be to me, I should not like the artistic effect of the memorial to be lessened out of consideration for my feelings. In any case the stone must be *raised* and the illegible lettering altered. Everybody here, with the exception of Marie, agrees that the stone *must* be left—but I am trying not to set my heart on this by telling myself that, before everything else, the monument must be a thing of simplicity and beauty. If that is possible *with* my stone I shall be all the better pleased, but if it is not possible I shall be resigned, because a monument belongs to the world and to future generations who will not care whether I or any one else put the stone there. Do not say *anything* about this to the members of the Committee, please—I am only mentioning it between ourselves, and I should like to know what you think about it.    Johannes thought the stone ought to remain!

My little gift will follow soon—and then I shall enclose the Variations for Rudorff, to whom please give my kind regards. . . .

### To Johannes Brahms

[LONDON, *April* 1876.]

Dear Brahms — Professor Macfarren (Bennett's successor as Professor of Music at Cambridge and Director of the Royal Academy of Music in London) will have written to you on behalf of the Rector of the University to know whether you will accept the distinction of Honorary Doctor of Music which they wish to confer on you.    The University wishes to honour me in this manner also, and I have said " Yes."    It is the first time the title of Doctor has ever been voluntarily offered to a foreigner.    Grove tells me that Haydn had to compose the prescribed exercise for Oxford before he was made a Doctor, and I think Grove is well informed in such matters.    But you can find out for certain from Pohl.    Although I think it would have been better if they had only offered you the distinction, I think you ought to accept it all the same.    It is a proof, at any rate, of how highly your things are thought of there, and indeed throughout the musical world in England.    All you have to do is to write a German letter in Roman characters to Macfarren, to say that you accept the honour with pleasure (or that you are delighted to accept), and you can add or not, as you please, that you regard it as a proof of sympathy with your artistic endeavours.    The next question is whether you will really come to England so that you may be created Doctor (a solemn ceremony at which the whole University is present). Without this you cannot be made Doctor. I shall not be able to manage it this year, and have postponed my visit to Cambridge until next year. They would be only too pleased if you would present yourself on May 18 (which has been the day for the conferring of the Doctor's Degree from time immemorial). I am sending you a letter on the subject from a very prominent member of Trinity College, and would draw your attention particularly to the *Postscript*. I am curious to know what you will do, and it would be nice of you if you sent me a line to Meran, Obermais, Pension Rainer, where I am going on Tuesday 11 to bring my wife back, I hope. I shall be four or five days in Meran. There is something fine in the thought of being accepted by a body of men which has included Bacon, Milton, Newton, Byron, etc. ; remember this, and do not regard it from too modern a standpoint. . . .

### To Richard Schöne

[BERLIN, *May* 1876.]

. . . I enclose herewith a note to the painter Leighton, whom I think you will like and who may be useful to you as regards artistic matters, more especially as he speaks German as though it were his mother tongue. You will see a large picture by him at the Exhibition, in case you should prefer to know beforehand to what type of mind his belongs. What I admire in him is that he never ceases to strive after perfection even in the minutest details, and I admire this all the more because he is in a fair way to be spoilt by attention and flattery. But I think he has delicacy and versatility as an artist to an unusual degree.

I shall be very much interested to know what sort of an impression is made on you by a landscape of Millais', which is also at the Exhibition — a large picture, in the foreground moorland (with details of grass and water), in the background a far-stretching country of a Scotch character.[1] The whole picture seemed to me original and significant, and a very great contrast to Leighton's in feeling and intention. I hope you will not be away *too* long, but I am delighted that you should be there for a short time! I missed you very much at the performance of the *Seasons*, but I will let your wife tell you all about it, as I saw, to my pleasure, that she was in the front row. I hope to have my wife back again with us this week.

### *To Ernst Rudorff*

[MANCHESTER, *March* 14, 1877.]

Dear Rudorff—After having sent you a copy of the programme of the concert at Cambridge (which was given on the occasion of my receiving the Doctor's degree), I must send a greeting to you and your wife and mother. I shall be coming myself in three weeks' time, and then I shall take over my share of the work again. Many thanks for doing it so faithfully for me! . . .

I have spoken to Manns and Hallé here in Manchester about your Serenade. The latter knows it already and means to do it without fail next autumn (when the concerts begin again). Next to Manns', his orchestra is the best in England. I have had no definite promise from Manns as yet, but I feel sure he will do it also. I shall draw Stanford's attention to it too. I have no time to tell you about musical

---

[1] "The Fringe of the Moor" possibly.—TR.

conditions in England. The most remarkable thing to my mind is the rapidity with which Brahms' works have become known, in a manner which far exceeded my expectations. Schumann made much slower progress here. Even the B major Quartette which was treated so scornfully at Berlin went down here. Note, on the last page of the programme, how charmingly the *Schicksalslied*, *Triumphlied* and *Requiem* have been used in Latin to express regret at Brahms' absence. You will be glad to hear that Petri's *début* was a great success. So, in spite of all difficulties, we do see some good results.

God be with you and keep you, my friend.— Always yours,                          JOSEPH JOACHIM.

### From Elisabeth von Herzogenberg

ALT-AUSSEE, *August 4,* 1877.

Dear Herr Joachim—Allow me to thank you, on the worst possible notepaper but none the less heartily for that, for having given me such a delightful excuse for writing to you. I must tell you I wanted to do so very much when first we heard that your dear wife had really recovered. I longed to write and tell you that we rejoiced with you, and that you would have to allow us to do so, just as you could not prevent us from sharing your anxiety. After all, we have a certain claim on any one to whom we owe a great debt of gratitude, and I owe this to your wife for some ineffaceable impressions. Years ago, when she sang the Brahms *Rhapsodie* at Leipzig, I sat there— very much ashamed of myself—melted to tears, among the flower of the Leipzig Philistines, who were far too polite to be moved. And then, when we went to the green-room, there stood the woman whom I longed to embrace.   Instead of that, of course, I could not utter a word, for, unhappily, I have always found that the mouth *cannot* speak out of the fullness of the heart.

I do not believe any artist could hear with indifference that some one has been deeply moved and delighted by him, and so I would ask you to tell Frau Joachim that which I was too stupid and too excited to say to her myself at the time.   All love and praise to the " Father of love " who has given her strength to recover from her severe illness !

As I have said, Frau Schwabe [1] was a very welcome excuse to write all this to you, without which I should hardly have ventured to trouble you with a letter. We are very grateful to you for having given us the opportunity of making such a pleasant acquaintance ; unfortunately I only saw Frau Schwabe once, but I felt very much drawn to her.

What a pity that her ill-health prevents her from walking to any extent ; I had looked forward so much to boasting to her of the beauties of Aussee.

I am expecting dear Fillu [2] in a few days ; when she was in Berlin she supplied me so nobly with news of Frau Joachim.   You can imagine how often we shall mention your name. . . .

### From Ernst Rudorff

LICHTERFELDE, *March* 3, 1879.

Dear Joachim . . . Last week Rubinstein drove people wild here again.   I did not go to his two concerts, and I felt annoyed afterwards because I

---

[1] The wife of a German merchant, who was very musical, and with whom Joachim often stayed when he was in England ; she was also a friend of Frau Schumann.   Joachim had given her an introduction to the Herzogenbergs at Aussee.

[2] The singer Marie Fillunger.

could not join in the talk about him, although of course the impressions I had formed of his playing on previous occasions were definite enough. But I heard him yesterday, when he gave an amazingly long and somewhat boring matinée, at which he launched out into his D minor Concerto and several small pieces of his own composition. His capacity certainly borders on the fabulous. He has a power, a temerity, and a temperament only attributed to demigods as a rule. But as to *what* he plays, that is a different question altogether. The things which I consider in the light of music and interpretation are, for the most part at any rate, on quite another plane. All the same, I have more respect now than I used to have for his colossal powers. Sauret was among the other performers. He played Ernst's *Air Hongrois* with great bravura, and after every variation he stood, like a true Frenchman, with outstretched bow, like a dancing-master making his bow, and he played the Bruch Concerto in such a disgustingly affected and ridiculously exaggerated manner that I liked him even less than I do Sarasate. . . .

## To Philipp Spitta

LONDON, *March* 17 [1879].

First of all, many thanks for sending me news; I was very glad to hear from you. As a matter of fact, I have never been so ill in my life; rheumatic pains which I felt every time I coughed or sneezed, and weakness and loss of appetite, and public engagements on top of everything! I am glad it is over; I have been much better for the last week.

Has the Cherubini Symphony,[1] which I sent off ten

---

[1] In D major. Cherubini wrote this Symphony in 1815 for the London Philharmonic Society, and conducted it on May 1.

days ago, arrived? I am anxious to know whether Rudorff will give it; it will interest you to do it at an orchestra practice, anyhow. I am sorry to say I have never heard it myself. A rumour from *Berlin* is going through all the papers here that I have accepted a post in London! As there is not the slightest foundation for this gossip, and as it was repeated recently in the Berlin papers, it must mean that an attempt is being made to lessen the attendance at the school next term. It might be as well if Engel contradicted it in a few lines under *Vermischtes* [Miscellaneous News]. Do you not think so too? The fact that, at the request of Cambridge University, I acted as one of the examiners of the candidates for the Doctor's degree in music may have misled some one. The expression, " Mr. Joachim has been 'appointed' an examiner," might have caused some ignorant person to spread the story without intending to do harm. Unfortunately, we have more reason to believe it was done intentionally!!! I shall bring the studies with me which were set for the examination; they will interest the Senate. . . .

*From Hermann Levi*

MAMERS (SARTHE), *July* 5, 1879.

. . . You ask me whether I am still a Wagnerian? When you heard *Tristan* with us that time I was still a timid beginner, a simple enthusiast. Now, after years of study and reflection, I feel I may really call myself a Wagnerian. Whether this change (from the opinions of my youth) should be attributed to lack of principle, weakness, felony, or to development and progress, I cannot say. But of this I am certain, that I bless the day on which my eyes were opened (dimly at first through the *Meistersinger*, and completely and finally through *Tristan*) and that I could never go back.

*Parsifal* certainly "carried me away," but all the same I am not one of those who at every new work by Wagner pronounce the previous ones to be "not quite on the highest plane." To me, *Tristan, Meistersinger* and the *Nibelungen*, although absolutely different in style, are all equally the emanations of the same great genius! *Parsifal* again is something absolutely new, but it is no more an advance after *Tristan* than is the C minor compared to the *Eroica* or the *Wahlverwandschaften* after *Werther*. But, from a purely musical standpoint, *Parsifal* (I only know the selections, which, however, are very extensive) seems to me of the greatest importance. But one cannot argue about Wagner any more than one can about religion. Every one sees it his own way. But I should be glad if you also were granted such a—change one day. (I said "granted" deliberately, because it comes quite of itself, and you need only to keep quiet and not to fight against it.) You must not shrink from the suffering and inner conflict of the transition period; that is all quickly forgotten in the joy of possession. I particularly want you to know that I do not belong to the futurists in the same sense as Richard Pohl or Porges. My estimate of Liszt will always separate me from those people. I have never been able to understand how any one could be a Wagnerian and a Lisztian at the same time. During the seven years I have been at Munich I have only had Liszt's name on my concert programmes twice; on both occasions the public met my wish that the items should be omitted. . . .

So we are to meet in the autumn? That will be delightful—but I fear you will go no further than

Munich station, as you have so often done these last few years? . . .

### From Ernst Rudorff

LAUENSTEIN (HANOVER), *September* 8, 1879.

. . . You have been surrounded by people, a great contrast to my quiet life here with my family.  I can well believe that you have gained something vital from the presence of Brahms and his music which you would not willingly have missed, more especially in respect of the Violin Sonata—and provided he really wished to give you of his best, as he seems to have done here. I am realising more and more by how many ties—not only of admiration but of love—this extraordinary man binds one to him, in spite of all his gruff ways.  I dream of him sometimes, and then, strangely enough, he is always so charming that I succumb to him entirely.  But apart from this man, and him mainly because he brought such magnificent music, I do not envy you all those dear delightful people, who have overwhelmed you in such herds, one bit.  Salzburg is too much on the high road, and Professor Joachim is too much common property of which every one thinks he can grab his share.  You yourself will have hardly any of that peace and quiet which one looks forward to enjoying in the holidays.

But I must tell you once more how much I value the few friendly words from you, and all the more so because in personal intercourse there is so seldom a chance of touching on anything more than super-ficialities.  I have brought Treitschke's new German history away with me and have read it with the greatest interest, I might even say edification.  The vigorous enthusiasm of it does one good.  You have probably got hold of the book too; if not I strongly recommend you to do so. . . .

### From Ernst Rudorff

[LICHTERFELDE, *about December* 23, 1879.]

Dear Joachim—I am extremely sorry we are not to meet, because I have things to say to you about which it is difficult to write briefly. Herr X. came to see me to-day to ask me if I would conduct the first part of the Synagogue concert. Although I always like to be where you are, and although I wish the people of Upper Silesia well from the bottom of my heart, and would gladly contribute to their assistance, I shall not conduct because the whole affair seems to me too disingenuous, and I dislike it too much. Moreover, I earnestly entreat you as an artist and as a man, for the sake of your position, to make up your mind even at this eleventh hour to withdraw from the matter, as it stands at present at any rate. Give a concert of your own, if you like, in another hall, at very high prices, for the same object.

My reasons are : 1. The programme seems to me absolutely unsuitable to a place of worship, and I do not think you ought to countenance the performance there of Beethoven Symphonies and Schumann's *Abendlied*. 2. The singing of the Aria " Jerusalem " from *Saul*, which comes after the stoning of Stephen by the Jewish enemies to Christianity, is objectionable. To me personally, although I am very tolerant, it is repellent, because it is not tolerance but complete thoughtlessness which makes such a thing possible. 3. The whole affair has obviously been devised to make a demonstration, but if any such demonstration does take place nowadays, which I think is inadvisable, you ought not to be on that side, but on the one directly opposed to it. You are among those of the Jewish race who, like Felix Mendelssohn, Neander, and others, have become so German that Germany claims you as her own and has the right to be proud of you as one of her noblest and greatest sons. You *cannot* make common cause with a Jewish coterie who want to make a boast of you and to use you *in majorem gloriam* of their *tribe*, so as to get a good attendance at the concert. That is what they are after, and nothing else besides. Those who really wish to do good do not want to be amused in return. If they are anxious to give up something for Upper Silesia they need not plunder other people to do so ; all they have to do is simply to open their purses again, however much they may have given already.

Incidentally, I hear that you have fixed a rehearsal for 11 o'clock on Christmas Day to which members of the school have actually been summoned. Forgive me for thinking that by doing this you are aiming a blow at universal customs and susceptibilities, which ought not to come from *you*.

And now forgive me for having read you such a lecture. I know it is your goodness which has led you to agree to all this, and to shut both eyes instead of only one when it is a question of helping your fellow-creatures. But I feel sure it is more important at the moment that you should honour truth and the dignity of art. I have been to see Spitta, and he agrees with me in every particular.

The fact that it was originally intended to have a chorus, as being particularly suited to the Synagogue, will make it all the easier for you to get out of giving the concert, there at any rate. I explained to Herr X. that it was out of the question now to rehearse the

chorus sufficiently, and he has accepted this. Now
go a step further and say there is no longer any sense
in using the Synagogue, that it is impossible to give a
satisfactory programme there, and that you would like
therefore to give a concert of your own, at which you
hoped you might count on the same degree of support
from Jewish circles as though it were given in the
Synagogue, since it would be for the same "good
cause."

Once more, forgive me for speaking so frankly.—
Yours always,                                    E. RUDORFF.


### To Ernst Rudorff

[BERLIN] *December* 24 [1879].

Dear Rudorff—You stand, to my mind, in the first
rank among those few people whose actions are a safe
indication of the trend of their inmost convictions, and
I honour you for this, apart from my affection for you.
And so, dear friend, I cannot take what you have said
to me amiss; but in the matter of this concert I must
go my own way. We can discuss the pros and cons
when we meet, but I will just mention two points: I
suggested myself that the concert should be given at
a later date, in a more dignified manner, and under a
different conductor, but it was not possible. Secondly,
do not make *me* responsible for the thoughtless choice
of "Jerusalem"; I know nothing about it and shall
take good care that the Aria is not sung. With all
best wishes for the season, and hoping to have a talk
with you soon, yours,               JOSEPH JOACHIM.

Remember that I am assisting my own race against
immoderate attacks, and endeavouring to relieve
boundless misery. *Under certain conditions* I have

no objection to instrumental music of a serious nature in a place of worship.

## From Johannes Brahms

[ISCHL., *July* 27, 1880.]

Dear Friend—I will not say much, but I had hoped that your letter would be more consoling and hopeful. It has made me very sad and is constantly in my thoughts. You had so much in common, which gave promise of a long and happy life together. And now!—I find it hard to believe there is any really serious cause for it, and probably there is not. I am always quick to see the dark side of such matters, but it is easier for two people to separate than to come together again, just as reason is lost more easily than it is regained. So I do not want to say much or ask many questions, but I shall wish with all my heart that something unexpected—only nothing bad—may give a good turn to the matter.

And, added to that, there is the dissonance of a broken friendship! I imagine you will not be in the mood now either for my work or your own. But I am sending you the things *with my card*, all the same, which I do all the more readily as Simrock is not in Berlin.

If there is anything fresh to tell me, do not keep it from me. I am continually thinking of you both, and a word from you to say matters had improved would be a relief.—Yours affectionately,     JOHANNES.

## To Philipp Spitta

[SALZBURG] *Sunday* [*September* 19, 1880].

Dear Friend . . . I have been playing with Brahms a good deal, and I went with him on the 13th to Berchtesgaden to see Frau Schumann on her birthday. He was here for three days, and besides the Hungarian Concerto, the arrangement of which he liked, we played one of Brüll's, the Dvořák Concerto, etc., etc. But best of all were two works by him, Overtures. One was composed for the Academy at Breslau, and makes use of students' songs (*Was kommt dort von der Höh', Landesvater, Gaudeamus*); the other is called a "tragic Overture." One more splendid than the other; the first is festive, the second tremendous. I saw the first movements of two Trios besides. This sort of thing does one good.

### From Philipp Spitta

BERLIN, *February* 14, 1883.

. . . The news of Richard Wagner's death reached us quite unexpectedly yesterday. Now that he is no more, one realises very clearly what a remarkable influence it was which has vanished from art. We know, of course, that he destroyed more good than he ever built up. But all the same there was in him a vital, creative spirit which caused a stir everywhere, and, if only because of this, artistic life will be poorer and more sluggish now. And where are the young spirits to whom one can look to maintain the glory of German music? I think the German Parnassus has never been so deserted as it is now. . . .

### To Philipp Spitta

MAINZ, *February* 23 [1883].

. . . On the day of Wagner's funeral I had a concert at Nürnberg, which I wanted to give up as I was not in the mood to play *there* of all places.    But, as this was impossible owing to the number of visitors (from Bayreuth even!), I made up my mind to make an explanatory and apologetic speech.    But it did not come off, because the people settled down to enjoy themselves so complacently at the first item, which was played by some one else, that my words would only have sounded like a reproach.    How thoughtless the public is!

### To Johannes Brahms

MAINZ, *November* 9 [1883].

Dear Brahms—I wanted to wait until I had turned my back on Berlin and its distractions before replying to your letter, which moved me deeply.    Now that I have played at Wiesbaden and Mannheim and am going to do so here to-day, I realise how hard it is to collect one's thoughts when one is travelling and stay-ing with strangers.    So this is just a line (so that you may not have to wait any longer for an answer, and I can breathe more freely) to tell you that, when I play your Concerto this evening I shall be taking your "proffered hand," and that I shall regard it as a great privilege if I can give the Symphony, *provided it will not give rise to the slightest difficulty between you and Wüllner*.    I will not consider anything in your letter except your reference to the proffered hand, which I cannot refuse.    So much for to-day.

If you can send me your score at once, and so give me all the sooner the enjoyment I always have in seeing something new of yours, my address from Monday onwards will be at Berlin again, Friedrich-Wilhelmstrasse, No. 5.

## To Clara Schumann

[SALZBURG] *September* 12 [1884].

. . . I talked a lot about you yesterday and had to give news of you and all your dear ones! Good Queen Marie of Hanover at Gmunden, where I paid her a visit, remembered you so warmly and kindly that it would have given you pleasure to hear her although you are so accustomed to homage. But there was something so touching and simple in the way in which, in her present circumstances, she recalled former, happier days, and thought so faithfully of you and your wonderful art. She has a fine nature, and trials have given it depth. I am glad I made up my mind at last to carry out my intention of paying her a visit. You ought to do so too one day. . . .[1]

## To Sir Charles Villiers Stanford[2]

[BERLIN, *April* 9, 1885.]

My dear Stanford—Your Overture[3] went very well yesterday evening, and was very well received. I like it very much and had great pleasure in studying it with the band. We rehearsed it twice; so that I think you would have been pleased. I conducted from the original score, as Pollini had not sufficient time for having it copied; to-day I sent it back, and will ask for a separate score, as the band will play the Overture in the usual concerts.

I shall play my Hungarian Concert on Saturday at

---

[1] From this time until his death Joachim spent a few days in September nearly every year as the guest of the Queen (and afterwards of the Duke of Cumberland) at Gmunden.

[2] Written in English by Joachim.—TR.

[3] To the Opera *Savonarola*.

Hanover.  Your plans for next year please me very much.

Let me hear good tidings soon, and give my best love to your dear own people.—Yours very sincerely,

JOSEPH J.

### From Elisabeth von Herzogenberg

[BERLIN] *Friday* [*October* 23, 1885].

You will be most welcome on Sunday at six, and you shall have some good Austrian coffee.

Do not think me officious for sending you the enclosed letter.  I had written somewhat warmly about half-hearted and whole-hearted, refined and unrefined musicians, and the real and the would-be Brahms disciples in general and in particular, and you must not take it amiss that when I came to the particular I turned to you as the finest example, and, as you were not listening, let myself go!  It will doubtless please you that Brahms the taciturn has responded so sympathetically, although it is really a matter of course.

Good-bye until Sunday.  The Finale is magnificent and as for the Adagio! . . .

### From Heinrich von Herzogenberg

[BERLIN, *end of October* 1885.]

Dear Friend—One thing is clear to us (and to you too), the enclosed concoction will not do![1]  If you cannot correspond with Brahms on the old footing and in the old tone (not merely superficially) you really ought not to write to him at all, as, in approaching

---

[1] The letter to Brahms which Joachim originally drafted was couched in stiff and formal terms.  See the following letter (p. 427) for the one he finally sent.

him on artistic grounds, the change of tone will be all the more painful.

My wife made a beginning last time. Perhaps you had better wait until occasion arises for another letter in which she can make a definite inquiry in your name, so that you may not lay yourself open to a refusal (which, of course, we none of us think possible after Brahms' last letter).

If he agrees about the Symphony, but if the wording of his letter leads us to believe he is expecting a letter from you on the subject, then—in our opinion— you ought to write to him *as you always did*, and this will be all the easier because you will be writing on a matter which never had anything to do with your personal relations with Brahms outside your art.

It would be better still if you wrote at once, as Brahms is a great enemy of circuitous methods, and will not see the necessity for any go-between after his last letter, which was doubtless *intended* to make an even better impression than is the case. You know how simple and downright he is, and how easily he loses patience if he thinks he is being dealt with indirectly.

In your place, for instance, I should address him as in the old days, and I should concentrate the warmth of feeling, which used to be personal also, on the *work*. In that way I should not be climbing down, and on the other hand I should not be giving the recipient the benefit of the spectacle of my endeavours to express a wish with some warmth and, at the same time, to put my letter in such a form as to avoid even the most conventional mode of direct address ![1]

[1] Joachim had contrived to write a letter in which he had avoided using the pronoun "you" or "thou" throughout, thinking in this way to get round an obvious difficulty !—TR.

You will say it is all very well to give advice. But we are ready to give any practical help you may require from us!

### To Johannes Brahms

[BERLIN, *November* 3, 1885.]

Dear Master—I hear that your new Symphony is not to be published immediately. But after having been given the opportunity of admiring your magnificent work on the piano, through the kindness of the Herzogenbergs, I have longed ever since to hear it played by the orchestra, and my duty to the Academy concerts, which are entrusted to my management, also compels me to ask you whether you could send me the manuscript of the E minor Symphony?

The concerts on December 11, January 4, and February 1 are at my disposal for this, and you know that there will be no lack of devotion or of the necessary rehearsing.—Hoping to hear from you soon, yours very sincerely,

JOSEPH JOACHIM.

### From Elisabeth von Herzogenberg

[BERLIN, *December* 30, 1885.]

Dear Friend—*Please forgive me!* It was so horrid of me to run away yesterday! But it looked more horrid than it really was; I did it out of diffidence. When you had gone into the florist's Frau von Beulwitz said, " Now the Professor is going to get you some flowers," and then I felt shy of waiting outside there until you came back with flowers in your hand, after the way you have spoilt us, especially lately. And it is a little aesthetic trait of mine that I

428 CORRESPONDENCE OF JOACHIM

never want to enjoy to the utmost the very things which give me most pleasure. But I had no sooner run away than I regretted it so much I would have liked to have gone back again if the thought of such a thing had not made me shyer *still.*

Now, will you be kind, and bring me six violets to-morrow as a sign of forgiveness? I should have written yesterday, but I felt that that would be presumptuous too, because I did not even know whether you had noticed my flight. But when Heinrich told me you were cross with me I felt very sad, and I beg you most earnestly to forget and forgive.

Do not laugh at me for writing this letter about a trifle—as it probably seems to you. It is not a trifle to me at all if you are only a little bit cross with me!

Looking forward to to-morrow.—I am, yours repentantly, ELISABETH HERZOGENBERG.

### To Sir Charles Villiers Stanford [1]

[BERLIN] *Sunday, February 7* [1886].

My dear Stanford!—Are you not afraid of the Elegische Ouverture? You feel so kindly towards me, I know, that I fear you might do it to give me pleasure. *In Kunstsachen sollte es aber keine Freundschaft geben!* [2] I earnestly say so, and will not be offended if you change your mind ; one is no judge in one's own matters. I have the parts required.

My second solo shall be :

(*a*) *Gartenmelodie,*
(*b*) *Am Springbrunnen,* } Schumann.
(*c*) *Abendlied,*

The two first are scored by Rudorff, No. 3 by

---

[1] Written in English by Joachim.—TR.
[2] "In artistic matters there should be no question of friendship."

myself, and you can say so in the book.   The Parisians
liked *a, b* very much.   How nice of you to know all
about my success ; it was really quite a genuine one,
all my colleagues heartily concerned in it.

The *Chaconne*, of course, for the Bach Concert !
And of course I will stay with you, if I do not take
away the pleasure from some friend, who could not
stay at Trinity.

I look forward to your Quintet with great interest ;
when is it to be, before or after Cambridge ?   Always
*most welcome* !

You should have heard Brahms new Symphony ;
it went splendidly, the band was heart and soul in it.
But also what a work !   One continuous passionate
strain ; the andante divinely sweet and yet original
etc., etc.   I am quite in love with it.   Best love to
you all and a kiss to Fräulein Stanford.—Yours
*bruderschaftlich,*                       JOSEPH J.

## *To Ernst Rudorff*

LONDON, W., *March* 22, 1887.

Dear Rudorff—With the best will in the world I
have not been able to answer your welcome letter, but
I think this note will be in time for you to make use
of the enclosed by Colonne.   I am living in a perfect
rush of concerts and travelling, as my concert agent
has crammed everything into six weeks.   I am very
glad to hear of your projected tour,[1] and that you are
to be lucky enough to go to beautiful Lisbon, which
Byron described so magnificently (*Childe Harold*).   I
shall be delighted to take over the entrance examination for your classes.

[1] Rudorff had been invited to Lisbon to conduct a series of orchestral
concerts there.

I am very sorry not to be in Berlin to-day,[1] and my thoughts turn in love and reverence to the old man who was so true to his principles. I am curious to see what impression Sullivan's Cantata will make. I thought it clever, but too superficial and not always in good taste. He has combined the mawkishness of Berlioz and Wagner with a good deal of originality and spontaneity in the conception. We have come very low if that is to be placed in the first rank. I enjoyed playing with Frau Schumann immensely; she plays more ideally than ever, it is a joy to hear her! Let me hear from you when you can manage it. I shall probably get back to Berlin on Easter Monday. I am playing in Paris on Good Friday and am going there on the 5th. . . .

### To Sir Charles Villiers Stanford[2]

BERLIN, *July* 23 [1887].

My dear Stanford!—I wish I had to conduct a series of Concerts, merely to come and ask you for your new Symphony! But you know that for reasons too long to recapitulate, I have given up the Concerts with the " Philharmonic band." I shall only give Concerts with Chorus in the Church (Cantatas of Bach, Psalms of Schütz, etc.). Now regarding your Symphony, I spoke to H. Wolff, the agent, who took up the Philh. Concerts and has engaged Bülow to conduct them. He says that Bülow will probably not give any new work without having seen the score. Are you on good terms with Bülow? I am sure if he does give the Symphony he will do it well, for although I have never heard any performance under

[1] The Emperor's birthday.
[2] Written in English by Joachim.—TR.

him, I know he is most rigorously conscientious in studying. When will your score be out? I long very much to see it; let me know if you please! I shall remain here another week, and after that I go first to Silesia, and afterwards to Gmunden in Austria. But letters addressed to Berlin, Friedr. Wilh. Strasse 5, always reach me. Let me know your plans; I suppose they are generous. *Monte generoso.*

I must not forget to congratulate you on being knighted; I am sure the Hausfrau must enjoy it. Remember me to Lady Stanford, and give many kisses to the dear little ones.—From your affectionate

BIGGLER JOE.

## To Ernst Rudorff

[AMSTERDAM] *Wednesday, January* 11 [1888].

Dear Rudorff— My address is Amstel Hotel, Amsterdam. It will be a week to-morrow (Thursday) since I came here, and the rest is doing me good. I have my hands massaged twice a day; the trouble seems to be something in the nature of gout. I cannot detect much difference as yet, but the doctor thinks the accretions in the joints are softening, and he hopes to distribute them. One good thing is that I am allowed to play, indeed I have to do so as much as possible, so I am practising the violin a lot, a thing I have not done for a long time! Dr. Metzger thinks it will *help on* his treatment, and I am not to mind if it hurts me; the more painful it is the better.

My colleagues, Röntgen and Konzertmeister Coenen, the father of our old pupil, are very pleasant, and do all they can to enliven my stay here, so that, in spite of the fog, I am enjoying myself. I took advantage of one or two bright afternoons to go to the Museum and the Zoological Gardens. Each in its own way is most interesting. You only realise to what a high degree of culture and creation Holland had attained 300 years ago when you see the works of all those masters (who were not even known to me by name), which show that largeness of conception and disciplined ability were universal here in those days. Van Dyck and Rembrandt certainly portrayed life with a peculiar refinement and warmth, but they would not have become the great artists they were if it had not been for the freshness and vigour of their artistic environment. (What a pity that comfort and luxury coarsened them in later years!) . . .

*To Philipp Spitta*

LEEDS, *March* 14 [1888].

Dear Spitta—Your telegram[1] was forwarded to me here. I have made up my mind not to go to Berlin, sorry as I am to give up all thought of paying the last honours to him whom I revered so deeply. I can honestly say that neither the wear and tear nor the loss of money would have prevented me, but there is a snow-storm going on here, which, added to other things, makes it very doubtful whether I could get there in time after all. And I do not suppose we should be present at the actual burial, as there will only be room in the Mausoleum for the royalties. Besides this, I had to remember that I could not cause other people, who have long been depending on my appearance at the concerts, loss and inconvenience for the sake of such an uncertainty. Faithfulness to duty is in keeping with the character of the old man who

---

[1] Giving news of the death of Emperor William.

has just died! At two concerts I was to have played "Hungarian Dances," but of course I have had these omitted from the programme. I have no concert on Friday. Are we going to do nothing at the school and the Academy to show our respect and sympathy? Please write to me in London and tell me. What about Händel's *Trauerhymne*? Brahms' Requiem needs too much practice. There is this consolation, we shall have seen the Crown Prince on the throne. His tragic fate which he bears so magnificently, fills me with infinite pity. . . .

## *To Philipp Spitta*

MARIENBAD, *August* 19 [1888].

Dear Spitta . . . On my way here I heard the *Meistersinger* at Bayreuth, chiefly because Frau v. B[eulwitz] and her daughter wanted so much to attend the Festival. I could not make up my mind to go to *Parsifal* also, as the two ladies did, when I remembered the performance three years ago. In spite of an excellent rendering by the orchestra and the magnificent staging of the whole thing, I found it more fatiguing than enjoyable, just as I did last time. The garrulousness in jest and earnest, and the vagueness of the melodies and the harmonisation spoil it all to my mind, although I cannot but admire much that is charming in it, and I would gladly surrender to the energetic spirit which dominates it. But it is impossible! You will be glad to hear that I managed to find time to spend a few days at Gmunden also, where I found the good Queen and Princess Mary as sympathetic and charming as ever. . . .

2 F

### From Philipp Spitta

BERLIN, 27. 2. 89.

Dear Joachim—We parted sooner than I expected yesterday, so I am writing to ask you something I had intended to say to you by word of mouth.

Will you please lend me for three days one of your violins,[1] the one on which you are playing least just now? You will know on Friday the reason why, and I shall only tell you now that it will be placed in pious and responsible hands and be well looked after.

If you consent, perhaps the bearer could take it away with her.—Always yours,

PHILIPP SPITTA.

### From Rudolf Grimm

POTSDAM, *Wednesday* [*about May* 1889].

Dear Joachim — I discussed the matter[2] with Herman yesterday, and I will tell you briefly what he said :—

" I am very sorry not to be able to see Joachim *at present*, it would upset me too much. I really cannot do it, I must save all the little strength I have for the lectures.

" Giesel always remained his friend. I have stated this in the introduction[3] on purpose to assure Joachim of it.

" If he wishes to dedicate the composition to Giesel it will give me great pleasure."—Yours, RUDOLF.

---

[1] Joachim's golden jubilee as an artist was celebrated on March 1, as he was in England on the actual date (March 17). Some former pupils were to play the three movements of his Hungarian Concerto on his violin.

[2] Joachim's wish to dedicate his G major Concerto (the first subject in which is based on a melody by Bettina von Arnim) to Gisela Grimm, who had died on April 4 of that year.

[3] To her play, *Alt-Schottland.*

## *To Philipp Spitta*

GENEVA, *November* 27 [1889].

My dear Spitta . . . I am feeling very unhappy about what you tell me of our concert, and as I only arrived here at one o'clock in the morning I could not get to sleep for worrying. I had arranged it all down to the smallest detail. . . . There was no question of a violin concerto by Bach, but of a piano concerto which Raif had on the stocks and was to conduct himself. Besides this, Bargiel had assured me most positively that his pupil's Sonata was well worth playing, and that he would accept the responsibility. Instead of that it is suddenly decided that Ernst's coquettish *Ungarische Lieder* are to be played by a girl who cannot even interpret their innate daring, however well she may overcome the technical difficulties. And this at a concert made sacred by Palestrina!! It sounds to me appalling. Was there no one out of all the piano classes who could have filled up the gap with something more suitable? Is our Institute a boarding school for girl violinists? I tormented myself with such thoughts as these the whole night long, and feel very depressed to-day. It is to be hoped the Schubert Quintette was a success, at any rate. . . .

## *To Frau Bendemann*

BERLIN, *January* 1, 1890.

Dear Frau Bendemann—What can your friends say to you in your bitter grief![1]

I cannot put into words how much I shall feel the

---

[1] Her husband had died on December 27, 1889.

loss of this beloved man and great artist, who always seemed to me the ideal example of intellectual concentration combined with the most genuine goodness, whenever I took myself seriously to task. And with him has gone one of the last survivors who reminded me of that happy time when I sat at the feet of the benefactor I can never forget, his friend Felix. They were worthy of one another.

Remember me kindly, dear lady, and be assured at all times of the faithful devotion of your grateful,

JOSEPH JOACHIM.

### To Emanuel Wirth

NEWCASTLE, *March* 20, 1890.

. . . I keep thinking of the Chancellor to-day, with some anxiety, because we had got used to feeling safe under his protection. What will happen now? Even if we did not always agree with him we always felt sure that his decisions were made after much thought and from the purest motives. Well, may God continue to watch over the Emperor and the Empire! I wish I could be with you on the 23rd, but I must content myself with sending you all my best wishes from this smoky hole where coal and the making of cannon predominate, but which cannot detract from the bright and sunny nature of my wishes. I am playing Beethoven's C major Quartette, Schumann's Quintette, and a Spohr solo here this evening. I shall think of your viola when I come to

 . . .

## To Clara Schumann

[BERLIN] 16*th* [*June* 1890].

My dear Frau Schumann—It is just like you to
write first to thank me when I derived so much real
happiness and benefit from my visit to you. You and
your dear children were so good to me and so ready
to accept what little I had to offer that it will be a
happy memory to me for a long time to come. It is
a week now since I left you! I started working again
at once, the result being the performance of the
enclosed programme, which was very satisfactory, so
much so that I even dared to wish you were there
sometimes; for the Rhapsodie, for instance. What a
magnificent thing it is! And what a deep impression
it made once more. If ever I have been wounded by
something Brahms has said or done, I only have to
think of the C major to realise what a great man he is.

I liked the first chorus in Bargiel's Psalm [1] particularly, although his works are never free from a certain
rigidity, unfortunately. I asked him to conduct it
himself, because I fancied he wished to do so, and I
think he was pleased. One cannot help liking him
because of his sincerity, and I have resolved to do all
I can to prevent him from becoming embittered. . . .

## To Clara Schumann

BERLIN, *May* 4 [1891].

. . . You have been so much in my thoughts since
the loss of our dear Arthur Burnand. You and the
children must have felt it very deeply, as I have done.
That charming house in Hyde Park Gate has so many
happy memories for us! Moltke's death grieved me

[1] XIII. Psalm, for chorus and orchestra.

too. But what a beautiful end for the great, brave, gentle man! How splendid to die like that after accomplishing such great things! He had long been prepared, and moved amongst us already one of the immortals, waiting calmly until he was called, and passing away without pain.

The day of the Memorial Service for him was Gertrud's[1] wedding day in London. I wanted very much to go over for it, as I had half promised to do. But the school prevented me again! At any rate, this time it was because I had the pleasant task of rehearsing for a musical evening, the programme of which I enclose. It really went very well, and I only wish you had been there to hear the grand Symphony with the Adagio so typical of Schumann, and one of my favourite melodies. I think you would have been pleased at the way the young people played it. I enjoyed practising the *Fritjof* very much, too. After Brahms, I do not know any modern work with such go about it, and I was glad to pay this homage to Bruch and give him this pleasure in the midst of his many troubles. He is very plucky, and a new violin concerto which he has written during the last few months, and which I am to play on May 31 at his benefit in Dresden, will do him credit. But I am sure I have chattered enough to you. I hope to hear again before long either from you or about you.—Always your sincerely devoted JOSEPH JOACHIM.

### From Clara Schumann

BADEN-BADEN, *May* 12, 1891.

Dear Joachim—Your welcome letter was delayed as I was already here in Baden. How nice of you to

---

[1] Joachim's niece, the daughter of his brother Heinrich.

have thought of paying me another visit—and I shall miss this because of the bad state of health in which I have been since March.   I had such a bad chill and rheumatic pains that the doctor finally sent me here, as he thinks very highly of the waters.   How lovely it would have been if you could have come *here*, but I cannot persuade you to do so when you have so little time at your disposal.   My plans for the summer are confined to Obersalzberg this year.   I shall not go to Franzensbad, as I am taking the waters here.   I am afraid you are not likely to be in this neighbourhood. . . . Burnand's death was a terrible shock to us.   You did not know, I expect, that Eugenie was staying with him, and that he had joked with her just before leaving the house.   A death like this is very desirable, but it is dreadful for those who are left behind.   Moltke's death was more beautiful still, surrounded by his family, in the full enjoyment of his home.   I wish I had known him, and Bismarck too.   What a shock his friend's death will be to the latter!   What lovely music you have been having, and I sit here longing to enjoy it without hindrance.   My hearing is causing me so much anxiety ; the chill has affected it so much for the last month that I feel as though my head were under water.   There is a noise like thunder in my ears day and night.   The doctor assures me it will pass when I have recovered from the chill.   But besides this, every note from the middle of the key-board to the bass sounds out of tune to me, and I cannot distinguish two intervals if they come close together, unless I know the work by heart.   Do not be cross with me for these lamentations ; but I know you will sympathise.

Thank God I can still enjoy Nature, which is particularly delightful here in her spring dress.   My

son-in-law, who is here with his family, has given me
a delightful surprise by hiring a comfortable carriage for
the whole of my stay, so that I can have a drive every
day, which I could not have afforded otherwise. . . .

Poor Frau Herzogenberg has had a bad winter—I
have thought of her constantly. A person of my age
ought not to complain, after all! Give them both my
*very* kindest regards—I am anxious to have news of
them. . . . Accept my sincerest thanks, dear Joachim,
for your kind words about Borwick. Yes, he is a
diligent, conscientious, and genuine artist; I hope
passion and warmth of feeling will come with maturity.
He has feeling for a good many things now, but not
enough for the old masters. In spite of this he was
my favourite pupil, and I really did give him all I
could! And so it is delightful to get such recognition
from some one like yourself. I must take this opportunity of telling you how pleased I am with Gabriele
Wietrowetz, who has really surprised us. She has a
fine future before her, in England perhaps, if Neruda
gives up playing, but she must take more care of
herself, and not put such an unreasonable strain on
her nerves as she did this winter. I should like to
give all young artistes the benefit of my experience,
but they do not want to have it—they will not *believe*
it. Soldat was just the same. . . .

### From Clara Schumann

FRANKFURT, *June* 8, 1891.

Dear Joachim—I have to tell you the sad news that
Ferdinand died peacefully the day before yesterday,
after much suffering. Death was a release for him, as
the doctors say he could only have continued to live
in misery, his internal organs having been quite

wrecked by the drugs. And so there is only the one son left to us, whom we must regard as buried alive! It is a cruel fate. But I tell myself that I still have much to be thankful for in my dear daughters, who are like real guardian angels to me, and are a great help to me in bringing up Ferdinand's children, even though they cannot banish my anxieties as regards money matters. After all, we have managed so far, and Heaven will aid us in the future also. This time last year you were with us, dear Joachim, and the memory of this fills me with gratitude.—All best wishes to you and your children from your old friend,

CLARA SCHUMANN.

### To A. Modes

BERLIN, *June* 23, 1891.

Dear Sir—The pleasure of playing a new concerto by Bruch, the delightful visit to Professor von Gebhardt, meeting my three children who are now living in the Rhine country—all this has made me regard my visit to Düsseldorf in the light of a holiday, so that I cannot consider the question of having my expenses refunded. —With many thanks for your kind letter, believe me, yours sincerely, JOSEPH JOACHIM.

### From Elisabeth von Herzogenberg

NAUHEIM, 27. 6. '91.

Dear Friend—Just a line to say how much you will be in my thoughts to-morrow. And with that I have said the best I am capable of saying, for, thank God, my thoughts are a little richer and less clumsy than my words. Particularly when I feel anything deeply, either great pleasure or great sorrow, I am absolutely tongue-tied, and I cannot tell you how often I have raged when you, more prodigal of your gifts than any one, have showered delight upon us, and we have stumbled along idiotically, and tried and tried—and have not got a word out. You see we are "ashamed"! It is only when we can get away from emotions and can turn to something concrete that we gain a little courage; then we take refuge in "a beautiful passage" and another still more beautiful, to which we can point, and Joachim says, with his head on one side, "Really, did I do it like that? I had no idea!" And so we walk like cats on hot bricks and try in vain to convey our impressions indirectly to the man who produced them. But the very best thing of all which is at the back of everything—the opening of the doors of the soul, the joy which one feels at any artistic revelation, and which you are the means of giving us—all this and many more secret things must always remain unspoken!

I think even Fräulein R. B.[1] must keep something to herself occasionally which she cannot express—I hope so, for her sake! . . .

### From Heinrich von Herzogenberg

STARNBERG, 17. 10. '91.

Dear Friend—Spitta will have told you that I am again at the parting of the ways. Although the final word has not been said yet, I have hardly any doubt that we shall not return permanently to Berlin this year—and therefore never again I suppose. It will not only be very hard to part from you all, we feel also that we shall be saying farewell to public life and work, and that we shall be entering upon our old age.

[1] A talkative old lady and a mutual friend.

If you do not know it already, I should like you to realise what my wife has been to me throughout my life.   There can be no question, therefore, of my sacrificing myself for her sake; and besides, apart from all the dear, good friends with whom I hope to keep in touch, I shall not be giving up so very much, because—if I find it impossible, for private as well as official reasons, to return to Berlin next autumn—I intend to enter seriously into competition with you by starting a little hot-bed of geniuses somewhere in South-west Germany!

I wrote and told Spitta there could be no question of leave now, just when we have recommended the four *Meisterschule* so emphatically—and his answer showed me I was right.   I hope Max Bruch will succeed me *immediately*, so that my youth may not have been given up for nothing, and that neglected duties may be made good.   I should like to recommend Herr *Anderson* (Barth) to his particular care; the others will get on quite well with Blumner.   There is nothing very great about them, but there are some good workers among them. . . .

I am expecting a decisive letter from Dr. Schmidtlein[1] to-morrow.   Meanwhile, I have made up my mind.   Rest and peace of mind are the first conditions for my wife's recovery, and so I must uproot her from her home and the surroundings she loves, and plant her where it is possible to fulfil these conditions without a daily struggle.   Whether we go to the south or not is a minor question; the main thing is a good, careful doctor.

Write a few kind words to us, but do not make it too hard for us, for we need courage!   We are going back to Munich on Tuesday—Hotel Marienbad.   If

[1] Herzogenberg's doctor in Berlin.

I feel I can safely go away, I shall probably go on to Berlin to see to things and say good-bye to you all.— Yours always, HERZOGENBERG.

### To Sir Charles Villiers Stanford[1]

[VIENNA, *December* 16, 1891.]

My dear Stanford—I have written to Chappell about the Quintet of Brahms, which is one of the sublimest things he ever wrote; a heavenly Adagio in it. Brahms is willing to have it performed in England, if we engage the Clarionet player, who has done it in Berlin, a Mr. Mühlfeld from the Meiningen band, a stupendous fellow; I never heard the like of his variety of tone and expression. If Chappell gets him perhaps six engagements (Cambridge amongst them) the thing might be arranged. I suppose you would help to it. Brahms could not send the Mscrpt. beforehand for an english player to practice, and besides there is so much of the Gypsy-stile in it: I don't think they would find the right expression.

I am going to Berlin to-day, and hope to play your Quartet through soon. We had a most lively Concert yesterday evening with a great deal of "tusi-musi."—Best love to all yours from Jo.

Tell Sedley Taylor that I am going to send him the Mozart programs.

### To Sir Charles Villiers Stanford[2]

[BERLIN, *December* 30, 1891.]

My dear Stanford!—At last we have tried your quartet, and I shall be very glad to play it at one of

---

[1] Written in English by Joachim.—TR.     [2] *Ibid.*

the Pops. in London, and, if you like, in Cambridge too.   The first and last movements are those I (and my partners also) liked best.   We think that you ought to consider whether the Adagio might not be condensed; it seems to me to drag in some places of a Recitative character:

When the passage comes a second time a cut might easily be brought about.

Chappell thinks there is no chance for getting the splendid Clarionet player Mühlfeld enough engagements to bring him over to England for the Brahms 5[tet.]

Is Egerton intelligent and spirited enough for playing a piece, in which there is much of a dramatic, phantastic character, that wants a great variety of tone, from $f\!f$ to $p\!p\!p$?   Tell me, and I might try to persuade Brahms when I see him in Vienna (in a fortnight) to send a copy over.   He made Mühlfeld a condition for giving the Mscrpt.

With many kind wishes for the new year and affectionate greetings to you, the Frau, and the chicks. —Ever sincerely yours,        JOSEPH JOACHIM.


*From Philipp Spitta to Joachim in Vienna*

BERLIN, 12. I. '92.

Dear Joachim—Here is the letter of condolence[1] to our poor Herzogenberg; please sign it on the first line after my name.   I must ask you to stamp the letter as we have no Austrian stamps here.   I heard indirectly from San Remo this morning that he felt her death (which was sudden and unexpected) terribly and was altogether crushed by it at first, but that he

---

[1] Frau von Herzogenberg died on January 7 at San Remo.

soon collected himself and regained self-control. His aunt and Hildebrand have gone to him from Florence. The burial appears to have taken place at San Remo. —Yours sincerely,        PHILIPP SPITTA.

### To Johannes Brahms

LONDON, *March* 30 [1892].

Dear Brahms—You will have had my telegram yesterday, but I must write and express, on behalf of Piatti, Strauss and Ries,[1] their great and respectful admiration for your magnificent Quintette. The piece gave them increasing delight at each one of the four rehearsals held by me. Mühlfeld was there for the last three. It had a remarkable success, we were called three times instead of once as we generally are. We shall play the Trio as well as the Quintette on Saturday, and the two pieces once more on Monday. But I thought it better, for Mühlfeld's sake, to begin by playing only the Quintette, and the result has justified me. People can appreciate the subtle things better if they have been carried away by something mighty first of all, and have confidence in the composer. There is a sensible, although enthusiastic, notice in the *Times* of the 29th. If you care to see it you can easily get a copy; I am sorry to say I have sent mine to my sister-in-law, and so have not got it here. It would please you to see how all the good musicians here—Stanford, Hubert Parry, Grove, etc., etc., love and admire you.

I will tell you about the Trio on Sunday.—Yours ever,        JOSEPH J.

[1] The members of Joachim's quartette in London.

*To Johannes Brahms*

[LONDON] *Tuesday 5th [April* 1892].

Dear Brahms—Your telegram of thanks gave great pleasure to all concerned. And now I have to thank you very much for your letter. We had the 3rd performance of your Quintette yesterday before a packed audience; even on Saturday people had to be turned away, and it was just the same yesterday. The Trio was played for the second time and much appreciated; even more so than the first time, and it was played with greater freedom too. Miss Davies entered into her part with the greatest devotion, and did it very well. I like the piece better and better, and I am sorry I cannot take part in it. Before Mühlfeld came I had the great pleasure of playing it through on the viola with the two others so that they might know it. I have got quite used to the C♯ and F major in the Quintette, it sounds to me like a *nota cambiata*. If one recognises the daring spirit behind it, the buffeting wave brings strength and refreshment. It is only capriciousness which offends (Hans, for instance, the republican fellow). I cannot give your messages to Stanford, because he has gone to Italy for a few weeks' holiday. But he heard the Quintette twice and was just as taken with it as Hubert Parry, Hallé and his wife, Grove, Chappell, etc. The latter was very grateful to me for so persistently opposing his prejudice against a strange clarionet player, in which I was finally successful because that excellent man Adolph Behrens guaranteed the financial part of the business. He is the same admirer of Brahms, an invalid I am sorry to say, who offered years ago to have your German Requiem copied and performed at his own expense. It sounds ridiculous now! Wilson, an

American, wants to carry me off to America, and says you are to be asked by the government to go too. I said if you went I would conquer my dislike of the idea. I think that was a good way of getting out of it! He was quite a nice man. Addio! J. J.

*To Johannes Brahms*

EDINBURGH, *March* 22 [1893].

Dear Brahms—Should Mr. Hadow, a very musical young graduate of Oxford University, wish to give you this letter, I have much pleasure in sending you a greeting from this land of fog, and in telling you how the glow of your genius has penetrated here and is warming and illuminating an ever-widening circle. It gives me great satisfaction to verify this year by year.

To return to the above-mentioned Mr. Hadow, I must tell you that he has done a great deal for music at the University, so that at Oxford it is now possible to hear not only chamber music, but also orchestral concerts. There is a real zeal for music among the students. Mr. Hadow has also composed, among other things, a string quartette which [Robert] Heckmann played in public at Cologne. I know nothing of his, however, except a biographical work on Schumann, Berlioz, and Wagner, and I believe he has designs on you now. So it would not be a bad thing if he were well informed! If you can spare a little time for this very charming young man, whom I am sure you will like, it will be very nice of you.

We have been playing a lot of your things. The day before yesterday at the Pop. Concert we had an excellent performance of your G major Quintette in which Piatti's playing was particularly happy. He is very much taken with the beginning, and I more especially with the deep and original Adagio, *one* of your most beautiful things. I have heard much of your delightful visit to Berlin (which I was extremely sorry to miss) from your godchild and others. What a pity it is we meet so seldom.—Always yours,

J. J.

### To Max Bruch

*Monday* [*May* 29, 1893].

Dear Bruch—I very much regret to hear that you have been suffering from influenza for such a long time. I meant to look you up, but I had guests and latterly my Marie was staying with me, although she could only stay for a few days, unfortunately. You will be glad to hear that her voice and delivery have developed to a surprising degree, every one who hears her is amazed at her progress.

She went from here to Bayreuth to study some parts with Frau Cosima ; for, of course, like all operatic singers she is under the spell of Wagner's creations. It is no good opposing this nowadays, and I must just put up with it and console myself with the reflection that at all events there is real seriousness of purpose at the back of it. . . .

### To Karl Halir at Weimar

[BERLIN] *July* 14 [1894].

Dear Colleague—We shall have to possess our souls in patience for a few days more ; I am told on reliable authority that His Majesty the Emperor's consent must be obtained for the salary you are asking in connection with the theatre.[1] I have no doubt this

---

[1] Halir hoped to be appointed teacher at the Berlin School of Music and *Concertmeister* to the Royal orchestra.

2 G

will be given, and that we shall be able to count you among our number.

I have a strange request to make, dear friend. A musician has told me of a remark made by [Richard] Strauss on the occasion of the Bülow Festival at Hamburg, which sounds to me incredible, and which I should like to hear denied. He is said to have met the suggestion that he should conduct Brahms' Requiem with the words: " I do not produce amateur music!" It is also said that when he happened to be seated opposite a photograph of Brahms at a friend's house, he requested the hostess to take it away, as otherwise he could not remain there! Both these tales sound to me like gossip, but I was told most positively that they were true.[1] Will you do me the favour of asking your friend, who is man enough not to deny it if both are true.

Possibly an answer in the affirmative would affect my personal relations with Strauss, but I should be sorry if this were the case, as I liked what I saw of him at Weimar very much.

With kindest regards,     JOSEPH JOACHIM.

### To Clara Schumann

[BERLIN] *October* 28 [1895].

My dear Friend—I am almost ashamed at the thought of your great kindness! I have been meaning to write to you for so long and have not done so. I found it very hard to pass through Frankfurt last Thursday without spending a little time with you; I wondered whether I could not miss a train and travel home at night. But as I had a bad cold, and as my herd of violinists were expecting me at the school on

---

[1] According to Halir they were untrue.

Friday at 9 o'clock, the head finally conquered the heart. I should have had many delightful things to tell you about the Musical Festivals at Zurich, and before that at Meiningen, where Brahms was honoured as one of the Immortals. I was absolutely carried away by all the magnificent works of his which were given, and I delighted in his good fortune in being there to enjoy to the utmost the perfect performances and the enthusiasm of the audiences. He is indeed to be envied and not least because he can say that he has not falsified the prophecies of his noble predecessor among our masters. Although a bitter fate has decreed that, humanly speaking, a barrier should rise between us, that has done nothing to diminish my genuine admiration of him. I was very glad to hear that you are much better and that you have even been delighting some of your friends by your playing just as before. Please God, I shall soon come to Frankfurt and see how much better you are for myself. Rest assured, dear Frau Schumann, that not a day passes on which I do not think of you, in the midst of all the work which presses on me here.

With all messages to you and your dear ones from your grateful and affectionate        JOSEPH JOACHIM.

## To Johannes Brahms

[BERLIN, *April* 1896.]

Dear Brahms—I came back from England the day before yesterday and I have a communication to make to you. A Mr. Adolph Behrens has died and, as a sign of gratitude and respect, he has left you £1000 (10,000 gulden) in his will. For the last twenty years he had been confined to his room, and if you knew how fine a character he was this proof of sincere attachment to you because of the pleasure your genius had given him, would rejoice your heart. As his sisters (whom I do not know personally) do not know your address I was asked to tell you the news, of which you will receive official notice from the executors later. I got to know Mr. Behrens thirty years ago at Pau, and, if I could fit it in, I always made a point of paying him a visit when I was in London, because this contemporary of mine, who was entirely devoted to art and science, always seemed to me the most perfect example of a gentleman. He has left me £1000 too, as also his former music teacher Bargiel, who taught him the whole of one winter at Cologne.

The family of Behrens has been settled in England for more than one generation and is very rich. Adolph Behrens was unmarried.

One more question. Have you got Haydn's " The Ten Commandments arranged as Canons " in the old Härtel edition ? If not, I should like to have the honour of giving it to you, I got a friend in London to give them to me for you. You see, I am always thinking of you, although I do not write to you.

Thank God there was better news of Frau Schumann from Frankfurt to-day. I cannot bear the thought of losing her, and yet we shall have to get used to it.

Please let me have a few words from you soon. I am very much taken up by school affairs so please forgive haste. J. J.

### From Johannes Brahms

VIENNA, *April* 10, 1896.

Dear Friend—A more delightful and desirable experience could not fall to any one's lot than that about which you have just written.

That a man I do not know, who has never, so far
as I can remember, even written to me, should think
of me in such a manner, has moved me deeply. I
have had the inestimable good fortune of experiencing
something similar before this — how small public
honours appear compared to such things as these.

But that is not the only pleasant part of your
letter! I have only got Haydn's Canons in my own
writing, and so the old edition is doubly welcome,
coming from you.

And now, I cannot call the other subject of your
letter sad. I have often thought Frau Schumann
might survive all her children and me—but I have
never wished that she might do so. The thought
of losing her cannot frighten us any more, not even
me who am so lonely and to whom so little is left in
the world.

And when she has left us, will not our faces light
up with joy at the thought of the splendid woman
whom it has been our privilege and delight to love
and admire throughout her long life?

Only thus let us grieve for her.

With affectionate regards—Your          J. BR.

### To Johannes Brahms

[BERLIN] *April* 20 [1896].

Dear Brahms—Friend Stanford, whose Opera,
*Shamus O'Brien*, was successfully performed in
London not long ago, wishes very much to have it
done in Vienna, and his agent, Sir Augustus Harris,
is in Vienna now with this object. I think [Hans]
Richter is sure to use his influence in the matter, but
Stanford fancies Richter is thought to be prejudiced
in favour of English compositions, and that I might

have some influence through you, if I told you I was very much interested in the Opera, which is indeed the truth. I am not so sanguine as to think this myself. But if you have an opportunity of expressing *my* good opinion in influential quarters, I shall be glad to have fulfilled my obligation towards my English friend. I think there is a good deal of sound and characteristic music in *Shamus O'Brien*, I am only afraid that people will say the working out of the second half of the book drags rather.

Forgive me for troubling you with a letter on the matter, but one is always glad to carry out the wishes of a fellow artist and friend if there is any chance of benefiting him by doing so.

I must thank you very much for your last letter, which gave me real pleasure. I shall send the Haydn Canons I promised you before long. The Musical Festival in May, added to all my school work, takes up every moment of my time.—Yours always sincerely,

J. J.

*To his Nephew Harold Joachim*[1]

NAPOLI, *June* 4 [1896].

Dear Harold . . . It was very sad to lose dear Mme. Schumann. I was present at the funeral service in her house at Frankfurt, but did not go to Bonn, where she was buried at the side of her husband. It was not possible to leave my travelling companions to Italy waiting longer, and so I went from Frankfurt to Trient. The sensation of seeing this country is enormous, it is beyond all my expectations, and just at this moment it is soothing to me. I have been at Naples since the 28th. In Prof. Dohrn's little yacht

---

[1] Written in English by Joachim.—TR.

(*Vaporetto*) I have been to Ischia, Capri, Sorrento, Salerno, sometimes for more than five hours, and seen more of the country and under Dohrn's guidance under more favorable circumstances than most strangers do. You must make Dohrn's acquaintance when he comes to Oxford for his B.C.L. degree; he is a most charming fellow. I have told him of you, and he looks forward to it. He will stay at Exeter College, I think, but you will easily find out. On Sunday morning we leave for Roma! Hotel Quirinal, and I mean to be back in Berlin on the 17th inst. Gerry Liddell is a delightful travelling companion.— Always your loving uncle                    Jo.

## To Karl Halir

HAINSTEIN BEI EISENACH, *September* 11 [1896].

Dear Friend and Colleague—I was very glad to hear from you, and your proposed tour[1] is the best of all signs that you are quite well again. Although I and others will miss you very much, I wish you success in the far West with all my heart. I am particularly glad to be able to be of use to you by lending you my English violin, it will be a charming bond between us whilst we are separated. One could confide anything to the care of your reverent, artistic hands! I am delighted to see that you are converted to Stradivarius, as his is the ideal tone to my mind also. No other maker has such great elasticity, I might almost say versatility of tone. I hope your successes will soon enable you to have a violin like this of your own, meanwhile please make use of your friend's. We might perhaps discuss the advisability of insuring the violin before you start. . . .

[1] A concert tour in America.

*To Sir Charles Villiers Stanford*[1]

BERLIN, *October* 9 [1896].

My dear Stanford—I was myself much alarmed by news about Brahms, that have spread about this week, so that I wrote the day before yesterday to Vienna. Fortunately a letter from Hanslick's, just received (about some detail he wants regarding Schumann's last illness), ends with the following account about Brahms, which I copy for you: *Leider ist Br. von seiner Gelbsucht* (jaundice) *noch nicht hergestellt. Da er aber gar keine Schmerzen fühlt, vortrefflich bei Appetit ist, Mittags und Abend wie gewöhnlich in seinen " Rothen Igel" geht und viel herumspaziert, so hoffen wir, dass er sich bald erholen wird.*[2]

Do tell this to all our friends, especially also to Chappell, who frightened me with having heard the worst news. The Hanslick letter is quite a relief! I can't tell how much I suffered. I hope every thing from Brahms' strong nature. Our quartet *is* coming to London. I thought the performance of your *Revenge* here was a settled matter; I will see Ochs about it. I beg to say that we do *not* hate the Britisher, though we disapprove greatly of Rhodes, Jameson, and that lot. I long to make the acquaintance of your Requiem, and trust to hear that you *did* like your new quartet, which I expect here. Goodbye, and much love to the Hausfrau and the bairns, as to yourself.—From                Jo.

---

[1] Written in English by Joachim.—TR.

[2] " Brahms, I am sorry to say, has not yet recovered from his attack of jaundice. But as he feels no pain whatever, has an excellent appetite, frequents the ' Rother Igel' every afternoon and evening as usual, and goes about a good deal, we hope he will soon be quite well again."

## To Julius Otto Grimm

[BERLIN] *December* 17 [1896].

Dear Ise—I thank you from my heart for having given me this sign that you still think of me. I, too, can honestly say that I often call to mind the happy time we spent together. I thought of you only last week in Vienna, where I saw a great deal of Brahms, who once made the third in the alliance at Hanover. You will be relieved to hear that his illness is not of the dreadful nature which the terrifying reports made us believe. The doctors are positive on the subject. All the same, his condition is somewhat grave. He is thin and sallow, and feels weak in consequence of the jaundice which has dragged on so long. But there is every reason to hope that, with his strong constitution and vitality, he will get well. He is to go to Karlsbad again in April. His interest in our quartette was quite delightful, and he generally stayed with us until late at night.

How much we have lost since last we met, my dear Ise! One lives on in one's children. . . .

## To Ernst Rudorff in Rome

BERLIN, *April* 29 [1897].

My dear Rudorff—Your kind letter touched me very much. I know hardly any one who can give such true consolation as you. I love to feel the influence of your thoughts and feelings, as I did the other day when dear, good Frau Marie Benecke told me what you had said about Mendelssohn's Variations for the Organ.[1] How is it you can always penetrate to one's

---

[1] A manuscript copy of some unknown Variations for the Organ, which Mendelssohn probably composed for a London organist. This copy had been

inmost soul! I only know that I am longing to see you again. Yes, the loss of Brahms was a cruel blow. I suffered much beforehand in seeing him gradually lose his hold on life, we must be thankful that his sufferings were not prolonged. The almost super-human energy with which he resisted death was amazing! I often think sadly of the last pleasure it was in our power to give him, and to which he responded with unusual gentleness. I have never heard him express his gratitude so warmly as after listening to his G major Quintette; he seemed almost satisfied with his work.

We still have his works—as an individual I counted for little with him during the last years of his life.

You will be interested in the draft of the programme for May at Bonn, and will enjoy it with us in spirit. We are also going to honour his memory at the Philharmonic here on May 7, so that all those who cannot go to the other concerts may take part in it. F minor Quintette, B major Quartette, Clarionet Quintette with Mühlfeld. The school is to do the Requiem in June, when I hope you will be able to be present once more. . . .

### To his Nephew Harold Joachim [1]

BERLIN, *May* 10, 1898.

My dear Harold—I have not yet thanked you for Hadow's interesting books. The article on Brahms is excellent, the views are so sound and his appreciation of his work based on thorough knowledge and love combined with justice.

I wonder whether it is beyond doubt that *all* the

---

sent to Mendelssohn's daughter. She had sent them to Rudorff for his opinion, and they had been declared genuine.

[1] Written in English by Joachim.—TR.

melodies quoted of Haydn's compositions are really Volkslieder, whether it is sure that they existed before his time, and whether they might not have found their way to the people through his works.   It takes nothing of the greatness of H.'s genius if he has made use of them, his inventive power is too many-sided for that ; but still it is difficult to believe in it!   I object to the expression "a little shallow it may be" for characterizing Haydn's sentiment, although he adds "pure and transparent as a mountain stream."   Surely even Beethoven and Bach have not invented deeper, more religious or more phantastic Adagios, than most of his, when he is serious.   I think in a new edition Hadow ought to modify the expression.   I cannot call Haydn Slavonic,[1] like lesser people (Dvořák, Smetana, Tschaikowsky), no more than I call Mozart Italian (in spite of the great Italian influence he does show).   He lifts the material into a higher sphere, and has the German gift to assimilate, so that it becomes a universal ideal thought, intelligible to all nations.   Göthe is essentially German in that sense.   Forgive, oh my dear Nephew philosopher, for blundering in your own department! fancy !

I am still a little rheumatic in my arm and scribble carelessly. . . .

### From Bernhard Scholz

Frankfurt a. M., *December* 9, 1898.

Dear Joachim—I cannot address you in any other way.   We parted in bitter anger nearly 30 years ago, but my thoughts go beyond this period to the

---

[1] In the margin Joachim wrote : " I think for the popular vein in his creations he might also be called a stirian (*steierisch*) or Tirolese musician."

happy, golden years, when a sincere friendship and a common aim united us, to the years before any great sorrow had fallen upon either of us.

We have grown old; we are among the few remaining witnesses of a finer, nobler epoch of our art. We are still united by the pursuit of the same ideal. Now you are one of those who have honoured a work of mine.[1] I should like to approach you personally, also. In my old age I long to stretch out my hand to you as of old, and to spend the evening of my days at peace with my old friend. I offer you my hand, if you grasp it you will gratify your brother artist,

BERNHARD SCHOLZ.

### To his Nephew Anton Singer [2]

[BERLIN] *Tuesday, February* 7 [1899].

My dear Nephew—To-day is indeed one of the saddest days of my life! I wish to tell your dear mother and you and your brothers and sisters myself, what you may have already learnt from the newspapers. My wife has succumbed under an operation (for gall stones) and is to be buried this afternoon.

We had separated—but I never realised more vividly the depth of my affection for her and her many splendid qualities, than on the two visits I paid her a few days before her operation. I knew it was a serious matter, but I trusted that my wife's strong constitution would stand the strain. The sudden end was all the harder to bear. I had been seriously considering whether we could not live together for the last years of our lives, for the good of the children. Providence has not permitted it! I know you will all

---

[1] As one of the judges at the Beethoven-Haus in Bonn, who awarded the prize to Scholz's Piano Quartette in F minor.

[2] Son of Joachim's sister Julie.

feel with me in my grief, and thank you from my heart for this as well as for your last sympathetic letter, in which however you should have addressed me as " *Du.* " Remember me to your dear wife.— Always your affectionate UNCLE JO.

My children are all with me with the exception of Josepha who is at Bern.

### *To Sir Charles Villiers Stanford* [1]

CHARLOTTENBURG, *March* 25 [1901].

My dear Stanford—I cannot refuse your invitation,[2] much as I feel that I ought to leave such festive occasions to younger people. However I will try my best for your sake, only I cannot promise a Spohr Concerto for the reason that my *staccato,* as wanted for his compositions, has left me. I am told that De Bériot was in the same predicament even at an earlier age. There are no staccato's in the Concerto (B minor) for two Violins, perhaps Arbós or Sutcliffe, or Grimson might play it with me. The Barcarole and Scherzo with Piano would probably not be important enough. And there will be no occasion for the Double Quartet in E minor?

I suppose there will be time to discuss program in April, when I come to London. Perhaps Schumann's Phantasie (dedicated to me) would do.

A thousand pities you were not here for our Bach Festival! So many unknown and beautiful works. The Fuller-Maitlands enjoyed them very much; it was nice to welcome them in Berlin. My entrance examinations call for me. You know what they are. —With best love to all yours, JOSEPH JOACHIM.

[1] Written in English by Joachim.—TR.
[2] To the Leeds Musical Festival.

*From the " Joachim Concerts Committee," London*

LONDON, *December* 18, 1906.

Dear Dr. Joachim—At a meeting held by the Joachim Concerts Committee on 6th of this month a proposal was adopted that our present Association should be constituted a "permanent body (with the assistance of the Joachim Quartet as long as possible) for the purpose of holding regular series of concerts in London for the performance of Chamber Music."

The following resolution was then proposed by Sir Lawrence Alma Tadema, R.A., O.M., seconded by Sir Alexander Kennedy, and unanimously agreed to : "That the title of the Association should be ' The Joachim Concert Society.'"

This resolution involves an extended use of your name for which we feel that we should ask your sanction. It seemed indispensable to mark the continuity of the undertaking in this manner; it also seemed right to us that not only your unrivalled career as a performer, but your work as a leader and teacher in maintaining the standard of pure and elevated musical art, should be commemorated, so far as within our power, in our endeavour to aid in preserving the tradition you have founded, and to encourage the following of your example in future generations.

Hoping, then, that you will honour our Association with your acquiescence in the aforesaid proposal, we remain, yours very sincerely,

For the Committee :

LAWRENCE ALMA TADEMA.
ALEXANDER KENNEDY.
FREDERICK POLLOCK.
EDWARD SPEYER.
EDWARD STREET.

THE JOACHIM QUARTET (JOACHIM, HALIR, WIRTH, HAUSMANN).

From the etching by Ferdinand Schmutzer.

## To Sir Lawrence Alma Tadema[1]

BERLIN, *January* 5, 1907.

My dear Sir Lawrence—I was sincerely touched by your and our other distinguished friends' proposal that the Association for a regular series of concerts for the performance of Chamber Music should continue under the title of the " Joachim Concert Society," even after my personal assistance must cease. I feel it to be a great honour for which I thank you and the other kind friends with all my heart. And yet after mature and conscientious consideration, I cannot but feel that I ought not to accept an honour, which involves no responsibility. I am perfectly sure that as long as the Committee in its present constitution exists nothing could happen, that would not find my approval; but circumstances may arise to bring about artistic changes for which I would not take the responsibility and then the title would be inconsistent.

May I ask you, dear kind friend, to accept my sincere gratitude and to convey the expression of my heartfelt thanks to the other members who kindly signed the proposal?

With many kind wishes for the New Year to you and all your dear ones, I remain, dear Sir Lawrence, your sincerely devoted friend,     JOSEPH JOACHIM.

## To Edward Speyer

BERLIN, W., *April* 1, 1907.

My dear Friend—I find it very hard to tell you of a decision to which I have come very reluctantly, but which is quite unavoidable. I had influenza in Vienna and was obliged to remain in bed there for more than

---

[1] Written in English by Joachim.—TR.

ten days, and although I have been considerably better since I came here there are still some minor troubles which necessitate great care.

The doctors both here and in Vienna strongly advise me not to expose myself to the uncertain climate in England during April. For the sake of the future, they are very anxious that, when I have fulfilled my most urgent duties in Berlin, I should take a real rest somewhere in the South.

They think that only in this way shall I be able to regain my full strength for next season. You can imagine how sorry I am to give up our fine London plans, and to put my dear friends into such an awkward position! But we shall be able to make up for it in May or June? Think the matter over and let me hear from you with regard to it before long, as I am, naturally, very concerned about it. My colleagues all urge me to take this step, which is, indeed, forced upon me.[1]

With kindest regards to you and yours, and to all the members of the Committee, from yours very sincerely, JOSEPH JOACHIM.

[1] A series of seven Joachim Quartette Concerts from April 13 to May 1 had been announced in London a considerable time beforehand. These took place at the end of June with the assistance of Klingler, as Joachim never recovered from his illness.

# INDEX

THE END